MYTH OF THE WESTERN

MYTH OF THE WESTERN

*New Perspectives on
Hollywood's Frontier Narrative*

Matthew Carter

EDINBURGH
University Press

Edinburgh University Press Ltd
The Tun – Holyrood Road
12 (2f) Jackson's Entry
Edinburgh EH8 8PJ
www.euppublishing.com

Typeset in 10/12.5 pt Sabon by
Servis Filmsetting Ltd, Stockport, Cheshire,
and printed and bound in Great Britain by
CPI Group (UK) Ltd, Croydon CR0 4YY

A CIP record for this book is available from the British Library

ISBN 978 0 7486 8558 5 (hardback)
ISBN 978 0 7486 8559 2 (webready PDF)

CONTENTS

ACKNOWLEDGEMENTS

I have enjoyed the advice and support of a great many colleagues, friends and students in the Department of Literature, Film and Theatre Studies at the University of Essex. I am grateful to all those whose ideas and opinions have undoubtedly made it into this book under the guise of my own opinions. Sadly, I cannot rightly recall who said what and when; I can only offer a general thank you and hope that this will suffice. A specific thank you should go to Jeff Geiger for all his help during the preparation of this book.

I am greatly indebted for the advice, criticism and encouragement given to me by David Musselwhite. David, you read every word when you did not have to, and it breaks my heart knowing that you did not live to see it realised. I can only hope that you would have been proud of me. I must also acknowledge my colleague and friend John Cant for all the fruitful and engaging discussions; for his brilliant observations on the Western and a great many other things besides. Whatever insights this book can lay claim to, he can lay claim to most of them first. John, I owe you a great deal. I am, of course, grateful to my parents for all their love and support, and for generally giving me the best upbringing I could have hoped for. I am happy to mention Sophie Cansdale, Shohini Chaudhuri, Maria Cristina Fumagalli, Richard Gray, John Haynes, Geoff King, Ildiko Olah and Andrew Patrick Nelson, all of whom have helped me in numerous ways over the years. I also would like to thank Gillian Leslie, Jenny Peebles and Rebecca Mackenzie of Edinburgh University Press for making the publication process run so smoothly.

Finally, I want to thank Caja Dan, my partner, best friend and the love of my life, without whom all this would be meaningless anyway.

A shorter and modified version of Chapter 4 was first published as '"I'm just a Cowboy": Transnational Identities of the Border Country in Tommy Lee Jones's The Three Burials of Melquiades Estrada', *European Journal of American Studies*, Online, 1 (2012), and reprinted in Andrew Patrick Nelson (ed.), *Contemporary Westerns: Film and Television, 1990–2010* (Lanham, MD: Scarecrow Press, 2013), pp. 149–69. An earlier version of Chapter 5 was first published as '"The Dismal Tide": Shoring up the Fragments in Joel and Ethan Coen's *No Country for Old Men*', *Icfai University Journal of American Literature*, 2(3/4) (August/November 2009): 73–89.

INTRODUCTION

I

As a consequence of decades of revisionist histories of the American West, the traditional frontier themes of the 'domestication of the wilderness' and 'Manifest Destiny' have been largely discredited. Many analyses of the politics of westward expansion have interpreted the process of 'nation-building' as nothing short of imperialism motivated by economic forces; imperialism that often resulted in wars of extermination against America's indigenous populations. The established history of the American West was addressed in the light of the narratives that became available as hitherto 'silent' groups – women, African Americans, Native Americans and other racial groupings – insisted that their presence 'on the frontier' be acknowledged and their voices heard. In short, the established history came to be seen as not so much biased as wholly mythic. The source of this mythology was a political discourse informed by notions of Anglo-American racial superiority and American exceptionalism. Together with a popular culture that demanded an heroic version of history, such 'frontier narratives' flourished first in the dime novels and stage shows of the late nineteenth century. But the principal medium whereby frontier mythology was popularised in the twentieth century was, of course, the cinema. And just as the grand narrative of the frontier had splintered under the weight of historical revisionism, so too was the cinematic Western understood to be anachronistic, leading to the common appellation 'post', as in 'post-Western'.

Although the first decade of the twenty-first century has seen a healthy number of Westerns being produced, and this output shows little sign (so far) of abating, the genre is generally regarded as a diminished form, its so-called 'classical' phase consigned to the 'Golden Age' of Hollywood's past. Writing in 2007, Los Angeles-based film journalist, John Patterson, declared that the Western 'is to all intents and purposes deader than Billy the Kid, Jesse James, John Ford and Sam Peckinpah put together.'[1] Patterson reiterates the common assertion that has been made since the 1980s at least; namely, that the Western was a 'political casualty of the Vietnam [War]', that the 'overthrow of the

Western's myths' necessarily means that the Western itself had also 'died'.[2] The Western had been found guilty by many of perpetuating the myth of the West; that is to say, the preconceived and erroneous notion that the settling of the frontier was the sole preserve of Anglo-American men, where racial and gendered 'others' served only to secure white male identity. The genre's heroic protagonist – the gunfighter – was now no longer viewed as the champion of civilisation, but as a dangerous relic, his individualism and masculinity now vilified rather than celebrated.

Furthermore, it is commonly accepted that the genre itself was largely responsible for its own decline, whereby historical revisionism was reflexively incorporated into a series of introspective 'revisionist' Westerns, which attacked the 'classical' phase's erstwhile triumphalism. In *The American West* (2009), Karen R. Jones and John Wills sum up this popular shift in historical opinion: 'Progress read conquest, and the frontier became the "f-word" in revisionist vocabulary.'[3] Conjoined with more established terminology, the genre that had once celebrated the American story of the coming of a 'Garden' of bountiful opportunity now depicted a 'Desert' of failed mythic promises: historical trauma, racial conflict, liminal identities.[4] The end logic of this argument essentially asserts that the Western participated in a self-defeating enterprise, which Stephen McVeigh describes in *The American Western* (2007) as 'the destruction of the genre's vital centre, even though the films [themselves] are a part of that destruction'.[5]

With specific regard to historical revisionism in the Western, and in one of the most accomplished contemporary studies of the genre that I have read, Patrick McGee writes that his book *From Shane to Kill Bill* (2007), 'participates in the shift away from the frontier myth in recent Western historiography and film criticism'.[6] This, he says, allows him to focus on the significant issues of 'class resentments' and 'social contradictions' that are evident (although largely disavowed) in contemporary US socioeconomic and political discourse. Popular culture, on the other hand, has few such constraints and, as McGee rightly suggests, it 'never stops finding new ways of saying the unsayable'.[7] Actually frontier mythology has never really 'left' the United States, although the terms by which it is rendered or assessed may have changed. Neither has the myth been absent from its popular culture, although equally its preferred forms may oscillate in popularity and productivity, depending upon a given period's cultural perceptions and moods and the popularity of particular genre cycles. Indeed, as far as many are concerned, the issues raised by the myth survived the so-called 'demise' of the Western through migration into other Hollywood genres, such as War, Action, and styles like film noir. (David Thompson argues as much in relation to *Chinatown* (Roman Polanski, 1974) and *Brokeback Mountain* (Ang Lee, 2005).[8]) Likewise, sci-fi franchises like *Star Wars* (1977–2005) and *Star Trek* (1966–) have been commonly interpreted (at least in part) as Westerns transposed into space.

That frontier mythology looms large in contemporary US popular culture is surely a truism, and a number of film scholars have recently taken account of the 'migration' of the themes of frontier mythology from the Western into numerous other Hollywood genres.[9] McGee acknowledges the importance of considering the pervasive nature of the myth in US popular culture forms when he writes that, just because his analysis of the Western 'participates [in this] shift away from the frontier myth [it] does not mean that it leaves the issue out of the account'.[10] While this 'shift' is apparent and, indeed, forms a valuable part of recent scholarship on the West *and* the Western, the political appropriation of frontier mythology in response to the shocking events of 11 September 2001 – coupled with the current level of Western film production – has encouraged me to foreground the sociocultural, historical and political dimensions of the myth in my own study.

In *Hollywood Westerns and American Myth* (2010), Robert B. Pippin argues simultaneously for the essentiality of the Western *and* frontier mythology for analysing the psychological dimension of US political philosophy. He claims that the Western is 'about America and the self-understanding of rapid American modernisation in the West in the nineteenth century'.[11] He also impresses upon the reader the serious consequences for the United States of shaping historical memory by myth and of filtering the historical experience of the West through the prism of popular culture:

> It is also true of course that while these events are foundings they are also the results of imperialist colonization or even wars of extermination. Thus the way these societies remember or mythologize their foundings, and their attempts to do so consistent with their own pacific, Christian, and egalitarian self-image, will make for a serious and complicated problem.[12]

It is because of similar sentiments that the so-called 'mythological' approach to the Western – that is to say, the use of frontier mythology as a framework or 'language' through which to 'read' the genre – has come under scrutiny within film scholarship during the last decade or so. As Steve Neale suggests, advocates of the mythological approach to the Western, 'view the latter solely as a vehicle for an unambiguous version of the former [and] stress the former's overarching characteristics . . . rather than the latter's local features'.[13]

It remains true that strong threads of this approach persist in academic studies of the frontier, and are tied to theories of the Western's development that insist that only revisionist Westerns criticised the myth. In *Coyote Kills John Wayne* (2000), for instance, Carlton Smith reiterates the view that frontier mythology promoted a kind of 'cultural exceptionalism' by which 'pop culture became the refractory point for oppressive colonialist allegories'.[14] Where 'traditional westerns have functioned as vehicles for an imperialist ideology', Smith argues, 'revisionist' Westerns from the 1960s onwards sought to 'critique' this myth and expose 'the way in which the West has always to a large degree been a historical construction, mediated by colonial concerns, and a violent response to difference'.[15] Smith utilises post-modernist theory in an attempt to interpret a contemporary set of 'marginalised texts' – both literary and cinematic – against traditional narratives of Anglo-American 'self-definition [and] projected fantasy about the self'.[16] Ultimately, he suggests that 'the texts in *Coyote Kills John Wayne* ... often give voice to an alternative history, and indirectly expose the dynamics of a historical memory predicated on forgetting'.[17] In *American Cinema in Transition* (2011), Martin Holtz similarly argues that the classical Western is ideologically conservative, and that the so-called 'New Hollywood' Westerns of the late-1960s to mid-1970s can be considered to be politically revisionist. His study seeks to analyse 'a representative corpus of Westerns in the two respective periods', before going on to argue (like Smith) that the Westerns of contemporary Hollywood ('Hollywood Now') have developed towards critical self-reflexivity.[18]

The central aim of this study is to offer a series of alternative arguments towards such popular interpretations of the Western. That is to say, I aim to question the professed aesthetic and ideological–mythological functions of the introspective categories: 'classical', 'revisionist' and 'post'. I do not seek to deny that such descriptives *can* be suitably applied to certain Westerns; rather, I seek to argue that they do not speak for the whole genre, and are inadequate terms for establishing a generic blueprint by which one can place films chronologically. I ally myself with the growing belief in film genre studies that attempts to discern 'blueprints', or formulas, often result in simplified or erroneous misreadings of whole rafts of film texts that are forced to fit what are essentially ready-made grids of reference. Intrinsic to such a line of analysis is a disputation of the general critical acceptance of a given genre's historical trajectory. In the case of the Western, that it 'evolved' during the course of the twentieth century from a rudimentary simplicity (the silent era) towards formal, thematic and ideological coherence ('classical'), and, finally, towards introspection, fragmentation and incoherence ('revisionist') – leading towards its demise ('post'). Under direct scrutiny is the suggestion that the classical Western is ideologically monolithic, that it *always* promoted a specious myth-historical memory aimed at Anglo-American 'self-definition', which justified a 'violent response to difference'. At the same time, this study questions the equally spurious assertion that revisionist Westerns *always* freed themselves from traditional notions of masculinity, heroism and Anglo-male bias.[19]

Of course, it should be noted that others have written on the Western without adhering to such schemas, but these are very much in the minority. Most notable of such scholars is Tag Gallagher, whose 1986 essay, 'Shoot-Out at the Genre Corral', was one of the first to scrutinise the evolutionary approach as it had been widely applied to the Western.[20] Gallagher argued for the cyclical nature of genres over any evolutionary pattern. He also pointed out the contingent nature of any cultural–ideological meanings that may be read into various periods of Western film production, and denied that classical Westerns were necessarily more simplistic in their narratives than later, more properly revisionist films. I will utilise Gallagher's essay as a basis for my own arguments in the chapters that follow, and try to expand upon his work as, although his essay is both convincing and provocative, few contemporary Western film scholars have utilised it to any great degree. In fact, most simply do not mention it at all.

Questioning the evolutionary approach to Hollywood genres in general has, of course, been established within the broader scope of film studies, most notably by Rick Altman and Neale (mentioned above).[21] Neale's account is perhaps the more compelling, and constitutes an excellent overview and critical analysis of the last few decades of aesthetic and thematic approaches to genre. He argues for a need to recognise 'the transience of genres, to deprive them of eternal or essential features, and to conceive these features instead as both historically provisional and empirically diverse'.[22] From remarks such as these, we can situate Neale's questioning of the evolutionary approach more broadly in the 'historical turn' in film studies. This is to say, the growing proclivity within contemporary film scholarship towards focusing on the specific contextual detail of individual productions (particularly their industrial contexts), as opposed to the use of teleological approaches or otherwise sweeping generalisations. Consequently, Neale's study suggests that the 'utility' of Hollywood genres with regard to historical shifts, changes in industrial practices, audience consumption/tastes and 'the socio-cultural contexts within which its films are produced and consumed[,] . . . needs to be re-examined, and that there is thus ample scope for more debate, more thinking and more research'.[23]

This study is intended as a contribution to such an overall approach. That such a study is valuable can be justified on the grounds that it becomes apparent that, despite Gallagher's valuable opinions on the Western *and* despite the broader developments in the field of genre studies, such as those provided by Altman and Neale, some of the more recent critical studies associated with the Western seem to have taken little notice of this development to the extent that they seem to fall back into the more sweeping and simplistic generalisations associated with the mythological and evolutionary approaches.[24] Although a comprehensive explanation as to why this seems to be the case is unlikely to be possible, a partial explanation might be found in the above-mentioned pervasiveness of frontier mythology in US society. After all, the Western is where these myths have been engaged with most directly in popular culture and for the longest period of time. The myth is certainly often considered to be the major thematic element in what the greater majority of Westerns are about, so to speak.

I wish to make it clear at this point that I do not deny all charges made against the Western. For much of what defines the genre has, undeniably, grown out of the myth of the West, and over the years the Western certainly has had a lot to answer for. However, I contend that, while it may have often celebrated this grand narrative, the Western has just as often also *reacted* to it. It did this by questioning the myth's legitimating pretensions, disclosing the darker currents of America's frontier legacy, and offering up cautionary tales for the cultural-hegemonic beliefs in American exceptionalism and Manifest Destiny. In short, it highlighted the symptomatic hubristic condition of US self-righteousness. In the very best efforts of the Western, and for every instance of the veneration of socially redemptive violence in the form of 'frontier justice', there exist counter-narratives that question and critique the sacred shibboleths of the United States. And yet, as indicated above and as this study seeks to further illuminate, a significant amount of academic criticism is still responsible for perpetuating what I would term the myth of the West*ern*. This is to say, the general acceptance as fact that the Western can be adequately defined in terms of a set of formulaic and thematic premises that can be easily identified and traced as the genre evolved by following its own 'internal logic', and/or in accordance with shifts in sociocultural, political and historical attitudes towards frontier mythology.

Indeed, when one looks more closely at a range of the most prominent Westerns produced during the course of the twentieth century, it becomes readily apparent that the pattern that seems to define the genre progressively disappears, to be replaced by a mosaic of varied narratives that reflect not only different times, but also different attitudes existing within any given time. I propose to investigate selected aspects of this mosaic with the intention of shedding new light onto the Western as a genre, and assessing how it can be interpreted culturally, historically and politically.

That the Western genre is capable of justifying such a diverse wealth of applied cultural analysis has already been considered by some notable film scholars. This is perhaps best summed up by Philip French who, in 1974, suggested that, thematically, the Western genre 'is a great grab-bag, a hungry cuckoo of a genre, a voracious bastard of a form, open equally to visionaries and opportunists, ready to seize anything that's in the air from juvenile delinquency to ecology'.[25] But before we take up the intellectual substance of the Western, it is necessary first to summarise the cultural, historical and political premises on which the Western (and the majority of scholarship on the Western) is said to be based, and to define in more detail the terms of analysis that this study will use.

II

The formal and thematic origins of the Western can be traced back at least as far as the novels of James Fenimore Cooper; in particular, to the Leatherstocking tales. The protagonist of these novels, Natty Bumppo – the original 'man without a cross' – is often regarded as the Western hero's progenitor; however, the time and location of the version of frontier mythology that was to become the preferred focus of Hollywood's West (one or two key instances notwithstanding) was not the eighteenth-century forests of Cooper's literary imagination, rather, it was to be the mid- to late nineteenth century during the US appropriation and settlement of the vast North American interior.

Voicing a typical opinion within Western film scholarship, Jim Kitses suggests that the 'raw material of the western' is drawn from this historical period:

> Hollywood's West has typically been from about 1865 to 1890 or so ... within its brief span we can count a number of frontiers in the sudden rush of mining camps, the building of railways, the Indian wars, the cattle drives, the coming of the farmer. Together with the last days of the Civil War and the exploits of the badmen, here is the raw material of the western.[26]

This temporal–spatial transfer amounted to nothing less than a paradigm shift in the terms of the popular mythology that would explain the process of westward expansion to US Americans as the nation stood on the cusp of the twentieth century.[27]

The causal factors for this shift can be related, in large part, to the start of an economic depression that was to affect most of the 1890s. This decade witnessed a period of social upheaval that, at least in part, grew out of a growing sense of panic and anxiety over the 'closing' of the frontier following a period of unchecked expansion matched only by unchecked immigration. America's sense of itself as a place of equality and opportunity was being threatened by the unprecedented rise of a corporate–industrial society in which growth had created wealth, but not general prosperity. Industrial monopolies and business cartels emerged to exploit the market, and fuelled political protest and conflict between labour and capital, and many in the United States became nostalgic for a simpler vision of America. This led to the deliberate construction of the myth of the West towards the end of the nineteenth century by a number of interrelated and mutually interdependent artistic, historical and political personalities.

William Frederick Cody

Standing prominent among these personalities was the figure of William F. Cody, aka, 'Buffalo Bill', whose much-celebrated show 'Buffalo Bill's Wild West and Congress of Rough Riders of the World' toured the United States and Europe from 1883 to 1916.

During its incredible run, Cody's 'Wild West' fused history with riotous legend in a series of action-packed extravaganzas that enthralled and 'educated' audiences with spectacles of 'Cowboys and Indians'. Also included were re-enactments of recent historical events, chiefly 'Custer's Last Stand', which typically segued into fantastical braggadocio fiction as 'Buffalo Bill' acted out the killing and scalping of an 'Indian' in a vengeance act entitled 'The First Scalp for Custer'. There were also various supporting acts, such as horse racing, stunt riding and marksmanship. The whole spectacle typically concluded with an action-packed 'Indian' attack on the 'historical Deadwood Stagecoach', with 'Buffalo Bill' riding to the rescue.[28] Essentially, the Wild West fuelled the public's imagination for a violent frontier filled with merciless savages and brutal outlaws, and then fed its desire for a hero to tame it.

Through a fortuitous encounter with the journalist Ned Buntline (real name, Edward Judson), Cody had been a dime novel character and stage actor in frontier melodramas since the 1870s. But the Wild West was an entertainment enterprise like no other. Exploiting the new era of mass communication technologies through advertising campaigns and even product-branding made 'Buffalo Bill' an internationally recognised symbol, what we would call a 'superstar' today. Richard Slotkin points out that the Wild West even became '"recognised" by "Governments, Armies and Nations" [achieving] something like diplomatic recognition'.[29] Joy S. Kasson describes the peculiar cultural significance of the Wild West on the public's perception of America's frontier history:

> By the last decade of the nineteenth century, as the Indian Wars faded into the past and the Great Plains began to open for settlement and tourism, the Wild West represented by Cody's show came to be understood by its audience as a nostalgic recreation rather than a representation of the world of the present ... Yet the Wild West created a special kind of memory landscape. It had the ability to persuade viewers that the past it depicted was *their* past, something they had viewed with their own eyes.[30]

The Wild West stands as an example of the complex relationship that American popular culture has with the frontier, encompassing within its broad range the myth of the West, the sponsorship of a particular cult of celebrity and the promotion of a triumphalist version of frontier history. Perhaps of most significance was the cultural status it gave to the cowboy. As a professional cattle drover, the cowboy was a marginal, even insignificant, historical figure, but through Cody's celebrity and the success and longevity of the Wild West, he was given new appeal as a symbol of the frontier. As David Hamilton Murdoch points out:

> by the mid-1890s the cowboy was on the edge of drifting into obscurity. Instead, he achieved immortality within a decade and became the final version of the hero from the frontier ... he became the focus of all the ideas which were coalescing into the definitive myth of the West.[31]

In many ways, what we now regard as the Western was 'born' on the cusp of the twentieth century through the appeal and impact of entrepreneurs like

Cody. Kasson points out that 'Buffalo Bill's Wild West had already assembled the tropes and images of the American West into a convincing and popular entertainment form [creating] the template early filmmakers could adapt and embellish'.[32] Slotkin claims that the Western's roots 'go deeper into the American cultural past than those of any other movie genre ... The West was already a mythologized space when the first moviemakers found it.'[33] *The Great Train Robbery* (Edwin S. Porter, 1903), contentiously described by George N. Fenin and William K. Everson as 'the first Western', undoubtedly drew upon the popular appeal of the Wild West. Supplanting the stagecoach attack with the outlaw's hold-up of an express train, the film's use of the developing cinematic techniques of close-ups and editing brought a new sense of immediacy to Cody's well-established action and adventure formula.[34] Cody himself attempted to incorporate the Wild West into the medium of film when he starred in a three-reel biopic of himself entitled, *The Life of Buffalo Bill* (Paul Panzer, 1912). Kasson again:

> The new medium of film gave the impression of 'real life' to scenes that were also highly dramatic; in holding these claims in balance and creating a convincing impression of shared memory, this early film sketched the contours that would define the film western for a half-century.[35]

Hers is an opinion shared by the majority of scholars writing on the Western: in creating a romanticised version of the nineteenth-century American West, the cinematic Western is, to a large extent, responsible for the erroneous idea that many people still have of that period.

Of course, Cody and his promoters were not solely responsible for the popularity, much less the credibility, of the myth of the West or the Western. The heroic version of the frontier story was contemporaneously given intellectual substance in the field of professional historiography by a young historian from Wisconsin.

Frederick Jackson Turner

It is generally considered that, in addition to disseminating the myth's ideological premises, the Western allowed for the clear articulation of an historical thesis. This thesis was famously delivered by Frederick Jackson Turner at a meeting of the American Historical Association (AHA), held at the World's Columbia Exposition in Chicago on 12 July 1893. Interestingly, on the same day as Turner's address, Cody's Wild West staged an unofficial performance outside the grounds of the Exposition, even extending special invites to AHA delegates (an invite that Turner declined).[36]

Turner insisted upon a direct relationship between successive frontiers in Anglo-American expansion across the continent, and of the consequent development of a uniquely American democratic civilisation. In what are now famous and often quoted words Turner illustrated what, for him, was evident in the title of his thesis, 'The Significance of the Frontier in American History': 'The existence of an area of free land, its continuous recession, and the advance of American settlement westward, explain American development'.[37] By this Turner actively sought to rupture popular consensus among his academic contemporaries, whose common advocacy lay with those such as Herbert Baxter Adams who believed in an evolutionary link between American institutions and their Anglo-Germanic ancestors in Europe. By stressing the differences rather than the similarities between Europeans and Americans, Turner was dispensing with so-called Teutonic 'Germ Theory' and, instead, promoted the frontier as a point of origin.[38]

Although not met with rapturous applause at the moment of its delivery, Turner's 'Frontier Thesis' (as it came to be known) undoubtedly captured the popular mood, subsequently becoming something of an ideological touchstone for many Americans on the cusp of the twentieth century. As with Cody and the Wild West, Turner's placing of the subject of the frontier at the forefront of the national consciousness came at the very moment it was coming to an end as a palpable geographical phenomenon.[39]

Of course, Turner's version of history did not materialise out of the ether any more than did Cody's. What can be said of it is that it galvanised a great proportion of contemporary popular, political, religious and historical opinion. Slotkin alerts us to the protracted legacy of the 'Frontier Thesis', suggesting that many of the 'elements' of Turner's address 'already belonged to the complex of traditional ideas that had accumulated around the idea of the "Frontier" since colonial times, including the concept of pioneering as a defining national mission'.[40] This 'national mission' relates to the overwhelmingly agricultural nature of the initial resulting economy of frontier settlement, and led to the equally overwhelming and long-held belief in America as the 'Garden of the World'.[41]

The notion of the Garden as a cultural ideal is, of course, not unique to North America as a whole or to the United States in particular. It stems from biblical mythology, itself a version of the wider 'myth of the pastoral' to be found in classical and other mythologies, rooted in societies for which agriculture was the principal economic activity. These ideas informed those who most effectively expressed the ideals of the new republic; most famously, Thomas Jefferson, whose defining moment as US president was to ensure the vast Louisiana Purchase from France in 1803. Jefferson believed that American land was now 'so extensive that the cupidity of a thousand generations would not be sufficient to exhaust it'.[42] He proclaimed the ideal American citizen to be the independent yeoman farmer, and the West as the place where countless numbers of settlers could find 'free land', employing axe and plough to create a 'natural democracy'. The myth of the 'American pastoral' was born. However, Jefferson had profoundly miscalculated, as 'during his own lifetime it was already apparent that the arable land available east of the 100th meridian was well on its way to being completely "taken up" and developed'.[43] The pretence of pastoralism was once more severely tested in the mid-nineteenth century. During the American Civil War, the industrial North defeated the agricultural South, and by the close of that century, the United States had firmly established itself as an industrial world power.

Written nearly a century after the Louisiana Purchase, Turner's thesis offered little suggestion of a 'frontier-less' future. Having placed so much emphasis upon its democratising influence – that is, its fostering of the individual exploitation of economic opportunity ('economic individualism') through the development of 'free land' – Turner could not account for the survival of democracy now that the frontier was gone. Instead of looking towards the future, Turner cast his gaze towards the past, and with an evident nostalgia for this Jeffersonian idealism mournfully consigned the frontier's agrarian values to the past. This move is reflected in the pessimistic tone with which Turner concludes the Frontier Thesis: 'Each frontier [furnished] a new field of opportunity, a gate of escape from the bondage of the past . . . But never again will such gifts of free land offer themselves . . . the frontier has gone.'[44]

Turner's assertion that 'the great shaping force of American life was now gone' contributed in no small way to the proliferation of a neo-Malthusian sentiment throughout many areas of US society. 'The essay was not just an original historical synthesis of the American past', argues David M. Wrobel, 'but a classic expression of frontier anxiety.'[45] At its most successful the Frontier Thesis professed to legitimate the vicissitudes of the American 'national character', or 'national identity', and Turner situated this theoretical composite firmly in relation to the frontier during the course of national progress. In doing so, he articulated a major historical theme that many scholars have discerned in the Western genre:

> This perennial rebirth, this fluidity of American life, this expansion west-
> ward with its new opportunities, its continuous touch with the simplicity
> of primitive society, furnish the forces dominating American character
> . . . In this advance, the frontier is the outer edge of the wave – *the
> meeting point between savagery and civilisation.*[46]

In spirit the Frontier Thesis marries a theory of national development with the philosophical underpinnings of Manifest Destiny, throwing its academic weight behind this great *fait accompli* of national predestination. In the nineteenth century, the United States' conception of itself as a force for good was married with a belief in the inevitability of expansion. This triumphalist version of Anglo-America was fully endorsed by Turner, who saw 'the need of a history of the continuous progress of civilisation across the continent'.[47] Turner firmly established the West as the crucible where America's exceptionalist mission – which had begun in 1620 with the

Puritan John Winthrop's 'City on a Hill' sermon – was played out, its end-game realised with the 'closing of a great historic movement [in] American history'.[48]

Thus envisaged, the Frontier Thesis served as an historical document, giving a secular gloss of legitimacy to the overt religiosity of Manifest Destiny. For this reason, the aggressive expansion into the West following the end of the Civil War was not to be understood within terms of imperialism. In expanding the nation, the pioneers were participants in the very momentum of history itself, working to fulfil America's exceptionalist mission. As free citizens of a uniquely constitutional government, these living examples of economic individualism advanced the ideals of freedom and democracy over a 'barbaric wilderness' environment. If some of his contemporary scholars balked at his maverick approach to historical practice, Turner's formulation of a national character was rarely questioned in any concerted fashion during the historian's own lifetime. Indeed, as John Higham is quick to remind us, as far as Turner and his academic disciples were concerned, 'the distinctive character of the nation was presupposed rather than argued'.[49]

The flaws in the Frontier Thesis as a work of historiography are, of course, plain to see. In 1950, Henry Nash Smith was one of the first American historians to point them out. 'The agrarian emphasis of the frontier hypothesis', he suggested, 'has tended to divert attention from the problems created by industrialisation for half a century during which the United States has become the most powerful industrial nation in the world.'[50] Not surprisingly, criticisms voiced by modern scholars focus less on Turner's lack of vision for the future than they do on his blatantly ethnocentric approach. Much like Cody's Wild West in this regard, the Frontier Thesis forwards Anglo-Americans as *the* actors in the great drive west; albeit Turner's heroes are the pioneering farmers, taming the wilderness with the 'plough' rather than Cody's cowboys taming it with the 'gun'. Turner's idea of the frontier as a crucible is, to most modern scholars, tantamount to Creationism. His selective brand of history had little time for the racial 'melting pot' from which all serious historians now accept modern America was forged. For instance, there is scant attention paid to the role played by women on the frontier; less still to the Chinese immigrants who laboured on the railways, or the Hispanic and African Americans, the latter of whom we are informed, 'comprised one third of all range riders' during the cattle industry's brief flourishing in the late nineteenth century.[51] Additionally, criticism abounds with regard to Turner's dismissive categorisation of the Native American as part of a declining savagery, a 'common danger, demanding united action' on the part of the nation to remove.[52] According to Smith, 'the virtual non-appearance of Native Americans in Turner's narrative indicates the extent to which [his] conceptions of a singular American "national character," were predicated on an absence'.[53] The significance of such elisions become clear if we consider that the grand narrative of frontier settlement as an Anglo-American story depended upon 'cultural exceptionalism and dominance [which] could only be asserted and defined against the liminal, the historically silenced'.[54]

Despite these obvious flaws, it would be folly to dismiss the cultural significance of the Frontier Thesis outright. As McVeigh and others have suggested, 'through the agency of writers like Turner ... the West was becoming a set of symbols that constituted not history, but an explanation of history, and in that sense a myth'.[55] And one must *always* take 'national myths seriously as a force in history'.[56] In this respect the Frontier Thesis proved itself to be more politically and culturally accurate than it was historically correct. This is to say, it presented an ideologically desirable (for Anglo-Americans at least) *idea* of America, rather than a 'real' history of America; yet, having successfully integrated itself into a significant proportion of the cultural mindset, it effectively *became* that history.

The 'effectiveness' of the Frontier Thesis upon US culture is attested to by the subsequent multitude of academics, politicians, artists, novelists and journalists who, '[i]n their allegiance to the Turnerian view of history ... fuel[led] the connection between national identity and frontier theory'.[57] One of the longest-lasting effects of Turner's historical philosophy was the fact of the expansion of US hegemony beyond its own continental borders. Naturally this was not seen within terms of imperialism, as the professed belief was one of humanitarianism and social progression: the bringing of democracy and freedom to the 'darker regions' of the world. Such nation-building pretensions have been repudiated by much contemporary historiography, as well as cultural and political discourses, but to this day there are those who still believe, to one degree or another, in America's exceptionalist mission on the international stage.

Theodore Roosevelt

In many ways Theodore Roosevelt is the critical political factor in validating Turner's Frontier Thesis. Roosevelt, the man who would become president of the United States in 1901, sought in the last years of the nineteenth century to elevate the Wild West cowboy to the status of national emblem. In so doing, he crucially helped to expand the concept of Manifest Destiny to embrace international conquest.

Roosevelt, himself a keen amateur historian, traded off his own real-life status as a cattle rancher in Dakota and drew on both Cody's Wild West and Turner's Frontier Thesis in order to shape his own vision of the national character.[58] His input into the creation of the myth of the West opposed Turner much less than it complimented him for his celebration of agricultural settlement. Although a great many of his political pamphlets and historical essays predate Turner's by some years, Roosevelt was quick to perceive the coalescing power of the Frontier Thesis, famously congratulating his professional counterpart for putting 'into shape a good deal of thought that has been float-ing around rather loosely'.[59] However, for Roosevelt it was not the yeoman farmer, but the cowboy who was to become the hero of frontier settlement. Through the cowboy he sought to assert a positive symbol of national identity in an age of rapid industrialisation, economic instability and growing social anxiety. Roosevelt sought to transform the image of the robust cowboy into an heroic symbol of unfettered individualism, galvanising mythic values for a modern industrial age. For him these ranch hands were 'as hardy and self-reliant as any man who ever breathed – with bronzed, set faces and keen eyes that look all the world straight in the face without flinching'.[60]

The masculine ethos of the cowboy was emphasised most vividly in Roosevelt's 1888 pamphlet, 'Ranch Life and the Hunting Trail': 'The whole existence is patriarchal in character. It is the life of men who live in the open … who go armed and ready to guard their lives by their own prowess, whose wants are very simple and who call no man master'.[61] In many ways, the cowboy was Roosevelt's symbolic response to the conundrum posed by Turner's frontierless future. The agrarian values of the West would at least live on in spirit through the honest values of the lone rider of the range: 'he is the grim pioneer of our race; he prepares the way for the civilisation from before whose face he must disappear'.[62]

It was during the Spanish–American War of 1898 that Roosevelt's own heroic persona began to resonate most profoundly, and it was where the role of the United States in the 'world community' was to be defined most delib-erately in terms of frontier mythology. Fighting in Cuba with his own cavalry troop, significantly named after Cody's 'Congress of Rough Riders of the World', Roosevelt self-consciously initiated his own national celebrity, which was enthusiastically taken up and ran with by his political allies and the numer-ous journalists who covered the conflict. The successes of Roosevelt's Rough Riders in Cuba – immortalised by his friend, the artist Frederic Remington in the famous (but wholly mythical) 'Charge of San Juan Hill' – worked to con-tinue Roosevelt's ideological association with the economic imperatives and political agendas that sought to extend the concept of 'westward' expansion overseas. From this perspective, the frontier was not so much 'gone' as it was transposed onto foreign military ventures; these new 'foreign wildernesses' would provide the necessary conditions for producing all that was good in American manhood. (Not insignificantly, Cody even incorporated Roosevelt's exploits in Cuba into the Wild West: 'ditch[ing] "Custer's Last Stand" as the finale set piece for the 1899–1900 season in favour of re-enacting the charge up San Juan Hill. The show … lionised Roosevelt as the ultimate cowboy hero abroad.'[63])

Roosevelt's own historical magnum opus was probably the multi-volume *The Winning of the West* (published between 1899 and 1906). If the 1890s saw the justification of overseas expansion as a continuance of the perceived benefits of the existence of a frontier of sorts, Roosevelt's most significant work of historiography adumbrated on an equally sinister and attendant attitude. McVeigh illuminates that 'for Roosevelt, westward expansion was an epic of racial conflict [and] a clear articulation of American exceptionalism'.[64] In the prevailing cultural mood of the time, it was generally understood that the natural individualist tendencies of the Anglo-Saxon race had, through its own biological gifts, been given the necessary conditions under which to flourish. These were, in Turner's words, 'the existence of an area of free land' that, in Roosevelt's opinion, the Anglo-Saxon race had earned the right to settle through conquest.

Where Turner had essentially elided the Native American, Roosevelt, like Cody, placed the continent's aboriginal inhabitants at the forefront of his version of frontier history. These distinctions are aptly summarised by Slotkin, who informs us that 'Turner's work is remarkable for the degree to which it marginalises the role of violence in the development of the Frontier'; conversely, 'for Roosevelt the history of the Indian wars *is* the history of the West'.[65]

For many film scholars, a general consensus can be discerned, suggesting that the Western combined Roosevelt's 'war centred and racialist historiography' with Turner's 'socio-economic analysis'.[66] Jones and Wills have suggested that, in fact, the 'gun' *superseded* the 'plough' as the primary symbol of the frontier in the Western:

> Hollywood promoted a carbine version of Fredrick Jackson Turner's 1893 frontier thesis . . . Where Turner had envisioned the farmer as hero, Hollywood instead forwarded the gun-toting cowboy as a symbol of Western (and national qualities) of individualism, justice, freedom and self-reliance.[67]

This suggests that Hollywood 'encouraged audiences to see their heritage through a cowboy's gun barrel', and thus engendered the culture of a 'gunfighter nation' (to borrow the title of Slotkin's book). Jones and Wills claim that the genre 'fed into a distinctly violent myth, a Wild West imagining whereby out of conflict came civilisation'.[68]

At its darkest, Roosevelt's take on the history of the American West promoted racialist theories of Anglo-Saxon superiority and the necessity of wars of extermination against the Native Americans. For him, Anglo-Saxon ascendancy constituted nothing less than the 'most striking feature of the world's history'.[69] This attitude clearly follows on from the violent cultural legacy of Cody's Wild West more than it does from Turner's Frontier Thesis. But whatever one's prognosis, it remains clear that the sociocultural, political and historical influences from which the myth of the West was shaped are themselves, deliberately, interrelated and interdependent.

III

As already suggested, the aim of this study is to refigure established critical consensus with regard to the evolution of the cinematic Western genre. As such, I provide less a critique of Western films themselves than I do a critique of the established scholarly readings of them. Also as suggested above, contemporary film genre studies provide a vital springboard into affecting such a critique. To reiterate some of these sentiments, as Neale suggests in *Genre and Contemporary Hollywood* (2002), genre is 'a multi-faceted phenomenon'. He continues thus:

> Genres can be approached from the point of view of the industry and its infrastructure, from the point of view of its aesthetic traditions, from the point of view of the broader socio-cultural environment upon which they draw and into which they feed, and from the point of view [sic] audience understanding and response.[70]

Other studies of genre have declared similar findings. For example, in *New Hollywood Cinema* (2002) and in one of the few specific references to Gallagher's 'Shoot-Out at the Genre Corral', Geoff King writes:

> Genres are not only shaped by internal processes of development. They owe many of their characteristics at any particular moment to broader social, cultural and industrial factors . . . Film history suggests that genres undergo various cycles rather than any linear process of evolution. More questioning or self-conscious versions of genre films can be associated with particular periods, but this is the result of particular contextual factors rather than any automatic or in-built dynamic.[71]

We might consider this statement in direct relation to the Western. However, and again as suggested already, despite the convincing arguments for the 'multifaceted' nature of Hollywood genres illuminated by scholars such as Neale and King in recent years, claims for the evolution of the Western – those which draw off older, teleological approaches – continue to be in evidence in contemporary Western film scholarship. Such claims are often married to the equally questionable assumption that the so-called classical Western wholeheartedly endorsed the Cody–Turner–Roosevelt frontier narrative, rather than interrogate its ideological function. Equally, the evolutionary approach suggests that Westerns from the mid-1960s onwards did little else *but* interrogate this function. Furthermore, a belief still holds that, in a so-called post-Western age, the genre has given over to pastiche to such a degree that all it can do is rehash traditional forms for the sake of nostalgia, or else remake itself within terms of a degraded, self-defeating – even self-*hating* – and utterly diminished form.

   In the chapters that follow I shall develop my critique. The study is divided loosely into two parts spread over five chapters, each of which deal with the genre's supposed 'classical', 'revisionist' and 'post' phases. Each chapter features detailed case studies that offer critical analyses of both individual films and of existing scholarship related to them, as well as to more general aspects of the Western genre as a whole. While it is structured chronologically, this is not to suggest acceptance of evolutionary schemas. Indeed, undermining patterns of development rather than supporting them, probing for narrative complexity rather than identifying narrative uniformity, are among this study's primary aims.

Although it claims to be representative, given the sheer number of Westerns, the range of themes the genre encompasses, and the approaches that have been taken to the study of the genre, this book does not (and cannot) claim to be exhaustive. Such attempts have been made in the past. But this is not such a book. Rather, it is intended as a contribution to the scholarly debate on the Western, and should be regarded as such. It does not, therefore, provide an expansive survey of the genre as much as it scrutinises existing Western film genre scholarship. For that reason, while this study provides a great depth of coverage, a greater deal of material is inevitably left out. For instance, it places little emphasis on the silent era Western; not entirely because of the unfortunate fact that only a small percentage of them still exist, but because this study's critical emphasis is on responding to the so-called 'decline of the Western' from its classical period onwards. (Some mention is made of a small number of applicable pre-Second World War sound films.) Though ample scholarship exists on this period of the Western, I hope this selective study adequately demonstrates that there is much yet to be explored. Rather than attempting a detailed analysis of the contemporary post-Western, the second part of this study – comprising Chapters 4 and 5 – offers an introduction into an exciting new cycle of production in the genre: the contemporary-set 'border' Western. Finally, offering an overall analysis of the Western's relation to frontier mythology together with its historical function is important, because for the majority of Western film scholars the genre is a form driven by myth at the *expense* of history. The approach taken in *Myth of the Western* therefore offers readers a greater understanding of the historical significance of the genre and – despite the numerous assertions of its demise – of its continuing artistic and cultural relevance.

Chapter 1 begins by discussing the terms by which the classical Western has been typically analysed in terms of its promotion of the myth of the West, along with the assumption that any pretence to historical dimension that this phase of the genre may possess is subsumed under an overriding mythological function. Defining key terms is the subject of the first section of Chapter 1. Drawing across a wide range of Western film scholarship, it describes the Western in relation to genre evolution theories and their political-allegorical variants. A case study that reads *Shane* (George Stevens, 1953) formally and thematically within terms of genre studies and the classical Western brings together the interrelated generic and sociocultural issues raised in this first section: heroism, individualism and the community, and the concept of the American national identity. A discussion of the classical Western's attitude towards the conquest of Native America is also initiated; it typically being defined through the Turnerian descriptive of '*the meeting point between savagery and civilisation*'.

The second part of Chapter 1 draws extensively on genre studies to provide a detailed critique of evolutionary approaches and of the classical schema. It does more than simply articulate the limitations of existing accounts; it offers a direct challenge to the premises upon which they rest. This section addresses, first, the arbitrary nature in terms of application of the formal attributes of the classical label. Then, it argues that this act of description constitutes the deliberate construction of categories by a process of selection and exclusion, distortion and effacement. Identified is a challenge to the proclaimed simplicity of the classical Western, both in its supposed adherence to triumphalist versions of frontier history *and* in its relation to genre evolution theories. Chapter 1 thus concludes by arguing that *Shane* contains a series of counter-historical aspects within its narrative that suggests that the film's sociocultural, political and historical dimensions are far more apparent and, indeed, far more complex than allowed for in classical schema or evolutionary and mythological readings.

Chapter 2 begins by discussing *Stagecoach* (John Ford, 1939) in relation to two interrelated themes that will frame its terms of debate: the 'captivity narrative' and the Western's methods of articulating Anglo-American sociocultural attitudes towards Native America. Its first aim is to offer a brief history of the captivity narrative and how the issues raised by it have been variously represented in popular culture. In *The Searchers* (John Ford, 1956), the cultural currency of the Rooseveltian 'race war', combined with the themes of abduction and captivity, raise issues about the role played by racial difference in structuring the myth of the West, as well as the nature of the Western's role in disseminating this mythology. The genre's portrayal of Native Americans is rethought in this section, arguing for the existence of a more complex consideration than is often attributed to either *The Searchers* specifically, or the classical Western more generally. These arguments are taken up in brief discussion of John Ford's 'Cavalry Trilogy' and some of the so-called 'pro-Indian' films of the period. These Westerns – along with *The Searchers* – are discussed alongside more contemporary films that boast sympathetic portrayals of Native Americans; chiefly, Kevin Costner's *Dances with Wolves* (1991). The purpose of this discussion is not to refute racist charges against the Western, but to provide a counter-argument to the evolutionary paradigms that identify socially progressive patterns in the genre's portrayal of the Native American. In other words, those claiming, over time, the existence of ever-more liberal or revisionist depictions of Native Americans as a *general rule*.

The second part of Chapter 2 considers *The Searchers'* complex depiction of both the hero and the pioneer community he nominally protects. In this respect, it develops some of the arguments outlined in Chapter 1, suggesting, once again, that the historical dimension of the classical Western is, indeed, complex and *overt*, requiring further critical re-evaluation. First, symptomatic readings of the historical significance of *The Searchers* are outlined before making the case for the existence of another, overlooked, dimension to its historical significance – one relating to its temporal setting. If read in this way, themes of miscegenation, captivity and race war, as channelled through the psychology of the film's hero, also relate to nineteenth-century notions of the American national identity in relation to Native Americans. While certainly not devoid of prejudice, *The Searchers*, by acknowledging imperialist conquest masked as historical progress, highlights Anglo-America's complicity in the genocide that lay behind the myth of the domestication of the wilderness. Overall, this chapter suggests that, along with all its flaws, *The Searchers* offers a powerful critique of the myth of the West, making it clear that the myth's values – and those who embody them – are beyond redemption.

Chapter 3 begins by providing a critical analysis of the asserted historical development of the revisionist phase of the genre. The commonly held view is that, from around the early 1960s onwards, the Western's best efforts became increasingly self-conscious *and* self-critical. This was seen in both the formal development of its own classical plot formulas, and in a critical shift in cultural attitudes towards its informing mythologies. As *The Man Who Shot Liberty Valance* (John Ford, 1962) is often considered to be the locus in the shift away from classicism, this chapter begins by scrutinising its deconstruction of the myth of individualist heroism as a specifically – and often asserted – revisionist trait. After *Liberty Valance*, a slew of films have typically been forwarded as opening up the floodgates on such issues as violence, gender, race and the darker aspects of Anglo-America's 'triumphant' march across the continent. The typical view held that such films consciously raised issues concerning their own status as Westerns, and of the genre's historical role in the construction of erroneous cultural attitudes and belief systems. Seen from this perspective, the West as depicted in the classical Western is largely a distortion of the 'real' experience of the frontier, while the so-called revisionist Western acts as an historical corrective.

The second part of Chapter 3 moves towards the close of the twentieth century. *Unforgiven* (Clint Eastwood, 1992) is often held up as an exemplar of the revisionist Western; moreover, as *the* example of the end logic of the genre's supposed formal and ideological self-critique. First is a contextual review of scholarship on *Unforgiven*, most of which fixes the film's chronology firmly in the genre's pessimistic 'late' period. Most analyses of *Unforgiven* tend to assume a set of classical generic codes and motifs that the film either successfully repudiates through a conscious semiotic and thematic revisionism, or else ends up succumbing to by the narrative's climax. This chapter scrutinises both approaches. It also critiques McVeigh's revisionist analysis of *Unforgiven*,[72] offering the counter-argument that, despite its pretensions, *Unforgiven* is far less revisionist (or post-modernist) than he suggests. Comparing it with older films, such as *Stagecoach*, *High Noon* (Fred Zinnemann, 1950), *The Gunfighter* (Henry King, 1950), and *Shane* and *The Searchers*, this chapter refutes the common revisionist contention that, over time, the optimistic vision that typified the frontier communities of the classical Western becomes darker and more complex.

Whereas Chapters 1, 2 and 3 share an overall thematic thread in seeking to undermine evolution theory through recourse to famous and much-discussed Western films, Part Two – Chapters 4 and 5 – brings us up to the current century and seeks to deal with the so-called post-Western through the analysis of two contemporary films set along the Mexico–Texas border: *The Three Burials of Melquiades Estrada* (Tommy Lee Jones, 2005) and *No Country for Old Men* (Joel and Ethan Coen, 2007). I argue that both films engage with an array of generic Western themes and tropes in order to provide complex articulations of the history, geography and legends of the American southwest. Equally, and in stark opposition to *Shane*, *The Searchers* and *Unforgiven*, neither film has (so far) received much in the way of scholarly attention.[73] Within the context of the theme of cultural hegemony and the growing academic field of trans-nationalism, these final two chapters argue for the continued sociocultural, political, and historical value of the Western against assertions that the genre is somehow 'dead', and that the post-Western exists as some kind of post mortem of the genre itself.

Chapter 4 begins by analysing the work of the New Western historians, notably that of Patricia Nelson Limerick. Specifically, it considers her attack on Turner's Frontier Thesis and her attempt to replace it with the more complex term, *la frontera*, as *the* defining paradigm of the historical West. It explores the extent of *Three Burials'* scrutiny of the myth of the West, suggesting that the film deconstructs the concept of a homogeneous and stable American national identity. *Three Burials* critiques America's 'dominant fiction' – this time in relation to Hispanic America – through its narrative focus on the borderlands. It reveals that myths abound on both sides of the border – of all borders; furthermore, that what the 'wetbacks' depicted in the film are chasing is their own myth of the United States.

The chapter concludes with a philosophical discussion of the inextricable status of myth and history. In this sense it develops the previous analyses of *The Searchers*, *Liberty Valance* and *Unforgiven*, addressing the question: what actually *counts* as history? Ultimately, I suggest that *Three Burials* offers a compelling and critical examination of the way in which the myth of the West has shaped the concept of national identity along racist and gendered lines; at the same time, it demonstrates the Western's long-standing capacity to oppose such a conception.

Chapter 5 develops Chapter 4's concerns describing the borderlands setting of *No Country for Old Men* as a term of both geographical *and* ideological reference. It also develops the theme of America's national identity in relation to the Western. It does this through recourse to *The Searchers*, as well as to more recent films with a contemporary setting, such as *Lone Star* (John Sayles, 1996). *No Country* has been regarded by the few critics and journalists who have discussed the film as an example of a post-Western. This chapter scrutinises this appellation, providing a short account of the supposed development of the Western in this direction from around the time of *Hud* (Martin Ritt, 1963).

The chapter then discusses the allegorical significance of *No Country* in (de)constructing the cultural rhetoric behind early twenty-first-century US foreign policies, specifically those in Afghanistan and Iraq. While certainly not comprising the whole of *No Country*'s significance, a discussion of these issues does provide an inroad into one of this study's primary focal points: the figure of the Western hero. The hero provides the lens by which the chapter observes how *No Country* assesses the role of myth in history and its sociocultural role in the contemporary world. Overall, the chapter argues that *No Country* utilises the Western's generic conventions in order to affect a critique of the cultural–ideological influence that the myth of the West still holds over the political trajectory of the United States in its self-assumed role as the world's figurative lawman.

That this selection of films under discussion is neither exclusive nor exhaustive seems too obvious a point to mention; however, given the nature of my criticisms, it needs to be addressed. The films provided as each chapter's main case study do provide me with representative examples of what have been termed the 'classical', 'revisionist' and 'post'-Western phases of the genre. That these films also provide me with suitable 'fences' upon which the narratives of other significant Westerns can be placed and discussed in context further justifies my selection of them as suitable films for analysis. (In truth, I could have chosen a dozen or so other films, and a further dozen beyond that.) Overall, I shall argue that these films help us to re-engage in a fuller discussion of the Western genre, the history of the American West and of the continued consequence of the adherence to myth in contemporary US culture.

NOTES

1. John Patterson, 'Whatever Happened to the Heroes?', Culture section, *The Guardian*, 16 November 2007, p. 6.
2. Ibid., p. 6.
3. Karen R. Jones and John Wills, *The American West: Competing Visions* (Edinburgh: Edinburgh University Press, 2009), p. 5.
4. I borrow the terms 'Garden' and 'Desert' from Henry Nash Smith, *Virgin Land: The American West as Symbol and Myth* (London: Harvard University Press, [1950] 1978).
5. Stephen McVeigh, *The American Western* (Edinburgh: Edinburgh University Press, 2007), p. 155.
6. Patrick McGee, *From Shane to Kill Bill: Rethinking the Western* (Oxford: Blackwell, 2007), p. xv.

7. Ibid. See also p. xvi.
8. David Thompson, 'The Cowboy's Last Stand', *The Independent on Sunday*, 30 April 2006, p. 8.
9. See, for example, Geoff King, *Spectacular Narratives: Hollywood in the Age of the Blockbuster* (London: I. B. Tauris, 2000), esp. pp. 1–69. See also McGee, *From Shane to Kill Bill*, pp. 235–44.
10. McGee, *From Shane to Kill Bill*, p. xv.
11. Robert B. Pippin, *Hollywood Westerns and American Myth: The Importance of Howard Hawks and John Ford for Political Philosophy* (New Haven, CT: Yale University Press, 2010), p. 21.
12. Ibid., p. 21.
13. Steve Neale, *Genre and Hollywood* (London: Routledge, 2000), pp. 135–6.
14. Carlton Smith, *Coyote Kills John Wayne: Postmodernism and Contemporary Fictions of the Transcultural Frontier* (Hanover, NH: University Press of New England, 2000), p. 3.
15. Ibid., p. 16.
16. Ibid., p. 6.
17. Ibid., p. 11.
18. Martin Holtz, *American Cinema in Transition: The Western in New Hollywood and Hollywood Now* (Oxford: Peter Lang, 2011), pp. 1–5, quote on p. 4.
19. A selected list of the conventional evolutionary critical accounts that I shall scrutinise in the chapters that follow are in chronological order: Robert Warshow, 'Movie Chronicle: The Westerner' (1954), reprinted in Leo Braudy and Marshall Cohen (eds), *Film Theory and Criticism: Introductory Readings*, 5th edn (Oxford: Oxford University Press, 1999), pp. 655–67; André Bazin, 'Évolution du western', *Cahiers du Cinéma*, 55 (December 1955), reprinted in Bill Nichols (ed.), *Movies and Methods, vol. 1: An Anthology* (London: University of California Press, 1976), pp. 150–7; Jack Nachbar (ed.), *Focus on the Western* (Englewood Cliffs, NJ: Prentice-Hall, 1974); John G. Cawelti, *The Six-Gun Mystique*, 2nd edn (Bowling Green, OH: Bowling Green State University Popular Press, [1971] 1984); Will Wright, *Six Guns and Society: A Structural Study of Myth* (Berkeley, CA: University of California Press, 1975); Thomas Schatz, *Hollywood Genres: Formulas, Filmmaking, and the Studio System* (New York: Random House, 1981).
20. Tag Gallagher, 'Shoot-Out at the Genre Corral: Problems in the "Evolution" of the Western' (1986), reprinted in Barry Keith Grant (ed.), *Film Genre Reader III* (Austin, TX: University of Texas Press, 2003), pp. 262–76.
21. Rick Altman, *Film/Genre* (London: British Film Institute, 1999); Neale, *Genre and Hollywood*.
22. Neale, *Genre and Hollywood*, p. 217.
23. Ibid., p. 5. See also Nick Browne (ed.), *Refiguring American Film Genres: Theory and History* (Berkeley, CA: University of California Press, 1998) and Steve Neale (ed.), *Genre and Contemporary Hollywood* (London: British Film Institute, 2002), esp. pp. 27–48.
24. Strong threads of genre evolution theory evident in more contemporary scholarship can be found in the following studies, some of which are discussed during the course of this study: Richard Slotkin, *Gunfighter Nation: The Myth of the Frontier in Twentieth-Century America* (Norman, OK: University of Oklahoma Press, [1992] 1998); Michael Coyne, *The Crowded Prairie: American National Identity in the Hollywood Western* (London: I. B. Tauris, 1997); John G. Cawelti, *The Six-Gun Mystique Sequel* (Bowling Green, OH: Bowling Green State University Popular Press, 1999); Smith, *Coyote Kills John Wayne* (2000, mentioned above); Will Wright, *The Wild West: The Mythical Cowboy and Social Theory* (London: Sage, 2001); McVeigh, *The American Western* (2007, mentioned above); McGee, *From Shane to Kill Bill* (2007, mentioned above); Jones and Wills, *The American*

West (2009, mentioned above); Jennifer L. McMahon and B. Steve Csaki (eds.), *The Philosophy of the Western* (Lexington, KY: University of Kentucky Press, 2010).

25. Philip French, *Westerns: Aspects of a Movie Genre* (New York: Viking, 1974), p. 24.

26. Jim Kitses, *Horizons West: Anthony Mann, Budd Boetticher, Sam Peckinpah – Studies of Authorship in the Western* (London: Secker & Warburg/British Film Institute, 1969), p. 8

27. Westward expansion is itself potentially a kind of myth that uses Manifest Destiny as a means to mask US imperial interests elsewhere: south towards Mexico and further 'West' into the Caribbean and the Pacific. For more on US imperialism, see Amy Kaplan, *The Anarchy of Empire in the Making of US Culture* (Cambridge, MA: Harvard University Press, 2002).

28. For a detailed account of the origins of Cody's celebrity, and of the Wild West itself, see Joy S. Kasson, 'Life-Like, Vivid and Thrilling Pictures: Buffalo Bill's Wild West and Early Cinema', in Janet Walker (ed.), *Westerns: Films through History* (London: Routledge, 2001), pp. 109–31. My descriptive of the typical aspects of the Wild West draws directly from her, pp. 113–18. For the cultural significance of the Wild West, see also Corey K. Creekmur, 'Buffalo Bill (Himself): History and Memory in the Western Biopic', in Walker (ed.), *Westerns: Films through History*, pp. 131–51; William G. Simon and Louise Spence, 'Cowboy Wonderland, History and Myth: "It ain't all that Different in Real Life"', in Walker (ed.), *Westerns: Films through History*, pp. 89–108; and Slotkin, *Gunfighter Nation*, pp. 63–88. For a detailed account of the international appeal of the Wild West, see Robert W. Rydell and Rob Kroes, *Buffalo Bill in Bologna: The Americanization of the World, 1869–1922* (Chicago, IL: University of Chicago Press, 2005).

29. Slotkin, *Gunfighter Nation*, p. 82. See also Janet Walker (ed.), 'Introduction: Westerns through History', in *Westerns: Films through History*, pp. 1–24. Walker notes that during a European tour in 1895 the 'Wild West Show', which comprised '600 men, 500 horses, 11-acre mobile showground, and 23,000 yards of tent canvas [and needing] 52 train cars to travel', toured '131 sites in 190 days, covering 9000 miles'. She also tells us that 'the German Army was ordered to study the operation'.

30. Kasson, 'Life-Like, Vivid, and Thrilling Pictures', pp. 116–17 (emphasis in original).

31. David Hamilton Murdoch, *The American West: The Invention of a Myth* (Cardiff: Welsh Academic Press, 2001), p. 62.

32. Kasson, 'Life-Like, Vivid, and Thrilling Pictures', p. 117.

33. Slotkin, *Gunfighter Nation*, p. 234.

34. George N. Fenin and William K. Everson, *The Western: From Silents to the Seventies* (New York: Penguin, [1973] 1977), p. 47.

35. Kasson, 'Life-Like, Vivid, and Thrilling Pictures', pp. 118–19.

36. For an in-depth discussion of Cody and Turner, see Richard White, 'Frederick Jackson Turner and Buffalo Bill', in James R. Grossman (ed.), *The Frontier in American Culture* (Berkeley, CA: University of California Press, 1994), pp. 7–67.

37. Frederick Jackson Turner, 'The Significance of the Frontier in American History' [1893], in Frederick Jackson Turner, *The Frontier in American History* [1920] (Tucson, AZ: University of Arizona Press, [1920] 1986), pp. 1–38, quote on p. 1.

38. For an account of 'Germ Theory', see Ray Allen Billington, *Frederick Jackson Turner: Historian, Scholar, Teacher* (New York: Oxford University Press, 1973), esp. pp. 64–6. Billington outlines the general historical consensus around 1870–80, which held 'that the Aryo-Teutonic peoples who had occupied the Black Forest of Germany in the days of Tacitus had developed the democratic institutions later to be shared by Great Britain, Germany, and the United States.'

39. Turner's delivery of the 'Frontier Thesis' came less than three years after the National Census Bureau for 1890 had declared the frontier officially closed.
40. Slotkin, *Gunfighter Nation*, p. 30.
41. Smith, *Virgin Land*, ch. 11, 'The Garden of the World and American Agrarianism', pp. 123–33.
42. Richard Slotkin, *The Fatal Environment: The Myth of the Frontier in the Age of Industrialisation, 1800–1890* (Norman, OK: University of Oklahoma Press, [1985] 1994), pp. 79–80.
43. Ibid., pp. 79–80.
44. Turner, *The Frontier in American History*, pp. 37–8.
45. David M. Wrobel, *The End of American Exceptionalism: Frontier Anxiety from the Old West to the New Deal* (Lawrence, KS: University Press of Kansas, 1993), p. 36.
46. Turner, *The Frontier in American History*, pp. 2–3 (emphasis added).
47. Billington, *Frederick Jackson Turner*, pp. 83–4.
48. Turner, *The Frontier in American History*, p. 1.
49. John Higham, 'The Future of American History', *Journal of American History*, 80(4) (1994): 1289–309, quote on p. 1295.
50. Smith, *Virgin Land*, p. 259.
51. Jones and Wills, *The American West*, pp. 93–4.
52. Turner, *The Frontier in American History*, p. 15. We may also note that Smith's *Virgin Land*, although it seeks to update and correct Turner's Frontier Thesis, similarly makes scant mention of Native Americans, only passing references to a series of 'bloody Indian wars' (p. 15).
53. Smith, *Coyote Kills John Wayne*, p. 2.
54. Ibid., p. 2.
55. McVeigh, *The American Western*, p. 26; see also Slotkin, *Gunfighter Nation*, p. 61.
56. Higham, 'The Future of American History', p. 1297.
57. Jones and Wills, *The American West*, p. 39.
58. Selections of Roosevelt's historiography and political philosophy are: *American Ideals, and Other Essays, Social and Political* (New York: G. P. Putnam, 1897); *The Winning of the West*, 6 vols (New York: G. P. Putnam, 1900); *The Strenuous Life*, from *The Works of Theodore Roosevelt in Fourteen Volumes* (New York: P. F. Collier, 1901); and *The Rough Riders* (New York: Da Capo Press, [1902] 1990). For an excellent biography of Roosevelt, see Edmund Morris, *Theodore Rex* (New York: Random House, 2001). For Roosevelt's views on the cowboy, see Sarah Watts, *Rough Rider in the Whitehouse: Theodore Roosevelt and the Politics of Desire* (Chicago, IL: University of Chicago Press, 2003).
59. Roosevelt's salutary remark has been widely quoted. As referenced chronologically in the works I have thus far cited, see Billington, *Frederick Jackson Turner*, p. 130; Slotkin, *Gunfighter Nation*, p. 29; McVeigh, *The American Western*, p. 25; Jones and Wills, *The American West*, p. 50.
60. Theodore Roosevelt, *Ranch Life and the Hunting Trail* (New York: Century, [1888] 1899), p. 9. Roosevelt, discussed in McVeigh, *The American Western*, p. 17.
61. Roosevelt, *Ranch Life and the Hunting Trail*, p. 6, discussed in Lee Clark Mitchell, *Westerns: Making the Man in Fiction and Film* (Chicago, IL: University of Chicago Press, 1996), p. 25.
62. Roosevelt, *Ranch Life*, p. 25, discussed in Murdoch, *The American West*, p. 72.
63. Jones and Wills, *The American West*, p. 97.
64. McVeigh, *The American Western*, p. 20.
65. Slotkin, *Gunfighter Nation*, p. 55 (emphasis in original).
66. Ibid., p. 60.

67. Jones and Wills, *The American West*, p. 61.
68. Ibid., p. 61.
69. Theodore Roosevelt, *The Winning of the West, vol. 1: From the Alleghanies to the Mississippi, 1771–1783* (Lincoln, NE: University of Nebraska Press, 1995), p. 1.
70. Neale, *Genre and Contemporary Hollywood*, p. 2.
71. Geoff King, *New Hollywood Cinema: An Introduction* (New York: Columbia University Press, 2002), p. 131.
72. McVeigh, *The American Western*, pp. 202–12.
73. For the most recent analysis of *Three Burials* at the time of writing, see Camilla Fojas, 'Hollywood Border Cinema: Westerns with a Vengeance', *Journal of Popular Film and Television, Special Issue: The Western*, 39(2) (2011): 93–101. For *No Country*, see William J. Devlin, '*No Country for Old Men*: The Decline of Ethics and the West(ern)', in Jennifer L. McMahon and B. Steve Csaki (eds), *The Philosophy of the Western* (Lexington, KY: University of Kentucky Press, 2010), pp. 221–41. As Devlin's essay's title suggests, his analysis broadly follows an evolutionary trajectory of declining ethics in the genre, arguing that the 'heroes' get darker, harder to distinguish from the villains than they were previously. (In my opinion, he takes too simplistic a view of earlier Westerns.) In discussing *No Country* he writes: 'we can no longer apply the terms "good" and "bad" to the "guys" opposing one another – and this shatters the order we recognise and assume in every western film' (p. 236).

PART ONE

PART ONE

1. A GOOD MAN WITH A GUN

'A man has to be what he is, Joey. You can't break the mold. I tried it and it didn't work for me. Joey, there's no living with . . . with a killin'. There's no going back from one. Right or wrong it's a brand, a brand sticks. There's no going back.'

I

George Stevens' *Shane* (1953) is a fairly tight adaptation of the 1949 novel by Jack Schaeffer, and has become celebrated as an archetypal Western, as *the* classical Western, in fact, an overtly mythic distillation of the historical migration of Anglo-American pioneers into the Wyoming Basin. *Shane* is set in the dying days of the West, mere months before the Superintendent of the US Census for 1890 would declare the frontier no more. It was, of course, this event that prompted Turner's compelling need to mark the 'significance' of the 'closing of a great historic movement [in] American history'.[1] It is often thought that with *Shane* the genre is 'recognised': Northrop Frye's concept of literary Romance, of a mortal hero who is, nonetheless, marvellous in his actions and superior to those around him, is combined with a profound sense of elegy of the passing of the agrarian frontier, usurped by the encroachment of urban-technological modernity.[2]

In this reading, *Shane* celebrates the 'Winning of the West' and the emergent civilisation at the same time as it mourns the loss of the sense of freedom and individualism that the frontier had supposedly engendered. Of course, such an ideological paradox is not peculiar to the Hollywood Western. It has its roots firmly embedded in a long tradition of popular American frontier literature and poetry, including the likes of Henry David Thoreau, James Fenimore Cooper and Ralph Waldo Emerson. 'For more than a century', Leo Marx informs us, America's 'most gifted writers have dwelt upon the contradiction between rural myth and technological fact.'[3] Such a contradiction manifests itself in the figure of the Western hero. While ultimately siding with 'progress', the hero remains ambiguous in his attitude towards civilisation, preferring instead the realm of wild nature with whose essence he feels a (false) sense of harmony. 'When such a hero dies', writes Douglas Pye, 'it creates the sense of a spirit passing out of nature, coupled with a melancholy sense of the passing of time, the old order changing and giving way to the new.'[4]

It is commonly argued that, by the late nineteenth century, the wilderness as the index of American social 'reality' was being replaced by the industrial cities. The West and the wilderness were now perceived as nostalgic remnants of a lost freedom, and this, of course, made them into concepts more popular than ever. First, I shall offer a description of this type of frontier narrative as it has been read into the Western. I do this insofar as the classical appellation has been defined and reinforced over the years by a large number of film scholars and cultural historians writing on, or referring to, the genre. Such scholars discuss how the classical Western's formulaic structures have become manifested as a series of visual and thematic tropes that have come to 'speak' the language of the genre, as it were. Such tropes, it is alleged, also came to 'speak' a nation's history, advancing a 'national iconography' and work to construct American national identity.

The Western genre has provided an authoritative voice to such a degree that, as far as many were (and still are) concerned, the Western *is* American history.[5] I shall show how film scholarship has read myth as history by 'discovering' these tropes in the genre and discuss how these tropes have been discerned in the narrative strategies of *Shane*. Additionally, I shall show how these fictional representations have been causally related to the triumphalist versions of US history (together with the various other forms of mythic expression) that I discussed in the Introduction. The sustaining premise behind my selection of *Shane* as an appropriate film for analysis can be justified on the following grounds. First, as its allegedly straightforward narrative structure is so often seen to typify the genre, its suitability for the application and articulation of classical Western tropes seems both logical and, moreover, obvious. Secondly, the classical definition of *Shane* offered by most formula analyses works together with the theory of genre evolution. I aim to use *Shane* as a primary text in order to affect a critical response to both of these approaches.

As a generalised notion, and as indicated in the Introduction, genre evolution theory has been taken up by a significant number of film scholars, and it is necessary at this point to offer a more detailed analysis of this approach to genre. It argues for the existence of an increased sense of introspection, self-awareness and self-reflexivity within the formal tropes of a given film category: first, as it establishes itself chronologically in a given period; and, secondly, as it develops formulas, tropes, plot types. That is, as it coalesces into a recognisable genre. According to Thomas Schatz, this is evidenced most profoundly in the Western by tracing the depiction of what he calls the 'changing hero'. In this reading, the hero's reasons for assisting the frontier community, in fact, his attitude towards society in general, evinces a 'growing incompatibility with civilisation'.[6] But the hero does not lose his romantic edge as, according to Schatz, 'he strikes a romantic pose even in the face of extinction'.[7] This pronounced formal development is typically combined thematically with a growing sense of cultural pessimism and increased narrative instability.

Overall, it is said that a mood of disillusionment afflicts the evolution of the Western. This development apparently came to dominate Hollywood film production as a whole by the late 1960s. The reasons posited for this are largely cultural and, according to Steve Neale, depend upon a mistreatment of 'genres simply as vehicles for "capitalist" (or the "dominant") ideology'.[8] Despite what Neale highlights as the obvious problematical issue of assuming the vehicular nature of Hollywood genres, what Ed Buscombe has described as the 'the economic and artistic imperatives of Hollywood' ensured that this approach to film studies has retained a sustained influence in Western genre criticism.[9] Specifically, this influence is felt in most analyses of *Shane*, especially in its relation to the study of diachronic changes within the Western genre as a whole.

The specific sociological causes often put forward for the evolution of the Western from the celebratory classical to the more pessimistic 'anti' or revisionist phases of the genre relate directly to domestic and foreign turbulence in cultural, political and ideological movements and counter-movements in the United States beginning in the 1960s. American idealism was severely undermined in this period by a series of high-profile assassinations, outbursts of racial antagonism and an increasingly unpopular war in Vietnam. It is suggested that this cultural 'turn' came to be reflected in the Westerns produced during this period, leading to darker narratives, ambiguous heroes, and revisionist attacks on the triumphalist, Anglo-American version of US history that classical Westerns were said to champion. When viewed from such a perspective, *Shane* seems like a relic from an older, more optimistic past; a time before the erosion of confidence in a shared national purpose.

The political-allegorical reading (whereby a given film was seen to have more to do with the era in which it was produced than it did with the era in which it was set) has become increasingly popular. The following example is from John H. Lenihan:

> The Vietnam War subsequently shifted debate from the issue of how best to respond to alleged communist expansion to the question of America's own expansionist impulses . . . From the end of World War II through the 1950s, Westerns increasingly reflected contemporary yearnings for peaceful co-existence by emphasising the desirability of negotiating with, instead of militarily destroying, enemy forces . . . until the sixties, when Westerns adopted much of the cynicism and dissent generated by America's policies in Southeast Asia.[10]

It should be noted that political-allegorical approaches to the Western are not automatically beholden to a relationship with genre evolution theory. As Alan

Williams has rightly pointed out, when it comes to Schatz's interpretive schema, the erroneous assumption is that 'it is not the filmmaking system or the social context that has changed, but the genres that have evolved'.[11] The pervading view on this, as summarised by Janet Walker, is that 'although informed by an historical consciousness', genre theories such as those offered by Schatz, 'do not purport in the final analysis to be historical studies'.[12] Walker suggests that, within this schema, the historical function of the Western becomes 'antiquated . . . usurped by formal and ideological issues'.[13] This is not a view of the genre to which Walker subscribes. For her, above all else, 'the western is a profoundly historical genre'.[14]

While the overall emphasis of evolution theory remains introspective genre developments over and above any specific change in historical context, this approach does share much in common with the political-allegorical approach. Both draw similar conclusions as to how and *why* the genre evolved in the way that it did. These similarities are perhaps best summed up by Michael Coyne in what he describes as 'the crucial relationship between era and artefact'.[15] Coyne's main focus is on 'an interpretive analysis of the social or political message underlying selected prestigious Westerns'.[16] Writing in 1997, Coyne's own prognosis of the 'relationship between era and artefact' is severe, ending as it does with the terminal proclamation that 'as a central force in the culture of contemporary American society, the Western is never coming back'.[17] The main reason posited is the Vietnam War. As far as Coyne (alongside numerous others) is concerned, this conflict 'made mockery of long-cherished national concepts of invincibility and righteousness, and the Western was a casualty of the accompanying cultural fallout'.[18]

Relating his political-allegorical readings to genre evolution theory, Coyne outlines his genealogy of the Western's 'birth and death' in organic terms:

> It strikes me that the genre in fact ran a course parallel to human life, with the difference that its birth and death cannot be exactly determined, whereas specific crucial areas of human experience which are frequently gradual and ongoing can, in the Hollywood Western, be pinpointed meticulously: onset of maturity (*Stagecoach*); increase of sexual awareness (*The Outlaw*); first full-blown sexual experience (*Duel in the Sun*); work (*Red River*); approach of middle age (*The Gunfighter*); assumption of greater responsibility (*High Noon*); disillusionment and midlife crisis (*The Man Who Shot Liberty Valance*); and intimations of mortality (most notably *The Wild Bunch* and *The Shootist*). Thus the genre's life cycle has now run its course.[19]

It is clear that Vietnam remains pivotal to such political-allegorical readings. Coyne even goes as far as to insist that 'Vietnam has killed the Western twice. The first time, the war in Vietnam debilitated the cinematic myth of the West. The second . . . the cinematic myth of the Vietnam experience is gradually supplanting the Western as America's most resonant historical moment.'[20]

Likewise, the 'relationship between era and artefact' remains 'crucial' to Schatz's evolution approach, specifically his attempt to discern an overall pattern of development within the genre. Despite shying away from overtly political-allegorical readings of films, implicit in his analysis is the suggestion that, in progressing towards self-conscious formalism, the Western ineluctably became embroiled in sociopolitical *and* historical issues. Thus, Schatz writes:

> As an element of our national mythology, the Western represents American culture, explaining its present in terms of its past and virtually redefining the past to accommodate the present. The image of the Western community in Hollywood movies tends to reflect our own beliefs and preoccupations, and the Western's evolution as a genre results both from the continual reworking of its own rules of construction and expression and also from the changing beliefs and attitudes of contemporary American society.[21]

In his opinion, such an evolutionary trajectory manifests itself in formal developments within the Western, from early rudimentary narrative transparency to eventual complexity and ambiguity:

> [During] the genre's gradual evolution ... It had grown from a naive, simplistic foundation ritual to a sophisticated formula in which American *history and ideology* – and the Western genre itself – could be reflected upon and examined in detail.[22]

Overall, most advocates of either the political-allegorical reading, and/or genre evolution, tend to adhere to John G. Cawelti's assertion that the revisionist narrative–ideological developments in the Western were due to an inability of the frontier mythology underpinning the genre to deal with the traumatic realities of the post-Vietnam War era.[23] Another such adherent was Jack Nachbar. In terms similar to Coyne, Nachbar describes the disintegration of the 'entire Western formula' by the 1970s:

> Like terrified shotgun riders on a Wells Fargo stage blasting away at shadows, the creators of contemporary Western movies are nervously aiming their genre in several directions at once. And like pellets from that shotgun, the Western formula is spreading out into a wide and confusing pattern.[24]

As a sustained critique of these attitudes provides the focal point of Chapter 3 of this study, I shall stave off in-depth discussion on this topic for the moment. Right now I want to consider aspects of the classical Western, and the question begging an answer here in relation to *Shane* is: to what extent is the so-called classical Western so overtly triumphalist or simplistic in either its formal, political-allegorical or historical content?

This question can be related to theoretical issues in film genre studies *writ large*. For instance, Janet Staiger argues against the commonly held assumption that 'Old Hollywood' (or 'Fordian Hollywood') films are somehow 'pure' and more 'easily arranged into categories' than those of the so-called 'New Hollywood' (or 'post-Fordian Hollywood').[25] 'It is one thing to claim, as Cawelti does', she writes, 'that genres are transforming in the early 1970s. It is another to propose that post-Fordian cinema is typified by its hybridity.'[26] Such an arbitrary distinction as Staiger highlights could easily be related to the equally arbitrary distinction between the formal and thematic differences asserted between classical and revisionist Westerns. The argument that earlier Westerns – *c.* 1930–60 – are instances of a somehow more 'pure classical genre', is to suggest narrative simplicity and even mono-ideological naivety. Likewise, to assert that Westerns of the New Hollywood era elicit 'transformation, deterioration, or hybridization of a pure essence or origin', is to be supportive of genre evolution theory's erroneous belief in the Western's 'growth, flowering, and decay'.[27] Neale criticises Schatz for considering genres as 'closed and continuous rather than intermittent systems'. This, he argues, 'is why [Schatz] rarely acknowledges the existence of hybrids'.[28] Neale continues by suggesting that 'the repertoire of generic convention available at any one point in time is always *in*-play rather than simply *re*-played'. This, he suggests, in further criticism of Schatz, 'is why it is so difficult to define genres in anything other than basic terms'.[29] Staiger argues likewise, insisting that, Fordian or post-Fordian, 'Hollywood films have never been pure'.[30]

As indicated above, *Shane*'s very status as a *locus classicus* of the genre enhances its suitability for providing a critical response to the proponents of both the classical reading of the film itself and of the Western's evolution as a whole. The counter-conventional reading that informs the latter part of this chapter takes its cue from Staiger and Neale, and acts as a reaction against established theoretical positions. As for Schatz's suggestion that early cinematic Westerns were 'naive' and 'simplistic' before evolving into a 'sophisticated formula', I contend that, despite a convincing surface appearance, such an argument does indeed amount to little more than conjecture. Furthermore, it depends upon the wilful omission of ambiguous aspects of form, character, plot and narrative in many of the most celebrated classical films, or the total elision of still others from the theoretical equation. This is done presumably in order to best suit the argument that later, or revisionist, Westerns are somehow darker, richer and more complex than their more properly 'pure' classical predecessors. In order to offer an adequate deconstruction of these attitudes, however, it is first necessary to outline the artistic, theoretical and cultural factors that have, and still do, inform such an influential and suggestive approach to the genre. To which end, I now offer a classical reading of *Shane*.

II

At the conclusion of *Shane*, the eponymous hero rides off, wounded and alone, and into the figurative ether of the frontier wilderness. He has just defeated Jack Wilson (Jack Palance), a professional gunfighter and one of the film's principal villains. And as he departs, the buckskin-clad Shane remains as majestic and as mysterious as the Teton Range from which he first emerged; his status as Western legend firmly secured. This image is consistent with the tone of Schaeffer's novel: 'He was the man who rode into our little valley out of the heart of the great glowing West and when his work was done rode back whence he had come and he was Shane.'[31]

Shane tells the story of how this iconic drifter ends up protecting a small Wyoming valley homesteading community from a brutal cattle baron called Rufus Ryker (Emile Meyer). Typically, the classical reading sees the film's ostensible historical inspiration – Wyoming's 1892 Johnson County War, where corporate cattlemen threatened brutal conflict against the region's homesteaders in defence of their economic interests – as merely derivative, transposed, or even reduced, to a personal conflict between Ryker and a small group of homesteaders. However, at the very least, the historical backdrop provides a catalyst driving the narrative action forward.

Desperate to fulfil a newly acquired government beef contract, Ryker means to dispossess the homesteaders (whom he regards as little more than 'squatters' on 'his' range) by any means necessary. His first efforts are aimed at Joe Starrett (Van Heflin), the unofficial spokesperson for the homesteaders. However, when his verbal intimidations (and even attractive bribes) fail, he hires the deadly Wilson to ensure his interests. Events soon escalate when Wilson incites Starrett's friend, Frank 'Stonewall' Torrey (Elisha Cooke Jr), into drawing his gun, goading him with insults about his being 'Southern Trash', before remorselessly gunning him down on the steps of Grafton's Saloon. In classical terms, this moment establishes Wilson as a sadist, a quick-on-the-draw villain who savours his execution of Frank. A professionally skilled hero is required to defeat him. Shane, who up until then had forsaken the 'gun' for the 'plough' by taking up work as a 'sodbuster' for Starrett, reluctantly commits himself to deadly action in defence of the homesteaders' plight. Learning from reformed Ryker cowhand, Chris (Ben Johnson), that 'Starrett's up against a stacked deck', Shane forcibly prevents Starrett from going to confront Ryker over the range dispute, noting that although he might be 'a match for Ryker' he is certainly 'no match for Wilson'. Shane once again takes up his six-gun, bids a tender farewell to Starrett's wife Marian (Jean Arthur), and begins the slow ride towards town.

The climactic shootout at Grafton's has since become iconic: following a tense standoff, in what seems like a heartbeat Wilson draws, but Shane is faster, and the force of his bullet drives Wilson's body to the saloon wall; he quickly spins round, dispatching Ryker, and, before leaving, seeing to Ryker's brother Morgan (John Dierkes), whose concealed rifle had been trained on Shane all along. In one fatal instance, Shane has eradicated the villainous elements of the town and made the valley safe for the homesteaders, a place where children like Joe and Marian's son Joey (Brandon De Wilde) can, in the words of Shane, 'grow up to be strong and straight'.

Cawelti once wrote of such an heroic intervention as an 'epic moment', which was fundamental to the classical Western formula.[32] This mythically constructed scenario, which highlights a major structuring opposition within the Western, typically sees the savage forces of the wilderness threaten an embryonic frontier civilisation, with the hero standing ever-ready to intervene on the pioneers' behalf, a stalwart sentinel 'poised against the threat of lawlessness or savagery'.[33] An important adjunct to the epic moment, to its very narrative functionality, was the so-called 'code of the West', the format for which was arguably established at the turn of the twentieth century by the novelist Owen Wister. In *The Virginian* (1902), Wister described a set of chivalrous attitudes and actions to which his eponymous hero would abide. A close friend of Roosevelt's, Wister is largely credited for bringing the politician's version of frontier history into the field of popular literature. The tone of *The Virginian* was one of romantic nostalgia for the mythic values of the passing frontier, a culturally elitist morality tale aimed at the modern finance capitalist: 'If he gave his word, he kept it; Wall Street would have found him behind the times. Nor did he talk lewdly to women; Newport would have found him old-fashioned.' For many scholars, writing years later, it was these very characteristics that came to embody the spirit of the heroes of Hollywood's 'silver screen': 'the horseman, the cow-puncher, the last romantic figure upon our soil'.[34]

The 'code' was, of course, another constructed fiction and, like the epic moment, a part of the myth of the West. Through it a paradigm was established that worked to synthesise the genre's combined promotion of civilised values, such as community and law, with its simultaneous, yet often antithetical, promotions of individualism and its celebration of violence. According to Cawelti, the code achieved this synthesis by insisting that the hero 'rarely engages in violence until the last moment and [that] he never kills until the savage's gun has already cleared his holster'.[35] In consonance with this, Robert Warshow once suggested that the Western 'offers a serious orientation to the problem of violence such as can be found almost nowhere else in our culture'.[36] His analysis was one of the first to link 'the values we seek in the Western' with a coded use of force:

> Those values are in the image of a single man who wears a gun on his thigh. The gun tells us that he lives in a world of violence, and even that he 'believes in violence'. But the drama is one of self-restraint: the moment of violence must come in its own time and according to its special laws, or else it is valueless.[37]

According to Warshow, the protagonist of the Western is in control of himself. He uses violence only when provoked and, ultimately, in defence of his vision of himself as a man of honour. For Cawelti, the hero's code and the epic moment (where an 'advancing civilisation met a declining savagery') worked to provide 'a fictional justification for enjoying violent conflicts and the expression of lawless force without feeling that they threatened the values or the fabric of society'.[38] Violence as a *moral force* therefore became central to the classical Western formula.

A formal analysis of the shootout in *Shane* will help to illustrate how these concepts have been applied to the Western. As Shane and Wilson standoff against each other, the establishing shot is on Wilson as he draws his gun; a reverse shot is immediately employed, revealing Shane reaching for his holster. Presumably they both draw at the same instant (as two highly skilled and experienced gunmen, seeking to draw first, that is, as quick as possible, would surely be the only way for each to ensure the best chance of their own survival), but the point to remember here is that, through a deliberate editing contrivance, Wilson is *seen* to make a move to draw first. This has the effect of positioning him as the aggressor, whereas Shane, drawing 'second' (only faster) occupies the moral high ground. Hence, *Shane* 'speaks' the 'language' of the genre, and Shane's slaying of Wilson and the Rykers (the epic moment) equates the hero's violence (his coded use of force) not with an act of aggression (which, ultimately, it is), but with an unavoidable and noble defence of the values of American civilisation.

Transforming acts of aggression into a noble defence highlights a common attitude in US society, and forms a major component of its assertion of its dominant ideology, one that is particularly pertinent to the political-allegorical reading of the Western. According to Coyne, the Western hero is 'like the nation's idealised self-image, friendly, benevolent, peaceable and slow to anger; yet once roused to violence he establishes his moral authority with a thorough and often terrible finality'.[39] Typically, the United States justifies its politically sanctioned violence by referral to this notion. It makes its military aggression different to that of other nations, rendering it exceptional within the concept of the national character. Hence, the historical events most celebrated in US society are not so much its military victories like Yorktown or Gettysburg (although these events *are* certainly celebrated), rather they are its *defeats* like the battle of the Little Bighorn, the Japanese attack on Pearl Harbor, and, most recently (and contentiously), the terrorist attacks of 11 September. In the case of the Little Bighorn (transformed by the myth of the West into Custer's Last Stand), an emphasis on the savage nature of the enemy's violence – scalping, decapitation, annihilation – transposes the Lakota, Northern Cheyenne and Arapaho's desperate defence of their ancestral homeland into an act of unbridled aggression. It therefore has the effect of rendering, as with Shane's violence against Wilson and Ryker, invasive violence as a noble defence of the values of American civilisation.

The sociological use of violence as it is depicted in the Western as an aspect of the hero's code has been analysed in-depth by Jane Tompkins. Tompkins, a feminist literary critic (and unashamed Western fan), claims that '[w]orking on Westerns has made me aware of the extent to which the genre exists in order to provide a justification for violence'.[40] She further remarks that, in the United States especially, '[v]iolence needs justification because our society puts it under interdict – morally and legally, at any rate'.[41] She suggests that this justification is teased out during the course of most Western narratives (including *Shane*'s, where the hero is goaded and insulted repeatedly) to 'the point where provocation has gone too far'. And in this instance, 'retaliatory violence becomes not simply justifiable but imperative: now, we are made to feel, *not* to transgress the interdict against violence would be the transgression'.[42] It is from similar such observations that Cawelti declared the Western's 'most obvious and recurrent theme [to be] the moral necessity of violence'.[43] He insists that 'Shane's killings are presented in such a way that violence is not only seen to be inevitable in relation to the plot – since the rancher will not give up his open range except over his dead body – but morally right and even transcendent.'[44] The paradox of the epic moment, therefore, can be summarised thus: the fatal violence of the gunfight, although illegal in the eyes of the laws of civilisation is, nevertheless, acknowledged as necessary for the foundation of law upon which civilisation is to be built. (Of course, the lingering cultural–ideological resonances of a Western like *Shane* are not lost on most contemporary film scholars; nor is it likely that would they have been lost on most audiences back in 1953 when *Shane* was thrilling cinemagoers across the United States. The right to bear arms in defence of one's person and property as enshrined in the Constitution is as powerful (and controversial) a belief today for many in the United States as it would have been back in the 1950s, certainly no less so than on the late-nineteenth-century Wyoming cattle frontier and during the Johnson County War.)

Perhaps the most meticulous account of the classical Western formula comes from Will Wright. His two influential structural studies of the Western, *Six Guns and Society* (1975) and *The Wild West* (2001), offer respective and related analyses of the genre's cinematic mode and of the power of the myth of the West (what he terms 'Wild West mythology') in contemporary US society. In *Six Guns*, Wright interrogates the relationship between individual film texts and the culture that produces them. Specifically, he focuses on the Hollywood Western and the twentieth-century United States. He correctly identifies this culture as existing within a market-based economy of mass industrial production and consumption. He also correctly identifies Hollywood cinema as a product inextricably related to both aspects of this culture. Therefore, his study is primarily a socioeconomic one in which the Western is understood as a mythic distillation that acts as a 'communication from a society to its members'.[45] In *The Wild West*, Wright extends his socioeconomic approach by incorporating a history of social contract theory in America. Wright complements his earlier argument – that Westerns function as modern-day myths for contemporary American society – by suggesting that '[m]yths always offer instructive, entertaining models of appropriate social actions, actions that are compatible with dominant institutions'. Furthermore, that these 'dominant institutions' are 'based on the [market] idea of rational individuals'.[46] In the case of Wild West mythology, it is Wright's contention that such a cultural story offered a 'vision of civil society [that] legitimated market ideas, the ideas of freedom and equality, [and] the idea of private property'.[47]

At once forgoing a complex psychological approach to the genre, *Six Guns* offers up a general theory that observes the Western maintaining a direct, uncomplicated relationship to both the film spectator and a particular period's dominant ideology. Drawing on the structural anthropology of Claude Lévi-Strauss, together with Vladimir Propp's formalist analyses of the plot functions of fairytales, Wright compiles a list of what he understands to be the key variations in the Western's plot structure.[48] These variations are then causally related to cultural, economic and ideological shifts in modern American society:

> [There exists] a clear pattern of change [within] the structure of the myth correspond[ing] to the conceptual needs of social and self-understanding required by the dominant social understandings of [a given] period; the historical changes in the structure of the myth correspond to the changes in the structure of these dominant institutions.[49]

Hence, tied to socioeconomic shifts, the Western undergoes a process of evolution from the 'classical plot' to the 'vengeance variation', the 'transition theme' and, finally, the 'professional plot', which apparently typified generic output in the mid- to late 1960s. The socioeconomic correspondence of the respective genre 'periods' are outlined thus:

> [T]he classical Western plot corresponds to the individualistic conception of society underlying a market economy ... the vengeance plot is a variation that begins to reflect changes in the market economy ... the professional plot reveals a new conception of society corresponding to the values and attitudes inherent in a planned, corporate economy.[50]

(The 'transition theme' is, apparently, 'more logical than temporal [and] includes three films in the early fifties'.[51]) Wright goes on to identify a series of plot structures as integral component parts of the myth of the West. 'For analysis', he writes, 'we can reduce each story to three sets of characters: the hero, the society, and the villains.'[52] Combined with this is his insistence on a series of four basic binary oppositions through which the Western genre is allegedly structured: 'inside society–outside society', 'good–bad', 'strong–weak' and, most pertinent to all structural studies of the Western, 'wilderness–civilisation'. This last is adapted from structuralism's 'nature–culture' master binary under which the 'three sets of characters' can interact within any given film text at any given sociohistorical moment. Of course, such a figuration is not limited to Wright or the Western. His insistence on structuring binary oppositions together with his conception of the genre's evolution is well supported in academic circles, and has long provided producers of popular culture in the United States with a comfortingly simplistic base from which to develop popular ideas of heroism. Within this paradigm, the narrative resolution of the nature–culture binary typically realises the protagonist's 'transcendence of the world of experience' following the ultimate triumph of 'good over evil . . . light over darkness'.[53] As already mentioned, this figuration is typically associated with the tradition of literary Romance. It is essentially utopian in that it seeks to perform a redemptory function. That is, for Frye, lifting man 'clear of the bondage of history'.[54]

Jim Kitses insisted that Frye's mode of literary Romance was central to the Western, 'insist[ing] on the idealisation of characters who wielded near-magical powers'.[55] Kitses also follows Frye's definition of archetypes, and his analysis of the genre is fully consonant with the spirit of literary Romance, providing 'the movement of a god-like figure into the demonic wasteland, the death and resurrection, the return to a paradisal garden'.[56] When interpreted in this manner, Shane and Wilson represent archetypes, and when Shane defeats Wilson it can be equated to good triumphing over evil at the most rudimentary (and Manichean) level.[57]

Kitses' analysis of the genre predates Wright's study by a few years; nevertheless, it strikes a chord with the latter through its similar utilisation of basic structural oppositions. Kitses privileged the opposition, wilderness–civilisation, as *the* master binary and combined *auteur* theory with structural analysis, drawing all opposing concepts under this grand rubric in what he termed a 'structuralist grid'. Schatz similarly relates Kitses' and Wright's structuralist model to *Shane*, interpreting it as 'a virtual ballet of oppositions [where] "open range" and fenced-in farmland manifest the genre's nature/culture opposition'.[58] Schatz's reading is supported by the political-allegorical approach of Lenihan, who declares that Shane's 'sad departure' from the valley at the end of the film 'reflects the classic Western's dichotomy between heroic, free individualism and the more enduring but constraining social order'.[59] This classical view of *Shane* has been reasserted by Ruth Griffin in her 2007 essay, 'Writing the West'.[60] Following her own detailed analysis of Wright's theories, Griffin claims that 'the essence of *Shane*'s narrative . . . can be comfortably mapped onto the classical plot category thereby working to reinforce its generic credentials'.[61]

It is hardly surprising that Wright considers *Shane* to be an exemplar of the 'classical plot', as 'the classic of the classic Westerns' no less.[62] According to Wright's *Six Guns* schema, this stage of the genre constitutes the dominant narrative mode of films produced from around 1932 to 1955. Plots typically involved 'a hero who is somehow estranged from his society but on whose ability rests the fate of that society. The villains threaten the society until the hero acts to protect and save it.'[63] In *The Wild West*, Wright extends the sociological function of this mythic individual, showing how this symbol of the national character developed over time. He identifies him as a 'market hero' in the Rooseveltian mode, a Progressive Anglo-Saxon who 'emerged from the wilderness to build a civil society':

> He symbolised freedom and equality, the end of class privilege, the end of sacred duties. He first appeared in early America as a scout in the eastern forests, knowing the Indians and blazing trails. He became most culturally resonant, however, and most mythically famous, when he changed to the lonesome cowboy wandering the Wild West.[64]

Within this central formal and thematic premise, Wright identifies a number of semantic narrative units, the ordering of which determine the basic syntactic structure constituting any given film or group of films. Within the 'classical plot' category these are said to include (but are by no means exhausted by): 'The hero enters a social group', 'The villains threaten the society', and 'The hero defeats the villains'.[65] Ostensibly, these semantic units are easily grafted onto the narrative of *Shane*, and it is Wright's overall contention that the 'classical plot ... defines the genre', and that all the other plot types, the 'vengeance', the 'transition', the 'professional', are 'built upon its symbolic foundation and depend upon this foundation for their meaning'.[66] Wright effectively suggests that the classical Western constitutes a generic yardstick, with *Shane* as its exemplary instance, the inference being the existence of a touchstone, a 'pure' Western.

Both film scholarship and recent historiography have tended increasingly to equate the classical Western's formal structures, together with its moral justification of individualistic violence, to those of an ideological sentinel seeking to legitimise through paeans to nationalist brands of freedom, democracy and economic individualism; the Anglo-American conquest of the North American continent and the dispossession of the Native Americans (aspects of which the classical Western is typically seen either to justify or to elide). This is certainly the view taken by Coyne, who states that 'Westerns typically enforced white centrality'.[67] Despite the occasional efforts of the genre to correct racial bias, Coyne maintains that such narratives were constructed 'as problems for white America to solve', ultimately suggesting that 'the Western remained a creature and a reflection of white America'.[68] In *The American West in Film* (1985), John Tuska provides us with the most vitriolic attack on the genre's racism, especially with regard to its treatment of Native Americans: 'I would hope that we may once and for all put to rest that killing "mythical" Indians is only so much "newspeak" for enjoying genocide.'[69] He insists that in general 'the

Western film as it has been made deserves the strongest censure which can be brought to bear for the lies it has told'.[70]

Tompkins suggests another form of genocide undertaken by the genre; one which relates directly to Tuska's and is apt for the kind of visual language peculiar to the cinema. She contends that, in constructing 'mythical Indians', the Western partook of a cultural elision of the real Native American so ruthless and so extensive that she felt compelled to leave them out of her analysis altogether:

> My unbelief at the travesty of native peoples that Western films afford kept me from scrutinising what was there. I didn't want to see. I stubbornly expected the genre to do better than it was, and when it wasn't, I dropped the subject ... I never cried at anything I saw in a Western, but I cried when I realised this: after the Indians had been decimated by disease, removal, and conquest, after they had been caricatured and degraded in Western movies, I had ignored them too. The human beings who populated this continent before the Europeans came and who still live here, whose image the Western traded on – where are they? Not in Western films. And not in this book, either.[71]

On the other hand, most of those writing on the Western (and the historical West for that matter) have convincingly argued that Indians are always *symbolically* present in Westerns – if only as degraded caricatures – and that this symbolism is fundamental to any serious study of the genre. For instance, Cawelti remarks that: '[t]he role of savage is more or less interchangeable between Indians or outlaws since both groups are associated [in the genre] with lawlessness, a love of violence, and rejection of the town's settled way of life'.[72] Leslie A. Fiedler reiterates such an assertion when he writes that 'the Redskins are present always by implication at least – even in the shootdown ... when the paleface in a White Hat, beating the paleface in a Black Hat to the draw, symbolically kills the wild Indian in us all'.[73] It is therefore clear, if only on the most prosaic of levels, to read into the homesteader's dispute with the Ryker brothers and Shane's duel with Wilson, this implied symbolic presence of the 'Redskins'.

Less prosaic is the emphasis Tompkins places on the genre's gender bias. For her, the main structuring binary in the Western is not that of wilderness–civilisation, but that between male and female – which we might term masculinity–femininity. In support of this assertion, Lee Clarke Mitchell argues that within the Western 'cultural meaning emerges through binary oppositions patterned on the cultural distinction of simple sexual difference'.[74] Perhaps unsurprisingly, this sexual difference is predicated upon an active, dominant masculinity over a passive, submissive femininity.[75] 'The Western *answers* the [nineteenth century] domestic novel,' argues Tompkins. 'It is the antithesis of the cult of [Christian] domesticity that dominated American Victorian culture

... Westerns either push women out of the picture completely or assign them roles in which they exist only to serve the needs of men.'[76] Furthermore, Tompkins argues that it is typical of most Western narratives that 'not only does the man do exactly what the woman has begged him not to do, but she takes him back after he has done it'.[77] This argument is apparently illustrated in her reading of *Shane*. Moments before the film's climactic gunfight, Marian Starrett 'dissolves into an ineffectual harangue ... unsuccessfully pleading with her man not to go into town to get shot. When the crunch comes, women shatter into words.'[78] Here Tompkins is insisting upon part of the tradition laid out (once more) by Owen Wister: that of the good woman who, despite her initial, seemingly intractable reservations, eventually acknowledges the social *need* for the hero's violence, just as Marion seems to accept what Shane has to go and do in her husband's stead.[79]

The racist and sexist charges made against the Western have been drawn together recently by Kitses, who adds monopolistic capitalism to the charge-sheet, suggesting that: '[t]he recasting of the frontier as a border between the powerful and the dispossessed, men and women, whites and people of colour has unearthed other meanings for the form'.[80] He finds that much contemporary scholarship has acted as a corrective to the 'ideologically innocent criticism of the past', and (in this respect he is echoing Tuska) he finds the genre 'guilty of bad faith'.[81] The gendered and racial bias of the classical Western highlighted by Tompkins and Coyne, respectively, is summed up by Kitses' suggestion that 'the feminine in the genre exists only to validate masculinity as the dominant norm. Encounters with the Indian, regardless of whether the latter is seen as savage or noble, ultimately function only to secure white identity'.[82]

Of course, Wright links racism to his own analysis. In *The Wild West* he describes how, during the late nineteenth century, popular social Darwinist theories of 'racial inferiority' were culturally linked to economic theories of market rationalism. 'They [Native Americans] are failures at rationality', he writes, 'and in terms of the Indian as symbol, that failure is based on race.'[83] Ultimately, Wright suggests that the same market exigencies that justified slavery were similarly utilised as an excuse in order to justify the Anglo-American conquest of the West: 'The savage/civilised distinction, then, could be used to justify conquering and killing non-whites for the sake of market expansion (rational destiny).'[84]

So, if *Shane* is indeed formally indicative of the classical Western, and furthermore, if the classical Western as a whole drew upon mythic structures in order to assert an ideological position that sought to glorify the history of post-Civil War US expansionism in such a fashion, then the ethical implications of this phase of the genre become rather ominous indeed. Put simply, it dictates that women must be subordinated to masculine authority, and that the wilderness and the racial other *must* be civilised, or else eradicated by morally justified and religiously ordained violence. Not only is this deemed an historical necessity, it is a necessity that is inexorably tied to the progress of western civilisation as a whole, and to the very foundations of American democratic civilisation in particular.

Richard Slotkin has comprehensively examined the importance of myth (specifically, frontier mythology, racialism and violence) in the culture, history and politics of the United States. In *Gunfighter Nation* (1992), he records the myth's importance to the complex ideological meanings to be found in the formal and thematic structures of the Hollywood Western. Slotkin considers myths as historically contingent (rather than archetypal, generated by either 'the nature of things' or 'the nature of language') and as working to assert dominant ideologies through metaphor rather than logic, their language figurative rather than scientific. He also emphasises the psychological dimension of myth that, despite Wright's contention that it is 'static', is considered as a socially determined function, as well as being an important plot structure or subgenre of the Western. Akin to Wright, however, is Slotkin's belief that myth essentially 'disarms critical analysis by its appeal to the structures and traditions of storytelling'.[85] Thus, he writes:

> Myths are stories drawn from a society's history that have acquired through persistent usage the power of symbolising that society's ideology and of dramatising its moral consciousness – with all the complexities and contradictions that consciousness may contain. Over time, through frequent retellings and deployments as a source of interpretive metaphors, the original mythic story is increasingly conventionalised and abstracted until it is reduced to a deeply encoded and resonant set of symbols, 'icons,' 'keywords,' or historical clichés. In this form, myth becomes a basic constituent of linguistic meaning and of the processes of both personal and social 'remembering.'[86]

Slotkin relates this definition of myth to US cultural perceptions of the history of the American frontier, painstakingly chronicling how it was expounded upon 'in a body of literature, folklore, ritual, historiography, and polemics produced over a period of three centuries'.[87] (It is worth noting that Wright takes no account of such a vast pre-cinematic legacy.) Asserting an effective ideology out of these 'various genres of mythic expression' was a formula that ensured widespread social and political support for promoting the 'progress' of Anglo-American civilisation over a succession of receding frontiers.[88] Slotkin suggests that this mythology should be understood as *the* major impetus behind such popular concepts as the 'redemption of American spirit' and the unique national character (identity), together with the powerful nationalist ideologies of American exceptionalism and Manifest Destiny. All of which came together to form what Slotkin calls the 'language of American myth'; permeating national policy, historical narratives, and 'reflected in the forms and practices of commercial culture-producers', including, especially, Hollywood Westerns.[89]

In remarks that are consonant with those of both Cawelti and Fiedler, Slotkin informs us that violence was a key ingredient in the mythology of the American frontier; especially symbolic violence against the Indian. He suggests that in 'each stage of its development, the Myth of the Frontier relates the achievement of "progress" to a particular form or scenario of violent action', or 'savage war', which was aimed against the 'non-White natives for whom the wilderness was home'.[90] Hence, for Slotkin 'the Frontier Myth is divided by significant borders, of which the wilderness/civilisation, Indian/White border is the most basic'.[91] He goes on to chart how such a 'scenario of violent action' became crystallised in the popular culture of the early republic through the figure of Daniel Boone (*the* heroic outrider of Manifest Destiny), whose legend sets the terms of the mythology that would explain the process of westward expansion for successive generations of US Americans. Slotkin explains that this process typically involves an exile from civilisation through 'a scenario of separation, temporary regression to a more primitive or "natural" state', and how this contact with nature, with the domain of the savage, causes regeneration of the spirit and earthly fortune. Ultimately, he who ventures into the wilderness becomes an agent for the further advance of civilisation *against* the wilderness. Slotkin terms this mythic process '*regeneration through violence*'.[92]

As suggested in the Introduction, James Fenimore Cooper's Leatherstocking tales provide us with oft-cited pre-cinematic examples of these ideological trends. Through these popular novels, Cooper provides the reader with a progressive explanation of the course of Anglo-American history. Although their generic status as literary Westerns remains highly contentious, Cooper's contributions to frontier mythology do in fact bear thematic comparison with the classical reading of *Shane*. For instance, the opening paragraphs of *The Pioneers* (1823) extol the project of Manifest Destiny:

> [P]laces for the worship of God abound with that frequency which characterises a moral and reflecting people ... The expedients of the pioneers, who first broke ground in the settlement of this country, are succeeded by the permanent improvements of the yeoman, who intends to leave his remains to moulder under the sod which he tills, or, perhaps, the son, who, born in the land piously wishes to linger around the grave of his father. Only forty years have passed since this territory was a wilderness.[93]

At the end of the novel, Leatherstocking leaves the pioneers behind, moving ever-westwards; the 'man without a cross', the advance guard of Anglo-American civilisation: 'This was the last they ever saw of Leatherstocking ... He had gone far towards the setting sun – the foremost in that band of pioneers who are opening the way for the march of the nation across the continent.'[94] Thus concludes Cooper's definitive statement of 1823. Such words find immediate resonance in *Shane* in the scene immediately following Frank's funeral.

Against their professed decisions to abandon the valley in the face of Ryker's now murderous tactics, and with the stalwart support of Shane, Joe implores the homesteaders to stay and defend their farms:

> We can have a regular settlement here, we can have a town, and churches, and a school . . . We can't give up on this valley and we ain't gonna do it. This is farmin' country, a place where people can come and bring up their families. Who is Rufus Ryker or anyone else to run us away from our own homes? He only wants to grow his beef and what we want to grow up is families, to grow them good and grow up strong, the way they was meant to be grown. God didn't make all this country just for one man like Ryker.

This scene resonates with a sense of the homesteaders' God-given right to civilise the wilderness. As Joe is speaking, the camera cuts first to a medium shot of Marian dutifully standing by her husband's side in a symbolic gesture of familial unity and feminine subordination. It then cuts to a close-up shot of young Joey's face, gazing up at his father and Shane, and we, the audience, might wonder too about the son 'born in the land', who, when the time comes, 'piously wishes to linger around the grave of his father'. Such a speech (together with the supportive input and very presence of Shane) rouses a sense of community among the harried and disgusted homesteaders. Its invocation of God automatically forges a link with the ideological precepts of Manifest Destiny, echoing the writings of journalist John L. O'Sullivan, whose own definitive statement came in 1845, the year the United States annexed Texas: 'Our manifest destiny is to overspread the continent allotted by Providence for the free development of our yearly multiplying millions.'[95]

Such alleged narrative simplicity is evocative of the 'conjuring trick' that Roland Barthes ascribes to the proper functionality of myth.[96] According to Barthes, 'myth is constituted by the loss of the historical quality of things: in it, things lose the memory that they were once made'.[97] Myth therefore simplifies, engaging the ideological in a purifying process of 'eternal justification' that 'abolishes the complexity of human acts', ultimately reducing them to a simplistic and 'harmonious display of essences'. In other words, a binary, either/or, 'good' versus 'evil'.[98] In this way, the ideological operation becomes naturalised, comes to be understood *not* as a social construct, but rather as 'a statement of fact'. And Barthes insists that, once integrated into a culture successfully, the validity of myth *'goes without saying'*.[99]

With this in mind, I turn once more to Cawelti's analysis of *Shane*. He explains how the hero's 'return to his role as gunfighter is clearly represented as an act of revitalisation and redemption in which, through an act of violence, the hero saves the . . . homesteaders and becomes one with himself'.[100] Here we find clear consonance between the film and the novel. Schaeffer's first-person narrative describes Shane moments before the shootout in explicitly existential terms:

Belt and holster and gun ... These were not things he was wearing or carrying. They were part of him, part of the man, of the full sum of the integrate force that was Shane. You could see now for the first time that this man, who had been living with us ... was complete, and was himself in the final effect of his being.[101]

It is for reasons such as this that *Shane* has so often been highlighted by film scholars as an archetype of the genre's cinematic mode: a fully-conscious distillation of the myth of the West supported by the cultural import of the hero's code, the epic moment, the wilderness–civilisation binary, and the myth of regeneration through violence.

More recent scholarship has seen such views on the film continue, with Rick Worland and Edward Countryman even going so far as to declare *Shane* the 'most Turnerian of Westerns'.[102] Griffin for her part suggests that '*Shane* can be seen to ... re-play the western as America's foundation myth, one that is rooted in the notion of Manifest Destiny.'[103] She reads the 'evolutionary trajectory' of Manifest Destiny into the film's narrative:

[It] begins with a wilderness inhabited by native inhabitants who have no God-given right to the land (according to the concept of Manifest Destiny). The wilderness is subsequently tamed by gunfighter heroes (Shane, both in his mysterious past and later when forced to defend the Starretts) and so made safe for the process of settlement (the Starretts, who do have a God-given right to settle the land) prior to frontier closure and the subsequent onset of 'civilisation' (land enclosure and the growth of domestic communities).[104]

Taking a broad perspective on the film, one could indeed read the valley homesteaders as Turner's 'outer edge of the wave', attempting to realise an agricultural miracle at the moment of transition between 'the cattle-raiser' (Rufus and Morgan Ryker) and 'the pioneer farmer' (Joe Starrett, Frank Torrey, etc.).[105] To reiterate Joe's legitimating summarisation of this social transition: 'He [Ryker] only wants to grow his beef and what we want to grow up is families ... the way they was meant to be grown.' In Turnerian terms, the link would seem clear: Ryker does not work the land and, being engaged in the outmoded and ecologically wasteful enterprise of free-grazing, he has no connection with it other than its monetary value. In mythic terms he is an affront to the civilising values of economic individualism that Turner saw as a foundation of the unique American democracy. He is, in this most vital of aspects, anti-Turnerian, anti-democratic and, therefore, anti-American.

From theories and interpretations such as those outlined above one can understand how the great ideological compound of frontier mythology acted as a catalyst that glorified national expansion into the West; how it highlighted these mass migrations as integral components in the realisation of an exceptional American national character. According to this supposition, it followed that the modern literary and cinematic Western genres grew from these nineteenth-century traditions to firmly establish the idea of *homo americanus* in the cultural mindset of the modern United States.[106] This it did by characteristically articulating the myth within terms of nation-building, and behind this ideological construct lay a belief in the moral necessity of violent confrontation between the savage forces of the wilderness (like Ryker and Wilson, who threaten the embryonic nation) and the torchbearers of civilisation (like Shane, whose regression into the wilderness provides them with the means to win the fight to realise it).

As far as some scholars were concerned this mythic figuration, long enshrined in American ideology and given its supreme voice by the cinema, was simplified almost to the point of contempt during innumerable repetitions, configurations and re-configurations. By the 1950s, this attitude was already apparent in some of the earliest film scholarship available on the Western. One of these scholars is Warshow, whose essay I have already mentioned. Indeed, when he bemoans *Shane*'s 'aestheticising tendency'[107] one feels that what he is *really* complaining about is that the film's mythic agenda is, if anything, *too* pronounced. Warshow writes that in *Shane* '[t]he legend of the West is virtually reduced to its essentials and then fixed in the dreamy clarity of a fairy tale, with the hero . . . hardly a man at all, but something like the Spirit of the West'.[108] For Warshow, *Shane* stood guilty of 'violating the Western form' precisely because of an *over*-identification with frontier mythology, yielding 'entirely to its static quality as legend'.[109] In advancing such sentiments, Warshow's work aligns itself with another pioneering film scholar of the time, André Bazin, who was the original advocate of the theory of genre evolution. Bazin put forward the concept of the 'superwestern' as the logical evolution of the genre following the 'introduction of new elements . . . social or moral theme[s]' after the Second World War.[110] Such elements he theorised on 'negative grounds' as some 'additional interest to justify [the Western's] existence – an aesthetic, sociological, moral, psychological, political, or erotic interest, in short some quality extrinsic to the genre and which is supposed to enrich it'.[111] For Bazin, *Shane* is the 'ultimate in "superwesternization"'. That is to say, the myth no longer provides the source of the Western, here 'the theme of *Shane* is the myth'.[112] Bazin bemoans this new trend of sociological and historical import into the apparent 'perfection' of the pre-Second World War Western form, and remarks disparagingly that, with *Shane*, 'George Stevens set out to justify the western – by the western'.[113]

By today's standards, both Warshow's and Bazin's analyses seem restrictive and unduly formalistic, as if the Western (or any other genre for that matter) ever stood exempt from the import of 'sociological, moral, psychological, political, or erotic' concerns. Such concerns were, according to Tag Gallagher, always apparent in the cinematic Western from the outset and did not signify anything like an evolution, or paradigm shift within the genre:

Any news event or fashion trend – labor actions, bloomers, Apaches, pro-hibition, female suffrage, Balkan crises, and a myriad of forgotten issues of the day – were zealously incorporated not only into westerns but into whatever genres were currently popular, the western hero and the nature of his struggles altered accordingly.[114]

Despite Gallagher's corrective, such an 'unhappy preoccupation with style' as *Shane* stands accused of by Warshow is neither a redundant critical concern, nor lost on more contemporary scholarship.[115] For instance, Bob Baker highlights that, in retrospect, the 'problem with *Shane* is the systematic, self-conscious way that George Stevens sets about it – a self-consciousness that, in the climate of the times, [even just] a decade on, contrived to diminish the movie and its director'.[116]

Despite such objections, it remains that the more common analyses of *Shane* follow the Turnerian paradigm that I have thus far outlined. As we have seen, this reading typically sees the narrative drive become a synecdoche, whereby one can interpret the homesteading Starrett family – Joe, Marian and their young son, Joey – as symbolising the germ of pioneering American civilisation, as reincarnations of de Crèvecoeur's 'western pilgrims', only in this case trans-planted from the late-eighteenth-century Hudson Valley to the late-nineteenth-century Wyoming Basin.[117] Thus interpreted, *Shane* becomes the means of elaborating an entire social system: the unique American democracy realised on the frontier through a common belief in the redemption of the spirit and the realisation of economic individualism.

An important caveat: we should bear in mind that, as a product of popular culture, *Shane* is unlikely to be an exact reconstruction of any historical thesis (Turner's own poetic style notwithstanding). The Frontier Thesis lacked a suit-able hero figure for the popular imagination to latch onto, therefore, lone gun-fighter figures like Shane and concepts such as regeneration through violence probably owe more to Cody's Wild West and to Roosevelt's validation of the cowboy as a new type of American hero. It stands to reason, therefore, that the Turnerian reading alone does not explain *Shane*. Although largely adhering to his chief maxim – that it was the creation of a civilisation from a wilderness that forged the most prized national characteristic of economic individualism – it is significant to note that *Shane*'s hero is *not* the yeoman farmer, nor even, strictly speaking, a member of civilisation. Shane might give pretence to the effort, but he is, in the final instance, not for farming. He is always an out-sider, adhering to the first two of Wright's 'classical plot' functions: 'The hero enters a social group' and 'The hero is unknown to the society'.[118] However, the Starretts are able to tame the wilderness only because of Shane – a sort of Emersonian transcendental figure – the 'good man with a gun', as Slotkin refers to him.[119] 'The West (and the future of America)', Lenihan concurs, 'belongs to the peaceful, ordinary citizen-settler, but it could not have been won without men like Shane.'[120]

There is another important cultural influence contributing to the power of both the myth of the West and the cinematic Western: frontier painting. It is well-known that Frederic Remington was a close friend of Roosevelt's, and produced hundreds of illustrations and lithographs for the latter's political pamphlets, as well as for numerous other journals, newspapers, galleries, etc. Remington's popular artistry celebrated the endeavours of various cowpunchers and frontiersmen, capturing mythic heroism in cinematic-like poses during a pre-cinematic age. He particularly emphasised movement and landscape, aspects that would soon transmute into the visual signifiers of the cinematic Western. To further this link, Mitchell suggests that another frontier artist, Albert Bierstadt, created paintings that 'reflect[ed] the crowding together of contextual fragments' whereby,

> The viewer is challenged by that excess into a kind of scenic unpacking, an unfolding of the paintings' mixed descriptive moments into relatively consistent temporal successions that resemble nothing so much as the unreeling of film. Scenes that appear simultaneous on canvas are transformed by their unusual perspective and conjunction, as if requiring a narrative explanation that only cinematic sequence can provide . . . Just as writers were developing materials for the Western, Bierstadt manufactured a 'West' in which fictional plots could unfold.[121]

With specific regard to *Shane*, Mitchell writes that 'the combination of Tetons and Technicolor automatically transmutes landscape into a Bierstadtian spectacle'.[122]

Like most of the more memorable Westerns, *Shane* comes across as a combination of these cultural–historical antecedents, which can be laced into the Turnerian reading. It would appear that Shane himself recognises his own fate in the 'procession' of Turnerian social epochs. In a telling scene moments before the shootout at Grafton's, Shane informs Ryker that his time of 'doin' things is over'. Ryker's retort is blunt and to the point: 'My time!? What about yours, gunfighter?' Shane replies by saying that the only difference between them is that, 'I know it.' Here *Shane* displays its intertextuality. The hero is certainly suggestive of a Roosveltian reading, with him being destined to fade away once the frontier has been settled. Such a reading posits Shane, like Leatherstocking and Boone before him, as a symbolic champion of Manifest Destiny. At the same time, Shane has a fraught and troubled relationship with that same civilisation. And as with Cooper's Leatherstocking, Shane has been viewed as a 'man without a cross'; a pathfinder, who straddles the divide between civilisation and savagery, between law and outlaw, between painful historical abstractions and utopian desires for the future American democracy.

As a writer of frontier tales, Cooper remains significant to any serious discussion of the twentieth-century Western if only for his role in the development of this basic narrative structure. But he also introduced a literary trait that would come to define the hero's persona in relation to the wilderness–civilisation binary: that of ambiguity. The spirit behind this ambiguity is one that places the hero at odds with the very civilisation that will, through his heroic efforts, ultimately come to supplant the wilderness through the hero's destruction of the savage forces contained within it. For Slotkin, 'Cooper's ultimate concern in the Leatherstocking tales is the problematic character of the frontiersman.'[123] He suggests that it was Natty Bumppo's 'troubling blend of European, American, and Indian elements that made him both a figure of promise and a nightmare to Cooper's contemporaries'.[124] From this we can infer that the hero was perceived as the agent of civilisation, and yet, like the very forces of savagery to which he is opposed, he threatens that civilisation with atavistic regression, a return to an undemocratic and uncivilised state of nature. As Fiedler rightly reminds us, despite Natty's ultimate status as torchbearer for the inevitable arrival of civilisation, the 'world of nature' – ergo, the wilderness – is all too often 'preferred to civilisation'.[125]

Transferring all this back to *Shane*, the classical reading would have it that Shane is a benign superhero who makes the valley safe for agriculture and settlement, and, in the words of Wright, 'gives up his status as gunfighter and saviour and chooses instead the dark night and the cold mountains'.[126] Indeed, the closing moments of the narrative echo the tragic realisation that Warshow (despite his objections to the film) informs us is felt by most Western heroes. 'As the reign of law settles over the West', he writes, 'he is forced to see that his day is over; those are the pictures that end with his death or with his departure for some more remote frontier'.[127] Thus is the end logic of the classical Western paradigm asserted as elegiac, if not overtly tragic (although one struggles to find a more moving scene than that in which Shane bids farewell to Joey). To reiterate Lenihan, '[Shane's] sad departure that concludes the film reflects the classic Western's dichotomy between heroic, free individualism and the more enduring but constraining social order.'[128]

III

The thesis adumbrated above is convincing enough that placing it under a critical microscope is no easy task. While I do not doubt the validity of certain of its aspects, the classical reading is merely one interpretation among many that can be applied to *Shane*. I have already suggested one potential limitation regarding the problematical nature of the hero and his relationship with the civilisation that he serves. Indeed, probing behind the self-generated folklore surrounding *Shane*, one uncovers ambiguities and fissures (un)contained within the narrative that open other possibilities for critical analysis. In their turn, these inherent contradictions help us to question the proclaimed simplicity of that problematical and unsubstantiated categorisation, the classical Western. This is so in its adherence to triumphalist versions of frontier history (be they Turnerian or Rooseveltian), prescribed narrative formulae, dominant myth ideologies, *and* in its relation to the theory of genre evolution.

The counter-conventional reading of *Shane* that follows relates directly to John Ford's much-celebrated Western, *The Searchers* (1956). As I offer an analysis of this film in Chapter 2, I shall confine myself for now to stating only that Ford's film is significant when placed in relation to *Shane*. This is so because in *The Searchers* the paradigm of the redeemer hero is ferociously dissected, suggesting that the relationship held by Westerns of the so-called classical period to their informing myth ideologies – or historical referents, for that matter – is rarely (if ever) reducible to a simplistic reflection or endorsement of dominant cultural, social or political trends.

In his study of the Western, Mitchell proposes an analytical method that resists 'the temptation of grand master narratives'.[129] For him, the popular Western genre often combines 'compelling issues in an exhilarating narrative mix'.[130] Contrary to the approaches of Slotkin, Coyne and Lenihan, he adds that this 'combination cannot be satisfactorily explained in terms of political allegory or social fable, of straightforward mutation of current anxieties into plots that stage or assuage them'.[131] Mitchell does not refute the political-allegorical connection completely – his study is, after all, concerned with the genre's complex responses to historically shifting patterns of gender politics during the twentieth century – but he refuses to identify this response in terms of simplistic binarism, or as *the* constitutional theme above all others. This is to say, Mitchell refuses to interpret the genre solely in terms of a masculine reaction against 'the advent of America's second feminist movement'. This is despite the fact that, as he sees it, 'the genre's recurrent rise and fall coincides more generally with interest aroused by feminist issues, moments when men have invariably had difficulty knowing how manhood should be achieved'.[132] Such a singular theoretical position, which would conceive of Westerns as instances of a wider cultural desire to 'marginalise and suppress' the feminine in favour of an assertion of masculine identity, is closer to Tompkins' approach to the genre;[133] instead, Mitchell proposes that successful Westerns 'won favor by sustaining *multiple* interpretations'.[134] Furthermore, by asserting the multiplicity of potential meanings that an individual film can simultaneously entertain, he also exposes the potential limitations in genre analyses of the kind practiced by Wright and Schatz. Accordingly, he argues that 'we need to explore not only the blunt plots so characteristic of texts but rather all the strange textures, the contours and grains, the idiosyncrasies that draw our eyes away from the center to unlit places where their power resides'.[135]

Such sentiments derive from the analytical approach known as deconstruction, which was made popular as a critical approach to literature with the advent of post-structuralism in the late 1960s. Deconstruction acts as a theoretical tool whereby the sort of binary oppositions asserted by structuralist analyses can be undermined or, rather, texts can actually be shown to undermine *themselves* by virtue of what their narratives exclude. According to Terry

Eagleton, deconstruction works to expose the ideological machinations that lay behind the either/or mentality encapsulating a rigid, intractable structuralist duality:

> Structuralism was generally satisfied if it could carve up a text into binary oppositions (high/low, light/dark, Nature/Culture and so on) and expose the logic of their working. Deconstruction tries to show how such oppositions, in order to hold themselves in place, are sometimes betrayed into inverting or collapsing themselves, or need to banish to the text's margins certain niggling details which can be made to return and plague them . . . The tactic of deconstructive criticism, that is to say, is to show how texts come to embarrass their own ruling systems of logic; and deconstruction shows this by fastening on the 'symptomatic' points, the *aporia* or impasses of meaning, where texts get into trouble, come unstuck, offer to contradict themselves.[136]

According to Staiger, a 'poststructuralist thesis would, of course, argue that every text inherently displays what it is not', and that we are alerted to the existence of so-called 'structuring absences' (that is, 'what a text cannot say but says in spite of itself'), instances of 'intertextuality' and 'over-determination', all of which shape the meaning of *every* text.[137]

Staiger's account ultimately draws from the writings of Michel Foucault. Foucault's work is concerned with what he calls 'discursive formations'. These are described as vast configurations of knowledge, providing culturally specific and historically contingent sets of rules which govern societies. For Foucault, social power is exercised through such discourses, which determine and articulate cultural attitudes, dominant ideologies, and the various forms and institutions of knowledge; they also determine and govern the criteria of 'truth'. However, because such a notion is inextricably bound up in the exercise of power, Foucault reasons that there can be no legitimate grounds for proclaiming absolute truth. In a display of his intellectual debt to Nietzsche, Foucault suggests that no discourse is ever absolutely true; it is either more or less powerful than the competing discourses against which it asserts itself. Within such systems, perspective substitutes truth and each discourse produces its own version of reality (that is, discursive formations produce 'realities' rather than reflect them). Inevitably, within such formations of power there exist those discourses that are considered illegitimate and that seek to operate outside of the rules governing 'official discourse'. As a result, such discourses are suppressed, their voices marginalised or silenced by the dominant discourse. However, without discursive formations we could not say anything, since, for Foucault, there is *no* perspective outside the social process; therefore, effective social change must be sought introspectively, through the discursive formations themselves. In his own writings, Foucault sought to undermine the legitimacy of established discourses by illuminating the elided discourses that necessarily lay suppressed within them, famously declaring that the 'manifest discourse is really no more than the repressive presence of what it does not say; and [that] this "not-said" is a hollow that undermines from within all that is said'.[138] Such a statement lies at the heart of post-structuralist theory, and its relevance to deconstructive criticism is clearly apparent: its primary tactic being a reading of the text 'against itself', in order to expose the textual unconscious (the 'not-said') that may be directly contrary to the text's surface meaning.[139]

I shall now adapt this schema to the Western genre. As one example, I would like to reiterate a frequently argued perspective: that the heroic version of frontier history that the classical Western espoused served to marginalise, or even silence, the voice of the Native American. In such a reading, the Indians have become conspicuous by their very absence, threatening to 'return and plague' the narrative from the 'text's margins', and, ultimately, cause us to question the historical validity of the official discourse of the frontier.[140] We could even argue that the very process of labelling *Shane* a classical Western (that is, as part of a fictional-wing that purportedly asserts an ideology that promotes a peculiarly Anglo-American version of history, one which glorifies and legitimates the expansionist policies of the United States) necessarily causes such a category to become inherently unstable and to (un)consciously undermine itself from within, ultimately creating a sense of *narrative confusion* that exposes the 'not-said' of the film's ostensible ideological meaning. For if *Shane* is an archetypal Western – one that utilises the recognisable tropes of the genre in order to render overt its informing mythological influences – then, as an inevitable by-product of this intent, a post-structural reading would have it that the film cannot but express the ideological contradictions and 'structuring absences' that it might otherwise might seek to contain.

The result of this, according to Forrest G. Robinson, is 'invariably an unstable compromise between assertions of prominent social and political ideals, on the one hand, and unsettling glimpses of lapses from those same ideals, on the other'.[141] Robinson analyses this 'unstable compromise' in relation to a number of prominent popular literary Westerns (including Schaeffer's *Shane*), suggesting that their plots betray 'a persistent pattern of doubleness, or self-subversion, in which conflicting moral perspectives compete for preeminence'.[142] Robinson suggests that an unconscious 'self-subversive tendency' works against the conscious narrative meaning of the text, working 'to undermine what it appears so clearly to approve'.[143] He further suggests that such texts have endured in the popular imagination 'because they give us a window on major cultural embarrassments, *and* because they open it no more than half way'.[144] Robinson puts it to us that 'we are compelled to return to these subtly mingled narratives precisely because we never see them fully through'.[145]

I argue that a number of counter-ideological, 'self-subversive' tendencies exist in *Shane*. It is my firm belief that the so-called classical Western often acts to highlight and contextualise ideological contradictions in the sociocultural, political and historical themes with which it engages, rather than merely to assimilate or elide them as some have suggested. I argue that *Shane* holds an ambiguous textual relationship with dominant ideologies; specifically, as embodied in the figure of the hero – Shane himself and the 'unlit places' of his mysterious persona. Initiating with a general critique of both the classical category and genre evolution theory, I shall draw upon recent scholarship to offer another interpretation of *Shane*, not one that claims to supersede any other perspective, but merely one that offers another interjection into the study of the Western's 'exhilarating narrative mix'.

IV

Aside from the intertextual complications that Staiger highlights in relation to specific genres, the concept of a classical Western is far from helpful even when judged on its own terms. This is so because it attempts to impose objective judgements upon a body of films that are actually derived from nothing more than an assemblage of subjective opinions. In 'Genre and Critical Methodology' (1974), Andrew Tudor highlights the paradox in attempting to define film genres in this fashion. In so doing, he exposes the limitations of formalist analyses such as those offered by Warshow and Bazin, and of contemporary structuralist projects such as Wright's:

> To take a *genre* such as a 'Western', analyze it, and list its principal characteristics, is to beg the question that we must first isolate the body of films which are 'Westerns'. But they can only be isolated on the basis of the 'principal characteristics' which can only be discovered *from the films themselves* after they have been isolated.[146]

It is precisely this sort of subjectivity (and, more properly, idiosyncrasy, as all such classificatory systems are, ultimately, created rather than objectively 'found') that allowed the diverse narrative structures and formal styles of *The Virginian* (1929), *Stagecoach* (1939) and *Shane* to be regarded as classical by Warshow, Bazin and Wright, respectively. This same subjectivity allowed for Warshow's criticism regarding *Stagecoach*'s 'unhappy preoccupation with style', while allowing Bazin to laud the very same film as 'the ideal example of the maturity of a style brought to classic perfection'.[147] It is also the same sort of approach that gave Alan Lovell the 'evidence' he required in putting forward John Ford's *My Darling Clementine* as 'the perfect example of the classic Western . . . rather than *Stagecoach*'.[148] However, Kathryn C. Esselman convincingly suggests that 'there is no one kind of true Western'. She compounds this sense of idiosyncrasy in a somewhat facetious fashion when she declares that, 'the search for the true Western is a little bit like the search for the perfect woman, always doomed to frustration by the reality of human nature'.[149] The same point is made more decisively by Gallagher. In relation

to how one defines classical Westerns, Gallagher points to the rather contentious nature of labelling Westerns according to certain formal characteristics
and plot motifs before placing them in a chronological framework within an
overall schema of generic evolution:

> A film is considered 'classic' when it matches a critic's paradigm of the
> ideal western. But the paradigm is entirely arbitrary, with the result that
> there is some disagreement about which pictures are 'classic' and which
> have evolved astray. Warshow, for example, is intent on showing how
> the 1943 Ox-Bow Incident (William Wellman), the 1950 Gunfighter
> (Henry King), and the 1952 High Noon (Fred Zinnemann) transformed
> the primeval western into a vehicle for social criticism, in comparison
> with Victor Fleming's naively archetypal 1929 Virginian. Thus he found
> an 'unhealthy preoccupation with style,' an 'aestheticising tendency,' in
> Stagecoach (John Ford, 1939), My Darling Clementine (Ford, 1946),
> and Shane (George Stevens, 1954) that he felt 'violat[ed] the Western
> form.' Later genre critics regard the last three pictures as 'classic' and
> regard as 'self-conscious' movies such as The Man Who Shot Liberty
> Valance (Ford, 1962), Hour of the Gun (John Sturges, 1967), Chisum
> (Andrew V. McLaglen, 1970), and The Wild Bunch (Sam Peckinpah,
> 1969).[150]

Gallagher argues that the Western has always been a complex genre, considering it axiomatic that perhaps 'older westerns, like olden times, will always
strike the modern mind as less complex, less amoral, and above all less vivid –
particularly when the modern mind feels it unnecessary to examine the past in
any detail'.[151] We may take the silent-era Westerns as a pertinent case in point.
I have already mentioned Gallagher's contention that silent-era Westerns
were shaped by and responded to contemporary sociopolitical issues, and it
seems that their formal composition was equally rich and complex. Although
Gallagher concedes to offering only a 'scant' survey of this period of film
production, he claims that '[w]ithout exaggeration, clichés were already an
issue'.[152] Thus he writes:

> Self-reflexivity in the early teens was often evident as well in the form of
> films within films: characters frequently fall asleep and dream, friends
> deceive friends with elaborate masquerades (put-on kidnappings and the
> like), Remington paintings (as in Ford's 1918 Hell Bent) come alive in
> an onlooker's fantasy – all methods of critiquing generic conventions.[153]

In sum, Gallagher contends that 'little evidence has been brought forward
to support the theory that there has been growing "self-consciousness" – or
any other sort of linear evolution – in and specific to the western'.[154] Alan
Williams also counters Schatz's belief that a progression 'from straightforward

storytelling to self-conscious formalism' is evident in the Western's development as a genre.[155] He writes:

> One can find self-conscious Westerns, such as [Douglas] Fairbanks' *Wild
> and Woolly* [John Emerson, 1917], as early as the late-teens. In fact, the
> entire mid-to-late silent cinema seems remarkably 'formalistic,' which is
> possibly one reason why it is wholly absent from Schatz's book.[156]

In relation to categories arbitrarily defined and then 'fixed' within a historical–
chronological evolutionary pattern of development, these approaches by
Tudor, Gallagher and Williams, as I have highlighted them, act as a corrective
to those formula analyses that claim to discern, define and then categorise the
Western genre's deep structures. As Gallagher insists, attempts to classify individual Westerns within a broader generic corpus (specifically within an evolutionary schema) result, all too frequently, in 'rich lodes of ambiguity [being]
overlooked in order to bolster a specious argument that "classic" westerns are
simple and naive'.[157]

Such charges have been rightly levelled at the sort of psychological impov-
erishment practiced by Wright in his structural study of the Western. Tuska,
for one, is highly critical of Wright's approach, where he finds 'the actual plots
of the films he selected to illustrate [the] basic plot types do not fit into his
categories at all without all manner of exceptions and unconventional interpretations'.[158] In sentiments that echo Tudor's objections to genre classification, Tuska finds that 'Wright encountered an insurmountable problem . . . in
trying to force all the Western films he labelled "classical" into this definition
as a category'.[159] He reminds us, for instance, that the final two of Wright's
plot functions for the classical Western – 'The society accepts the hero' and
'The hero loses or gives up his social status' – often fail to fit the very films that
Wright himself has labelled classical.[160]

One can easily apply such criticisms to the narrative structure of *Shane*.
First, 'The society accepts the hero'. According to Wright, one of the initiatory
'classical plot' functions insists that 'the society does not completely accept
the hero', and that his eventual acceptance is won by his making the society
safe after his defeating of the villains.[161] Coyne has it that 'Shane's alienation
stems from his own emotions rather than rejection or marginalisation by the
community'.[162] However, in my opinion, Shane is *never* really accepted by
the homesteaders. They eye him with suspicion and treat him as an outsider
throughout. Not only is he made to feel alienated from their clandestine meet-
ings (in one instance, he stands outside in the rain until Marian takes pity
on him and takes him inside the farmhouse), but upon rumour of Wilson's
arrival in the valley (all 'pow-wow' with Ryker) things take a darker turn.
The revelation that Shane knows who Wilson is (or, at the very least, he has
heard of him) compels one of the homesteaders to question him in an accusatory tone, 'You seem to know a lot about this kind of business, Shane?'

Another even goes as far as to equate all 'gun-slinging' with 'murder', suggesting that, at the very least, the community is suspicious of Shane's deadly credentials.

Actually, it is only really Joey who fully accepts Shane for who he is, perhaps because he does not really understand *what* Shane is, at least not with the same depth as Marian. In reference to Shane's vagueness about his own mysterious (but inevitably violent) past, Marian says, 'I think we know . . . Shane.' Indeed, while being undoubtedly sympathetic and even romantically attracted to Shane, Marian is suspicious and despairing of his existential link to the six-gun. This is evidenced when she catches Shane teaching Joey how to shoot. Unconvinced by Shane's declaration – 'a gun's just a tool, Marian . . . as good or as bad as the man using it' – she replies that 'guns aren't going to be my boy's life'. Further adding that 'we'd all be better off if there wasn't a single gun in this valley . . . including yours'. Marian's view on this issue is made slightly puzzling by the fact that the opening sequence of the film depicts Joey, young as he is, with rifle in hand stalking a deer outside the homestead. (Presumably Marian and Joe are aware of their son's playtime activities?) As Joey aims the rifle, the deer he is tracking angles its head towards him, framing the tiny figure of Shane emerging from the Tetons within its antlers. This perspectival alignment automatically associates this mysterious stranger with the wilderness. We soon learn that Joey's gun is not loaded – 'Joey's too young for that' – as Joe is quick to inform Shane; however, the idea of the United States as a gunfighter nation is clearly in evidence here in this scene *before* Shane's arrival. Shane may well bring death with him in the form of the six-gun, and Joey might be 'too young' for the moment, but the hard fact is that, from the very outset, the child is being culturally indoctrinated, as it were, for a masculine social trajectory with violence at its core.

Despite the common assertion, which has been reiterated most recently by McGee, that Shane's relation to the six-gun is problematic and 'conflicted', he does seem to enjoy the sense of identity and social role that it gives him.[163] As Shane tells Joey before departing the valley for good, 'A man's gotta be what a man's gotta be. You can't break the mold. I tried it and it didn't work for me. There's no living with a killing. Right or wrong, it's a brand, and a brand sticks. There's no going back.' Such a statement is laden with a sense of predestination, as if being a gunfighter – a 'killer of men' – is all Shane ever could be. We might wonder, however, just how much Shane really did *try* to give up his gunfighter identity. When he first encounters Wilson at Joe's homestead and later on in Grafton's moments before the so-called epic moment, Shane smiles at his adversary. These two brief moments are scarcely mentioned in critical writing on *Shane* (except for Slotkin), much less discussed; however, to my mind they hold significance. It is as if Shane is relishing the coming fight, is edging for a chance to re-acquaint himself with his own past. After all, it is his role as gunfighter that gives him an identity, a sense of history. (I will return to the significance of Shane's psychological motivation and his status as a political-allegorical figure later, but first I want to consider other aspects of the classical reading in relation to *Shane*.)

While none of this exactly undermines Tompkins' argument that the Western 'exists to provide a justification for violence', these aspects of *Shane* do indicate that the film's narrative does not hold so simplistic a relationship to the epic moment, nor, indeed, to the hero's code, as a classical reading would have us believe. One could easily (and, quite probably, correctly) argue that Shane ultimately improves the valley by eliminating the threat posed by the Rykers and, therefore, the film adheres to Wright's 'classical plot' *and* to Slotkin's concept of regeneration through violence. On the other hand, one could just as easily point to the lack of effect that this violence has with regard to the 'society accept[ing] the hero'. In particular, we see no shots the homesteaders, of Joe or Marian, *after* the epic moment in Grafton's. In fact, Joe's and Marian's involvement in the film ends after Joe's fight with Shane (Joe is left concussed and reduced to child-like dependency upon Marian, who nurses him tenderly).

The belief that the classical Western unambiguously reflected values and themes central to dominant US ideology (that is, the belief that it symbolised a triumphalist version of American progress) persists. Writing in 2009, Jones and Wills followed Cawelti, Wright, etc. by suggesting that 'the inevitability of progress resided in the backdrop to each [classical] Western'.[164] As far as they are concerned, this was the theme behind the narrative drive of *Shane*: 'In *Shane*, the gunfighter hero departed from town because he recognised that he was no longer needed. The frontier was about to close and move on elsewhere, his shooter skills consigned to a past era. A better future lay ahead.'[165] Jones and Wills see nothing beyond this interpretation. Like Schatz, their analysis of the genre pertains to evolution theory, categorising films like *Shane* as 'traditional Westerns' before making their account of 'the demise of the Western' which, by the 1970s, 'seemed out of touch with society'.[166] For them, *Shane* was representative of the classical Western, providing an 'idyllic platform of Americana, both nostalgic for the past and optimistic in its portrayal of national direction, assur[ing] general confidence in the American experiment'.[167] But how far does *Shane* really adhere to such a generalised perspective, or blue-print?

I have already indicated the homesteader's lack of reaction to Shane's use of violence, but equally there are no sequences indicating their making good the valley for American settlement following his departure: no 'churches', no 'school', and no framing device suggestive of any kind of Joe's hoped-for 'regular settlement'. Contrast this ambiguity for a moment with Ford's version of a bleak frontier township in *My Darling Clementine*. In the rough township of Tombstone, the church – albeit only half-built – is prominent throughout, symbolising the eventual emergence of a community-driven 'regular settlement', of the emergence of a religiously ordained and legitimated American civilisation. In *Shane*, there is no such visual analogue. (This is not to suggest that *Clementine* unambiguously endorses the myth of the West, either. Although Ford's film is filled with images that signify civilisation – not least the dedication of 'the first church of Tombstone' – *Clementine* also suggests the myth's darker side, whereby the spectre of death remains a constant on the frontier; the church being only half-built.)

If *Shane* aimed to be so overtly triumphalist, that is, if it pertained to a Turnerian thesis that sees the defeat of the savage forces of the wilderness as tending towards emergent culture, democracy and economic individualism, if 'a better future' really 'lay ahead', then why is the audience denied its visual realisation? Similarly, there is no evidence that Joey grew up to be 'strong and straight'. The last we see of him he is hopelessly calling after Shane, begging him to 'come back!' What kind of society has Shane left behind him exactly? What kind of civilisation is it that he has helped to create? If the frontier depicted in *Shane* is to be read as a celebration of Turnerian economic individualism, or if its homesteaders are to be considered as resembling some form of Jeffersonian 'natural democracy' even, then what are we to make of this conclusion? As Wright has it now '[t]here is no law for a hundred miles', and we know that the homesteaders have already proven their inability to thrive without the intervention of a hero figure. Joey speaks more truth than perhaps he realises when he tells Shane, 'We *need* you.'[168] Now the valley has no power structure at all, no government, 'no law', none of the constituent elements required for an emerging civilisation, and the Starretts, along with the other homesteaders, are rendered helpless in the face of any potential future threat.

If we read these ideas into the text, then we do so through assumption only, as, ultimately, the film's attitude towards violence as a regenerative 'tool' is held in ambiguity. As I have already mentioned, Wright suggests that 'Shane could, of course, stay in the valley and maximise the rewards of his power and the farmer's gratitude; but he gives up his status as gunfighter and saviour and chooses instead the dark night and the cold mountains.'[169] I have already considered the 'farmer's gratitude', or lack thereof, and I am willing to concede that such a reading may be, in and of itself, contentious, speculative or even insignificant. But to claim, as Wright does, that Shane 'gives up his status as gunfighter' is to provide a distorted, even erroneous account of the film's plot.[170] On the contrary, it is precisely because Shane *cannot* give up 'his status as gunfighter' that makes his leaving the valley at the film's conclusion a *necessity* rather than a choice. His re-assumption of the role of the gunfighter – a role he had never really abandoned – merely reasserts his basic incompatibility with the social order that relies on his 'power' at the very same time that it disavows it. The homesteaders may '*need*' Shane, as Joey insists, but they cannot admit to that need, else they would have to brand themselves hypocrites, and acknowledge their reliance on 'gun-slinging' and their own complicity in acts of 'murder'.

If anything, and if one were forced to categorise *Shane* in this fashion, by leaving the valley at the end of the film, Shane is acting more in line with the hero of Wright's 'vengeance plot' than he is with the classical formula. 'Unlike the classical hero who joins the society because of his strength and their weakness', argues Wright, 'the vengeance hero leaves the society because of his strength and their weakness.'[171] As we know, Shane does not 'join the society' at all; to my mind he is *never* a part of it. In the end he leaves, apparently in accordance with the 'vengeance' plot type – because 'his strength' is incompatible with 'the values of society'.[172] However, clearly this plot type does not suffice as an explanation either. As I have previously indicated with Joey's 'pre-Shane' familiarisation with a rifle, 'the values of society' do *not* preclude violence, they *embody* it. Society's disavowal of violence being a hypocritical element of the myth of American civilisation that the narrative of *Shane* happens to expose. If one argues (as many have) that, in slaying Wilson and the Rykers, Shane eradicates from society its savage elements and causes regeneration through violence, the same progressive reading cannot so easily be applied to Shane himself. As he rides off wounded (possibly dying) and alone, he has absolutely failed to 'give up his special status', and it is this fact that ensures both his personal failure and, ironically, the validation of his philosophical musing to Joey that you cannot go back from a killing.

According to Wright, 'in the classical plot only the hero is associated with the wilderness'.[173] He declares that it is this unique relationship with nature that provides the 'hero's source of strength, both physical and moral; he is an independent and autonomous individual because he is part of the land'.[174] This interpretation is also evident in Slotkin's analysis of *Shane*. He suggests that Shane be allegorically associated with nature, 'an aristocrat of violence . . . an alien from a more glamorous world'.[175] He further suggests that Shane's reasons for helping the homesteaders 'are chivalric and romantic'; however, 'because Shane's motives . . . are unique and arise from no visible history or social background, they appear to be expressions of his nature, signs of a nobility which is independent of history'.[176] McGee also re-emphasises the interpretation that Shane is without history:

> Ultimately, a man without history has no real identity because identity is a function of history, of the stories we tell about ourselves . . . when it comes to Shane, no one seems to know anything for certain . . . because he has no story that can explain his being.[177]

Again, Shane's only palpable identity is as a gunfighter. The six-gun provides his only existential link to history, but it is a violent aspect of his own and America's past that must be disavowed if the nation is to succeed in the domestication of the wilderness and realise its own exceptionalism. And if, like Ryker, his 'time is over' and he cannot change, then he too must be swept away by the tides of history.

Let us further consider Wright's thematic association of the hero with the wilderness in relation to the wilderness–civilisation binary, as well as *Shane*'s relation to frontier history. Drawing directly from Wright, Mitchell discusses the narrative theme of Shane's association with the wilderness in terms of the

film's formal construction. 'Because Joey's prepubescent angle of vision domi-
nates the film', argues Mitchell, 'characters are metonymically equated with
the spaces through which they move.'[178] He continues:

> Scenery imparts a mythic power that is accepted by Joey as natural,
> explaining why Shane *is the only figure* filmed alone against the moun-
> tains, the villainous Rikers [sic] *never appear this way*, and the farmers
> only with Shane. So closely is this standard observed that when Shane
> and Joe Starrett ride into town, the road they take faces the mountains,
> while the Riker [sic] gang rides down the same road filmed from the
> opposite direction. Other characters are likewise bound to identifying
> locales – the saloon, the store, or simply (in the case of the homesteading
> wives) buckboard wagons.[179]

I wish to take issue with this aspect of Mitchell's analysis. Quite apart from the
irony of him utilising a 'cinematic conceit' first adumbrated by Wright (a man
whose approach to the Western Mitchell claims 'suffers from theoretical incoherence'), his claim that the Rykers never appear framed against the mountains is, in any case, incorrect.[180] Rufus Ryker *does* appear framed against the
mountains. This slippage in his own analysis goes against Mitchell's otherwise
correct insistence that 'Wright's exchange of isolated texts for a master plot
ends up confirming instead how much individual details always do matter.'[181]
In an erudite attention to the language of the cinema, Mitchell continues by
impressing the importance of the 'the non-sequential minutia of scenery and
cinematography, the evocations of music and sound track, the idiosyncrasies
of casting, that also make for successful films'.[182] By applying such a close
reading, one attentive to *Shane*'s 'minutia of scenery and cinematography', one
can deconstruct Mitchell qua Wright's suggestion that 'Shane is the only figure
filmed alone against the mountains'.

The scene under consideration is Ryker's night-time speech to Joe at the
Starrett homestead. The occasion of its delivery is the evening of the Fourth
of July, following the valley's Independence Day celebrations (from which
the Rykers are conspicuously absent). Unsurprisingly, the subject of Ryker's
speech concerns the question of who has legitimate rights to the valley:

> When I came to this country, you weren't much older than your boy.
> We had rough times. Me and other men that are mostly dead now. I got
> a bad shoulder yet from a Cheyenne arrowhead. We made this country,
> we found it and we made it, with blood and empty bellies. Cattle we
> brought in were hazed off by Indians and rustlers. They don't bother
> you much any more because we handled them. We made a safe range
> out of this. Some of us died doing it, but we made it. Then people move
> in who never had to raw-hide it through the old days. They fence off my
> range and fence me off from water. Some of them plough ditches, take

out irrigation water so the creek runs dry sometimes and I gotta move my stock because of it. And you say we have no right to the range. The men that did the work and ran the risks have no rights? I take you for a fair man, Starrett.

As Ryker delivers his speech he is held almost entirely in a medium close-up shot, clearly framing him against the stunning backdrop of the Tetons. Therefore, not only is Shane *not* 'the only figure filmed alone against the mountains', this scene suggests that Ryker – the ostensible villain of the piece – is also to be 'metonymically equated' with the wilderness. To my mind, Ryker's physical position in this scene, combined with the content of his speech, makes his association with the wilderness undeniable.

Joe's reply is courteous but, ultimately, unsympathetic:

I'm not belittling what you and the others did, but at the same time you didn't find this country. There were trappers here and Indian traders before you. They tamed this country. They weren't ranchers. You talk about rights. You think you've the right to say nobody else has got any. That ain't the way the Government looks at it.

The historical significance of this scene is played down by Slotkin, for whom issues such as 'rights' and 'progress' are merely 'palaver' for what the film is really all about. That is to say, the epic moment between Shane and Wilson, and the civilising process of regeneration through violence. During the scene between Ryker and Starrett, Slotkin writes that 'the camera is watching Shane and Wilson size each other up'.[183] He continues:

They [Shane and Wilson] say nothing; they merely look and smile a little smile. They know that the talk of rights and wrongs has become meaningless. ... Violent force alone will settle the issue, and the gun-fighters are the ones who best understand that truth. Ryker and Starrett and their original objectives are reduced to mere premises from which the action will arise, but the action itself will be entrusted to professionals.[184]

Slotkin interprets the debate over land rights between cattle baron and home-steader as superfluous to the generic demands of the shootout between Shane and Wilson. In other words, the film's mythic function serves its generic requirements and supersedes any historical dimension,[185] which is here relegated to 'meaningless' background noise.

'The politics of "saving the valley" have now become "stylized" as well', insists Slotkin, 'reduced to the formally necessary confrontation of two professionals who belong to neither of the contending classes.'[186] Slotkin is quite correct in arguing that 'the action itself will be entrusted to professionals [and that] the gunfighters are the ones who best understand that truth'.[187] This truism is pointed out earlier in the film in rather sardonic fashion by Wilson. Sitting in Grafton's, Ryker claims that 'I like Starrett ... but I'll kill him if I have to.' Wilson quickly corrects him, 'You mean *I'll* kill him if you have to.' I do feel that Slotkin's analysis tells only part of the story, however, and here is where I would differ from him. Ryker's 'Independence Day' speech and debate over land rights with Starrett seem significant on multiple levels. To relegate them as Slotkin does runs the risk of underestimating *Shane*'s potential for 'sustaining *multiple* interpretations'. The film should be seen as simultaneously pertaining to both generic *and* historical, or even counter-historical, interpretations. In formal terms, Slotkin's suggestion that 'the camera is watching Shane and Wilson', is not completely accurate as at least half of the shots that constitute this scene focus on the discourse between Ryker and Starrett.[188] Visual emphasis is, at the very least, distributed equally between the film's generic function (Shane and Wilson) and its historical dimension (Starrett and Ryker).

I would even suggest that the scene of Ryker's speech foregrounds a historical theme. As I have already mentioned, Griffin has outlined the narrative of *Shane* in relation to Manifest Destiny, and she has it that Ryker's speech 'effectively encapsulates Turner's vision of progress, the stages by which America was won and which the western genre charts so evocatively'.[189] She suggests that here can be seen 'the standard trajectory of western settlement, from mountain men and trappers to ranchers and town tamers', with the eventual succession of the homesteaders, 'to the pinnacle of "civilisation", land enclosure and the settlers'.[190] In my opinion, *Shane*'s attitude to frontier history is more complex than the classical reading allows for, and there is a counter-historical thread one might pick up. I return again to the subject of Ryker's speech. Consider such a scene: a convincing monologue delivered by the villain that, as Mitchell astutely reminds us, is 'based on values otherwise clearly associated with Shane'.[191] Mitchell does not exploit this 'fissure' within the narrative, beyond suggesting that 'Riker's [sic] night-time speech in defence of his rights ... is oddly persuasive', but I believe that he has missed a point worth discussing.[192] What I propose is that this scene discloses the darker aspects of the history of nineteenth-century US expansion. For one, Ryker's defence of his hard-fought position in the valley, together with his contention that the homesteader's 'fence off my range and fence me off from water ... plough ditches ... so the creek runs dry', places him, ironically enough, as victim. His existential link to Shane, the hero, is clear in this regard as historical 'progress' is forcing him, like Shane, to recognise that his 'time of doing things is over'. I wish to make clear that I am not suggesting that Shane and Ryker be read as one and the same, or even two sides of the same coin; Ryker is *not* a hero, *not* the 'dark half' of Shane, but while he may lack an heroic capacity neither is he completely unsympathetic. He is a threatening bully, but he is also a man who is threatened by others and whose entire way of life is at risk. (It is worth noting that all this comes before Ryker's adoption of murderous tactics, that is, before Wilson kills Frank, so our sympathies are somewhat aroused at this point.)

Baker has argued that, despite this exchange between Ryker and Starrett, *Shane* mitigates our sympathies for Ryker, arguing that 'the audience is to some extent headed off from arbitrating the semi-legalistic conflict of settlers *versus* ranchers or the rights and wrongs of the Homestead Act and instead corralled into the easy ethical framework of peaceful settlers *versus* terrorising ranchers'.[193] His main reason for thinking this is the implication that the Rykers are both without wives and children. With this lack established in the narrative, 'the way is open for a clear-cut resolution of the story: a clutch of dependent Rykers would certainly make for an anomalous ending'.[194] Baker is not wrong, of course, but I argue that there are other elements simultaneously in play. Mitigated or not, Ryker's appeal to Starrett gives the lie to Wright's contention that 'in classical Westerns, no villains are sympathetic, no heroes or society is unsympathetic'.[195] Actually, the location of individual characters within these structuring oppositions is complex. We might recall that Wright takes little to no account of the psychological complexities of character motivation. For him, the hero and the villain are at opposite ends of a binary division, fixed as mythic archetypes. It becomes apparent, however, that such an interpretation does not apply to the narrative of *Shane*. The result is a distorted reading that fails to accommodate a rich, in-depth analysis of either the hero or, in this case, the villain. On yet another level, while Starrett's rebuke to Ryker may well ape Turner's Frontier Thesis, this does not mean that the film necessarily endorses this version of history. In indicating that the 'trappers' and 'Indian traders' were the ones that tamed the country first, Starrett is inadvertently acknowledging the inevitability of his own demise once 'the frontier has passed by'.[196] He too will become a victim of this deterministic view of historical 'progress', cast aside with the coming of the industrial era, where corporate 'agribusiness' was to replace the individual homesteaders.

The history of the spread of agriculture into the West is plagued by an irony. It was widely believed that the huge agricultural production it would generate would lead to corresponding increases in the wealth of individuals (economic individualism) and of the nation as a whole. In fact, the effect was the opposite. Over-production was so great that world prices for grain and other crops collapsed, and US agriculture passed into the hands of corporate monopolies, as only very large-scale operations could compete. In their belligerence towards one another, Ryker and Starrett are symbolically prefiguring this historical exploitation of the land and its resources which resulted in environmental, social and economic disaster. The over-grazing and over-production of arid soils, of course, eventuated in the 1930s Dust Bowl. It can be argued that Ryker inadvertently hints at environmental despoliation when he complains that, even with their low-level farming, the homesteaders sometimes cause the creek to run dry, forcing him to move his stock.

Another significant counter-historical aspect of the narrative relates to the racial aspects of frontier settlement. Ryker's reference to his 'bad shoulder', the result of a 'Cheyenne arrowhead', tacitly acknowledges that Turner's proclamation of so-called 'free land' was a misnomer from the start – the product of a wilfully deliberate historical deceit. For under the vast rubric of Manifest Destiny the constructed fiction of 'free land' sought to assuage any guilt regarding the expropriations and conflicts with the Native Americans. The land had, of course, never been free and was instead acquired as the result of a series of brutal and protracted military conquests. It is certainly ironic, but perhaps all too predictable, therefore, that neither Ryker nor Starrett – 'cattle-raiser' nor 'pioneer farmer' – miss a stitch upon the mention of 'Indians' in their dispute over who has the legitimate 'right to the range'. In fact, as McGee astutely observes, 'even more than Ryker does, Joe assumes that the conquest of the West was a form of natural progress'. Consequently, Joe 'shows no sympathy for the Native Americans who occupied and used the land before any of these so-called Westerners appeared on the scene'.[197]

Of course, the 'revelation' that the land was never free can hardly be claimed to be a latent aspect of the Western. Turner may have made only scant reference to the Native American, but this attempted elision from the official history of the frontier cannot rightfully be claimed to apply to Hollywood's West. The fate of the Native Americans is often regarded as an unpalatable fact that returns to plague US culture, but in actuality even so-called classical Westerns usually acknowledge quite openly the acts of conquest required in the founding of modern America: Ryker's 'bad shoulder' together with his contention that a 'safe range' was achieved only through 'blood and empty bellies' constitutes instances of such an acknowledgement. The expropriation of Native Americans from their ancestral homelands is a thematic constituent of *Shane*'s articulation of the national character, of American national identity.

Shane also lays bare this unpalatable fact: 'Law and Order' and the domestication of the wilderness is in fact the result of a ruthless social Darwinian struggle for power between competing interests. The claim of 'Rights' comes down to the application of force and, as McGee notes, 'violence [is] the ultimate basis of social power'.[198] Violence permitted the new Americans to tame the West, it is what allows Ryker to assert his authority over the valley, and it is what allows Shane to take that authority from him. Therefore, the generic violence of the shootout – the epic moment – in *Shane* foregrounds an historical dimension, rather than sublimates it under the function of myth.

V

We come now, finally, to an analysis of Shane himself – his psychological motivation and political-allegorical dimension. McGee is persuasive in his suggestion that the hero recognises the fundamental opposition between 'the values of community and the values of power', and how this is manifest in the 'visual composition' of the film.[199] However, we have seen how the survival of the community depends on power at the same time as it disavows the agent of that power. Central to this issue is Shane's shootout with Wilson. Aesthetically, the stark realism of the moment, which sees actor Palance's body being jerked backwards (courtesy of an elaborate harness) by the force of Shane's bullet, is undercut by the scene's inherent melodrama. On his ride to town, Shane is photographed from a distance, silhouetted against the Tetons. Symbolically dressed in tasselled buck-skins, he emerges out of the wilderness as a cinematic re-imagining of Daniel Boone. Victor Young's musical score does nothing to diminish this metatextual description of Shane. It plays over the sequence and slowly rises to an arresting crescendo as the hero nears Grafton's. When he finally enters the saloon filtered lights darken the already murky interior, and low-angled shots increase Shane's and Wilson's stature. Such visual effects are suggestive of *noirish*, even expressionistic tones, which complement the initial deathly silence as Shane squares-up to Wilson. Wilson leeringly smiles at Shane, Shane smiles back – a smile indicating that Shane will enjoy this epic moment of ritualised violence.

Peeking unseen through the saloon doors is young Joey Starrett. I have already mentioned how some scholars have argued convincingly that the film's narrative is structured around his perspective. This is either literally, as when Shane first arrives in the valley, or if not through strict point-of-view structures, then the boy is present in most of the significant scenes. Structuring the majority of the narrative around Joey's gaze is important when considering the film's contradictory effects, especially in relation to Shane's character. Slotkin suggests that emphasising the boy's perspective has the result of 'abstracting and stylising every person and action . . . looking through history to find a mythic archetype'.[200] Similarly, Mitchell reasons that both the film's realism, and its deliberate emphasis on mythological tropes, 'result[s] from the film's investment in Joey's gaze'.[201] He further suggests that this 'sense of preadolescent consciousness'[202] helps 'to explain why violence seems required and yet is so often deferred'.[203] It also adds to spectator desire and expectation:

> From the beginning, [Joey's] aimless gaze at Shane's body arouses a longing for action – 'Bet you can shoot. Can't you?' – followed by impetuous queries and exclamations that prompt the viewer's longing as well: 'Aren't you goin' to wear your six-shooter, Mr. Shane?' . . . 'Let me see you shoot, Shane.' The repeated deferral of Joey's desires prompts a regressive response in the viewer, whose own generic expectations are stymied yet sharpened by curbs on the boy's consciousness – as if we were being co-opted into wanting the exhibition of violence that the genre always promises. When violence finally does erupt, its presentation only confirms a child's mixed perspective, appearing at once realistically brutal and yet magically inconsequential.[204]

Mitchell's assessment of *Shane* is firmly based in a study that has as its overall objective the divination of a 'common strategy' in early Cold War Westerns. The section I have drawn from for the above quote, Chapter 7: 'Sentimental

Educations', argues that Joey's purpose in the narrative is to provide a 'juvenile condensation of impulses toward both the real and the mythic' by relating the film to the post-Second World War sociocultural issue of 'how a boy is to become a man'.[205] To this he adds issues of fatherhood, cultural initiation and the nuclear family, to which Shane, in however diminished a way, is interpreted as an 'external threat'.[206] This threat is visualised in the film by two moments in the narrative when Shane reaches for his gun. The first is when he spins to draw on Joey upon hearing the boy open the breach on his empty rifle. The second moment is when Marian drops some pans in the kitchen; Shane's first instinctual reaction is to reach for his holster. When he realises there is no threat he looks around at the Starrett family and bows his head in shame. This import of the threat of violence and danger into the domestic realm alerts us to the possibility that Shane has the potential to be a disruptive force to the Starrett family (the microcosm of frontier community), and that he does not really belong in the civilised domain.

For Joey, Shane can be said to represent the desired father figure the boy can never have, an ego-ideal for a male child on the verge of adolescence. McGee suggests that 'Joey functions as the allegorical embodiment of a generation of young boys who have been imprinted with this phantasmic idealisation of masculine identity and violence.'[207] This identity was another aspect of the national character for, in Coyne's political-allegorical reading, Shane is read in terms of an ideal national image (one that the younger generation can look up to and identify with), and that he is clearly an 'instance of the American hero who is keen to avoid trouble if possible but who ultimately finds he must resort to violence'.[208] Coyne has it that *Shane* be read in the context of the Cold War, where Ryker represents a charismatic authoritarianism (Soviet communism) threatening the democratic principles of the homesteaders (American capitalism), 'with Ladd's Shane as [the] personification of the sleeping giant in the age of atomic weaponry'.[209] For Marian, Shane could be seen to represent the ideal embodiment of a figurative heroic husband: a charismatic type so far beyond the existential constraints of her actual husband, the dependable but plainly 'average' Joe. This is suggested (perhaps unwittingly) in the subtext of Joey's final call to Shane: 'Mother wants you! I know she does!' Coyne makes an interesting point that 'a curious expression crosses the boy's face [as if he realises] the significance of what he has just said'.[210] It is at this moment that 'Joey loses both his boyhood hero and his childhood innocence'.[211]

Most commentators insist that Shane is far too honourable to act on his own attraction to Marian, and they are probably right, however, it is curious to note that a man who resolutely refuses to be goaded into violence until it is literally unavoidable erupts with rage at mere insinuation. Following Shane's refusal to accept Ryker's lucrative offer to come and work for him ('whatever Starrett's paying you I'll double it!') he asks of him, 'What *are* you looking for?', Ryker pauses and then smiles sardonically, 'Pretty wife

Starrett's got.' Shane explodes, 'Why, you dirty, stinkin' old man!' Coyne suggests something similar when he proposes that Wilson is 'the dark side' of Shane, and that Shane's slaying of Wilson constitutes an act of repression.[212] Making reference to the attraction between Shane and Marian, he asserts that it is such an amoral familial disruption that Shane seeks to repress by his fatal actions: '[Shane] could disrupt the Starretts' marriage; for Shane has the potential to be either Galahad in Camelot or the serpent in Eden.'[213] Even Starrett remarks with a somewhat melancholic tone that, should he meet his end fighting Ryker, he knows that Shane could look after Marian and Joey better than he ever could. In other words, he knows that Shane could literally supersede him as father of the family, and that (on some level at least) this may even be a desired outcome for him and his family. Tompkins hypothesises about how this (un)conscious wish-fulfilment might have panned out:

> When Joey calls out at the end of *Shane*, and the call echoes, 'Come back, Shane!' we want Shane to come back just as much as he does. But suppose Shane *had* come back and had gotten Marian Starrett away from Joe, Sr. What would it have been like to live with him? Shane was a man of few words, mysterious, catlike, sexually appealing, with something a little deadly in the background . . . What would it have been like to spend long days with this edgy, introverted person, with hair-trigger reflexes and an undigestible past? How much did Shane like living with himself?[214]

These are all interesting aspects of Shane's psychological motivation, especially when considered in conjunction with Joey's plea for Shane to 'Come back!' But, of course, Shane cannot 'come back' for, as we have seen, his very presence threatens to disrupt not only the marital sanctity of the Starrett family, but also the whole social order that the homesteaders symbolically represent. Pressing the political-allegorical reading further, one could tease out another aspect of Shane's character which is not befitting his role as all-American hero. There is a strong possibility that Shane may well be a violent outlaw on a self-imposed path of redemption. As McGee relates, in his past Shane may well have been 'a gunman for hire to someone like Ryker, a servant to power and property. Something brought about a change, and more than likely it was an act of violence that disrupted Shane's perception of himself and the world.'[215]

It is telling that redemption for such a figure can come only through exile and (possibly) death. In any case, Shane's departure from the valley in the film's final shot allows us to muse over a deeply complex narrative with an even deeper ambivalence regarding that narrative's attitude towards both its hero and triumphalist brands of frontier mythology.

NOTES

1. Frederick Jackson Turner, 'The Significance of the Frontier in American History' [1893], in Frederick Jackson Turner, *The Frontier in American History* (Tucson, AZ: University of Arizona Press, [1920] 1986), pp. 1–38, quote on p. 1.
2. Northrop Frye, *Anatomy of Criticism* (Princeton, NJ: Princeton University Press, 1957). Frye, discussed in Douglas Pye, 'The Western (Genre and Movies)' (1977), reprinted in Barry Keith Grant (ed.), *Film Genre Reader III* (Austin, TX: University of Texas Press, 2003), pp. 203–18, quote on pp. 204–7.
3. Leo Marx, *The Machine in the Garden: Technology and the Pastoral Ideal in America* (New York: Oxford University Press, 1964), p. 354.
4. Pye, 'The Western', p. 207.
5. For an example of this assertion, see Jim Kitses, *Horizons West: Anthony Mann, Bud Boetticher, Sam Peckinpah – Studies of Authorship within the Western* (London: Secker & Warburg/British Film Institute, 1969), p. 8.
6. Thomas Schatz, *Hollywood Genres: Formulas, Filmmaking, and the Studio System* (New York: Random House, 1981), p. 58.
7. Ibid., p. 59.
8. Steve Neale, 'Questions of Genre' (1995), reprinted in Grant (ed.), *Film Genre Reader III*, pp. 160–84, quote on p. 179.
9. Edward Buscombe (ed.), *The BFI Companion to the Western* (London: British Film Institute, 1988), p. 13.
10. John H. Lenihan, *Showdown: Confronting Modern America in the Western Film* (Urbana, IL: University of Illinois Press, [1980] 1985), pp. 24–5.
11. Alan Williams, 'Is a Radical Genre Criticism Possible?' *Quarterly Review of Film Studies*, 9(2) (1984): 123–4. Williams, discussed in Neale, 'Questions of Genre', p. 173.
12. Janet Walker (ed.), 'Introduction: Westerns through History', in *Westerns: Films through History* (London: Routledge, 2001), p. 5.
13. Ibid., p. 5.
14. Ibid., p. 10.
15. Michael Coyne, *The Crowded Prairie: American National Identity in the Hollywood Western* (London: I. B. Tauris, 1997), p. 13.
16. Ibid., p. 13.
17. Ibid., p. 189.
18. Ibid., p. 189.
19. Ibid., p. 189.
20. Ibid., p. 191.
21. Schatz, *Hollywood Genres*, p. 58.
22. Ibid., p. 64 (emphasis added).
23. John G. Cawelti, *The Six-Gun Mystique Sequel* (Bowling Green, OH: Bowling Green State University Popular Press, 1999), pp. 143–6. Cawelti, discussed in Neale, 'Questions of Genre', p. 179.
24. Jack Nachbar (ed.), 'Riding Shotgun: The Scattered Formula in Contemporary Western Movies' (1973), reprinted in *Focus on the Western* (Englewood Cliffs, NJ: Prentice-Hall, 1974), p. 102.
25. Janet Staiger, 'Hybrid or Inbred: The Purity Hypothesis and Hollywood Genre History' (1997), reprinted in Grant (ed.), *Film Genre Reader III*, p. 185.
26. Ibid., p. 195. A similar point is made by Rick Altman in relation to genre theory. Altman suggests that the fact of genre hybridity 'is typically forgotten for genres created in the past, leaving us with what seems like an uncomplicated genre identified by a single name.' Rick Altman, *Film/Genre* (London: British Film Institute, 1999), p. 149. See also Geoff King, *New Hollywood Cinema: An Introduction* (New York: Columbia University Press, 2002), pp. 139–46.

27. Hans Robert Jauss, *Towards an Aesthetic of Reception* (Brighton: Harvester Press, 1982), p. 88. Jauss, discussed in Neale, 'Questions of Genre', p. 173.
28. Neale, *Genre and Hollywood*, p. 211.
29. Ibid., p. 219.
30. Staiger, 'Hybrid or Inbred', p. 185.
31. Jack Schaeffer, *Shane* (London: Bantam Pathfinder, [1949] 1963), p. 119.
32. See John G. Cawelti, 'Savagery, Civilisation and the Western Hero' (1971), reprinted in Nachbar (ed.), *Focus on the Western*, pp. 57–63. See also Michael Marsden, 'The Modern Western', *Journal of the West*, 19 (1980): 54–61.
33. Cawelti, 'Savagery, Civilisation and the Western Hero', p. 58.
34. Owen Wister, *The Virginian: A Horseman of the Plains* (Oxford: Oxford Paperbacks, [1902] 2009), p. 7.
35. Cawelti, *The Six-Gun Mystique Sequel*, p. 40.
36. Robert Warshow, 'Movie Chronicle: The Westerner' (1954), reprinted in Leo Braudy and Marshall Cohen (eds), *Film Theory and Criticism: Introductory Readings* (Oxford: Oxford University Press, 1999), pp. 654–79, quote on p. 666.
37. Ibid., p. 667.
38. Cawelti, 'Savagery, Civilisation and the Western Hero', p. 57.
39. Coyne, *The Crowded Prairie*, p. 76.
40. Jane Tompkins, *West of Everything: The Inner Life of Westerns* (New York: Oxford University Press, 1992), p. 227.
41. Ibid., p. 227.
42. Ibid., p. 228.
43. John G. Cawelti, 'Myths of Violence in American Popular Culture', *Critical Inquiry*, 1(3) (1975): 521–41, quote on p. 526.
44. Ibid., p. 526.
45. Will Wright, *Six Guns and Society: A Structural Study of Myth* (Berkeley, CA: University of California Press, 1975), p. 16.
46. Will Wright, *The Wild West: The Mythical Cowboy and Social Theory* (London: Sage, 2001), p. 2.
47. Ibid., p. 3.
48. See especially Claude Lévi-Strauss, *The Savage Mind* (London: Weidenfeld & Nicolson, [1962] 1966); Vladimir Propp, *The Morphology of the Folktale*, trans. Laurence Scott (Austin, TX: University of Texas Press, [1928] 1968).
49. Wright, *Six Guns and Society*, p. 14.
50. Ibid., p. 15.
51. Ibid., p. 15.
52. Ibid., p. 40. These three plot structures are discussed in greater detail in Cawelti, *The Six-Gun Mystique Sequel*, pp. 29–45.
53. Hayden White, *Metahistory: The Historical Imagination in Nineteenth-Century Europe* (Baltimore, MD: Johns Hopkins University Press, 1973), pp. 8–9.
54. Frye, *Anatomy of Criticism*, p. 347.
55. Kitses, *Horizons West: Anthony Mann, Bud Boetticher, Sam Peckinpah*, p. 15.
56. Ibid., p. 20.
57. For an example of *Shane* being read in this manner, see Ed Andrechuck, *The Golden Corral: A Roundup of Magnificent Westerns* (London: McFarland, 1997), pp. 40–7.
58. Schatz, *Hollywood Genres*, p. 55.
59. Lenihan, *Showdown*, p. 18.
60. Ruth Griffin, 'Writing the West: Critical Approaches to *Shane*', *Literature Compass*, 4(1) (2007): 24–47.
61. Ibid., p. 38.
62. Wright, *Six Guns and Society*, p. 34.
63. Ibid., p. 15.

64. Wright, *The Wild West*, p. 3.
65. Wright, *Six Guns and Society*, pp. 41–8.
66. Ibid., p. 32.
67. Coyne, *The Crowded Prairie*, p. 5.
68. Ibid., p. 5.
69. John Tuska, *The American West in Film: Critical Approaches to the Western* (London: Greenwood Press, 1985), p. 260, see esp. ch. 16.
70. Ibid. p. 260.
71. Tompkins, *West of Everything*, p. 10.
72. Cawelti, *The Six-Gun Mystique Sequel*, p. 35.
73. Leslie A. Fiedler, *The Return of the Vanishing American* (London: Jonathan Cape, 1968), p. 140.
74. Lee Clark Mitchell, *Westerns: Making the Man in Fiction and Film* (Chicago, IL: University of Chicago Press, 1996), p. 138.
75. For a deconstructionist reading of this gender binary in literature, see Hélène Cixous, 'Sorties' (1975), reprinted in David Lodge and Nigel Wood (eds), *Modern Criticism and Theory: A Reader* (London: Longman, [1988] 2000), pp. 263–71. For how this gender binary has been appropriated and articulated in Hollywood narrative cinema, see Laura Mulvey, 'Visual Pleasure and Narrative Cinema', *Screen*, 16(3) (1975): 6–19.
76. Tompkins, *West of Everything*, pp. 39–40.
77. Ibid., p. 144.
78. Ibid., pp. 61–2.
79. For specific reference to Wister's *The Virginian*, see Leslie A. Fiedler, *Love and Death in the American Novel* (London: Penguin, [1960] 1984), p. 259.
80. Jim Kitses, *Horizons West: Directing the Western from John Ford to Clint Eastwood* (London: British Film Institute, [2004] 2007), p. 21.
81. Ibid., p. 21.
82. Ibid., p. 21.
83. Wright, *The Wild West*, pp. 158–71.
84. Ibid., p. 168.
85. Richard Slotkin, *Gunfighter Nation: The Myth of the Frontier in Twentieth-Century America* (Norman, OK: University of Oklahoma Press, [1992] 1998), pp. 5–6.
86. Ibid., p. 8.
87. Ibid., p. 10.
88. Ibid., p. 6.
89. Ibid., pp. 24–6.
90. Ibid., p. 11.
91. Ibid., p. 14.
92. Ibid., p. 12 (emphasis in original). For a more detailed account of the Daniel Boone legend in frontier mythology, see Richard Slotkin, *Regeneration through Violence: The Mythology of the American Frontier, 1600–1860*, new edn (Norman, OK: University of Oklahoma Press, 2000), esp. pp. 21–2 and ch. 9.
93. James Fenimore Cooper, *The Pioneers* (New York: Signet Classics, [1823] 1964), pp. 13–14.
94. Ibid., p. 436.
95. See David S. Heidler and Jeanne T. Heidler, *Manifest Destiny* (London: Greenwood Press, 2003), p. 23. See also pp. 132, 137, 175–6, 200.
96. Roland Barthes, *Mythologies*, trans. Annette Lavers (London: Vintage, [1972] 1993), p. 142.
97. Ibid., p. 142.
98. Ibid., p. 142.
99. Ibid., p. 143 (emphasis in original).

100. Cawelti, 'Myths of Violence', p. 539.
101. Schaeffer, *Shane*, p. 101. Cawelti also makes this observation in 'Myths of Violence', p. 539.
102. Rick Worland and Edward Countryman, 'The New Western, American Historiography and the Emergence of the New American Westerns', in Edward Buscombe and Roberta E. Pearson (eds), *Back in the Saddle Again: New Essays on the Western* (London: British Film Institute, 1998), p. 195, fn. 5.
103. Griffin, 'Writing the West', p. 28.
104. Ibid., p. 28.
105. Turner, *The Frontier in American History*, p. 1. See also pp. 2–3, 12.
106. For elaboration of *homo americanus*, see Johan Gultang, 'The Meanings of History: Enacting the Sociocultural Code', in Jörn Rüsen (ed.), *Meaning and Representation in History* (Oxford: Berghahn Books, 2006), p. 98.
107. Warshow, 'Movie Chronicle', p. 664.
108. Ibid., p. 664.
109. Ibid.
110. André Bazin, 'Évolution du western', *Cahiers du Cinéma*, 55 (1955), reprinted in Bill Nichols (ed.), *Movies and Methods, vol. 1: An Anthology* (London: University of California Press, 1976), pp. 150–7, quote on p. 153.
111. Ibid., p. 152.
112. Ibid., p. 153.
113. Ibid., p. 153.
114. Tag Gallagher, 'Shoot-Out at the Genre Corral: Problems in the "Evolution" of the Western' (1986), reprinted in Barry Keith Grant (ed.), *Film Genre Reader III*, (Austin, TX: University of Texas Press, 2003), pp. 262–76, quote on p. 266.
115. Warshow, 'Movie Chronicle', p. 664.
116. Bob Baker, '*Shane* Through Five Decades', in Ian Cameron and Douglas Pye (eds), *The Movie Book of the Western* (London: Studio Vista, 1996), pp. 214–20, quote on p. 215.
117. J. Hector St John de Crèvecoeur, *Letters from an American Farmer* (New York: Oxford University Press, [1782] 1998), p. 44.
118. Wright, *Six Guns and Society*, p. 41.
119. Slotkin, *Gunfighter Nation*, p. 396.
120. Lenihan, *Showdown*, p. 18.
121. Mitchell, *Westerns*, pp. 69–70.
122. Ibid., p. 194.
123. Slotkin, *Regeneration through Violence*, p. 493.
124. Ibid., p. 493.
125. Fiedler, *Love and Death in the American Novel*, p. 192. On Cooper's significance to frontier mythology, see Slotkin, *Regeneration through Violence*, ch. 13; Edwin Fussell, *Frontier: American Literature and the American West* (Princeton, NJ: Princeton University Press, 1965), ch. 1.
126. Wright, *Six Guns and Society*, p. 47.
127. Warshow, 'Movie Chronicle', pp. 657–8.
128. Lenihan, *Showdown*, p. 18.
129. Mitchell, *Westerns*, p. 12.
130. Ibid., p. 8.
131. Ibid., p. 8.
132. Ibid., p. 152.
133. Tompkins, *West of Everything*, p. 39.
134. Mitchell, *Westerns*, p. 12 (emphasis in original).
135. Ibid., p. 13.
136. Terry Eagleton, *Literary Theory: An Introduction* (Oxford: Blackwell, [1983] 1995), pp. 133–4.

137. Staiger, 'Hybrid or Inbred', pp. 188–9. Staiger also makes useful reference to Thomas O. Beebee's assertion that *any* act of genre classification is 'always already unstable', due to the fact that 'a 'single' genre is only recognizable as difference, as a foregrounding against the background of its neighboring genres.' And as a consequence of this, an individual text typically 'involves more than one genre, even if only implicitly'. Thomas O. Beebee, *The Ideology of Genre: A Comparative Study of Generic Instability* (University Park, PA: Pennsylvania State University Press, 1994), pp. 27–8. Beebee, discussed in Staiger, 'Hybrid or Inbred', p. 189.

138. Michel Foucault, *The Archaeology of Knowledge* (London: Routledge, [1969] 2002), p. 28.

139. This is, of course, dealing on an individual level with what Foucault is concerned with on a wider sociopolitical and cultural–historical level. 'In attempting to uncover the deepest strata of Western culture', writes Foucault, 'I am restoring to our silent and apparently immobile soil its rifts, its instability, its flaws; and it is the same ground that is once more stirring under our feet.' Michel Foucault, *The Order of Things: An Archaeology of the Human Sciences* (London: Tavistock, [1966] 1970), p. xxiv

140. As I shall argue below, the voice of the Native American haunts the narrative of *Shane* in a not insignificant measure.

141. Forrest G. Robinson, *Having it Both Ways: Self-Subversion in Western Popular Classics* (Albuquerque, NM: University of New Mexico Press, 1993), p. 3.

142. Ibid., p. 3.

143. Ibid., pp. 2–3. He argues, for instance, that Jack Schaeffer 'gives no evidence of glimpsing the penetrating critique of male hegemony that [the novel] *Shane* so brilliantly performs', ibid., pp. 2–3.

144. Ibid., pp. 2–3 (emphasis in original).

145. Ibid., pp. 2–3.

146. Andrew Tudor, 'Genre and Critical Methodology' (1974), reprinted in Nichols (ed.), *Movies and Methods*, vol. 1, pp. 118–26, quote on p. 121 (emphasis in original).

147. Warshow, 'Movie Chronicle', p. 664. Bazin, 'Évolution du western', p. 151.

148. Alan Lovell, 'The Western' (1967), reprinted in Nichols (ed.), *Movies and Methods*, vol. 1, pp. 164–75, quote on p. 169.

149. Kathryn C. Esselman, 'From Camelot to Monument Valley: Dramatic Origins of the Western Film' (1974), reprinted in Nachbar (ed.), *Focus on the Western*, pp. 9–19, quote on p. 13.

150. Gallagher, 'Shoot-Out at the Genre Corral', p. 264.

151. Ibid., p. 263.

152. Justification for a 'scant' survey becomes apparent when one considers the condition of artefacts from this period of film production. According to Nachbar, as of 1974, 'the American Film Institute estimates that less than 20 percent of silent films are in existence', and that, among Westerns, the 'percentage of loss is probably even higher'. Nachbar (ed.), 'Introduction', in *Focus on the Western*, p. 8.

153. Gallagher, 'Shoot-Out at the genre Corral', p. 266.

154. Ibid., p. 264.

155. Schatz, *Hollywood Genres*, p. 38.

156. Williams, 'Is a Radical Genre Criticism Possible?'; Williams, discussed in Neale, 'Questions of Genre', pp. 123–4.

157. Gallagher, 'Shoot-Out at the Genre Corral', p. 272.

158. Tuska, *The American West in Film*, p. 14.

159. Ibid., p. 14.

160. Wright, *Six Guns and Society*, p. 42.

161. Ibid., pp. 41–8.

162. Coyne, *The Crowded Prairie*, p. 74.
163. McGee, *From Shane to Kill Bill*, p. 10.
164. Karen R. Jones and John Wills, *The American West: Competing Visions* (Edinburgh: Edinburgh University Press, 2009), p. 235.
165. Ibid., p. 235.
166. Ibid., pp. 231–40.
167. Ibid., p. 235.
168. Wright, *Six Guns and Society*, p. 47.
169. Ibid., p. 47.
170. In Wright's schema, a necessary function for the 'classical plot': 'The hero loses or gives up his social status'.
171. Wright, *Six Guns and Society*, p. 59.
172. Ibid., p. 59.
173. Ibid., p. 121.
174. Ibid., p. 189.
175. Slotkin, *Gunfighter Nation*, p. 400.
176. Ibid., p. 400.
177. McGee, *From Shane to Kill Bill*, p. 6.
178. Mitchell, *Westerns*, p. 194.
179. Ibid., p. 194 (emphasis added).
180. Ibid., p. 11. See also pp. 305–6 and fn. 12.
181. Ibid., p. 11.
182. Ibid., p. 11.
183. Slotkin, *Gunfighter Nation*, p. 398.
184. Ibid., p. 398.
185. Slotkin terms this the 'progressive epic'. Ibid., p. 398.
186. Ibid., p. 399.
187. Ibid., p. 398.
188. Not forgetting little Joey, of whom there are numerous cut-away shots, and to whom Ryker even addresses part of his speech, an appeal to the next generation of settlers – 'How about it, son?' Thus, from 'Joey's prepubescent angle of vision' we see Ryker's association with the wilderness as much as we do Shane's.
189. Griffin, 'Writing the West', p. 31.
190. Ibid., p. 31. Turner writes: 'Stand at the Cumberland Gap and watch the procession of civilisation, marching single file – the buffalo following the trail to the salt springs, the Indian, the fur-trader and hunter, the cattle-raiser, the pioneer farmer – and the frontier has passed by.' *The Significance of the Frontier in American History*, p. 12.
191. Mitchell, *Westerns*, p. 195.
192. Ibid., p. 195
193. Baker, 'Shane through Five Decades', pp. 218–19.
194. Ibid., p. 219.
195. Wright, *Six Guns and Society*, p. 55.
196. Turner, *The Frontier in American History*, p. 12.
197. McGee, *From Shane to Kill Bill*, p. 12.
198. Ibid., p. 11.
199. Ibid., p. 14.
200. Slotkin, *Gunfighter Nation*, p. 397.
201. Mitchell, *Westerns*, p. 195.
202. Ibid., p. 196.
203. Ibid., p. 195.
204. Ibid., p. 195.
205. Ibid., pp. 206–7, 218.
206. Ibid., p. 202.

207. McGee, *From Shane to Kill Bill*, p. 18.
208. Coyne, *The Crowded Prairie*, p. 76
209. Ibid., p. 76.
210. Ibid., p. 74.
211. Ibid., pp. 74–5.
212. Ibid., p. 75.
213. Ibid., p. 75.
214. Tompkins, *West of Everything*, p. 128.
215. McGee, *From Shane to Kill Bill*, p. 16.

2. A FINE GOOD PLACE TO BE

'Fetch what home? The leavings of Comanche bucks sold time and again to the highest bidder with savage brats of her own?! Do you know what Ethan will do if he has a chance? He'll put a bullet in her brain. I tell you Martha would want him to.'

I

During the climactic chase sequence in John Ford's *Stagecoach* (1939) there occurs a moment which is crucial in the film's status as a Western. It speaks of the genre's relationship to frontier mythology and of the myth's significance in shaping the cultural attitudes of both the nineteenth-century and mid-twentieth-century United States. With ambushing Apaches closing in on the stagecoach and with its beleaguered occupants running low on ammunition, Southern 'gentleman', Hatfield (John Carradine), is seen pointing his pistol at Lucy Mallory (Louise Platt), a white woman and recent mother who is praying for rescue. Before Hatfield can shoot his last bullet into Mallory's brain he is, himself, mortally wounded by an Apache rifle shot. A close-up shows the pistol falling from his grip, while the oblivious Mallory continues praying. Almost immediately following this near-death experience, and as if in divine answer to her prayers, the US Cavalry arrive to drive off the attacking Apache and rescue those aboard the stagecoach.

The cultural significance of this scene for the Western is to be found in the long-held belief that one is better off dead than falling into the hands of 'Indians'. The very thought of a white woman (especially) being captured by 'savages' – of suffering 'a fate worse than death' – is cinematically referenced as far back as D. W. Griffith's *The Birth of a Nation* (1915). This example from *Stagecoach* exists as but one such articulation of this fear of the racial 'other'.

Contemporary audiences might well balk at the racist implications of this scene. By today's standards Hatfield's intended action, undoubtedly motivated by his culture's fear of the Native American 'other', comes across as somewhat perverse. However, from the moment of the arrival of European settlers into the New World, such fears became formalised in the 'captivity narratives' that have continued to feature heavily in American literary output. The captivity narrative was developed in response to the experiences of white captivity among Native Americans in colonial America. These narratives existed long before the Western genre came into being, and it is highly likely, therefore, that Ford was drawing on a long-standing and ideologically ingrained societal awareness to make this scene from *Stagecoach* not only dramatically engaging, but culturally *intelligible*. According to Slotkin, the captivity narrative mythologises the historical confrontations between Anglo and Native American cultures. In *Regeneration through Violence*, he suggests that it provides 'a variation on the great central myth of initiation into a new world and a new life that is at the core of the American experience'.[1] He further argues that: '[f]rom the moment of its literary genesis, the New England Indian captivity narratives[s] ... reduce[ed] the Puritan state of mind and world view, along with the events of colonisation and settlement, into archetypal drama'.[2] From the very outset, the issue of race was ingrained within captivity narratives; it both constituted and, moreover, *justified* them. Thus, Slotkin writes:

> The culture and literature that we call American was borne out of the confrontation between cultures that embodied two distinctly different phases of mythological evolution, two conflicting modes of perception, two antagonistic visions of the nature and destiny of man and the natural wilderness.[3]

This 'confrontation between cultures' set the tone for the rhetoric of a 'race war' between European settlers and Native Americans that would concern the various forms of Anglo-American cultural expression. As I have mentioned in Chapter 1, Slotkin insists that the so-called 'Indian wars' constitute the 'original generic form of the Frontier Myth'.[4] In terms of popular culture he explored this idea through the concept of regeneration through violence. I have already engaged with the complex ways in which the cinematic Western has interacted with this mythic concept along with the domestication of the wilderness through my analysis of *Shane*, and it would certainly be erroneous to think that popular culture forms and, indeed, the popular imagination itself, has dealt with the 'confrontation between cultures' unambiguously.

It is often said that the wilderness and its occupants caused European settlers to 'project onto the Indians [their] own latent desires for freedom, sensuality, and escape from the spiritual rigours of the Christian community'.[5] Therefore, such fears as those manifested in the Anglo-American figure of Hatfield are expressive of an ideological fear symptomatic of, as Arthur M. Eckstein explains it, 'how quickly the [captivity narrative] tradition became characterised by anxiety caused by white captives' surprisingly easy "conversion" to Indian ways'.[6]

This unacceptable attraction to the lifestyle of the racial other may well account for the on-going appeal of the captivity narrative in popular culture, and for the construction of the powerful myth of Native American savagery as a means to counter it. The historical phenomenon of 'willing conversion' surely contributed to the designs evident in the nineteenth-century United States that sought to subjugate or annihilate Native Americans and their 'unfettered' cultures. The destruction of the Indian in literary and cinematic expressions of the captivity narrative was, according to John G. Cawelti, 'also symbolically a destruction of the captive's own feared desires for lawlessness and the lascivious freedom of the wilderness'.[7] Slotkin suggests that, for the Puritan settlers of the seventeenth century, such destruction constituted nothing short of an act of '*exorcism*', whereby European settlers' desires to succumb to the temptations of the wilderness 'are treated as if they were representations of the id, being sought out and recognised only that they might be repressed or destroyed'.[8] Hence, the overriding cultural attitude in the face of this socioreligious anxiety: 'The cross is thrust upon the Christian – to love it, accept it, and be saved; or to rail against it and perish. The situation of the Puritan soul, for all its outward security, is thus extremely precarious.'[9]

This notion of the 'precarious' state of the Anglo-American soul has a particular thematic resonance in John Ford's *The Searchers* (1956). Here the complexities of the captivity narrative, and its ambiguous and contradictory representations in popular culture, are brought to the fore in what many consider to be his finest Western. The cultural currency of race war and the captivity narrative are here exploited by Ford in order to ask pressing questions about the role played by race in structuring the myth of the West, and of the Western genre's role as a product of popular culture in disseminating this mythology to twentieth-century audiences. The overriding thematic concern that many scholars have identified in *The Searchers* appears to be the opposing of 'blood kinship' to a culture of kinship by adoption, where originary concerns over racial purity are surmounted through a culture based on racial interaction and tolerance. In both instances, the historical issue of race as a major component of American national identity is brought into stark relief. Equally ambiguous and contradictory is the film's interpretation of the Western hero who, as Douglas Pye points out, 'is both monstrous *and* John Wayne'.[10] The film posits an ambiguous hero through highlighting his symbolic links to Anglo-America's Manifest Destiny; specifically, his mythic role in the race war so crucial in the narrative of the domestication of the wilderness. I shall develop my argument for how *The Searchers* relates to these aspects of the trope of the hero during the course of this chapter. First, I aim to provide some exposition and analysis through which I can identify the complex nature of *The Searchers*' relationship with issues of race, and how we can situate the film within the Western genre as a whole.

II

Overall, much has been written on *The Searchers* and, invariably, not all of it is consistent, in agreement or even accurate. A case can be (and, indeed, has been) made that *The Searchers* is an over-determined film, and I do not (and cannot) propose to deal with *all* the published criticism here, let alone all the film's themes and nuances of plot. I shall, however, adumbrate some of the most prominent or 'representative' perspectives during the course of this chapter.

As indicated in Chapter 1, Roland Barthes tells us that myth serves an ideological purpose by flattening history, simplifying its complexities and reducing them to a binary between opposing forces, typically that of Good against Evil. In the case of the myth of the West, its purpose is as a justification of Manifest Destiny. Within the terms of this myth, the ancestral European pioneers are religiously legitimated as the forces of Good, coming to represent American exceptionalism, democracy and economic individualism. They were, in other words, the vanguard in the onward march of civilisation. Conversely, the Native Americans are typically cast as the Evil that resists the forward march of the pioneers and, therefore, they oppose the very momentum of history itself.

Many film scholars have interpreted the Western itself as championing this project, providing a palatable and exciting 'myth of origins' by which the United States can readily interpret its own past. For example, Richard Maltby conflates frontier mythology and the Western genre to argue for a 'Western myth [that] made available a rhetoric[al] discursive framework by which a national self-image of the self-righteousness of Manifest Destiny could be maintained.'[11] In this understanding of the genre, Native Americans are reduced to mere 'props', as Tompkins calls them, generic tropes emptied of any historical signification beyond that of legitimating Anglo-American conquest. In other words, they become either representations of that otherness that the dominant culture both need *and* fear, or else, in accordance with Slotkin's account of the Puritan mindset, metaphors for that within themselves that they wish to repress. Either way they never represent 'real' Native Americans, but, rather, symbolic 'Indians'. Pye concurs with this view, suggesting that, despite the fact that the,

> history of the Western is littered with movies that attempt to develop liberal perspectives on the historical treatment of native Americans . . . the racism that is inherent in the traditions of the genre makes almost any attempt to produce an anti-racist Western a paradoxical, even contradictory, enterprise. It is, in effect, impossible to escape the genre's informing White supremacist terms.[12]

However, such an argument depends upon conceding to the cynical belief that the Western *is* American history.[13] By this I mean the assumption that the 'real' history of the frontier has long been sublimated to the Western genre, which exists essentially as a conduit for mythology parading as history: the myth of the West. The belief here is that the Western exists almost as a simulacrum, a self-reproducing narrative that provides its own source of meaning, at once depicting several attendant myths, namely, regeneration through violence, the domestication of the wilderness, and the emergence of the 'Garden of the World' from the 'Great American Desert'; ultimately providing an audio-visual analogue, a paean, if you will, to Anglo-centric historical narratives such as those provided by Turner and Roosevelt.

Maltby goes even further, suggesting that myth precedes historical narrative in such a way that the two become indistinguishable.[14] This follows his claim that '[t]he history of the West is in a sense a subgenre of the western, and revisionist history a subgenre of that'.[15] If Maltby is correct, then the historical validity of any discourse concerning the frontier is destined to be stymied by the omnipresence of an indelible and insurmountable mythological discursive formation. Maltby is in many ways persuasive, yet Slotkin has argued that the opposite is the case. He suggests that frontier mythology actually provides the source of the Western genre. That is to say, the myth existed long before the Western and will outlast it, its terms transferable to other modes or genres of cultural expression. In Slotkin's view the Western exists as but one genre by which to express Anglo-America's myth–ideology systems. Implicit in this line of argument is the potential for a historical revision of the racism underpinning the myth that is beyond being a mere 'subgenre' of the history of the West, or even of the Western genre itself.[16] However, Slotkin doubts the ability of the Western in this task. His deterministic political-allegorical thesis in *Gunfighter Nation* concludes with the belief that, due to its Anglo bias, and ever since the cultural–political fallout following the Vietnam War, the Western genre has ceased to be the popular culture form through which this historical revisionism will be expressed. (He actually concurs with Maltby and Pye in this respect.) Like so many other scholars, Slotkin believes that the Western is essentially Anglo-centric and has long since lost its explanatory power with regard to making American history comprehensible to US citizens.[17]

Slotkin's analysis of the genre is certainly compelling, but perhaps overly fatalistic. As I have attempted to show in Chapter 1 through my analysis of the interacting historical and mythic narrative themes of *Shane*, there is no guarantee that the individual films that make up what we call the Western genre will regurgitate the myth of the West entirely from an Anglo-American perspective. And even if they do, they rarely do so in a straightforward, unproblematic manner. Post-structuralist analyses have taught us that so-called 'resistive' narratives and ideological agendas that muddy the clear waters of the myth can, more often than not, be found in most Westerns. And yet, far from undermining the power and significance of the genre, this complex articulation of the myth's ideological purpose, often manifested through a sense of what I have termed 'narrative confusion', actually enhances its status as a platform for ideological *and* historical debate. In other words, the Western can exist as a vehicle for a radical critique of the myth's 'White supremacist terms', and thereby work to expose the sinister underbelly of the paradoxical ideological machinations that promoted Manifest Destiny.

Often a narrative is confused to the degree that a single film text can be said to exist simultaneously as both promulgator of the dominant ideological discourse *and* as consciously expressing its antagonistic counter-ideological narratives. Myth and anti-myth, if you will, thus become one and the same thing (to lesser or greater degrees, of course). This proposition follows the suggestion made by Susan Kollins that 'the Western [is] a genre structured by competing and contradictory impulses [whereby] the concept of a purely faithful or fully critical text loses its explanatory power'.[18] Such a perspective, which does away with the terms classical and revisionist, may indeed account for the completely opposing conclusions that many scholars have come to in their analyses of *The Searchers*.

Ford's most prominent Westerns tend to be instances of such extremely complex texts. Indeed, it can be said that they stir far more debate among film scholars than they do consensus. Regarding the depiction of Native Americans, his films undoubtedly stand guilty of some of the charges levelled by scholars such as Maltby and Pye, but these alone never tell the 'whole story'. Ford's Indians are contradictory and inconsistent figures (as I shall go on to discuss below, it is this aspect of *The Searchers* that proves to be one of the most difficult to interpret), and yet the ongoing desire to discern socially progressive patterns of meaning within the genre as a whole has also caused some of his films to be misinterpreted. As one example of this, I refer to a 1998 essay by Jacqueline K. Greb titled, 'Will the Real Indians Please Stand Up?' Within an evolutionary schema Greb seeks to discern an ever-more liberal attitude in Ford's treatment of Native American culture. When it comes to assessing the three films of his so-called 'Cavalry Trilogy', Greb writes that: '[in *Fort Apache* (1948)] John Ford "confronts Indian culture on its own terms" ... Captain York, played by John Wayne, not only shows respect for Cochise, played by Miguel Inclan, but he also treats him as an equal'.[19] Few would argue with this assessment; however, it is the next sentence with which I wish to take issue. 'In *She Wore a Yellow Ribbon* and *Rio Grande* (1950)', Greb continues, 'Indians gain more culture, normal life experiences, human traits.'[20] Greb provides no justification for this comment, and if one looks even briefly at *Rio Grande*, the reverse seems to be the case. In this, the final film in the Cavalry Trilogy, the faceless Apache antagonists (for here there are no Indian characters in the manner of Inclan's Cochise) attack a wagon train carrying women and children (the wives and daughters of the cavalry regiment headed by Colonel Kirby Yorke, played once more by John Wayne), and take them across the Mexico–Texas border.

Again, we see here how the captivity narrative plays on Anglo-America's worst nightmares: women and children at the mercy of a savage race enemy are threatened with 'a fate worse than death'. But here there is no attractive alternative culture or legitimate political concern as evident in *Fort Apache* through Cochise's dignified proclamation, delivered in fluent Spanish, to Colonel Owen Thursday (Henry Fonda) on display here. There is nothing of the sort that would typify such 'pro-Indian' Westerns contemporary to *Rio Grande* as Delmar Daves' *Broken Arrow* or Anthony Mann's *Devil's Doorway* (both 1950). Instead, and in an extraordinary turnaround by Ford, there is only a justification for the fear of the racial other and a promotional stance towards the theme of race war. Such a fear is realised when it is revealed that the all-male group of Apaches have raped and murdered one of their captives before crossing the border. In response Yorke initiates an illegal crossing of the Rio Grande in order to save the remaining hostages. The renegade Apaches are holed up in a deserted Mexican village and are generally depicted as aggressive, drunken savages, intent on committing further atrocities against the defence-less captives. The realisation of Anglo-America's worst fears is avoided by Yorke's cavalry, who come to their rescue and wipe the Apache out to a man. This annihilation of the other is presented in the film firmly within terms that justify Manifest Destiny. At one point, US soldiers occupying a church even use cross-slits in the windows as vantage points for shooting; thus visually affirming the link between Anglo-America's use of annihilatory violence and the will of God.

On the one hand, then, and in two films from the same director, we are presented with a sympathetic view of the plight of the Apache Nation (with a hint towards liberal co-existence with the racial other) in the earlier *Fort Apache*; on the other hand, representatives of the same Nation are depicted as one-dimensional savages in the later *Rio Grande*, that is, as ruthless kidnappers of white civilians and possessive of an overtly savage nature that justifies their annihilation within the rubric of race war and the religious auspices of Manifest Destiny. Perhaps Tag Gallagher sums it up best when he writes that 'John Ford ... *is* the worst possible paradigm with which to illustrate the evolution of the western'.[21] This is especially so when one bases this paradigm on the existence of ever-more liberal, or revisionist, depictions of Native Americans as a *general rule*.[22]

When it comes to *The Searchers*' treatment of the captivity narrative and of Anglo and Native American communities, things prove to be extremely complex. The psychological motivation of the film's characters (both Anglo and Native American) extends to encompass the very cultural climate within which the film was made. Indeed, the historical significance of *The Searchers* has often been linked to the era in which it was produced rather than that in which it is set. This has a profound effect on the allegorical significance of the Comanche. Brian Henderson provides us with perhaps the most representative version of such a reading. His 1981 essay, '*The Searchers*: An American Dilemma', utilises the work of Claude Lévi-Strauss and Vladimir Propp to provide a structuralist reading of the film. This, of course, places his study alongside

Will Wright's *Six-Guns and Society* (discussed at length in Chapter 1). Unlike Wright, however, who clearly erred in applying Lévi-Strauss' anthropological studies of myth and kinship unproblematically to modern commercial cinema, and who neglected study of the psychological dimension of character motivation, Henderson both acknowledges Lévi-Strauss' shortcomings and indicates where his binarism and Propp's formalism fail to account for aspects of *The Searchers*' plot. For instance, Henderson points out that considering Propp's analysis of folktales assumes that 'the feelings and intentions of the dramatic personas do not have an effect on the course of action in any instances at all ... [t]here is a Proppian problem in the film's doubled hero: it is Martin who kills Scar, recovers Debbie, and marries Laurie'.[23] Additionally, where Wright ignored certain instances of plot in numerous films so as to make them better fit his overall evolutionary schema, Henderson's analysis highlights certain areas of theoretical concern (which is to the strength of his analysis rather than to its detriment). According to Henderson, the film's powerful appeal to audiences can be explained by reference to the theories of Lévi-Strauss with regard to the film as myth. 'But if myth is viewed as a collective phenomenon', he writes, 'then the power of myth can only be explained by reference to the community that responds to it ... [t]he operation of myth – both its construction from actual conflicts and its impact on audiences – always has to do with the time in which the myth is told, not with the time that it tells of.'[24] Most consider it to be the case that films contribute to and adapt cultural perceptions in the present, and Henderson's reserved use of Lévi-Strauss concerns the latter's insistence that 'myth operates by transposing the terms of the actual conflict into other sets of terms, usually in the form of binary oppositions'.[25]

Thus is Henderson able to place *The Searchers* firmly within the US culture of the 1950s with its concerns over race relations in the early years of the Civil Rights Movement. However, the fact that (as even a scant observation of the film would suggest) the various characters in *The Searchers* do not lie easily on either end of any assumed binary is testament to the shortcomings of structuralist theory in its application to contemporary popular culture and, moreover, to the powerfully complex and ambiguous statement that *The Searchers* makes about race.[26]

If Henderson's use of Lévi-Strauss *is* applicable, however, then he is persuasive in his claim that the power of *The Searchers* 'becomes explicable only if we substitute black for red and read a film about red–white relations in 1868–1873 as a film about black–white relations in 1956'.[27] To support his argument, Henderson notes that Frank Nugent's film script (written in close collaboration with Ford) was being adapted and prepared from Alan Le May's 1954 novel during that crucial period between May 1954 and May 1955 when the US Supreme Court was embroiled in *Brown* v. *Board of Education of Topeka*.[28] It was ultimately decided during this period that segregation in the schools of the American South be constitutionally outlawed, thus furthering the United States' movement away from its history of racial apartheid. Henderson's political-allegorical interpretation becomes problematic, however, if placed in the context of some aspects of the overall plot of *The Searchers*, especially in relation to themes of captivity and race war.

The film is nominally set in Texas in 1868; although the moment it starts we are confronted with the now famous buttes of Monument Valley, Utah. Almost all the action in the film (like the greater majority of Ford's Westerns) is shot in this location, but the action in the film is supposed to encompass much of the Texan southwest. The Edwards family – husband, Aaron (Walter Coy); wife, Martha (Dorothy Jordan); teenage son, Ben (Robert Lyden); and younger daughters, Lucy (Pippa Scott) and Debbie (Lana Wood) – along with their neighbours, the Jorgensens – Lars (John Qualen); his wife, Mrs Jorgenson (Olive Carey); their son, Brad (Harry Carey Jr); and daughter, Laurie (Vera Miles) – nominally herd cattle, but there is no grass anywhere to be seen; there appears to be nothing that could sustain stock. This does support Henderson's contention that the film is to be regarded as myth. That is to say, *The Searchers* gains its mythic status and meaning by being set in a metaphorical space: between civilisation and wilderness, represented in the narrative by interior and exterior spaces. The precarious state of civilisation is underscored near the beginning of the film by the brutal massacre of the Edwards family carried out by a band of Comanche. During the attack, both Aaron and Ben are killed; Martha (it is inferred) is raped and then killed; both Lucy and Debbie are abducted (it turns out that Lucy suffers the same fate as Martha not long after her capture); the ensuing pursuit to recover Debbie lasts (depending on which critic you read) between five and seven years. The two main 'searchers' are Ethan Edwards (John Wayne), the estranged brother of Aaron, and Aaron's adopted son Marty Pauley. Marty is a young man of mixed race. He is 'one-eighth Cherokee', with the rest being 'Welsh and English'. Marty's racial ancestry is, significantly, rendered ambiguous: 'at least that's what they tell me'.

A straightforward (if dangerous) mission to recover a missing child becomes much more complex when, following years of fruitless searching, it is revealed that Debbie (now 'of age' and played by Lana Wood's older sister, Natalie) has assimilated into Comanche culture and has even married the man who led the 'murder raid' on her family's farm, Chief Cicatriz (Henry Brandon), aka Scar. When Ethan and Marty have their first encounter with the adult Debbie, she states her disinclination to come back to the folds of Anglo-American civilisation. As a child she had hoped for rescue, but when Marty says that she should come back with him to her people, as an adult she declares that the Comanche '*are* my people!' As the narrative progresses, it also becomes alarmingly clear that Ethan's intentions towards Debbie shift. He does not aim to rescue her, as originally planned, but is now intent on killing her. Ethan appears exasperated by Debbie's betrayal of her race. In his mind, living with Scar and the Comanche is, indeed, a fate worse than death. Hatfield's fears for Lucy Mallory in *Stagecoach* become realised here in *The Searchers* and consumes

Ethan's mind to a singular, psychopathic intent. As far as Ethan is concerned, by becoming one of Scar's wives, Debbie has lost her virtue and defiled the memory of her dead mother.

Henderson reasons that since 'there were very few anti-miscegenation statutes regarding Indians at any time ... the emotional impact of *The Searchers* can hardly come from the issue of the kinship status and marriageability of an Indian in white society in 1956'.[29] Taken in the context of films produced during this period that held less antagonistic views towards Native Americans, Henderson's political-allegorical reading is credible in its suggestion that *The Searchers* speaks to and of its times. He argues that the film's status as an articulator of frontier mythology sublimates its historical function to its contemporaneous context. In other words, the period in which *The Searchers* was produced constitutes its historical significance and the history of the 1868–73 Texas southwest is understood to be essentially mythic. However, Eckstein (echoing the terms of Maltby) cautions that substituting black for red in this fashion 'once more annihilates the Native Americans, by taking [Indians] not as themselves but as "empty signifiers": Native Americans are denied their own existence and become mere symbols of somebody else'.[30]

Joanna Hearne has suggested another way to interpret such films. She reasons that the absence of 'anti-miscegenation statutes' did little to dissipate long-standing US cultural prejudices towards Native Americans. Indeed, she argues that so-called the 'Termination policies' of the 1940s and 1950s were frustrated by 'unfair wages, restrictive voting laws, stereotyped representations of Indians in the media, and other discriminatory practices'.[31] All of which suggested that '"mainstream" American culture would not welcome full participation of native peoples as citizens'.[32] She argues that films such as *Devil's Doorway* might well be 'discussed as an allegory for early civil rights', but that, moreover, they often resonated 'with the problems facing returning Native American veterans after World War II, including references to poor reservation conditions, chronic local prejudice, racist and outmoded government supervision ... and, most important, a federal assault on tribal lands, sovereignty, and treaty rights'.[33] In short, while Hearne concurs with Henderson in that the historical significance of 1950's Westerns is often to be found in their contemporaneous context, she argues that the allegorical function should not be reserved for African Americans and that it works equally well for issues affecting Native Americans. Such issues include 'tribal identity, sovereignty, and land rights that were central to federal Indian policy shifts in the late 1940s and early 1950s'.[34]

Convincing as both these arguments are, one should not dismiss a film's temporal setting when considering its historical significance, and there are certainly more than *a priori* grounds for attempting to read *The Searchers* within terms of the nineteenth-century frontier, therefore, inverting Henderson's terms by reading the film as a 1950's retrospective attitude towards 'red–white relations in 1868–1873'. If read along these lines, themes of miscegenation,

Indian captivity and racial conflict also relate to nineteenth-century notions of American national identity in relation to the Native American other. Recent studies, such as those provided by Hearne, imply that the issues raised in the nineteenth century by westward expansion, particularly the resultant interaction between US settlers and Native Americans, have not been laid to rest; there have always been indications in popular culture that this is the case. Although hardly a 'pro-Indian' Western, *The Searchers* does provide a counter-narrative to America's 'dominant fiction': an acknowledgement of Anglo-American imperialist conquest masked as historical progress; hence, the irony implicit in Mrs Jorgenson's claim that the country will one day be 'A fine good place to be'.

III

That many Westerns deal with sexual interactions between Anglos and Indians is surely testament to the continued cultural relevance of the captivity narrative and of the complex way in which the genre articulates characteristic aspects of the American national identity. Debbie's desire to stay with the Comanche suggests that *The Searchers'* depiction of attitudes towards the Native American is far more complex than a mere cinematic *repetition* of the captivity narrative that casts them in the role of 'savage', more than simply realising Anglo-America's worst fears.

We may note several curious aspects of *The Searchers'* narrative that manifest the historical fact of miscegenation. For one, Marty's mixed-race status and Ethan's overt hostility towards him: 'Fella could mistake you for a half-breed!' Regarding Debbie, Ethan denies Marty's familial connection to her through adoption into the Edwards family: 'She's your *Nothing*!', and that adoption 'don't make you kin!' What makes narrative confusion in this regard is the fact that the Anglo-Americans, Aaron and Martha, have adopted this 'half-breed' with no consideration that his blood is 'polluted' in any way. He is, as far as they are concerned, one of *them*. Further confusion is aroused by the fact that it was Ethan who apparently found Marty as a child after his own family was massacred by Comanches, and who subsequently brought him to his brother's home for adoption. Ethan plays down this connection with Marty. 'It just happened to be me,' he insists. 'No need to make more of it!' In another complex revelation towards the end of the film, it is revealed that it was none other than Scar himself who was responsible for the massacre of Marty's family. Again, this becomes significant when considering aspects of race and miscegenation in *The Searchers*, and some critics have even suggested that Marty is actually Ethan's biological offspring and, therefore, a product of his own transgressive sexual liaisons with the racial other.[35] Although this cannot be proven, it is interesting to speculate on; indeed, the film would appear to invite as much.

I suggest that we do see the speculation supported (on some level at least) when Ethan confronts Scar face to face for the first time. In response to Ethan's sarcastic remark that he 'talks pretty good "American", for a Comanch', insisting that someone (that is, a white person/captive) must have taught him, Scar replies with mirrored sarcasm of his own, 'You speak good Comanche, someone teach *you?*' The significance of this mutual belligerence is twofold. On the one hand, it hints at miscegenation. Indeed, Scar's alleged historical inspiration is the Comanche Chief Quanah Parker. Quanah Parker was the son of Cynthia Ann Parker, who was abducted by Comanches in 1836. Like Debbie, Cynthia went on to marry her captor and did not wish to return to white society, even following her 'rescue' by US soldiers several years later. Like Quanah Parker, Scar has blue eyes and is possibly the offspring of an Anglo-American and Comanche sexual union.[36] He has undoubtedly learned what English he has from his interactions with Anglo-Texans and his grasp of Spanish from commercial dealings with Mexican traders like the flamboyantly named Emilio Gabriel Fernandez y Figueroa (Antonio Moreno), who sets up the first meeting between Scar, Ethan and Marty. On the other hand, Scar's response to Ethan highlights the fact that Ethan *does* indeed know a lot about Comanche culture (that is, not just their language). This makes plausible the suggestion that Ethan has had, at one time or another, intimate relations with the objects of his racial hatred. Perhaps he has, indeed, had a Native American wife in the past. Could this then have been Marty's own mother? The idea gains more credence if we consider the scene in Scar's tent where Debbie extends a lance hung with numerous scalps, victims of the Comanche's own race war. Ethan will later reveal to Marty that one of them ('long and wavy') belonged to Marty's long-dead mother. This is a more than curious narrative oddity for, as Patrick McGee pointedly asks, 'how could Ethan recognise someone's scalp unless he was on the most intimate terms with that person?'[37] Of course, one cannot base an argument on this alone, but it does at least give one pause to consider the nature of Ethan's claim that he 'found' Marty following a massacre. What is more suggestive is that, in highlighting the interlaced cultural, economic and sexual interactions between Anglo, Mexican and Native Americans along the borderlands, *The Searchers* highlights white hypocrisy in its hero's assertion of superior self-righteousness based on racial purity. *The Searchers* disabuses us of the myth that such concrete distinctions could be made between races, certainly not at this late stage of the history of the American West.

Much of what I have suggested above is conjectural; however, one thing seems, to my mind at least, certain. In *The Searchers*, while the fear of miscegenation is of extreme thematic importance to a 1950's US culture where the Civil Rights Movement was gaining momentum, the same theme is also central in its relation to frontier mythology, popular representations of the late-nineteenth-century southwest, and the racism specific to that period in America's history. The film's adoption (and adaptation) of the more contemporary theme of black–white relations (also red–white relations) is, in my opinion, essentially *combined* with the historical themes of race war and the captivity narrative, itself derived of the ancient Homeric quest for the lost female.[38]

So, how does one consider the characters of Ethan and Scar in relation to each other? It has often been remarked that Ethan and Scar are two of a kind: the central figures of a drama which represents the racial polarisation that characterised the conflict between Anglo and Native Americans. And yet, when *The Searchers* is read like this – with Ethan and Scar as two symbolic avatars that represent the respective mythic tropes of civilisation and wilderness – certain issues are highlighted that cannot be so easily incorporated into such binarism. Primarily, and as I suggested above, neither figure stands clearly at either end of this dichotomy; either racially or *ethically*. To this end, Slotkin puts forward Ethan as a person always at odds with civilisation. Linking him thematically to Robert Montgomery Bird's protagonist in his 1837 novel, *Nick of the Woods*.[39] Slotkin suggests that, like the protagonist of Bird's novel, Ethan is an inversion of the 'man who knows Indians', the 'evil twin of Cooper's Hawkeye whose knowledge of Indians engenders a profound and undying hatred rather than sympathetic understanding'.[40] Some commentators have gone so far as to suggest that Ethan divorces himself from civilisation entirely because he becomes irredeemably savage following his eventual scalping of Scar. Thereby, the traditional paradigm of the Indian's association with savagery is maintained *and* displaced onto Ethan, who appropriates it and who must, therefore, remain a part of the wilderness.[41]

Another common and similar interpretation along these lines sees Scar as Ethan's 'dark-half', in Freudian terms, his id.[42] This would be in keeping with Slotkin's assessment of the Puritan mindset as outlined above and, much like Shane's slaying of Wilson in *Shane*, the destruction of Scar and his warriors has been understood by many as being constitutive of an act of both exorcism and *repression*; primarily a repression of Ethan's own anti-social and morally unacceptable desires towards Martha *and* Debbie, but also of society's exorcism of the racial other. This reading is persuasive, but the end logic of the psychoanalytic approach is extreme to say the least and sees the Edwards family massacre as symbolically being carried out by Ethan's id, as the realisation of his nightmare wish fulfilment. That is to say, his unconscious self carries out the annihilation of the family, the woman, and the domestic realm of civilisation that he desires, but can neither possess nor be a part of. Slotkin aligns such an analysis with his own political-allegorical reading and, in the process, illuminates some of the possible reasons providing the impetus for Ethan's expressed desire to kill the adult Debbie rather than save her; or, rather, to kill her *in order* to save her:

> From the start of the search, love and hate are confounded with each other in Ethan's mind. He loves Debbie not only as his niece but as the only surviving daughter of his beloved Martha. But his feeling for Martha has been twisted by guilt into the rage that keeps him solitary

and at odds with his society. Now all that rage can be focused on Scar, whose rape of Martha and destruction of Aaron's family is a horrific, nightmare enactment of Ethan's repressed desire. By rescuing a pure and unsullied Debbie from Scar, Ethan can symbolically expiate his own guilt toward Aaron and in a sense redeem Martha's sin as well, since her living avatar will be a virgin daughter.[43]

Of course, it is highly unlikely that Debbie is 'pure and unsullied' by this point, but when linked to the above suggestion that Ethan incorporates savagery into himself this reading might explain why Ethan finally decides *not* to kill Debbie. As summed up by McGee: 'Ethan saves Debbie by sacrificing himself on the alter of savagery when he scalps Scar . . . When Ethan picks her up in his arms, Debbie ceases to be the grown woman who has lived with a buck and becomes the little girl to whom Ethan gave his war ribbon.'[44]

Compelling as all this is, psychoanalytic readings incorporate their own problems, and so-called 'canned Freudian' explanations of the film are hardly in short supply. There are two big issues at play here. First, *The Searchers* displaces (if not dilutes) Ethan's suffering at the hands of Comanches by making it not his own family slaughtered – as is the case in Bird's *Nick of the Woods* – but that of his brother, Aaron. Although no doubt the advocate of such an approach would suggest that this only adds to the illicit and pathologically frustrated nature of Ethan's desires, his forbidden love for Martha facilitates the return of a repressed, murderous creature from the depths of his unconscious mind to wreak unmentionable horrors upon that which he jealously covets. Secondly, unlike Shane who *does* kill Wilson, Ethan does *not* kill Scar. As Henderson and others have pointed out, it is Marty who kills Scar while recovering Debbie from the Comanche camp. Surely then it is Marty who takes over the role of hero, the protector of Debbie, while Ethan becomes more and more a flawed, abject figure concerned only with revenge. In this reading, surely Ethan's desire for revenge is frustrated through the denial of mortal combat with his dark-half? Or, as McGee suggests, by scalping Scar does he actually eradicate Debbie's transgression in his own mind? However, there is yet another 'snag' here regarding formulaic plot trajectories: as Henderson noted, it is neither Ethan *nor* Marty who find Scar's camp. This crucially 'heroic' task falls to Mose Harper (Hank Worden), the nominal 'fool' of the film, a man who admits to 'playing crazy' in order to escape from Scar's camp in order to alert, not Ethan, but Marty of the Comanche's return. Is *this* significant? Perhaps Mose believes that Ethan's intentions towards Debbie are indeed as diabolical as Marty fears.

The figurative holes created by such narrative confusion are not easily negotiated by psychoanalytical readings, which while they may (or may not) adequately explain Ethan's motivations (if not Ford's in creating such sinister psychological complexity and narrative sophistication), they fail to adequately explain the complex nature of the film itself. Nor, as we have seen, are such complexities happily incorporated into a formula analysis of the genre as a whole. As if to exemplify this, and in what is surely a clear instance of how far so-called Western genre conventions (such as Wright's insistence that 'the hero defeats the villain') remain entrenched in the critical psyche, Kathryn C. Esselman gets the plot of *The Searchers* spectacularly wrong. In drawing her own thematic comparison with *Nick of the Woods*, she writes: 'Ethan pursues and ultimately kills in personal combat the chief who had led the massacre of his brother-in-law's [sic] family and kidnapped his niece. The family included the woman Ethan loved – his brother's wife – so, like Nick, Ethan avenges them.'[45]

In my opinion the film's mirroring of Ethan and Scar seems to serve the purpose of exposing the redundancy of such a mythic trope, as if there could ever be so clear a distinction between civilisation and wilderness or, indeed, between Anglo and Native Americans. Indeed, the strength of *The Searchers* undoubtedly comes from its refusal to polarise in such a fashion. Such narrative confusion as the film displays is precisely what makes *The Searchers* significant in terms of placing it within the Western genre and in its relation to the myth of the West. At one and the same time it appears to embody mythic tropes and, through its use of *generic* tropes, holds them up to critical inspection. As such, claims to provide *definitive* explanations of character motivation, or, indeed, of aspects of the plot or of the film as a whole are always only partial explanations, accompanied, inevitably, by significant and debilitating caveats, deviations, misreading and conjecture.

IV

I shall now consider *The Searchers'* attitude towards Native Americans more directly. Primarily, I wish to take issue with the deterministic belief represented by Maltby, above, that Native Americans in Westerns are to be consigned to the status of 'empty signifiers'. Such an argument is not surprising, however, when one considers that it has often been said that frontier mythology generally sought to either disguise the fate of the Native Americans (to silence their voice), or else to justify their demise under the vast rubric of Manifest Destiny. Actually, the Western genre as a whole has dealt with this mythic–historical elision in a number of intricate ways, and its attitude towards Native American cultures is hardly univocal or ideologically monolithic; the incontestable fact of unflattering stereotypes not withstanding. The myth itself cannot completely silence the plurality of history. Melinda Szaloky rightly reminds us that 'since history is always anchored in what it has marginalised, omitted, or exorcised, these silences are essential structural constituents of each story told about the past and, thus, cannot be completely ignored'.[46]

Of course, the omission of the Native American is not a phenomenon that can be rightfully applied to most Westerns. If we consider that well over a third of all Westerns produced contain narratives that involve Indians directly, then we can understand that the Western embodies the theme of race war rather than leaving it 'marginalised, omitted, or exorcised'. One film's take on this theme is often an idiosyncratic matter and there are significant differences between individual film texts. How then is *The Searchers* historically anchored with respect to Native Americans?

Before attempting to answer this question, I wish to make clear that I do not mean to forward *The Searchers* as a revisionist Western with regard to its depiction of Native Americans. Nor do I aim to 'save it', so to speak, for a liberal perspective; for it is certainly not a liberal film in the tradition of say *Devil's Doorway* or *Broken Arrow*. As already mentioned, the Western has often had a paradoxical, inconsistent and sometimes deeply insulting attitude towards Native American culture, and *The Searchers* is certainly no exception. Nevertheless, and as we have seen with essays like Greb's above, numerous scholars have attempted to discern a progressive pattern of development towards the Native American as his image allegedly evolved from an erroneous depiction of one-dimensional motiveless malignancy towards an equally erroneous proud and noble eco-friendly warrior in line with the counter-culture of the 1960s and 1970s. Of course, the 'good Indian–bad Indian' dichotomy has always remained as either an implicit or overt factor in Hollywood's brand of Native Americana. As Cawelti points out, since the earliest encounters in the seventeenth century 'there has always been a certain ambivalence about Native Americans which manifested itself in divided portrayals of native peoples as diabolical savages on the one hand and noble innocents on the other'.[47] Such ambivalence with regard to the Western's construction of 'Native American identity' is especially evident in the most overtly liberal examples of the genre.

To take a relevant example, Kevin Costner's *Dances with Wolves* (1990) is typically considered to be the film that exemplifies the socially progressive, revisionist re-appropriation of the Native American into popular culture. The film gives full characteristics and histories to its Native Americans, a tribe of Lakota Sioux. It is filmed on location on the Great Plains, and the Sioux are played by respected Native American actors like Rodney A. Grant and Graham Greene. Moreover, it has them speaking in their native Lakota tongue. It is true that this opposes Ford's Comanche who, as Native American scholar Tom Colonese correctly points out, bizarrely speak Navajo, which, he rightly reminds us, 'is not a small point to Indians'.[48] But Costner's vision of the nineteenth-century frontier ultimately proves itself to be fully embroiled in the polarisation of the Native American in popular culture and not, therefore, necessarily a revisionist Western in its treatment of them.[49]

Janet Walker draws attention to this polarisation by highlighting the distinction that the film draws in its depictions of the Lakota, on the one hand, and their 'blood enemies', the Pawnee, on the other. In one illustrative scene we see a flashback to childhood memories of the white woman, Stands-With-A-Fist/ Christine (Mary McDonnell), who has been adopted and raised by the benevolent Lakota. In brutal and disjointed sequences, and without any discernable motivation, we witness the Pawnee viciously attack and murder her family. We hear her mother's voice cry out to her as she flees the homestead for the wilderness. (One could argue here that Costner gives visualisation to that which Ford more unnervingly inferred with the Comanche 'murder raid' on the Edwards' homestead.) As opposed to the human characteristics given the Lakota, the Pawnee are depicted as cowardly savages, waiting for Christine's father to turn his back on them before cutting him down with their tomahawks.[50] Walker sees this as a continuance of an 'earlier generic paradigm [where] long-held stereotypes erupt through the thin crust of liberal sentiment, belying the film's pretence to present an enlightened picture of Native Americans'.[51] Thus, the film seeks to displace, rather than deconstruct, a culture of racial prejudice towards the Native American; depicting a noble race in the Lakota, while denigrating the Pawnee as natural savages. In Costner's West, the historical propensity of the Sioux as savage must be hidden from the viewer, displaced onto the Pawnee as 'bad-Indian' if the Sioux as 'good-Indian' – as historical victim and rightful defender of his territory – is to be envisioned.

In addition to Walker's criticisms, I would go as far as to say that *Dances with Wolves* is both ideologically *and* historically disingenuous. For instance, the film's only in-depth depiction of a Sioux wife indicates a monogamous culture, whereas in reality polygamy was typically practised. *The Searchers* is at least more honest in this aspect, with Scar having multiple wives. Moreover, *Dances with Wolves*' primary agent, Lieutenant John Dunbar (Kevin Costner), is still a white male hero. The narrative is structured around Dunbar's diary excerpts, delivered in the form of a series of voice-overs; the story still *told*, therefore, from the Anglo-American perspective. It has to be said also that Dunbar's attitude strikes one as more befitting a late-twentieth-century revisionist historian of the American West than it does the jaded nineteenth-century Civil War veteran he is supposed to be. Furthermore, the Sioux were a far cry from the 'noble savages' that *Dances with Wolves* depicts them to be. In the 1700s, having themselves been driven west of the forests by Algonquian tribes allied to French traders, the Sioux arrived on the northern Great Plains and, armed with weapons traded for furs with the United States, immediately attacked the warring Cheyenne and Crow Nations in a merciless decades-long struggle for the Black Hills. Historians Robert V. Hine and John Mack Faragher inform us that the whole history of the American West was characterised by such a 'collision of cultures', and that, 'by the late eighteenth century [the Sioux had established themselves as] the most powerful mounted group on the northern plains'.[52]

In spite of all this, Colonese praises *Dances with Wolves* for its historical accuracy, arguing that, if compared with *The Searchers*' Debbie, Stands-With-A-Fist comes across as a 'far more rounded character . . . integrated totally into the [Sioux] community'.[53] And yet, in a not-so-deft feint, *Dances with Wolves* avoids full-on confrontation with the captivity narrative as Stands-With-A-Fist was never, strictly speaking, 'in captivity', but rather benevolently adopted by the Sioux. She is simply with them as the story begins, we learn nothing of how she escaped the Pawnee, how she came to be discovered by the Sioux, and very little (beyond how she got her name) of what her early life with them was like.

The issue of miscegenation is also avoided in *Dances with Wolves* for, unlike Debbie and Scar, the romance between Dances-With-Wolves/John Dunbar and Stands-With-A-Fist/Christine is, in the final analysis, a sexual union between two Anglo-Americans (Stands-With-A-Fist's previous Lakota husband conveniently already dead before her character is introduced into the narrative). Both *The Searchers* and *Dances with Wolves* do deal critically with the myth of the US military as an heroic force for historical progress, although, perhaps unsurprisingly, *Dances with Wolves* takes its critique further. As a curious aside on this last point, the soldiers in *Dances with Wolves* are largely depicted as irredeemably sadistic, murderous and stupid – 'savage' in other words – and, at the same time, woefully inadequate in combat. The civilised–savage dichotomy here has not been transcended at all, it has merely been inverted, with the US military assuming the Indian role that Colonese insists is typical of most Westerns: 'the Indians aren't just *bad* – they are, in battle, *incompetent*'.[54]

Rick Worland and Edward Countryman have sought to link more contemporary Westerns with a strong Native American presence to the revisionism they see as apparent in recent historiography of the American West. With specific reference to Michael Mann's *The Last of the Mohicans* (1992) and Bruce Beresford's *Black Robe* (1991), Worland and Countryman champion these film's liberal-revisionist credentials. 'The Mohawks of *Black Robe* and Wes Studi's Magua of *Mohicans* may be forest horrors of the sort that viewers of older Westerns know only too well', they write, 'but in both cases there is an explanation for what they do, rather than mere assertion that they are evil by their very nature.'[55] Yet just how far precisely is all this a revision of 'older Westerns'? Well, Magua's reason for his incessant desire to murder Cora and Alice Munroe (Madeleine Stowe and Jodhi May) is because his family suffered terribly at the hands of their uncle, a British Army officer, Edmund Munroe (Maurice Roeves). Together with his Huron followers, Magua will go on to annihilate Munroe's command and cut the still-beating heart out of his chest; horror, indeed. With regard to Scar's reason for *his* murderous rage, it is, as he reveals to Ethan and Marty, in response to his 'two sons [having been] murdered by white men'. My point here is that Magua's and Scar's 'explanation for what they do' is essentially the same (vengeance) and, as this brief thematic comparison suggests, there is little indication of revisionism in either character.

I have already suggested that *The Searchers* cannot itself be labelled as either a liberal or 'cult of the Indian' Western, that the consternating issues regarding its erroneous depiction of the Comanche remain, and that Colonese and others are certainly right to highlight them. But the point I wish to hold up as significant for my concerns here is the fact that *The Searchers* refuses to romanticise in the manner that *Dances with Wolves* does. I suggest that the refusal of liberalist sentiment adds to the power of the film's critique of savage aspects of Anglo-American civilisation. I will return to the significance of Anglo-American savagery later, but first I want to consider other aspects of the representation of Native American culture in *The Searchers*.

The Searchers proves itself to be a film that exposes the complex 'collision of cultures' that Hine and Faragher insist constituted the long history of American settlement in the southwest.[56] They remind us that 'the mounted warrior of the plains – the ubiquitous and romantic symbol of native America – was in fact not an aboriginal character at all but one borne from [this] collision of cultures'.[57] They describe how the Comanche, who lived on the fringes of the Great Plains as an adjunct of the Shoshone, 'adopt[ed] the horse [and] migrated onto the plains, and over several generations they gradually moved southeastward toward present-day Oklahoma and Texas'.[58] In what they describe as one of the many 'fascinating ironies of frontier history, [the] first settlers of the Great Plains during the colonial era were not Europeans but Indians'.[59] The Comanches in particular 'circulat[ed] within territories from five to seven hundred miles in diameter [and] because of their ferocity they [like the equivalent Sioux in the north] became legendary rulers of the southern plains, raiding Indian and Mexican villages from the Mississippi all the way west to the Rio Grande'.[60] I have already referenced scholars who suggest Scar's mixed-race heritage as evidence of the complexity by which *The Searchers* deals with the concept of race in structuring American national identity; this is opposed to the Lakota of *Dances with Wolves*, who are seemingly racially 'pure' as well as being culturally naive. Even as late as 1864, they are apparently ignorant of firearms and, more amazingly, coffee; whereas cultural mixing seems evident from the very outset of *The Searchers*. Consider Mose's 'Indian feather hat', Ethan's 'Indian rifle cover', Marty's bare-back horse riding and topless state when we first encounter him, and, not to forget such foregrounded 'subtleties' as the 'Indian weave blanket' outside Aaron's homestead (which is hanging in the front of the Edwards' ranch when Ethan first emerges from the desert). All point to a hybridity of Anglo and Native American cultures that is entirely absent from the supposedly revisionist *Dances with Wolves*.

If we now consider the murder of Scar's two sons, which essentially acknowledges Anglo-American atrocities during its own aggressive expansion into the West, then we witness yet another layer of historical significance. Just as Hines and Faragher inform us, the whites were not innocent parties in this 'collision of cultures', and neither were the Indians. In *The Searchers*, the Anglo settlers *and* the Comanche seem to be bound up in a social Darwinian war of annihilation, comprising ever-degenerating spirals of massacre and counter-massacre. *The Searchers* depicts the human cost of settling 'free land', land like that which the warring factions in *Shane* will eventually dispute 'legitimate' ownership of once this stage of frontier history is over.

At the same time, the group that suffers the most in *The Searchers* is still the Comanche. What is a personal trauma for Edwards and the Jorgensen families is, of course, a national trauma for Native Americans; implicitly or explicitly

The Searchers acknowledges this historical fact. When considered from this perspective, the film seems to exist as a resolute critique of triumphalist brands of frontier history and its concomitant myth of the West; not to forget the curative discourse of regeneration through violence. Nevertheless, some scholars such as Jon Tuska insist that the film endorses the racial violence characteristic of the history of Anglo-American expansionism. '*The Searchers* [is]', he declares, 'one of the most viciously anti-Indian films ever made.'[61] He goes on to say that 'Ford deliberately although erroneously portrayed Indian captivity as generally driving to insanity most whites unfortunate enough to have undergone the experience', and that 'the entire film is in effect an argument in favour of killing Indians as the only solution to the "Indian problem".'[62]

The key issue one may take with Tuska's analysis is the difficult fact that Debbie is *not* driven to insanity by her 'Indian captivity'. As Joseph McBride and Michael Wilmington have it, Debbie, 'like Martin . . . has accepted her dual heritage. . . . Miscegenation has not destroyed her identity, but deepened it.'[63] Tuska responds to this very excerpt by reference to Martin's 'dual heritage', suggesting that, to the contrary, it is because 'Debbie has co-habited with an Indian [that] at the end she could only be linked with a man who is, if not morally, at least racially dubious.'[64]

Tuska is right to query McBride's and Wilmington's belief that Debbie's sense of identity has been 'deepened' by her life among Scar's Comanche, as there is little indication one way or the other whether she has 'accepted' it or merely *adapted* to the situation as best she could. As Gaylyn Studlar suggests:

> Although Debbie is ostensibly in a family (her Comanche one), Ford never allows us to see any affective qualities that he normally associates with happy domesticity . . . Like Dallas [Claire Trevor] in *Stagecoach*, Debbie may accept her situation, but there is precious little proof that she is contented in it.[65]

However, Tuska's claim that Marty is 'racially dubious' seems, to me, to be an untenable position to take, especially considering that Marty is primarily 'linked' with Laurie, who is of Anglo-Saxon and Nordic ancestry, and whom he will go on to marry, presumably with the full consent of her parents who, like his own adoptive parents, the late Aaron and Martha, do *not* regard him as 'racially dubious'.

With regard to Tuska's other point, the 'whites unfortunate enough to have undergone the experience' of captivity must be in reference to the women recovered from a raid by US cavalry on a Comanche winter encampment. Critics typically discuss this scene, and that of the climactic Ranger attack on Scar's camp, as referencing George A. Custer's massacre of Cheyenne at the Washita River in the winter of 1868. Perhaps the winter attack sequence is more likely Ford's reference of the Washita; indeed, the military band in *The Searchers* plays 'Gary Owen', the song of the 7th Cavalry, which Custer famously had his band play during the Washita massacre. The regiment's guidon is also clearly visible at the cavalry headquarters and when the soldiers herd Comanche prisoners along with bull-whips. It is at this point that Ethan and Marty find the body of 'Look' (Beulah Archuletta), the Comanche woman Marty had mistakenly married during a trade with some agency Indians (he thought he was purchasing a blanket). He literally kicks her out from under his blanket one night and Ethan roars with laughter as she falls down a hill. A number of critics (including Tuska) have analysed the characterisation and treatment of Look in such instances in terms of both racism and misogyny.[66] Now, in the next scene this woman, treated as a commodity by both her own people and the Anglos, has been murdered by US cavalry. Marty expresses his disgust. 'Why'd them soldiers have to go and kill her for, Ethan?! She never done nobody any harm!' Even Ethan shows signs of distress as he gently wipes his gloved hand over Look's hat and appears pale, upset even. The overriding sense from both men (as well as, perhaps, for the audience) is that of shame for having engaged or colluded in her earlier abusive mistreatment depicted in comedic terms. Again, the narrative is unclear: *how* are we supposed to read such a juxtaposition of sequences? These scenes surely dilute (at least) Tuska's declaration that *The Searchers* is 'one of the most viciously anti-Indian films ever made'.

Historically, Custer's men gunned down the Cheyenne at the Washita River without distinction, and of the estimated 103 victims, the majority are considered to have been women and children as most of the men were off hunting buffalo at the time of the attack. Eckstein provides further illuminating insight into this historical link, revealing that Frank Nugent's version of the shooting script even included a follow-up scene in which Ethan meets none other than Custer himself and berates him for allowing the massacre of women and children. This confrontation was to be played out in full view of a group of eastern journalists, thus undermining Custer's heroic braggadocio of a 'brave battle' with himself in the lead. Most insightful is Ethan's remarks to the effect that, 'should any female white captives have been killed during the fighting . . . they were probably killed by the panicky soldiers, not by the Indians'.[67] This is an astonishing thing to say, not because it appears in a so-called classical Western, but because it is an accusatory remark made by Ethan, an unregenerate racist, towards Custer, the traditional symbol of US military heroism and self-sacrifice.[68] However, as this scene was ultimately cut from the final edit, I shall not (and cannot) base my response to Tuska's criticism of *The Searchers* on it alone. According to Eckstein, the whole 'Custer sequence' was ultimately discarded by Ford to assist in the 'darkening' of Ethan's character and to make the follow-up scene – Ethan's encounter with the recovered white women at the 7th Cavalry headquarters, which includes the now famous 'John Wayne look' moment – more ambiguous.[69] Ethan's 'look' – intensified by the camera's slow-zoom towards his grizzled expression – is certainly enigmatic, but seemingly embodies both hatred *and* pity towards the women. (Various scholars have regarded it in varying degrees of either emotion, but seldom both together.)

Of the three visible white women recovered, one grins like an idiot as the second woman clings to her like a baby. The third older woman appears to pine hysterically after a lost child, being calmed only after a soldier hands her a doll. 'It's hard to believe they're white,' the soldier says to Ethan. 'They ain't white, not no more,' he replies. 'They're Comanch.' The scene would appear to emphasise Ethan's racism, however, it is not enough to assume that the women's perilous psychological state has been caused by their captivity alone. Yet again, the film proves itself to be unclear. I suggest that the narrative confusion evident in *The Searchers* makes it ultimately ambiguous as to what this scene truly signifies in terms of a wider thematic or ideological stance on miscegenation. As a consequence, it is not enough to suggest, as Tuska does, that this scene explicitly indicates Ford's personal racist views towards Indians and to leave it at that. Pye considers this scene in more depth than Tuska, but ultimately comes to the same conclusion. 'We may be distanced here from Ethan', he writes, 'but there seems little or no ambiguity in the presentation of these women . . . there is no real support for a view markedly different from what Ethan thinks he sees.'[70] But if we take these women in the context of Debbie's experience of captivity, as surely we must, then we have to acknowledge that the latter is not in a deranged state at all. What then, precisely, is it that has driven *these* women 'to insanity'?

To attempt an explanation (for I doubt a precise *answer* is possible), I would like to take as my starting point the film's penultimate scene: the Ranger attack on Scar's camp – in which the Comanche chief is ultimately killed and Debbie recovered – then retroactively apply this sequence to the winter cavalry attack – in which Look is killed and these white women recovered.

Slotkin describes the final sequence in some detail, reading it in terms of US Cold War political terminology: a 'surgical strike' or 'tactical fantasy' in which 'Ford backs away from fully visualising the implied parallel between the Ranger attack and the cavalry's massacre of the Indians at the Washita'.[71] He summarises thus:

> The Rangers charge at top speed through the village, firing left and right as the 7th Cavalry did at the Washita – the composition of individual shots in fact mirrors the image of Custer's battle in popular prints and posters . . . Yet in the battle itself we see only Indian men falling from the shots, as if the Rangers had special powers to kill both comprehensively and selectively. This tactical fantasy, coupled with Debbie's rescue, indicates the limits of Ford's demystification of the savage war and rescue myth.[72]

Slotkin is, in many ways, correct in his belief that Ford, 'though rejecting race-hatred and the spirit of extermination it begets, [nevertheless] accepts as valid

... a more "meliorative" violence'.[73] He argues that, since we see no 'Indian prisoners – not even women and children – in the comic after-battle scene [in which the Revd Captain Samuel Clayton (Ward Bond) is stabbed in his backside by an over-enthusiastic cavalry lieutenant]', what we are essentially presented with instead is a 'paternal love' on the part of Ford, who 'condescendingly recognises Look's humanity, wishfully spares Comanche women and children while slaughtering the men'.[74] However, surely Look's fate undermines this notion of 'tactical fantasy' for we know already what Anglo-Americans are capable of in the name of the domestication of the wilderness. In light of the fact that the earlier cavalry raid does depict Comanche prisoners being herded like animals into captivity, that we do not 'see any Indian prisoners' following the Ranger attack is, therefore, a chilling fact in itself. From this, another level of signification can now be identified.

On the eve of the Ranger attack Marty fears for Debbie's safety, protesting to Clayton that, should the Rangers just go charging in, 'they'll kill her and you know it!' It is generally understood that Marty is referring to the Comanche here yet, in light of the earlier cavalry attack with the indiscriminate and reprehensible nature of the killing, 'they' could just as easily mean the Rangers themselves. Marty reasons that Debbie would likely be shot by 'friendly-fire' during the inevitably confusing melee. Ethan and Clayton both reluctantly allow Marty to attempt to sneak into Scar's camp in an effort to rescue Debbie prior to launching a full-scale assault. But rescuing Debbie is not their primary objective, and Clayton is quick to remind Marty that 'there's more at stake here than your sister'. As Slotkin argues, 'the rescue simply does not mean as much to them as it does to Martin. [Ethan and Clayton] still believe that the destruction of Scar is more important than the rescue of the captive.'[75]

I have mentioned Slotkin's suggestion that the Ranger sequence constitutes a 'tactical fantasy' of selective violence, however, Eckstein correctly points out something that Slotkin fails to mention: Ethan 'riding over an Indian woman holding a baby' moments before taking Scar's scalp.[76] It is true that the woman is not killed (she immediately gets up and flees still holding her baby), so Slotkin's general assessment is hard to dispute. However, this 'slippage' in what *is* essentially a 'tactical fantasy' of violence is surely enough to acknowledge at least the potentiality of a more sinister outcome. That this potential has already been realised (resulting in the reprehensible slaughter of innocents like Look) surely supports this assertion. One can certainly suggest that the slaughter of the Comanche seems to have been the primary aim. With the sort of frenzied blood-lust that results in the murder of women and children, it is not too far-fetched to imagine a similar scenario in which a white woman and her baby are trampled by a cavalryman's horse, only the outcome here was more tragic, with the surviving mother reduced to an hysterical state. Again, this is conjecture, yet I would suggest it entirely plausible that the woman's hysteria is caused, not by the experience of captivity, but rather by the violence inflicted on them by the US Cavalry, themselves only ostensibly aiming for the rescue of such captives.

In avoiding the liberal sentiment of the 'cult of the Indian' Western, Ford, as Eckstein suggests 'left his Comanches as savages'.[77] But in so doing, he affected a penetrating and more honest critique of Anglo-America's own propensity towards savagery. This critique is realised primarily through utilising recognisable institutions of the Western canon – in this case, the US Cavalry and the Texas Rangers – in order to undermine their heroic credentials and thus undermine Anglo-America's heroic version of frontier expansion and settlement. This social critique is primarily realised, however, not through the genre's portrayal of Native Americans, but through a relentless introspection of the figure of the white male hero – both in his mythic role as symbolic outrider of Manifest Destiny and as agent in the domestication of the wilderness.

V

In a film so full of complexity and contradiction, it is perhaps fitting that its protagonist proves to be its most enigmatic element. The opening scene of Ethan's arrival (or return) to his brother's homestead reveals through a wonderful economy of style many complex aspects about his character and, by extension, the complexities of American national identity. Like Shane and many other Western heroes he emerges from the wilderness landscape, appearing from behind a hillock as if out of the very ground itself; his association with the wilderness seemingly organic.[78] He is an unreconstructed Confederate soldier who never formally surrendered. Indeed, he still wears his grey cavalry coat and verbally honours his oath taken 'to the Confederate States of America'. He is therefore associated with the 'outlaw' tradition of the genre, and it is quite likely that he has recently robbed a 'Yankee' stagecoach, as if, like former 'bushwhacker' Jesse James, he considers himself a Southern guerrilla in a war that never ended. Just what Ethan has been doing in the three years since Appomattox remains a mystery, but it is partly answered by way of the medal he gives to little Debbie. The medal reveals him to have been a mercenary fighting for the Mexican Emperor Maximilian, which, Slotkin informs us, would be 'a cause perfectly consistent with his racism'.[79] Furthermore, Ethan's traditional heroic disdain for money is highlighted by his casually tossing a bag full of 'Yankee dollars' to Aaron, while his unheroic hatred of Native Americans is soon established through his openly aggressive attitude towards Marty.

Overall, Ethan provides us with gallery of Western hero types. His past, like Shane's, is mysterious and a little bit deadly. Cinematic cues confirm that he is clearly in love with his brother's wife, Martha, and that she is clearly in love with him, forging another thematic link to Shane's and Marian's mutual but forbidden attraction. He is a threat to the domestic realm and brings anti-social violence, illicit sexual desire and racism with him. To confirm the enigma, Ethan is an unregenerate racist, but is also the story's hero, if a terribly flawed one. He breaks the so-called hero's code on numerous occasions. For example, he shoots people in the back (both Anglos and Natives), wilfully engages in the mass slaughter of humans and buffalo, defiles the corpses of his 'race enemy', and seems intent on murdering his own niece. Pye argues that such actions, together with 'Ethan's obsessive hatred of Indians and the idea of mixed blood are presented in ways designed to distance us from him.'[80] Yet he also argues it both ways, suggesting that the film 'allows no comfortable identification with *or* disengagement from its hero'.[81]

As many commentators have recognised, one of the principal ways in which we come to terms with Ethan's dark character is that he is played by Hollywood's most celebrated Western actor. As Slotkin suggests, 'Ford's casting of John Wayne deliberately invokes the star's heroic on-screen persona . . . Ethan's point of view also determines the way in which much of the action is seen.'[82] It is because of this narrative alignment that it has 'been easy to mistake [as many have done] Ethan's racism for John Ford's'.[83] Slotkin also suggests that 'the heroic associations of Wayne's screen persona reinforce our tendency to give Ethan's actions the best possible interpretation'.[84] And, furthermore, in reference to the actor's wider cultural significance:

> Wayne's 'Ethan' does not die or dissolve with the final fade-to-black: he is re-absorbed into the on-going life of John Wayne-as-movie-star and becomes part of an ever-growing heroic persona that would finally make Wayne a 'living legend,' a cultural symbol whose role in public mythology is akin to that of figures like Daniel Boone, Davy Crockett, and Buffalo Bill.[85]

Slotkin's suggestion that, through our understanding of Wayne as a cultural symbol, we are compelled to sympathise and, in many ways, rationalise Ethan's pathologies is convincing enough to some. Indeed, Wayne's status as a paradigmatic American hero could well account for those who associate the Western solely with him, and who are therefore mistaken in the view that Ethan's racism is typical of the genre as a whole.[86] Pye suggests that this dual attitude towards Ethan is due to the inherent racism of the genre: 'in wrestling as a Western with the ideological and psycho-sexual complex that underlies attitudes to race, [*The Searchers*] is working *within* almost intractable traditions of representation'.[87] Actually, Ford skilfully positions Ethan in such a way that his racist mania and obsessive quest to find Debbie illuminates the prevalence and terrifying consequences of racism in American society and, particularly, its difficultly in overcoming its own fears over miscegenation. I argue that the character of Ethan holds a mirror up to this systemic racism, working as a corrective, therefore, to Maltby's insistence that the Western exists as 'a discursive framework by which a national self-image of the self-righteousness of Manifest Destiny could be maintained'.

The majority of scholars suggest that, while *The Searchers* exposes aspects of institutional racism, in the final analysis they reason that Ethan's racism is more extreme or, at least, more overt than that of white society. Still others suggest that Ethan's racism has no place whatever in Anglo-American civilisation and that this is why Ethan must be excluded from it at the end. In David Grimsted's opinion, *The Searchers* seeks to promote an American society based on racial tolerance. In depicting its Anglo community as devoid of prejudice against Native Americans, he insists that '[e]ven at those points where some Indian-hating would seem humanly logical, Ford turns anger elsewhere ... Ford's society in the film, rather than racist, is notably free of racism even where circumstances would lead one to expect it.'[88] He argues that, through Ethan, Ford depicts 'racism [that] grows from personal rather than social pathology', and that 'Ethan's racism is what cuts him off from the rest of the family/society'.[89] Grimsted also sees Ethan in sympathetic terms, arguing that his 'flaws are made shocking but Ford lets us know, mostly through the quiet shots that punctuate his fury, [his hatred's] deeply humane connections'.[90] Expunging Ethan from civilisation at the film's end, symbolised by the final fade to black, is therefore expressive of an idealised society. Ethan's racism, although a necessary, even humane, product of race war, is not welcome in the kind of civilised nation that the United States likes to think of itself as being. The baton, as it were, is being passed on to the figure of Marty: himself a product of miscegenation and whose unproblematic integration into Anglo-American civilisation will be symbolically 'rubber-stamped' by his marriage to Laurie. The coming of a society based on racial tolerance and kinship by adoption, rather than obsessions about kinship by blood appears to have been achieved here, on the frontier, Turner's and Roosevelt's crucible of modern American democratic civilisation.

I would like to suggest now that this ending is itself, a myth. Furthermore, that the film renders this myth in ironic terms, exposing it as a false consciousness, a dangerous delusion.[91] It is here that the powerful ideological critique, the 'counter-narrative' of the nation offered by *The Searchers*, comes into fruition. As I have already detailed, *The Searchers* illuminates the powerful issue of race in structuring American national identity. On an immediate historical level, Ethan is a returning soldier who fought for the racist, slave-holding South in America's great fratricidal Civil War. The difficult historical issue of reconstruction and re-integration of the secessionist states and of those who fought for them is thus embodied in the hero from the outset. The film's supposed location in the 'sovereign State of Texas', together with Ethan's subsequent role as a hired mercenary, gives further persuasive support to this reading. Also, the homesteaders refer to themselves as 'Texicans' rather than Americans; a consensual *united* identity within terms of post-Civil War reconciliation is thus rendered extremely precarious. However, far from offering a simplistic reduction of sociohistorical contradiction and complexity, recapitulated as myth, and with a resolved conclusion tantamount to social fantasy (that is, that Debbie is reincluded into white civilisation at the end of the film), *The Searchers* wilfully embodies these contradictions and uses the hero as a symbol through which to problematise the mythic terms by which civilisation is founded. That is to say, it is through Ethan that the film exposes America's disavowed racism, and the myth of a cultural geography that distinguishes its civilisation from the wilderness in the form of idealised, racially tolerant familial communities like the Edwards and the Jorgensens.

Ethan's slaughter of the buffalo provides me with my first illustrative case in point. This scene has typically been understood as a shocking instance of Ethan's personal racism and of his descent into madness. Certainly, the scene is constructed to signify as much, with a maniacal, wide-eyed Ethan firing repeatedly into the herd in order to scatter it and deny winter food to the Comanches, violently striking Marty to the ground when he tries to stop him. Grimsted contends that this scene 'illuminates well Ford's dramatisation of "personal" racism' and that Ethan's 'shooting at the buffalo was clearly a gesture of fury at the costs and frustrations of the [racial] conflict'.[92] Furthermore, he contends that 'it was far from an exterminating plan like that which was briefly US Cavalry policy, or its casual enactment as white man's sport'.[93] I do not doubt Ethan's personal pathology; however, the placement of this scene within the narrative as a whole suggests something altogether more sinister and wide-ranging than Grimsted allows for. Ethan is interrupted by the sound of a cavalry bugle and we cut immediately to the aftermath of the aforementioned massacre of the Comanche (where Ethan discovers Look's body). Pye is surely right when he suggests that this juxtaposition 'marks eloquently the way in which Ethan's racial hatred is repeated at the institutional level in the genocidal actions of the US Cavalry'.[94] But there is, despite Grimsted's dismissal, a further and more direct level of historical significance in Ethan's animal slaughter.

During this period of Anglo-American expansion, hunters and trappers were engaged in a systematic extermination of the buffalo herds all along the Great Plains. The result was a booming economy for frontier settlements, individuals and trading companies alike; conversely, the effects on the Native American tribes of the Great Plains were irreversibly catastrophic. In his 1970 book, *Bury My Heart at Wounded Knee*, Dee Brown references federal government representative, General William Tecumseh Sherman's public response to this wholesale slaughter: 'Let them kill, skin, and sell until the buffalo is exterminated, as it is the only way to bring lasting peace and allow civilisation to advance.'[95] Sherman's response is shocking and reveals that a policy based on both cultural and literal genocide – as denoted in *The Searchers* by this juxtaposition of slaughter – flowed directly from Washington in terms utterly commensurable with the ideological precepts of Manifest Destiny. In depicting this terrible story, *The Searchers* can be said to reveal human *and* environmental costs as well as the irony implicit in the domestication of the wilderness;

a societal critique, therefore, rather than solely the result of one individual's 'fury' and 'frustration'.[96]

VI

I shall conclude my discussion on *The Searchers* with the scene that is most suggestive of societal racism. The scene in question immediately follows Laurie's abortive wedding to comical 'hick', Charley McCorry (Ken Curtis), in which Charley and Marty literally fight over her. When Marty informs an exasperated Laurie that he will leave her again the following day, still intent on 'fetching' Debbie home, she suddenly explodes at him:

> Fetch what home? The leavings of Comanche bucks, sold time and again to the highest bidder with savage brats of her own?! Do you know what Ethan will do if he has a chance? He'll put a bullet in her brain. I tell you Martha would want him to.

Pye convincingly suggests that 'Laurie's hideous outburst locates the disgust and loathing of miscegenation not simply in Ethan but at the heart of the White community. Ethan is, in this respect at least, not an aberrant but a representative figure.'[97] In his more recent analysis, however, Grimsted sees it differently. He suggest that, although Laurie's 'words are as snarlingly vicious as any of Ethan's . . . they don't have the same impact'.[98] This, he reasons, is because her racist tirade is placed in the context of her desire for Marty, a desire that for years has been frustrated by his refusal to give up on the search for Debbie and settle down with her. 'We know they are really voiced out of love of part-Indian Martin – to keep him home,' he argues. 'She says them to hold a man whose racial ancestry bothers her and her family not a jot.'[99] He concludes by arguing that 'no one feels a touch of surprise when Laurie joins in leading Debbie – and Martin – back into the sheltering community' represented by the Jorgenson homestead.[100]

Interpreting the film in terms of gender politics, Studlar similarly suggests that 'Laurie's hate-filled speech reveals her desperation to keep Marty home from what she regards as a pointless search for someone now beyond the pale of white society's norms.'[101] While agreeing with the personal context within which Grimsted interprets Laurie's outburst, Studlar refuses to justify it as he does, aligning Laurie instead 'with masculine values that reduce female worth to sexual and racial purity'.[102] She goes on to remark:

> Laurie would initially seem to represent the generic ideal, the sexually innocent, sympathetic woman who brings civilisation to the frontier. But Laurie becomes the voice of patriarchal sexual norms that condemns the captive female who assimilates – culturally and sexually – into Indian society.[103]

Laurie's outburst automatically re-ignites the issue of female captivity, and it seems to me that the film's overall interpretive attitude towards the captivity narrative hinges, to a large extent, upon how one contextualises her words. For Studlar, to 'say that Martha would want Debbie dead is, as Marty (and the audience) immediately knows, a misinterpretation of Martha Edwards's values'.[104] She insists that, while 'the white woman's sexuality may be what is at stake in the Western's conventional war between white "civilisation" and red "savagery" ... Ford demonstrates in *The Searchers* [that] the claims of the genre for the meaning of female purity can be held up for scrutiny, even for a film in the classical mode'.[105] Obviously, I dispute Studlar's suggestion of a 'classical mode' in respect of *The Searchers*, but her assessment that the film works 'in critiquing racism ... through the framework of "feminised" values [specifically those of Martha as a structuring absence] that are brought into open conflict with the established generic appeal of "masculine" values associated with violence and vengeance [as represented by Ethan]' are very persuasive.[106] On the other hand, it seems incredible that Grimsted could suggest that Laurie's outburst is based solely on Marty's 'naive interpretation of Ethan's stance'.[107] He writes that 'Laurie's speech functions in the narrative not to condemn her, much less her family/community, for sharing Ethan's racial hate, but to help convince the audience that Ethan may really attempt to kill Debbie.'[108]

Marty's naivety relates directly to Grimsted's insistence that Ethan *never* intended to kill Debbie and that we, the audience, only *think* that he will due to our alignment with Marty's gross misreading of the events that structure most of the latter part of the search. 'Nowhere in the film', he argues, 'does Ethan say or suggest he plans to kill Debbie.'[109] To me, this reading seems absurd and, therefore, Grimsted's attempts to explain away two significantly related moments in the plot in accordance with this view are unconvincing. The two moments in question are when Ethan and Marty first encounter Debbie outside Scar's desert camp, and later in the film when Marty appeals to Clayton to let him go in ahead of the Ranger attack in order to rescue her. In the first scene, Ethan draws his gun on Debbie and orders Marty to 'step aside'. Grimsted argues that 'we really have no indication of whether [Ethan] intends to shoot her or to try to keep her from running away. Again, Ford lets Martin – arms outstretched in front of Debbie and face terrified – impose his fears on us.'[110] Actually, Debbie is saved from Ethan only by a timely arrow fired by Scar. It strikes his shoulder, spinning him around, his gun shot (a shot that he had already committed to firing) harmlessly embedding itself in the desert sand. The second moment immediately follows Marty's protestation: 'If we go charging in there they'll kill her and you know it!' Ethan's response is to say, 'That's what I'm counting on.' To me the nature of Ethan's intentions seem rather unambiguous here; however, Grimsted attempts to explain this away by suggesting that, while Ethan says that 'he counts on the raid killing Debbie, and Martin chastises him for it ... he actually shows no personal wish to do it – only brief opposition to Marty's plan to slip into Scar's camp to rescue Debbie'.[111]

Overall, I believe Grimsted is right in how he positions Laurie's outburst within the context of her frustrated relationship with Marty; however, I do not agree that the film itself endorses such a position. Equally, like Studlar, I doubt that *The Searchers* pertains wholeheartedly to the masculine ideological paradigm of chaste female 'purity'. If Laurie represents a mythic ideal of womanhood, then she must also symbolise the future of American civilisation following the settlement of the frontier. One could link Laurie to Ethan in that, if the myth of the domestication of the wilderness represses the historical fact of Anglo-America's originary crimes (both against nature and the aboriginal populations themselves), then the figure of Ethan marks a return of this historical repressed. Therefore, Ethan's crimes mirror those of Anglo-America – the US military, the Rangers, the hunters and the pioneers who settled the 'free land' – and expose their (largely) unacknowledged complicity in expropriation and genocide. Equally, Laurie's outburst strikes out from the heart of white civilisation, confirming that civilisation's willing complicity in such crimes. Indeed, it exposes Anglo-American hypocrisy in denying this aspect of themselves and placing it all onto the shoulders of a figure like Ethan before branding him abject, singular, an aberration.

McGee extends the theme of Ethan's moral burden to encompass the related socioeconomic factors existing as a historical and ideological function within the narrative. He argues that 'the apparent innocence of the Edwards and Jorgenson families hinges on Ethan's assumption of the burden of shame for the sin of primitive accumulation; their legitimacy depends on his lawlessness, their sexual propriety on his transgressive desire'. Furthermore, that 'Ethan Edwards embodies the contradictions at the origin of the capitalist culture of the United States.'[112]

On the one hand, then, as McGee informs us, Ethan 'expresses the racism that historically justified the primitive accumulation of capital in the form of expropriated land [from the Native Americans] and labour, particularly the labour of slaves', while, on the other, he cares nothing for monetary wealth and, more importantly, by 'finally bringing Debbie back to the enclave of the family, he gives birth to a racially mixed community from which he must be symbolically excluded'.[113] But surely, with Laurie's explosion of racism against Debbie, the myth of overcoming kinship structures based on blood for one based on adoption and tolerance is destroyed in *The Searchers*. Eckstein and others have uncovered sufficient evidence to suggest that Ford purposefully 'darkened' Ethan's character, but why include this racist tirade from Laurie *unless* he was trying to make an equally powerful point about Anglo-America's hypocritical attitude to its own racist stance?[114]

Perhaps the enigma of Ethan Edwards and, by extension, *The Searchers* as a whole, can be at least partly explained by how Slavoj Žižek defines a functioning ideology. Žižek suggests that 'an ideological identification exerts a true hold on us precisely when we maintain an awareness that we are not fully identical to it, that there is a rich human person beneath it . . . *is the very form of ideology*, of its "practical efficiency"'.[115] He puts forward the term 'trans-ideological kernel' to explain how, if an ideology is to 'seize' a culture, 'it *has* to batten on and manipulate some kind of "trans-ideological" vision which cannot be reduced to a simple instrument of legitimating pretensions to power'.[116] If I read him right, then he suggests that, for an ideology to function effectively, one must be, to a certain extent, ignorant of its operating mechanisms. This feeds well into Barthes' naturalising function of myth which, itself, can be adapted to the ideological purpose of the myth of the West. That is, of course, the attempt to justify the project of Manifest Destiny and to promote the myth of the domestication of the wilderness, regeneration through violence and American exceptionalism.

Since this mythic 'vision' of the history of the founding of the United States cannot operate if 'reduced to a simple instrument of legitimising pretensions to power', it must engage with sentiments of national identity, group solidarity, justice and the greater sense of belonging to a community. These are the results of an ideology that actively seeks to disavow that which sustains it, and that necessarily relies on a disavowing or thwarting of those aspects that forms its key component. Equally, Žižek argues that 'an ideological edifice can be undermined by a too literal identification, which is why its successful functioning requires a minimal distance from its explicit rules'.[117] Ethan lacks a sense of this 'minimal distance', whereby his overt and incessant racism and violence becomes unacceptably abject, becomes disturbing, or even *dangerous* to a civilisation when made public or explicit. However, at the same time it forms a necessary but unacknowledgable element of its cultural–ideological functionality. For Žižek, an ideology's power mechanism relies on this self-censorship, 'it relies on a mechanism which is operative in so far as it remains censored'.[118] What we can identify in *The Searchers* is the emergence of this censored functionality: in Ethan, in the narrative's linking of his actions to US policies (the slaughter of Comanche and the destruction of their cultural ties to the buffalo herds) and its instruments of power (the Cavalry, the Rangers), its contradictions of a Christian religiosity married to war (the figure of Revd Captain Clayton), and, perhaps more revelatory, the racist invective delivered by a representative of the domesticity of the settled wilderness – Laurie herself. With all this in mind, it seems incredible that the 'winning of the West' as it is described by Ford in *The Searchers* could be understood as anything but ironic.

In the film's final movement Debbie is returned by Ethan to the folds of Christian civilisation in the form of her new home at the Jorgenson's ranch. In light of what I have argued above, we may well 'feel a touch of surprise' when Laurie joins her in entering the house with her part-Cherokee groom-to-be. Debbie looks fearfully around at her new surroundings and becomes shrouded in an ambivalent darkness which hides the traditional warmth of the domestic, interior space. Personally, I wonder for the outcome of her reintegration into a white community that disavows its own prejudices and, like the representative Laurie, fails utterly to overcome them. Ethan stands outside, holds his arm in that oft-cited gesture of pain; perhaps this is the pain of a man who is, at one and the same time, a savage racist *and* a man who embodies so much civilised compassion that he cannot, finally, bring himself to murder little Debbie. He is, therefore, a figure who openly embodies the contradictions and hypocrisies of a community that pointedly ignores both its need for him and its own racism, and who he turns his back on in the final fade-to-black.

NOTES

1. Richard Slotkin, *Regeneration through Violence: The Mythology of the American Frontier 1600–1860*, new edn (Norman, OK: University of Oklahoma Press, 2000), p. 179.
2. Ibid., p. 94.
3. Ibid., p. 25.
4. Richard Slotkin, *Gunfighter Nation: The Myth of the Frontier in Twentieth-Century America* (Norman, OK: University of Oklahoma Press, [1992] 1998), p. 461.
5. John G. Cawelti, 'Myths of Violence in American Popular Culture', *Critical Inquiry*, 1(3) (1975): 521–41, quote on p. 538.
6. Arthur M. Eckstein, 'Introduction: Main Critical Issues in *The Searchers*', in Arthur M. Eckstein and Peter Lehman (eds), *The Searchers: Essays and Reflections on John Ford's Classic Western* (Detroit, MI: Wayne State University Press, 2004), p. 10.
7. Cawelti, 'Myths of Violence in American Popular Culture', p. 358.
8. Slotkin, *Regeneration through Violence*, p. 179 (emphasis in original).
9. Ibid., p. 104.
10. Douglas Pye, 'Double Vision: Miscegenation and Point of View in *The Searchers*', in Ian Cameron and Douglas Pye (eds), *The Movie Book of the Western* (London: Studio Vista, 1996), p. 229.
11. Richard Maltby, 'A Better Sense of History: John Ford and the Indians', in Cameron and Pye (eds), *The Movie Book of the Western*, p. 39.
12. Pye, 'Double Vision', p. 229.
13. The phrase 'the Western *is* American history' has been used, critiqued and parodied by numerous film scholars. See, for example, articles by Andre Bazin, Jim Kitses, Richard Slotkin and Janet Walker.
14. Maltby, 'A Better Sense of History', p. 39.
15. Ibid.
16. Slotkin, *Gunfighter Nation*, p. 10.
17. Ibid., pp. 624–63.
18. Susan Kollins, 'Genre and the Geographies of Violence: Cormac McCarthy and the Contemporary Western', *Contemporary Literature*, 42(3) (2001): 557–88, quote on p. 560.
19. Jacqueline K. Greb, 'Will the Real Indians Please Stand Up?', in Gary A. Yoggy (ed.), *'Back in the Saddle': Essays on Western Film and Television Actors* (London: McFarland, 1998), pp. 129–44, quote on p. 132.
20. Ibid., p. 132.
21. Tag Gallagher, 'Shoot-Out at the Genre Corral: Problems in the "Evolution" of the Western' (1986), reprinted in Barry Keith Grant (ed), *Film Genre Reader III* (Austin, TX: University of Texas Press, 2003), pp. 262–76, quote on pp. 272–3.

22. For more in-depth analyses of the depiction of Native Americans on film, which includes an interesting analysis of *Fort Apache*, see Michael Valdez Moses, 'Savage Nations: Native Americans and the Western', in Jennifer L. McMahon and B. Steve Csaki (eds), *The Philosophy of the Western* (Lexington, KY: University of Kentucky Press, 2010), pp. 261–91.
23. Brian Henderson, ''The Searchers': An American Dilemma', *Film Quarterly*, 34(2) (1980/1): 9–23, quote on p. 10.
24. Ibid., p. 10.
25. Ibid.
26. Henderson does acknowledge that Lévi-Strauss' structuralist insistence on binary oppositions does not bear up well under contemporary theories of popular culture. Hence, he writes: 'Lévi-Strauss' binarism . . . has been much attacked. The consensus now seems to be that binarism fits some situations well but as a universal principle of the formation of culture it is untenable.' Ibid., p. 12.
27. Ibid., p. 19. Michael Coyne makes a similar political–allegorical point, see *The Crowded Prairie: American National Identity in the Hollywood Western* (London: I. B. Tauris, 1997), p. 70. John H. Lenihan similarly assesses Native Americans in Westerns of this period as allegorical representations of African Americans. See Lenihan, *Showdown: Confronting Modern America in the Western Film* (Urbana, IL: University of Illinois Press, [1980] 1985), pp. 23–81.
28. For an in-depth study of *Brown* v. *Board of Education of Topeka* within the context of the Civil Rights Movement, see Waldo E. Martin Jr, *Brown v. Board of Education of Topeka: A Brief History with Documents* (Boston, MA: Palgrave Macmillan, 1998).
29. Henderson, 'Double Vision', p. 19.
30. Eckstein, 'Introduction: Main Critical Issues in *The Searchers*', pp. 1–47, quote on p. 9.
31. Joanna Hearne, 'The "Ache for Home": Assimilation and Separatism in Anthony Mann's *Devil's Doorway*', in Peter C. Rollins and John E. O'Conner (eds), *Hollywood's West: The American Frontier in Film, Television, and History* (Lexington, KY: University of Kentucky Press, 2005), pp. 126–60, quote on p. 137.
32. Ibid., p. 137.
33. Ibid., p. 126
34. Ibid., p. 127. Steve Neale forwards a similar argument. He suggests that 'what is occluded in the substitution of "red for black" in the reading of 50s and 60s pro-Indian and Indian Westerns is not just the possibility of any discussion of contemporary Native Americans and of contemporary relations between native Americans, Euro-Americans and the Euro-American government, but the possibility of any address to the particular, indeed, unique position of Native Americans vis-à-vis Euro-American liberalism, vis-à-vis segregation, vis-à-vis integration and vis-à-vis civil rights in the late 40s, the 50s and the early 60s.' See Steve Neale, 'Vanishing Americans: Racial and Ethnic Issues in the Interpretation and Context of Post-War "Pro-Indian" Westerns', in Ed Buscombe and Roberta E. Pearson (eds), *Back in the Saddle Again: New Essays on the Western* (London: British Film Institute, 1998), pp. 8–29, quote on p. 11.
35. Peter Lehman considers this along with the possibility that Debbie herself is Ethan's biological offspring from an affair with Martha. He does not forward these as definite, merely considers them as possibilities. See Lehman, ''"You Couldn't Hit It on the Nose": The Limits of Knowledge in and of *The Searchers*', in Eckstein and Lehman (eds), *The Searchers*, pp. 239–65, quote on pp. 246–7.
36. Some would put Scar's blue eyes down to the fact that he is played by Henry Brandon, an Anglo-American actor of Germanic descent, and would say no more beyond Hollywood's racially biased casting policies at that time. Nevertheless,

I owe the insight about Scar's blue eyes to Gilberto Perez's review of Robert Pippin's, *Hollywood Westerns and American Myth: The Importance of Howard Hawks and John Ford for Political Philosophy* (New Haven, CT: Yale University Press, 2010). Perez writes: 'we see that [Scar's] eyes are blue. Not, as may be supposed, because Hollywood Indians are played by white actors – that wasn't Ford's practice. Scar's eyes are blue for a good reason: they tell us that the Comanche chief is part white . . . Ford does not explain, he just shows: he wants Scar's blue eyes to give us pause.' Gilberto Perez, 'House of Miscegenation', *London Review of Books*, 32(22), 18 November 2010, pp. 23–5. On Quanah Parker as Ford's historical inspiration for Scar, see James F. Brooks, '"That Don't Make You Kin!": Borderlands History and Culture in *The Searchers*' (pp. 265–89), and Tom Grayson Colonese, 'Native American Reactions to *The Searchers*' (pp. 335–43), both in Eckstein and Lehman (eds), *The Searchers*. For an excellent biography of Quanah Parker and the Comanche Nation, see S. C. Gwynne, *Empire of the Summer Moon: Quanah Parker and the Rise and Fall of the Comanche Tribe* (London: Constable & Robinson, 2010).
37. Patrick McGee, *From Shane to Kill Bill: Rethinking the Western* (Oxford: Blackwell, 2007), p. 102.
38. For discussion of *The Searcher*'s Homeric links, see two essays by Martin M. Winkler (ed.), 'Tragic Features in John Ford's *The Searchers*', in *Classical Myth and Culture in the Cinema* (Oxford: Oxford University Press, 2001), pp. 118–47, and Martin M. Winkler, 'Homer's *Iliad* and John Ford's *The Searchers*', in Eckstein and Lehman (eds), *The Searchers*, pp. 145–71.
39. Robert M. Bird, *Nick of the Woods; or, Adventures of Prairie Life* (Hamburg: Tredition Classics, [1837] 2007).
40. Slotkin, *Gunfighter Nation*, p. 462.
41. For analysis along such lines, see Armando Jose Prats, *Invisible Natives: Myth and Identity in the American Western* (London: Cornell University Press, 2002), pp. 63–70.
42. For what is perhaps the earliest version of this type of analysis of *The Searchers*, where Scar is understood as Ethan's 'dark-half', see Joseph McBride and Michael Wilmington, 'The Prisoner of the Desert', *Sight and Sound*, 40(4) (1971): 210–14.
43. Slotkin, *Gunfighter Nation*, p. 466.
44. McGee, *The American Western*, p. 107.
45. Kathryn C. Esselman, 'From Camelot to Monument Valley: Dramatic Origins of the Western Film' (1974), reprinted in Jack Nachbar (ed.), *Focus on the Western*, (Englewood Cliffs, NJ: Prentice-Hall, 1974), pp. 9–19, quote on p. 13.
46. Melinda Szaloky, 'A Tale N/nobody Can Tell: The Return of the Repressed Western History in Jim Jarmusch's *Dead Man*', in Janet Walker (ed.), *Westerns: Films through History* (London: Routledge, 2001), pp. 47–71, quote on p. 53.
47. John G. Cawelti, *The Six-Gun Mystique Sequel* (Bowling Green, OH: Bowling Green State University Popular Press, 1999), p. 105.
48. Colonese, 'Native American Reactions to *The Searchers*', pp. 335–43, quote on p. 340. Although Ford's Cochise in *Fort Apache* more accurately conducts his meeting with the US military in fluent Spanish via an interpreter, in *Rio Grande*, the Apache are largely unintelligible, making stereotyped 'whoops' and 'hollers'. More inconsistency.
49. Ward Churchill, for instance, disparagingly re-titled the film 'Laurence of South Dakota'. See Ward Churchill, *Fantasies of the Master Race: Literature, Cinema and the Colonisation of American Indians* (Monroe, ME: Common Courage Press, 1992); Churchill, discussed in Walker (ed.), *Westerns*, p. 248, fn. 5.
50. Janet Walker (ed.), 'Captive Images in the Traumatic Western: *The Searchers*, *Pursued*, *Once upon a Time in the West*, and *Lone Star*', in *Westerns*, pp. 219–53, quote on p. 222.

51. Ibid., p. 222.
52. Robert V. Hine and John Mack Faragher, *The American West: A New Interpretive History* (New Haven, CT: Yale University Press, 2000), pp. 138–40.
53. Colonese, 'Native American Reactions to *The Searchers*', p. 341.
54. Ibid., p. 337 (emphasis in original).
55. Rick Worland and Edward Countryman, 'The New Western American Historiography and the Emergence of the New American Westerns', in Buscombe and Pearson (eds), *'Back in the Saddle Again'*, pp. 182–97, quote on p. 186.
56. Hine and Faragher, *The American West*, p. 138.
57. Ibid., p. 138.
58. Ibid., p. 139.
59. Ibid., p. 138.
60. Ibid., p. 139. See also Gwynne, *Empire of the Summer Moon, passim.*
61. Jon Tuska, *The American West in Film: Critical Approaches to the Western Genre* (London: Greenwood Press, 1985), p. xix.
62. Ibid., p. xix.
63. Joseph McBride and Michael Wilmington, *John Ford* (London: Secker & Warburg, 1974), p. 162.
64. Tuska, *The American West*, p. 57.
65. Gaylyn Studlar, 'What Would Martha Want?: Captivity, Purity, and Feminine Values in *The Searchers*', in Eckstein and Lehman (eds.), *The Searchers*, pp. 171–97, quote on p. 191.
66. Tuska, *The American West*, p. 57. See also Peter Lehman, 'Looking at Look's Missing Reverse Shot: Psychoanalysis and Style in John Ford's *The Searchers*', *Wide Angle*, 4(4) (1981): 65–71; Lehman, discussed in Douglas Pye, 'Double Vision: Miscegenation and Point of View in *The Searchers*', in Cameron and Pye (eds), *The Movie Book of the Western*, pp. 231–2.
67. Arthur M. Eckstein, 'Darkening Ethan: John Ford's *The Searchers* (1956) from Novel to Screenplay to Screen', *Cinema Journal*, 38(1) (1998): 3–24, quote on p. 9.
68. It was not until the 1970s and films like *Little Big Man* that Custer was portrayed explicitly as an egotistical murderer; although Ford's *Fort Apache* does attack his legend and exposes the cultural collusion necessary in its promotion. His version of 'Custer's Last Stand' is, of course, the fictitious Colonel Owen Thursday's demise at the hands of Cochise's Apaches. In fact, the whole 'Custer sequence' in *The Searchers* could be seen as Ford's response to his own cavalry–journalist sequence at the end of *Fort Apache*; where, in the earlier film, John Wayne's character defends the myth of military heroism, his outburst here explodes it. For discussion of how the Custer legend grew in the United States as a cultural symbol of heroism and sacrifice, see Slotkin, *The Fatal Environment: The Myth of the Frontier in the Age of Industrialisation, 1800–1890* (Norman, OK: Oklahoma Press, [1985] 1998).
69. Eckstein, 'Darkening Ethan', pp. 9–13. Certainly, if Ford had retained the 'Custer sequence' in which Ethan defends Comanche women and children, it would have undermined the audience's sense of anxiety in its fear that Ethan will go on to carry out the horrific act of murder against Debbie.
70. Pye, 'Double Vision', p. 233.
71. Slotkin, *Gunfighter Nation*, p. 471.
72. Ibid., p. 471.
73. Ibid. For example, the Washita massacre is envisioned with more honesty in *Little Big Man*, where women and children are considered as 'fair game' by Custer's men who slaughter indiscriminately and without mercy in what, to all intents and purposes constitutes a 'free-fire zone'.
74. Ibid.

75. Ibid., p. 470.
76. Eckstein, 'Introduction: Main Critical Issues in *The Searchers*', p. 13.
77. Ibid., p. 13.
78. Richard Hutson makes a similar point with regard to the Comanche when they encounter the searchers for the first fight sequence; they 'appear to peel off the rocky depths of the buttes [of Monument Valley] and march in processions that echo the formations of the earth and rock'. See Richard Hutson, 'Sermons in Stone: Monument Valley in *The Searchers*', in Eckstein and Lehman (eds), *The Searchers*, pp. 93–109, quote on p. 105.
79. Slotkin, *Gunfighter Nation*, p. 470.
80. Pye, 'Double Vision', p. 229.
81. Ibid., p. 229 (emphasis added).
82. Slotkin, *Gunfighter Nation*, p. 463.
83. Ibid., p. 463.
84. Ibid., p. 473.
85. Ibid.
86. Undoubtedly, Wayne's own right-wing, conservative politics helped to encourage this misperception.
87. Pye, 'Double Vision', p. 229.
88. David Grimsted, 'Re-Searching', in Eckstein and Lehman (eds), *The Searchers*, pp. 289–335, quote on pp. 313–14.
89. Ibid., pp. 304, 313.
90. Ibid., pp. 316–17.
91. Like numerous other scholars, I am willing to concede that the film's subtleties may have been lost on most audiences in 1956, or even on many contemporary viewers of the film.
92. Grimsted, 'Re-Searching', pp. 329 fn. 19, 316.
93. Ibid., p. 316.
94. Pye, 'Double Vision', p. 229.
95. Dee Brown, *Bury My Heart at Wounded Knee: An Indian History of the American West* (New York: Henry Holt, 1970), p. 265.
96. Brown also suggests that, 'of the 3,700,000 buffalo destroyed from 1872 through 1874, only 150,000 were killed by Indians'. In another historical link, Brown informs us that, when the Comanche decided upon 'a war to drive the white hunters from the grazing grounds', it was none other than Quanah Parker – Ford's alleged historical inspiration for Scar – who led 'the Comanche warriors into battle against the white hunters'. Ibid., p. 265.
97. Pye, 'Double Vision', p. 230.
98. Grimsted, 'Re-searching', p. 313.
99. Ibid., p. 313.
100. Ibid.
101. Studlar, 'What Would Martha Want?', p. 187.
102. Ibid., p. 186.
103. Ibid.
104. Ibid., p. 187
105. Ibid., p. 192.
106. Ibid., p. 193.
107. Grimsted, 'Re-Searching', p. 313.
108. Ibid., p. 314.
109. Ibid.
110. Ibid.
111. Ibid., p. 315.
112. McGee, *From Shane to Kill Bill*, p. 103.
113. Ibid., pp. 103–4.

114. Eckstein, 'Darkening Ethan', pp. 3–24.
115. Slavoj Žižek, *The Plague of Fantasies* (London: Verso, 1997), p. 21 (emphasis in original).
116. Ibid., p. 21 (emphasis in original).
117. Ibid., p. 22.
118. Ibid., p. 25.

3. RETHINKING REVISIONISM

'It's a hell of a thing, killin' a man. You take away all he's got, and all he's ever gonna have.'

I

In a review published shortly after the release of Clint Eastwood's *Unforgiven* (1992), Harvey R. Greenberg offers the following summary:

> *Unforgiven*'s apocalyptic conclusion constitutes an insanely logical outcome – and send-up – of the bellicose John Wayne machismo so frequently celebrated by the genre ... *Unforgiven* underscores how fragile a reed is civilisation, with no hero on a white horse or in a cop car to redeem the threat of humanity's supreme undefendedness. The indomitable thrust to push back the frontier, tame the wilderness, 'build houses', seems pitiable or risible against this recognition ... appears galactically remote indeed from John Wayne triumphalist pieties.[1]

It is clear that Greenberg considers *Unforgiven* as a highly conscious response to both the formal structures of the so-called classical Western and the genre's celebration of its most famous heroes: be they mythologised historical figures such as Wyatt Earp, fictitious national allegories like Shane, or that most curious and uneasy synthesis of the two – John Wayne. Critical responses to *Unforgiven* have tended to fall into one of two broad categories. On the one hand, there are those who, like Greenberg, evidently see in David Webb Peoples' gloomy script an apocalyptic repudiation of the classical Western's 'bellicose' glorification of violence. On the other hand, are those like Daniel O'Brien, who see the film's eventual repudiation of its own 'anti-violence' logic – by collapsing back into a conservative glorification of 'masculinity' and 'individualism' – as expressive of the typical conventions of the genre: 'a man having to do what a man has to do'.[2] Michael Coyne shares similar, if more vitriolic, sentiments, which act as a summary of his overall position on

Eastwood's efforts in the genre. Despite initiating a 'dark, savage tale about a reformed killer', he writes, *Unforgiven* fails at the last hurdle where, at 'the final showdown, [it] degenerated into the same old *High Plains Drifter/Pale Rider* nonsense about the man who cannot be killed'.[3]

Whatever one's opinion, *Unforgiven* remains Eastwood's most critically and commercially accomplished Western to date, garnering four 1993 Academy Awards, including Best Motion Picture and Best Achievement in Directing for Eastwood. But where Greenberg sees the film as a revisionist triumph against the classical Western and O'Brien sees an ultimately flawed narrative, both are united in their placing the film in the genre's revisionist phase. Whether successful or not, *Unforgiven* represents a throw-down against the traditional values of frontier mythology that, as far as the above critics are concerned, have informed not only the narrative logic of most Hollywood Westerns, but an ideology that for centuries has preached an heroic version of history.

I have already discussed how this mythology was expressed in various formats over the course of three centuries, and how it coalesced into the myth of the West on the cusp of the twentieth century. Briefly reiterated – through a series of pamphlets, sermons, paintings, speeches, dime novels, etc., it typically preached a belief in the inevitable progression of Anglo-American civilisation ever-westward across the North American continent. Religious legitimacy for this protracted series of conquests was achieved through the meta-narrative of Manifest Destiny, which sought to foster belief in the young nation's exceptionalism: first, through the trials and tribulations of the ardent-hearted yeoman farmer; and, latterly, through the heroism of the white male cowboy or gunfighter as its principal agent of progress. Westerns typically featured both these symbols of American exceptionalism, with the individualist hero usually employing deadly force to protect the pioneering frontier community from the threat posed by the savage forces of the wilderness.

Of course, it is the attempt to 'tame the wilderness' through such 'triumphalist pieties' that Greenberg is referring to as being so 'frequently celebrated by the genre'. Evidently, for him *Unforgiven* realised an apotheosis of revisionism: the end logic of a long process of mythic introspection and generic self-critique. With *Unforgiven*, the Western had come a long way from Buffalo Bill rescuing the Deadwood Stage from savage 'redskins' towards realising a stark rendering of 'humanity's supreme undefendedness'.

For reasons that I shall discuss shortly, the precise beginning of the revisionist phase of the genre is hard to pin down. However, the commonly held view is that from around the early 1960s onwards the Western's best efforts became increasingly self-conscious *and* self-critical. This was seen in both the formal development of its own classical plot formulas, and in a critical shift in cultural attitudes towards its informing mythologies. John Ford's *The Man Who Shot Liberty Valance* (1962) is commonly mentioned as a progenitor of revisionism. Although one can discern such criticism in much earlier films such as Howard Hawks' *Red River* (1948), Ford's own *Fort Apache* and William

Wellman's *The Ox-Bow Incident* (1943), it is a view that still holds currency. For instance, Patrick McGee declares that *Liberty Valance* 'brings to closure the classic Western itself'.[4]

Following on from *Liberty Valance*, a slew of films have been put forward as opening the floodgates on such issues as gender, race and the darker aspects of Anglo-America's 'triumphant' march across the continent. Seen from this perspective, the West as depicted in the classical Western is largely a distortion of the historical experience of the frontier. Focus on the Native American as signifier for contemporary sociopolitical issues informed the narrative themes of films such as Arthur Penn's *Little Big Man* (1970) and Robert Altman's *Buffalo Bill and the Indians; or, Sitting Bull's History Lesson* (1976). Such cultural–ideological agendas were also accompanied in the field of exploitation cinema, most notably in the Western with Ralph Nelson's notorious film, *Soldier Blue* (1970). Nelson bluntly (and somewhat confusingly) reworked the Mylai massacre into a counter-cultural re-imagining of atrocities committed by the US Cavalry against the Cheyenne during the 1870s. Belief in the idea of such a new sense of generic self-reflexivity held that such films consciously raised issues concerning their own status as Westerns, their own historical role in the construction of erroneous cultural attitudes and beliefs, and the nature of their relation to the myth of the West and towards contemporary events.[5]

These alleged generic insights were accompanied (at more or less the same time) by advances in the field of academic historiography, chiefly by the proponents of what would eventually come to be known as the New Western History. Led most notably by Richard White and Patricia Nelson Limerick, the New Western historians were sceptical of Hollywood's capacity to develop more balanced treatments of the West. For example, Limerick's view of popular cultural depictions of the late-nineteenth-century frontier is one of open disparagement:

> In the popular imagination, the reality of conquest dissolved into stereotypes of noble savages and noble pioneers struggling quaintly in the wilderness. These adventures seemed to have no bearing on the complex realities of twentieth-century America. In Western paintings, novels, movies, and television shows, those stereotypes were valued precisely because they offered an escape from modern troubles . . . An element of regret for 'what we did to the Indians' had entered the picture, but the dominant feature of conquest remained 'adventure'.[6]

Limerick's remarks, although by no means unjustified, remain typical of a large number of cultural historians whose attitude to the popular arts is dismissive at best. In the case of the above quotation, it results in the reduction of the entire formal and thematic scope of the Hollywood Western to that of an ideological sentinel, proffering escapism and fantasy instead of holding a serious concern for 'the complex realities of twentieth-century America'.

In the previous two chapters I have warned against such a view. Hollywood and the popular cultural material it produces have often been unjustly reduced in status to that of a servile accomplice to dominant ideologies. For one, if we consider the common argument that Westerns have often had a great deal to say about the period in which they were made over that in which they are set (consider Brian Henderson's analysis of *The Searchers*, for example), then they automatically call into question Limerick's assertion that the genre merely 'offered an escape from modern troubles'. On the contrary, as part of an industrial mass-medium, cinematic Westerns cannot but be affected and, to some extent, conditioned by 'modern troubles'; their historical perspectives unavoidably influenced by contemporary cultural, political and even economic trends. The extent to which the cinematic Western wholeheartedly endorsed either the triumphalist version of Anglo-American history *or* the dominant contemporary ideologies prevalent at any given period remains, of course, a matter of rigorous debate. It is a debate that transcends specific genre concerns and is virtually as old as serious academic film criticism itself.

In 1967, Alan Lovell advanced the sociological concerns voiced by Robert Warshow and André Bazin a decade earlier by raising the issue of 'the problem of the relationship between the Western and social reality'.[7] Ultimately, and in terms similar to Limerick's assessment, Lovell asked the question: 'do Westerns distort reality, is their purpose essentially that of social propaganda[?]'.[8] Such a question was responded to that very same year by James K. Folsom, who briefly ruminated on the Western's potential for setting up 'an alternate standard of values to the often shabby ones of modern finance capitalism'.[9] This, of course, recapitulates the generic binary between West and East, frontier purity and eastern corruption, and Folsom mentions such films as *One-Eyed Jacks* (Marlon Brando, 1961) and *High Noon* – where Sheriff Will Kane (Gary Cooper) finds the town of Hadleyville 'not worth defending' – as socially conscious critical texts.[10] More pointedly, Folsom interprets the conclusion of *Shane*, 'where Shane rides away from the grubby town in which the action of the film has taken place ... [as] a statement of a similar theme'.[11] It is in this sense that Westerns are seen, not so much as nostalgic for a simpler past, an 'escape from modern troubles', or necessarily 'social propaganda', but, rather, as actively critical of the industrial–capitalist *present*. Folsom suggests that, in fact, Westerns 'often represent ... a political point of view which is at the very least profoundly suspicious of the development of modern American democracy'.[12]

However, the conception of the Western as 'social propaganda' seems to be a popular position, and one assumed most forcefully by Will Wright. We may remind ourselves that Wright assumed a straightforward, one-way relationship between the individual film text and the socioeconomic conditions of its production. He asserted that 'myth depends on simple and recognisable meanings which reinforce rather than challenge social understanding'.[13] However, I have previously made clear in my readings of *Shane* and *The Searchers* that while

Wright's schema may hold true for oral folklore and tradition, it loses much of its theoretical credibility (and coherence) when transposed onto a contemporary and complex art form like film. In a review of *Six-Guns and Society*, Janey Place remarks that 'Wright fails to allow the relation between a society and its popular culture the complexity which is necessary to its operation.'[14] She goes on to say that, although '[m]ovies both reflect the values and ideology of the culture and are a means of reproduction of that ideology ... [t]he ability of popular culture to reflect and express a wide range of contradictions that arise from the tensions of our socio-economic structure is awesome.'[15] She insists that Wright's adoptive myth structural analysis fails to adequately account for the complex industrial–commercial vicissitudes of cinema, finally suggesting that 'any attempt to locate the meaning of an entire basic myth may be naive, regardless of the theory and method used'.[16] One would be wise to keep such sentiments in mind when considering any analytical approach to the Western as some of the genre's best efforts *have* questioned the glorification of national expansion.

As I have already shown through analysis of *The Searchers*, ideological contradictions are laid bare in its exposure and fierce critique of the racism underpinning the rhetoric of nineteenth-century US expansionism. This introspection occurs in *The Searchers* on both a formal and thematic level and has, significantly, often been articulated in the Western genre as a whole *through* the figure of the white male hero. As in the case of Ethan, the Western has often held a mirror up to the myth of such heroes, undermining their status and, as a consequence, questioning the very morality of the nation that they had come to represent. Similar sentiments have been reiterated by McGee, who writes that 'although the Western has often been described as a conservative film genre, one that stresses extreme versions of masculinity and individualism ... there has always been another side to the Western, another shadow that it casts'.[17] This being said, McGee essentially aligns himself with the theory of genre evolution by insisting that this development within the genre is a consequence of US civil and political strife during the late 1960s and beyond. The symptom of which is that 'the late westerns from directors like Sam Peckinpah, Sergio Leone, Clint Eastwood, and others are more pessimistic than the films of the classical period'.[18]

Most critical literature on *Unforgiven* (as exemplified by Greenberg and O'Brien) fixes the film's chronology firmly in this pessimistic 'late' period. What few writers seem to scrutinise, however, are the very classical or revisionist conventions that are liberally applied to the genre with regard to its relation to frontier history and to cultural attitudes in contemporary US society. There is typically assumed some kind of increasingly anti-mythological stance and generic self-critique that developed from the early 1960s and proliferated as the twentieth century drew to a close. As a consequence of this, the most prominent writing on *Unforgiven* tends to assume a set of traditional or, rather, classical generic codes and motifs that the film either successfully repudiates through a conscious semiotic and thematic revisionism, or else ends up succumbing to by the narrative climax.

As *Unforgiven* is so often held up as an exemplar of the revisionist phase of the genre, moreover, as the end logic of the Western's supposed formal and ideological self-critique, it would be constructive to first contextualise such a theoretical approach before beginning my own analysis of the film proper. In what follows, I shall seek to briefly outline my general sentiments of the Western genre beyond what has been outlined thus far and draw it onto the sociohistorical moment of *Unforgiven*'s release. Specifically, by discussing more properly classical Westerns I shall seek to continue my counter-argument to the common revisionist contention put forward by Schatz and others that, over time, 'both the frontier community and its moralistic standard-bearers are depicted in increasingly complex, ambiguous, and unflattering terms', along with the accompanying belief that '[t]he gradual fading of this optimistic vision, more than anything else, characterises the evolution of the Western genre'.[19]

To accompany this, I shall outline a 2007 analysis of *Unforgiven* offered by Stephen McVeigh. Within the pessimistic logic of genre evolution, McVeigh's analysis draws on a political-allegorical approach to the Western in order to relate, through a deconstructive comparison, *Unforgiven*'s narrative with that of *Shane*'s. Ultimately, McVeigh offers up Eastwood's film as '*the* postmodern Western'.[20]

II

Previously I applied Tag Gallagher's argument against genre evolution in order to establish *Shane* and *The Searchers* as two reflective examples of the so-called classical Western that questioned dominant mythological paradigms.[21] That is to say, they are two films whose narratives express what would come to be known as revisionist traits. I argued that both films demonstrate narrative confusion through the release of contending (often contradictory) sign systems. In analysing these iconic Westerns, I sought to question the whole theory of generic evolution insofar as it pertains to a tendency to utilise formal and ideological-based distinctions that define individual films chronologically as either classical, revisionist or, more increasingly of late, post-Westerns.

To further this line of critical enquiry, I incorporate into my analysis a theoretical contention put forward by Fredric Jameson. Jameson argues that *any* 'cultural artefact' is ineluctably connected with the historical circumstances surrounding its inception, including its industrial–commercial production and its social reception.[22] From this we can suggest that, in the Western, the individual film text 'speaks', as it were, through its 'form', obliquely articulating the various ideological contradictions of its sociohistorical moment: variously distorting, repressing and transforming such articulations, and exposing the latent meanings behind any ostensible meaning promoted by the text.

We can perceive already in Jameson a movement beyond the social and formal reductionism of Wright's structural analysis. Where Wright asserted the existence of binary oppositions and patterns with the aim of establishing unity, coherence and a fixed pattern of development within the genre, Jameson highlights the potential in popular culture for textual disunity. As I have shown, such a rigid approach as Wright offers reduces the oft-times rich and ambiguous relationship between individual film texts and the socioeconomic institutions from which they emerged to one of unproblematic ideological reflection. This approach to the Western falls within what Altman and Neale have both termed the 'ideological' approach to genre.[23] According to Neale, the ideological approach, 'open to the charges of reductivism, economism, and cultural pessimism', refuses the very possibility that an individual film text could resist dominant culture, much less articulate its ideological contradictions.[24] This led inevitably to formulaic and simplistic (mis)readings of whole rafts of film texts. For Jameson, such indeterminate aesthetic qualities, so often in evidence in artefacts of popular culture, are to be utilised as lenses through which one can seek to clarify and lay bare a particular artefact's political, social and economic roots.

Jameson insists upon the priority of the 'political perspective' for the interpretation of narrative, while simultaneously arguing that history rejects any given attempt to represent it 'totally'. Hence, the ideological manipulation of history to suit particular individual or collective class, economic or other interests is, as a consequence, never complete, never as *simple* as Wright's approach would have us believe. (Jameson's relation to Foucault here should be apparent.) '[A] given artistic process', Jameson contends, 'is informed by contradictory sign systems and, as sedimented content, it carries ideological messages of its own, distinct from the manifest content of the text [and] display[s] such formal operations from the standpoint of what [we] will call the "content of form"'.[25] The 'content of form' relates directly to another of Jameson's terminologies. It is similarly rooted in what he calls the *'ideology of form'*.[26] And this he defines as 'the symbolic messages transmitted to us by the coexistence of various sign systems ... as a determinate structure of still properly formal *contradictions*'.[27] Here there is a 'determinate contradiction of specific messages emitted by the varied sign systems which coexist in a given artistic process as well as in its general social formation'.[28]

By the time of the release of *Shane* and *The Searchers*, the most dominant issues of the 'social formation' being asserted as ideology in the United States concerned the cultural transition from post-Second World War to early-stage Cold War sociopolitical environments. We are reminded here of Robert Warshow's ethical claim for the Western as offering a 'serious orientation to the problem of violence such as can be found almost nowhere else in our culture'.[29] In making this claim, and despite his well-known reservations with regard to the import of 'social problems' into the post-Second World War Western, he thus identifies the genre as *the* major popular cultural expression of the modern American *zeitgeist*. It is from this premise that, years later, Richard Slotkin could regard *Shane*, *High Noon* and *The Gunfighter* (1950) as all having their roots in the post-Second World War phase of the genre he calls 'renaissance' Westerns. He reasons this by their apparent '[addressing of] ... the complex of ideological problems that we may call "social justice"'.[30] For Slotkin, this era heralded an increased sense of self-consciousness among producers of Westerns, often resulting in overtly 'stylised' films whose principal narrative concerns were structured around the image of a lone male hero. Sometimes this would manifest itself to the point of 'fetishisation', whereby 'a single element of the Western (e.g. prowess with a gun, or the gun itself) is isolated from its original context and made the subject of exaggerated attention and concern'.[31] The suggestion here is that these films achieved this emphasis by incorporating stylistic elements from film noir (and other urban detective formats), with their particular narrative concentration on the personal psychology and morally duplicitous motivation of their protagonists.

Slotkin's suggestion that the Cold War Western adopts some of the formal characteristics of film noir points towards hybridity within the genre and a wider intertextual interplay within cinematic genres as a whole. Indeed, though *Gunfighter Nation* is predominately about Westerns, Slotkin shows how other genres (particularly the War film and the Epic) play off the structure of both frontier mythology *and* the Western. In addition to this exaggerated mythical image, and in accordance with the aspects of Jameson's theoretical approach I outlined above, Slotkin suggests that there was often a 'consonance between the formal character of the gunfighter' and a wider 'ideological content'.[32] This last was concerned with expressing cultural attitudes towards violence, both through its expression and the situations that justified its use. Interpreted in this way, the figure of the gunfighter becomes 'an important symbol of right and heroic action for filmmakers, the public, and the nation's political leadership'.[33] Slotkin suggests that this 'renaissance' spirit caused, among the 'best' directors at least, a 'highly developed sense of the genre as *genre*', and he cites Anthony Mann's *Winchester '73* (1950) as emblematic of this introspective development.[34] He describes Mann's 'organising of each episode ... around the theme or setting of a different subtype of Western, including the town-tamer, the stagecoach journey, the outlaw Western, and the Cavalry/Indian Western'.[35] This is presented as evidence of 'the self-conscious sense of genre convention' apparent as a *new* development in the post-Second World War Western.[36]

While I do not deny the validity of Slotkin's reading of *Winchester '73*, could not the same self-consciousness also be applied in equal measure, for instance, to John Ford's *pre*-Second World War *Stagecoach*? *Stagecoach* is, after all, beholden to a similarly modernist sensibility as that of its post-Second World War and Cold War counterparts. By self-consciously incorporating many formal and thematic tropes from both feature Westerns and the raft of the contemporary 'B' movies that preceded it (its 'stagecoach journey', attendant

'Cavalry/Indian' chase, and its incorporation of the 'outlaw Western' with the Ringo Kid's revenge against the Plummer brothers in Lordsburg – a subplot which, not incidentally, eventuates in some 'town-tamer' exploits of its own), the same 'sense of genre convention' Slotkin attributes to *Winchester '73* applies to Ford's *Stagecoach* in equal measure. It is curious to note, therefore, that Slotkin writes of Ford's 'return to the Western genre' with *Stagecoach* as being 'undertaken with revisionist intentions', and that Ford 'wanted to develop and expand the latent capacities of the old form as a vehicle for cinematic expression'.[37] I agree with Slotkin's contention that *Stagecoach* is an example of generic self-consciousness, yet such a contention seems at odds with his own insistence on an increased sense of the 'genre as *genre*' beginning only *after* the Second World War and the early years of the Cold War.

Quite apart from this chronological glitch, *Stagecoach*'s commonly asserted status as a classical Western also becomes questionable if we scratch under the narrative's surface and apply Jameson's concept of the content of form. In Schatz's reading, the romantic union of the outlaw, Ringo Kid (John Wayne), and the prostitute, Dallas (Claire Trevor), is essentially optimistic, as 'the uncivilised outlaw-hero and a woman practicing society's oldest profession have been united and go off to seek the promise of the American West's new world'.[38] However, Gallagher alerts us to the significance of the fact that Doc Boone (Thomas Mitchell) insists that, in being forced to flee the United States for sanctuary in Mexico at the close of the narrative, Dallas and Ringo are '*saved* from the blessings of civilisation'.[39] Actually, they are not permitted to stay in Lordsburg by the town's authorities. Despite Ringo's heroism in protecting the occupants of the stagecoach from Apache attack, and despite Dallas' help in delivering Lucy Mallory's baby, they are branded outcasts – *personae non gratae* – and forced to live an outlawed existence on the run in Mexico. This is as opposed to being free to seek 'the promise of the American West's new world'. For Gallagher this is hardly the 'optimistic vision' beneath a superficial 'veneer of cynicism' that Schatz proposes.[40]

Perhaps Schatz's terms could even be inverted, where a veneer of *optimism* masks a particularly *cynical* vision, a complex and ambiguous apperception introspectively based on past Westerns *and* on the contemporary socioeconomic climate from which *Stagecoach* drew its narrative inspirations. To me it seems difficult to discern optimism from the film's conclusion. This is, indeed, signposted from the outset of the narrative with Dallas initially forced out of the township of Tonto by the Puritanical intolerance of the women of the 'Ladies' Law and Order League', and ostracised from 'polite society'. This suggests the very opposite of Schatz's interpretation where, in fact, the so-called 'promise of the American West's new world' is something categorically *denied* both Ringo, 'the uncivilised outlaw-hero', and Dallas, the prostitute 'practicing society's oldest profession'. There is, therefore, an undoubted irony in *Stagecoach*'s view of the ideology asserted through the myth of the West, a subtle undermining of Greenberg's assertion that, traditionally, the

Western 'celebrated' the 'indomitable thrust to push back the frontier, tame the wilderness . . . "build houses"'.

In agreement with this hypothesis and in keeping with the spirit of Folsom's approach to the genre as outlined above, Lenihan writes:

> *Stagecoach* actually conveys as much social criticism as did *High Noon*. Ringo's departure from Lordsburg and [the] 'blessings of civilisation' at the film's conclusion are as much a condemnation of society's weaknesses as was Marshal Kane's departure from Hadleyville – a point that also appears to have escaped John Wayne when he criticised *High Noon*'s denigration of American heritage.[41]

Such ironic closing sentiments as *Stagecoach* displays suggest that a cynical view of the coming of civilisation is discernable in Westerns of a much earlier period than those produced during the first years of the Cold War; it is, after all, a Depression-era film that critiques bureaucracy, banks and social repressions. Ford's film stands in defiance to Schatz's argument that classical Westerns are essentially optimistic, let alone being narratively simplistic or culturally 'naive'. *Stagecoach* problematises the commonly held argument that depictions of frontier civilisation in the Western steadily deteriorated as the genre underwent a process of increasingly self-conscious introspective revisionism. Such insights prove to be invaluable when engaging with a critical reassessment of *Unforgiven*'s revisionist status, a status reaffirmed in 2007 by Steven McVeigh.

III

As mentioned above, McVeigh explores the political-allegorical functions of the Western at the close of the twentieth century. He also proposes that the majority of prominent Westerns released from the early 1960s onwards were, to one extent or another, revisions of *Shane* and its eponymous hero. He traces a line of 'transcendental' Western protagonists, foregrounding their ideological function, and grades them against Shane as heroic models for US political leadership:

> The character of Shane resonates in the culture and finds common ground with Kennedy. In the wake of Kennedy's assassination, the western generally, but *Shane* in particular, is subverted, the innocent values lost, along with the possibility of heroic leadership and all of this compounded by American involvement in Vietnam.[42]

He thus assesses *Unforgiven* in a revisionist vein, as an expression of 'the genre's fragmentation' in this tumultuous period. For McVeigh, '*Unforgiven* . . . contains multitudes, and as such . . . attempts to speak to and of many different perspectives'.[43] This is, presumably, in a way that earlier, more properly classical, Westerns do not. It is for these reasons that McVeigh makes his claim for placing *Unforgiven* among those revisions of *Shane* that 'resonat[e] with the outlook of the New Western History'.[44] He declares *Unforgiven* '*the* postmodern Western', a brutally introspective deconstruction of stock Western types and the 'archetype' of Shane. '*Shane* is remade in the decades following the original release,' McVeigh insists. 'But the question emerges, what kind of *Shane* is produced?'[45] He asserts *Shane*'s 'timeless' credentials, while simultaneously suggesting it as contingent upon changes in cultural attitudes, as an 'updating of traditional mythic and generic patterns'.[46]

In attempting to establish the 'difference that exists between the classic Hollywood Western and these revisions of *Shane*', McVeigh establishes a paradigm that asserts either an elegiac mourning of past frontier ideals or a nostalgic celebration of what has been lost. For him, this distinction also marks the distinction between the 'classic Hollywood Western', which now appears as 'anachronistic' in the post-Kennedy period, and the elegiac concerns of the 'new "*Shanes*"', which 'are born from a mourning for the loss of frontier values'.[47] For him, *Shane*'s overtly mythical aesthetic gives the film a transcendental power:

> The movie's intention to place a mythical agenda over simple narrative function, and the archetype that is the character Shane, means that the film transcends its generic Western limitations and emerges as an important American cultural artefact . . . [*Shane*] does not fit into an easy chronology of the gunfighter mystique and it does not remain locked up in its generic Western confines.[48]

McVeigh's use of the term classical and his particular concentration on *Shane* as ur-narrative – 'a point of origin' – remains, for me, unsatisfactory.[49] Aside from the dubious assumption here that narrative is a 'simple' function of the film, McVeigh puts forward a contentious, but all too common, belief that popular genres act as 'limitations' for creativity, surmountable only by a great filmmaker or a visionary artist. After all, in asserting *Shane*'s status as 'an important American cultural artefact' through this transcendence, McVeigh, whether he intends to or not, is implicitly suggesting that other Westerns simply fail to achieve this level of cultural significance.

McVeigh's focus on *Shane* reduces the influence of such socially significant and related films as *High Noon* and *The Gunfighter* from the theoretical equation. Along with *Shane*, Slotkin interprets these films as forming part of a loose 'trilogy' of 'gunfighter' Westerns, which emerged in the early 1950s. Not so for McVeigh, for whom *Shane* is, 'contrary to Slotkin's depiction of it as the third link in a chain of similar films, [an] original Hollywood Western'.[50] He continues by claiming that *Shane* 'is a world away from even such exceptional Westerns as *High Noon* and *The Gunfighter*'.[51] What is most significant about the context of McVeigh's analysis of *Shane* (and, by implication, *Unforgiven*) is what he neglects to analyse. Foucault's 'not said' returns here with a vengeance, as mention of that important film, *The Searchers*, is missing from his argument. In fact, the film does not feature in McVeigh's study of the Western genre at all.

Omissions of important film texts aside, McVeigh's interpretive schema fails him even with respect to the films he discusses. The following excerpts from *The American Western* make clear the procrustean nature of forcing films to fit a developmental political-allegorical pattern of ever-pessimistic mythological introspection and narrative evolution:

> During Kennedy's thousand days in the White House, there were no cinematic attempts to revise *Shane*. There was not the cultural need to investigate alternative models of leadership or heroism. A brief exploration of the Western in the early 1960s demonstrates that the genre was content to reflect, however fleetingly, contemporary social and political concerns without questioning the figure of the leader.[52]

Such a 'brief exploration' McVeigh provides a mere two pages later, offering his ideological interpretation of *Liberty Valance*:

> If *High Noon* and *Shane* created models of heroic leadership that could be discerned in Eisenhower and Kennedy, then *The Man Who Shot Liberty Valance* posed questions that Americans would come to ask of the nature of heroic leadership, questions such as: on what do we base assumptions about an individual? What happens if the individual becomes too powerful and abuses the power of the position or trust of the people?
>
> In construction, *The Man Who Shot Liberty Valance* is similar to *Shane*. Both Shane and Stoddard [James Stewart] come to a community and ultimately improve it through a series of violent episodes.[53]

Such a reading of *Liberty Valance* appears strange if one takes into consideration McVeigh's earlier assertions that, during the Kennedy administration, there was a lack of a 'cultural need' to criticise the figure of the hero. And it must be noted that this film was released well over a year *before* Kennedy's assassination and, therefore, *during* his 'thousand days in the White House', a time when, apparently, there was no 'need to investigate alternative models of leadership or heroism'. This contradiction ruptures the smooth, self-reflexive revisionist chronology McVeigh would otherwise seek to establish. *Liberty Valance* undoubtedly draws on many Westerns, including *Shane*, though I doubt that their narrative 'construction' is as similar as is being suggested here. Indeed, the analyses of *Shane* and *The Searchers* that I have already offered suggest that these 'models of heroic leadership' *were* being self-consciously critiqued from within the genre decades before Kennedy was a major player in US politics, let alone elected president.

I feel that McVeigh attributes too much credence to this political-allegorical reading of *Shane* as a 'plan', or 'model', for heroic leadership that would come to inform the popular myth surrounding Kennedy. This is especially so if one considers how Slotkin's own approach details how the 'gunfighter' plot habitually slipped into the 'revenger' plot, towards even greater psychological complexity of character pathology, and 'was accompanied by the de-emphasis (and for a while virtual abandonment) of the social/historical formulas of motivation that had previously shaped Western scenarios'.[54] In this particular narrative scenario, it is alleged that 'the private dimension determines the whole significance of the story'.[55] While I do not entirely agree with this either, I shall argue below that the narrative of *Unforgiven* concerns itself more with this so-called 'psychological' or 'revenger' Western formula, which Slotkin associates with the 'outlaw' mode of the genre, than it does with exposing – much less deconstructing – a cultural symbol of heroic leadership modelled on the figure of Shane.

Jon Tuska states that the political-allegorical interpretation of the genre 'cannot ever really be verified: not by asking the director, the screenwriter, other critics . . . When encountering them, you either agree or disagree; beyond that . . . they are ultimately useless.'[56] In this sense, one feels that McVeigh – like Slotkin – tries too hard to read contemporary politics into Westerns. In a review of *Gunfighter Nation*, New Western historian Richard White suggests that the flaw in Slotkin's approach lies in its very use of history:

> [T]he historical techniques Slotkin deploys sometimes seem to amount only to chronological serendipity . . . His tactic is to describe a political situation and then show how a nearly contemporaneous movie is like it or comments on it. This makes possible seemingly arbitrary comparisons between apparently unconnected events without demonstrating any actual connections between their producers or a common popular interpretation.[57]

The relevance of such a criticism, if applied to McVeigh's analysis of *Liberty Valance*, is clear where even such an instance of 'chronological serendipity' appears to be lacking.

I wish to make my position clear. I do not, like Tuska, refute that ideological self-critique occurs within the genre as a result of changes in societal attitudes and historical–political circumstances or, indeed, that the drawing of such parallels is always serendipitous, as White suggests. Nor do I seek to deny the fact that the Western (like any other cinematic genre) reinvents itself with each successive generation, can be uncompromisingly introspective or that it is anything other than ideologically labile. McVeigh, Slotkin, Coyne, etc. are otherwise very illuminating in elucidating the oft-times rich and multifarious ways in which the genre responds to changes in sociopolitical circumstances, *and* how it interacts with its informing mythic discourse. My major caveat is just that, on occasion, arguments structured by the political-allegorical approach seem too forced, suggestive of an (unconscious) ideological correlation between producers of popular culture, policymakers in the United States and historical events that is simply not borne out in the films themselves.

It is with the above issues in mind that I now offer my assessment of *Unforgiven*. I investigate the film's pretensions to historical, myth and genre revisionism, and consider how far its narrative themes resonate with those of the New Western History. Finally, I establish how far one can qualify McVeigh's assertion that *Unforgiven* stands as '*the* postmodern Western' by analysing the individualist hero in his role as gunfighter and the film's articulations of violence within the broader context of the genre as a whole.

IV

It is important to note from the very outset that *Unforgiven* is not, strictly speaking, a revisionist Western, at least not in the manner prescribed by the advocates of the New Western History. That is to say, it does not pretend to offer a variant of the genre or a view of the late-nineteenth-century frontier that is more *historically* accurate. (Of course, this is *not* the same as saying that it bears no relation to history whatsoever.) As a consequence, many have suggested that *Unforgiven* be read along intertextual lines. That is to say, as a response to the Westerns of the past, the film asserts its own ideological stance based to some extent on anti-myth. This type of approach makes no pretensions to objectivity; it just assumes a different mythic guise in order to respond to that of the old. (This, of course, refers back to the discussion in Chapter 2 of the simultaneity of myth and anti-myth as is evident in *The Searchers*. The extent to which this anti-myth, as is apparent in *Unforgiven*, is a deconstruction or outright repudiation of the myth it would seek to supplant, merely an extension of it through different formal motifs, or a fundamental and systemic part of the Western genre's cultural–ideological dialectic is a matter of contention to which I shall respond during the course of this chapter.)

Unforgiven structures its narrative around the figure of lonely ex-gunfighter turned pig farmer, William Munny (Clint Eastwood), a man who – so the initial crawl informs us – is 'a known thief and murderer, a man of notoriously vicious and intemperate disposition'. It situates itself in 1880 Wyoming two years after the death of Munny's wife Claudia. 'Not at his hands as her mother might have expected', so we are told, 'but of smallpox. That was in 1878.' Despite initiating an historical allusion (the well-documented 'Yellow Fever Plague' of that year), this event actually appears to serve within an existential context, one that has more to do with Munny than it does the broader scope of the history of the West. Much like *The Searchers* did with Martha, *Unforgiven* establishes the deceased Claudia as a nineteenth-century feminine ideal, a 'structuring absence', at least so in Munny's mind, who on numerous occasions claims that she 'cured' him of his past of 'drink and wickedness'.

However, these initial anti-mythic sentiments are undercut by the establishing shot of Munny's Wyoming farmstead. Silhouetted against the romanticised backdrop of an impossibly golden sky, it provides a stark contrast to the avowedly unromantic information contained within the crawl. This shot's mythic nature is reinforced by the accompaniment of Lennie Niehaus' nostalgic musical score. Much like the Edwards farmstead in *The Searchers*, with its version of the popular Civil War song 'Lorena' playing on the soundtrack and its Monument Valley backdrop set in 1868 'Texas', *Unforgiven*'s opening sequence makes clear from the very outset that the film is situated firmly in mythic terrain.

Such mythic terrain is replicated throughout *Unforgiven* as glorious sunsets silhouette the characters against stunning Wyoming and Alberta landscapes. Masterfully rendered by cinematographer Jack N. Green, such shots are reminiscent of the painted canvases of Frederic Remington, Charles Russell and Albert Bierstadt from whom such filmmakers as Ford drew their visual inspiration for pictures like *Stagecoach* and *She Wore a Yellow Ribbon* (1949). In *Unforgiven*, the landscape imports itself into the psychology of the characters themselves, creating what we might call an 'existential geography'. It also serves a more prosaic function by providing a contrast to the sense of restriction engendered by the film's urban spaces.

First and foremost, however, in *Unforgiven* Eastwood revisits his own myth, which had been cemented in the mid-1960s by a number of truly mythical lead roles. In a fruitful collaboration with the Italian filmmaker, Sergio Leone, Eastwood's star persona was established in *A Fistful of Dollars* (1964), *For a Few Dollars More* (1965), and *The Good, the Bad, and the Ugly* (1967). One area of theoretical consensus on these Italian Westerns was their self-conscious detachment from such notions as the domestication of the wilderness and Anglo-America's Manifest Destiny. With Leone, the notion of community gave way to a fetishistic concentration on the favoured trope of the gunfighter. Here the hero's moral position in relation to the code was ambiguous to say the least, and his isolationism and self-interest was often taken to the extreme.

Leone's depictions of violence were brutal and comical in equal measure, but they managed (more or less) to make a distinction between the hero's use of violence and that of the villain – a distinction that McVeigh insists is absent from *Unforgiven*, where it 'is impossible to decide categorically who is good and who is bad'.[58] Leone's Westerns are often charged with reducing to depthlessness the figure of the gunfighter and re-imagining him as some kind of supernatural avenging angel: the atavistic Man with No Name. This figure has no history, no past, no story. Any sense of history (either personal or otherwise) is wilfully suppressed in favour of social fantasies of elaborate and violent 'fast-on-the-draw' shootouts. It is this aspect in particular that led many theorists to offer post-modernist readings of Leone's work.

Leone's Westerns proved to be extremely popular in the United States, and inevitably fed back into Eastwood's Hollywood output. This gave the actor/ director a star persona with a very definite history from which to contextualise his own career. By conflating two major aspects of the US cultural mindset – the popularity of the Western and the accessible narrative conduit of frontier mythology – Eastwood, like John Wayne before him, established himself as a part of this culture, directing and/or starring in some truly iconic Westerns such as *High Plains Drifter* (1973), *The Outlaw Josey Whales* (1976) and *Pale Rider* (1985). As a consequence of this, it would be difficult (I would argue nigh-on impossible) to interpret the sad figure of Munny – ailing farmer and knee-deep in pig shit – without an introspective reference to these films, as few (if any) moviegoers could conceivably have watched *Unforgiven* without being mindful of such a culturally significant cinematic legacy.

The first indication that the Western genre and the myth are being discussed in *Unforgiven* is provided by the names of the characters, beginning with Munny himself. Although I have not read it mentioned anywhere, Will Munny seems to relate to the name Will Penny – a down-and-out westerner from a 1968 film of the same name.[59] More significantly, William Munny is also a very obvious allusion to William H. Bonney, more commonly known by his alias, Billy the Kid – popular folk legend of the Lincoln County War. With the possible exception of Jesse James, Billy is *the* mythical figure *par excellence* of cinema's Wild West. This attribution is accompanied by the presence of the Schofield Kid (Jaimz Woolvet) – the young criminal braggadocio who is in awe of Munny's notorious legend as 'the meanest goddamned son-of-a-bitch alive'. It is the Kid who prompts Munny out of retirement for a $1,000 bounty and who is clearly more fascinated with the idea of the gunfighter than he is with financial profit.

The Kid is one of the characters through whom the audience can assess *Unforgiven*'s statement on the power of the myth in mediating cultural–historical experience. Believing Munny's brutal credentials through the strength of rumour and hearsay alone, the Kid constructs an image of Munny much akin to the way the audience constructs a popular–cultural image of Eastwood. And much like our own perception, the Kid's is hopelessly flawed (this is suggested through the all-too obvious metaphor of the Kid needing eye-glasses). By the time the Kid meets Munny, this 'bad-ass' image has set in his own mind, much like Eastwood's has in ours. It is in this regard that, upon meeting this unobtrusive and apparently weak old man, his disappointment can be said to mirror our own: 'You sure as hell don't look like no mean-assed son-of-a-bitch cold-blooded goddamned killer to me!'

In addition to the Billy the Kid allusion, Munny's surname could also be a pun on money, a signification that would indicate the reasons for his violent past, and his reason for taking on the proverbial 'one last job' with the Kid and his old friend and partner-in-crime, Ned Logan (Morgan Freeman). McGee provides perhaps the best account of this:

Munny (Eastwood), Little Bill (Gene Hackman), and English Bob (Richard Harris) all have names that allude to currency; and [that] the plot of [the] film is driven by the desire for money and the need to defend or resist the concept of private property that determines the value of everything.[60]

Although this hypothesis is strongly supported by the blatant economic interests of several of the characters in *Unforgiven*, I would ultimately side with Carl Plantinga, whose own review of the film suggests that its overriding concern is with depicting masculinity, in that 'much of *Unforgiven*'s violence stems from threats to male potency and power'.[61] The majority of revisionist readings of *Unforgiven* contend that it is the myth of the heroic avenger who brings justice with his six-gun that is repeatedly ridiculed, and several separate episodes within the narrative deal with masculinity in this regard. The starkest of these occurs when Ned asks Munny if he has been with a woman since the death of Claudia. Munny looks sheepishly to the ground and gives the slightest shake of his head; the answer is evidently a no.

Many of the remainder of *Unforgiven*'s cast have standard Western names – so standard in fact that they appear as clichés. Strawberry Alice (Frances Fisher) is far from as sweet as her nickname suggests. She displaces her hatred towards men for a lifetime of prostitution onto the two cowboys – Quick Mike (David Mucci) and Davey Boy Bunting (Rob Campbell) – responsible for a vicious assault on Delilah (Anna Thompson-Levine). It is Alice who becomes the driving force behind raising the $1,000 bounty to place on the cowboy's heads and, in so doing, sets in motion the slow spiral of violence and revenge that structures the narrative. Mike's nickname is also significant in terms of masculinity. 'Quick' could refer to his ability to draw a gun; however, in relation to his 'teensy little pecker' that Delilah ridicules (thus prompting his brutal attack upon her), it is more likely a reference to premature ejaculation.[62] Finally, the name of (supposedly) professional gunfighter, English Bob – 'The Duke of Death' – appears as a terrible cliché. Bob is initially accompanied by a dime novelist, W. W. Beauchamp (Saul Rubenik), who is writing a biography of the Duke's 'heroic' exploits. As the film's very own mythmaker, this irksome hack compliments the Kid's avid consumption of popular folklore. It is, after all, Beauchamp who creates the fascinating stories about noble gunfighters and who admits to 'adding a certain "poetry" to the language'. (Beauchamp also shares the Kid's literal short-sightedness, sporting thick spectacles through which he perceives and constructs his myopic view of the frontier.)

Much of the narrative's action takes place in the fictional Wyoming township of Big Whiskey, which is run by Sheriff Little Bill Daggett. Daggett's name has also been seen as a pun on both money (the Dollar bill) and on manhood (little 'willy'). Indeed, one wonders why the bulky Daggett would be nicknamed 'Little' in the first place. This is especially so since he turns out to be one of the narrative's more genuinely tough and violent characters. Daggett's brand of law is indeed brutal, direct, and resides in the logic of deterrence: 'No

Firearms in Big Whiskey, Ordinance 14'. English Bob is the first of the would-be assassins lured by the promise of 'whore's gold' to arrive in Big Whiskey. He arrogantly ignores the edict and is promptly surrounded by the Sheriff and his armed deputies. Stripped of his pistols he is beaten to a bloody pulp by Daggett who, in front of numerous shocked townsfolk and a terrified Beauchamp, warns all would-be assassins to stay away from Big Whiskey:

> I guess you think I'm kicking you, Bob. But it ain't so. What I'm doing is talking, you hear? I'm talking to all those villains down there in Kansas. I'm talking to all those villains in Missouri. And all those villains down there in Cheyenne. And what I'm saying is there ain't no whore's gold. And if there was, how they wouldn't want to come looking for it anyhow.[63]

Just before being rode out of town, Bill returns Bob's Colt .45, the barrel now comically twisted in an obvious symbol of emasculation. Leighton Grist suggests that Daggett's brutal deconstruction of Bob's masculine image is completed when Bob leaves, cursing the townsfolk, 'his measured, "aristocratic" speech is [now] replaced by peevish insults and a coarse Cockney accent'.[64]

As for Daggett, whether his name is merely a reminder of what initiates the violent chain of events depicted in *Unforgiven* (that is, in relation to Quick Mike's insulted manhood) or is a comment on his own sexual impotency remains unclear. However, it is important to note that Big Whiskey's sheriff, prone to such psychotic outbursts, is also an unmarried man who, without the traditional domesticating image of the female, is building a house as unstable as his temper.

Reading Daggett in this fashion supports Grist's popular contention that male violence in the film can be explained by a lack of sexual fulfilment.[65] Such is similarly suggested when, in an attempt to lure Logan into a share of the bounty, Munny states that they had done killings for money in the past: 'Yeah', replies the now settled Logan, gazing past Munny at his wife, 'we *thought* we was doin' it for money.' A broad observation of the film in this regard would surmise that the sexually fulfilled Logan proves incapable of killing, whereas the sexual unfulfilled Munny proves the opposite. This observation is borne out in the narrative when Logan attempts to shoot Davey. Crouching from a vantage point high above a valley, he has the cowboy clearly in the sight of his Spencer rifle, but cannot bring himself to pull the trigger. As I shall discuss in more detail below, the murder of Davey will be left to Munny, who has no such moral scruples.

V

Big Whiskey itself is certainly foreboding and is worth discussing in relation to *Unforgiven*'s revisionist status. Dark, murky and ramshackle, its denizens scurry about its mud-sodden streets, all the while cowering under a seemingly unending barrage of thunderstorms. The principal economy seems to be based on booze and 'billiards' at Greeley's Saloon.[66] It constitutes a repudiation of Turner's historical image of the pioneering community as vanguard in the westward progress of Anglo-American civilisation. As Greenberg has it: 'the railroad stops here.'[67] On the whole, Big Whiskey goes some way towards vindicating Slotkin's contention that the 'gunfighter' narrative borrows the stylistic elements of film noir for its dominant aesthetic. Here is the conclusion of Greenberg's revisionist descriptive:

> No church is seen in Big Whiskey, nor God mentioned. The daunting milieu presented by David Peoples' script exists in a kind of moral pre-history, where raw aggression is regularly answered by talion vengeance. *Macbeth* and *Lear* are not far from the conception.[68]

Other scholars have understood Big Whiskey in intertextual terms, suggesting that it follows in a similar vein to Eastwood's other mythic frontier townships, most notably the coastal settlement of Lago in *High Plains Drifter*. Lago is a ramshackle community that houses corrupt and murderous citizens, and whose buildings Eastwood's mysterious avenger famously has painted red and renamed 'Hell' following his instigation of a brutal, climactic massacre. The Drifter is Eastwood's first response to Leone's direction of him as No Name, although this time the metaphorical associations of him with death have become literal. Jim Kitses suggests that, with Big Whiskey, as in 'Leone's West, savagery has invaded the community'.[69] Plantinga supports this view, remarking that when the audience is first introduced to the township, 'they find a corrupt version of American society, driven by a capitalism blind to humane values . . . [protecting] private property at the expense of human rights'.[70] One might be forgiven for seeing in all this a revisionist repudiation of the triumphal myth of the pioneering community. But we should ask the question: how far does this aspect of *Unforgiven* really lend itself to an increased sense of critical awareness of mythological values in the genre as a whole?

I have already discussed *Stagecoach* in relation to Schatz's attempt to establish proof of an evolutionary model within the Western. We might remind ourselves that he sees in its narrative an essentially positive view on the synthesis between civilisation and wilderness. His overall formula assumes that a greater sense of 'optimism' and social values is to be found in Ford's earlier Westerns like *Stagecoach* than they are in the 'cynicism' of later films like *Liberty Valance*.[71] As I have already suggested, however, the historical chronology of a genre is no guarantee of linear shifts in cultural mood, much less of an evolutionary schema. This has been argued to devastating effect by Gallagher, who dismisses Schatz's 'extended' but thoroughly 'invidious' comparison between the two films' depictions of civilisation as proof of any such evolution within Ford's corpus.[72] Gallagher inverts the terms within which Schatz regards these two Fordian communities. He declares that in *Stagecoach*, 'civilisation is corrupting', and, furthermore, that 'in malodorous, dirty, sleazy Lordsburg and Tonto, full of the mean, intolerant, aggressive people . . . one finds nothing of the idealism, progressivism, and enlightenment shared by virtually everyone in *Liberty Valance*'s Shinbone'.[73] Such observations are partly justified when one recalls *Stagecoach*'s townships in any detail: the mean streets of Lordsburg, host to three brutal murders courtesy of Ringo, do not hold up too well to Schatz's assertion that *Stagecoach* 'offers the promise of an ideal frontier community'.[74]

Despite providing a more comprehensive view of Tonto and Lordsburg than Schatz, Gallagher might well be accused of over-simplifying the community of Shinbone to best suit his own argument. Indeed, it must be admitted that it is difficult to marry his utopian vision of 'progressivism and enlightenment' with what we see on the screen. After all, Shinbone is a place where prospective visitors are mugged and viciously beaten on their way in via stagecoach; where a comically inept Marshal (Andy Devine) is utterly powerless to prevent Liberty Valance (Lee Marvin) and his cronies from running wild; and where the ostensible hero, Tom Doniphon (John Wayne), seems quite content to let it all go on without a singular care for the community of which he is nominally a part. His willingness to shoot Valance over something as trivial as a steak while turning a blind-eye to the thug's brutal 'stand and deliver' terror tactics, is surely testament not to a hero, but to a selfish individual in a similarly selfish and lawless community.

It is not my intention here to intensely scrutinise these specific readings, but offering brief comparative analyses of these frontier communities as they are presented in two major Westerns from both the so-called classical and revisionist phases of the genre, respectively, together with their relation to *Unforgiven*'s Big Whiskey (not forgetting *Drifter*'s Lago), reveals two things above all else. First, it gives further lie to the theory of the evolution of the Western, specifically defined here through Schatz's belief that 'as the [Western] formula was refined through repetition . . . the society becomes more insulated and self-serving'.[75] On the contrary, all the townships mentioned above – Lago, Tonto, Lordsburg, Shinbone – appear to be 'self-serving', and Big Whiskey is surely not as irredeemable as Lago. Secondly, these readings suggest that the Western (as its best efforts make clear) is a genre acutely aware that the domestication of the wilderness – the very mantra of triumphalist and progressive frontier mythology – is never a straightforward process. Moreover, like the community in *The Searchers*, they suggest that Anglo-American civilisation itself is flawed. That it is, in other words, a fertile ground for engendering and then propagating the sort of savage elements that it would otherwise claim to have expunged following the settling of the frontier and denied through its exceptionalism.

These descriptives as offered give weight to my suggestion that the Western expresses the paradox that lies at the heart of the myth. That is to say, the frontier is both Garden and Desert. Savagery has not so much 'invaded' the community, as Kitses suggests, rather, it was always already there, brought along by the so-called emissaries of progress themselves. What Plantinga describes as a 'corrupt version of American society' is not particularly a revisionist corrective, therefore, it is an aspect of US history that the Western has always articulated, sometimes only by mere implication, at other times, as in *The Ox-Bow Incident*, where justice gives over to fascism in the form of a lynch mob, it is rendered in explicit terms.

Although I have thus far argued for the existentialist nature of *Unforgiven*, it is worth mentioning that both Kitses and Plantinga impress the 'Americanness' of the scene where Daggett beats Bob to a bloody pulp: it is Independence Day with US flags lining the shop fronts along Big Whiskey's main street, significantly held in frame behind Bill, establishing him as the New World authority against Bob's Old World 'Englishness', which easily translates into cultural 'otherness'.[76] If, indeed, the Western is to be understood as a mythologised version of US history in microcosm, and if the frontier communities under discussion here are anything to go by, then the genre's attitude towards the birth of the nation is none too flattering, expressed as it is on a basis of exploitation, violent intimidation and theft.

VI

Foremost among the exploited in Big Whiskey are the prostitutes managed by Skinny Desbois (Anthony James), proprietor of Greeley's. Alice and the rest of the prostitutes directly under her charge are regarded by all as Desbois' property. After Delilah has been assaulted by Mike, Desbois shows Daggett a 'lawful contract', declaring that Delilah represents 'an investment of capital' that, as a result of injuries, now constitutes 'damaged property'. Tuska relates that history has taught us that 'women on the frontier had to endure all sorts of hardships' and, in direct reference to the Western, suggests that 'the kind of personal fortitude it required has hardly been represented'.[77] The depiction of the prostitutes in *Unforgiven* would seem to indicate a nod in this direction, and in fact Eastwood has been praised for foregrounding the plight of the 'women of Big Whiskey'.

In appearing to take seriously the issue of the dehumanising of women, the assault on Delilah is to be 'regarded as a business matter pure and simple'.[78] Daggett's administered punishment – seven horses to be given as recompense by Quick Mike and Davey Boy to Desbois, *not* Delilah – underlines this, and is proposed after the saloon owner's callous appeal to Daggett that 'nobody's gonna pay money for a cut-up whore!' The exchange between sheriff and pimp holds the former in a close-up as he knowingly utters the word, 'property'; thus does Daggett pronounce a sacred shibboleth of the United States – the right to private property. In this case, however, this property right is at the expense of Delilah's rights as an individual. She is regarded as a commodity, equivalent to a 'ham-strung cow pony', to be paid for by her attacker's own commodities in turn.

One could justifiably regard Alice's outright refusal of Davey's apparently genuine effort at recompense (having already compensated Desbois as ordered by Daggett, he offers his last, best horse to Delilah) as morally righteous. To reduce the assault on Delilah to the amoral economic concerns of the male-dominated power structure in Big Whiskey would be to legitimate the female's perceived commodity status. It is a suggestion that Alice deems to be an outright insult. 'A pony!? She ain't got no face no more and you wanna give her a pony!?' This alone does not make *Unforgiven* a feminist (let alone revisionist) narrative, however, as Kitses rightly asserts, to see in this act 'evidence of a praiseworthy independence and nascent feminism is to overlook its consequences', which are that Alice is acting out of vengeance 'for the most despised of women'.[79] Indeed, it soon becomes apparent that Alice's vengeance is not so much designed for Delilah's benefit as it is for herself; a displacement of impotent rage for all the years that men have abused and degraded her. When Alice and the other prostitutes pool their money into the bounty, Silky (Beverley Elliot) asks Alice, 'If Delilah don't care one way or the other, what're you so riled about?' Alice retorts sharply, 'Just because we let them smelly assholes ride us like horses, don't mean we gotta let 'em brand us like horses!' Alice may not be greedy for money and the commodity value of 'property', but the vindictiveness of her intentions shows that she too fails to transcend the vengeful spiral of violence that engulfs the film's male characters. Kitses condenses her narrative purpose thus:

> It is Alice's thirst for blood that triggers the cycle of violence, the expanding arc of savagery and death that structures the film's action – the brutal beatings and messy executions finally culminating in the ... finale's slaughter. 'We all got it coming': the design of the film is to show how violence begets violence, how the appetite for blood grows.[80]

Kitses continues in relation to Davey's rejected offer of a horse with the insightful observation that 'Alice is aghast that such is being volunteered [but] how much might such a fine animal be worth towards a new life for Delilah? The question does not arise in the context of the thousand dollars the women have amassed as a reward.'[81] Both Kitses and Plantinga rightly draw attention to this important episode in the narrative, and are probably correct in describing Davey's offer of his best horse to Delilah as a genuine act of 'penance', but in suggesting (as Plantinga does) that this is an offer that 'the women angrily reject' is to provide an over-simplification of this scene's significance.[82] In a similar misreading, Ed Andrechuck notes that, 'even the prostitutes, especially their leader Strawberry Alice and the disfigured Delilah react with their own unforgiving sense of frontier justice by calling in the gunmen'.[83] A detailed look at the shot construction of this scene lends itself to a different interpretation.

During the women's refusal of Davey's offer of 'penance', and between the constant barrage of mud and shit that Alice cajoles them into pelting him with, a series of cut-away shots focuses on Delilah and Davey. Neither Plantinga nor Kitses mention these shots in their analyses, although they are, one feels, fundamental to the meaning that both of them seek to draw from this scene. The sequence of shots reveals that, significantly, Delilah is not involved in this attack on Davey who, although not completely innocent, at least tried to hold back Mike once he realised that the latter was cutting into Delilah's face with his knife. If Alice was acting out for her friend's welfare then surely she would respond as Delilah does, as Delilah seems to *want*, with a quiet and poignant dignity whose obvious compassion rests with the forgiving rather than the 'unforgiving' that Andrechuck suggests. In fact, Delilah looks ashamed as a number of quick shot/reverse shots establish a stolen glance between her and Davey as the latter, guilt-ridden and humiliated, casts his dejected gaze toward the ground and rides away. The next shot holds Delilah in a medium close-up as she similarly averts her gaze from Davey's receding figure, and turns to walk inside the saloon and away from this depressing spectacle.

The role of women in *Unforgiven* is not technically restricted to the prostitutes, although it is fair to say that, despite their dehumanised status as 'property', they (more specifically, Alice) constitute the film's only active female agency. One is thinking here, specifically, of Logan's Native American wife Sally Two-Trees (Cherrilene Cardinal). If one points to the positives of Sally's inclusion in the narrative (as many scholars have), one must also point out the fact that she still *does not* have a voice. She acts as a kind of thematic match to Claudia, a silent presence to her structuring absence, if you will, but *not* a character in and of herself. For his part, Logan appears to need no real encouragement in deciding to leave Sally and his pastoral idyll, preferring instead to head off with Munny on what Sally seems to rightly recognise from the outset as a fool's errand (giving Munny her 'evil eye' glance and touching his rifle butt forlornly before he rides away with her husband). And as he leaves, Logan is acting *exactly* as the genre (and its audience for that matter) expects: his love for money/Munny, whichever, easily overrides his love for his wife, to whom he never even bids farewell.

One should reiterate also that Alice wilfully imbricates what agency she does possess with the male-dominated cycles of bloody revenge. Plantinga asserts that the role of women with regard to issues of sexuality and power in *Unforgiven* is explored from diverse perspectives:

> [Woman is depicted as] the Redeeming Feminine (allied with nineteenth-century evangelical Christianity), as prostitute and property, as threats to male power and the male ego, as victims of patriarchal capitalism, and as a utopian subgroup valorised for its communal practices.[84]

As discussed thus far, I concur with most of the 'roles' that Plantinga assigns to women in *Unforgiven*. I would, however, seriously query his attribution to the women of the role of 'utopian subgroup'. To be fair, Plantinga does concede shortly after this statement that 'the women of *Unforgiven* are either powerless to prevent violence . . . or complicit in it'. He goes on to suggest that the film 'considers the redemptive power of the feminine' before dismissing this as a 'possibility of real change'.[85] Grist would disagree on this point, stressing that Delilah be allied with Davey and the Kid as representative of a younger generation devoid of 'the destructive attitudes of the older generation [representing] in its margins . . . an implicit faith in the future'.[86] To my mind the role of female agency in the film is hardly revised from most of the more prominent Westerns that preceded it. However, *if any* characters embody the attribute of 'utopian subgroup', then Grist is probably right in naming Delilah and Davey. I argue, though, that such 'faith in the future' is not manifest in the narrative and is purposefully placed at its 'margins'. (To paraphrase Mitchell, we might say – where this text's power resides.)

Davey would appear to genuinely seek forgiveness and Delilah would seem to genuinely offer it in her dignified refusal of vengeance. Despite largely denying her a narrative voice, the film is at pains to include shots of her scarred face that in many ways 'speak' her story. This is a point well made by Grist, who writes that such a 'device . . . lends her the function of a silent moral chorus'.[87] In fact, for every mention of revenge or spectacle of violence displayed in the narrative, there is an accompanying cut-away shot depicting Delilah, never approving, always despondent and sad. She is powerless, torn between the gratitude she feels towards her fellow prostitutes and fear, both of the male-dominated power structure of Big Whiskey and, indeed, of Alice if ever she was to criticise her motives.

McGee also makes an interesting point when he writes that 'Delilah's facial expressions . . . suggest that, without knowing how to articulate it, she is looking for something else besides revenge, something [where] a different kind of social relationship is possible.'[88] Delilah had attributed something like 'a different kind of social relationship' to Munny and his deceased wife (although initially, of course, she assumes that Claudia is alive as Munny still speaks of her in the present tense). This is suggested in Munny's brief but poignant exchange with Delilah, which takes place soon after his recovery from a violent fever and an equally violent beating he sustains at the hands of Daggett. The conversation between them hints at the possibility of romance as Delilah, conscious of her facial scars, shyly offers Munny a 'free one' as a down-payment on the $1,000 reward. Although he has clearly been looking at her with desire, Munny declines her offer (both Logan and the Kid have accepted similar such down-payments with the other women already). Assuming that it is because of her scars rather than his puritanical abstinence, Delilah covers up and looks hurt, 'I didn't mean . . . with me.' Munny immediately attempts to redress his unintentional insult, 'It ain't like that at all. You're a beautiful woman an' . . . if I was to want a free one, I guess I'd want you more than them others. I can't have no free one on account of my wife.' By insinuating that his wife is still alive I suggest that Munny has precluded this possibility and, by extension, *Unforgiven*'s narrative has precluded any such feminised 'utopian subgroup' as a site of potential social change.

The role of women in *Unforgiven*, like the film's pretensions to so-called ethnic revisionism – specifically, the African American Logan and, once again, his Native American wife Sally – I relate to what Jameson describes as 'the artificial reconstruction of the voice'.[89] Here Jameson alludes to narratives typically repressed by the ideology of the dominant class: 'the oppositional voices of black or ethnic cultures, women's and gay literature, "naive" or marginalised folk art, and the like'.[90] According to Jameson, these oppositional 'voices' are 'for the most part stifled and reduced to silence, marginalised, [their] own utterances scattered to the winds, or re-appropriated in their turn by the hegemonic culture'.[91] It remains for 'the individual text, the individual cultural artefact [through the] pluralistic rediscovery of other isolated social groups', to rewrite 'these utterances in terms of their essentially polemic and subversive strategies'.[92] This would, Jameson contends, 'restore them to their proper place in the dialogical system of social classes [and] restore vitality to ... the aesthetic realm'.[93] My contention is that *Unforgiven* simply does not do this, and actually ends up promoting what Jameson refers to as 'cultural universalisation', which 'implies the repression of the oppositional voice, and the illusion that there is only one genuine "culture"'.[94]

My reasons for using Jameson here are primarily to offer a counter-argument to McVeigh's post-modernist and evolutionary reading that suggests that *Unforgiven* 'contains multitudes' and that it 'attempts to speak to and of many different perspectives'.[95] For the most part, as far as I see it, *Unforgiven* merely pays lip-service to the inclusion of erstwhile elided 'voices', while actually assigning them marginalised roles that allow only for the emergence of a single discourse, that of the gunfighter as an instance of 'cultural universalisation'; rather than saying it 'contains multitudes', we might say that it *re*-contains multitudes. Of course, *Unforgiven*, like any other text, betrays itself in its assertion of a single, 'stable' meaning, it is just that any such argument must be read here *against the grain*, it is not organic to the text as it is with, say, *The Searchers*, and it does not seem intentional on the part of the filmmaker (or else, if that were the intention, then the film must be read as a failure). This is hardly *the* example of introspective generic revisionism.

In my reading, the women exist only to serve the greater need of that version of the mythic narrative with which *Unforgiven* concerns itself. Of course, Logan, as an African American, is equally embroiled in the gunfighter discourse. In this respect, the narrative displays the opposite of post-modern plurality, attempting, as indicated, to re-contain multitudes. The marginalised voice is, as a consequence, denied the subversive free-play typically associated with a post-modernist *jouissance*. Indeed, for all the narrative screen-time afforded women in *Unforgiven*, their voice remains surprisingly marginalised, silenced or, as with Alice, 're-appropriated' into the 'hegemonic culture' of Big

Whiskey's male-dominated power structure; their presence seeking to re-affirm rather than undermine masculinity and the mythology of redemptive violence. Let us further consider some of these assertions.

The concept of the Redeeming Feminine is worth discussing in relation to Munny's deceased wife. I have already mentioned that Claudia is established in the narrative through her non-appearance as a structuring absence for the ex-gunfighter (a woman who, in life, supposedly cured Munny of his drunken violence). In this regard, and combined with his vigils at her graveside, *Unforgiven*'s Munny suggests a homage to Nathan Brittles (John Wayne) in Ford's *She Wore a Yellow Ribbon*. Aside from this intertextual reference, Munny is just as keen to impress Claudia's redemptive powers on his two young children. 'Your departed mother, God rest her, showed me the error of my ways'; and 'remember how the spirit of your departed maw watches over you'. However, unlike Brittles, and despite always speaking fondly *of* Claudia, Munny never speaks *to* her, even when alone at her graveside. The 23 April 1984 shooting script with Eastwood's revisions (eventually abandoned in favour of Peoples' original 1976 screenplay) bearing the title, *The William Munny Killings*, is very revealing on this issue:

> The headstone is under a couple of shade trees fifty yards from the sod hut. Munny is sitting on a rock under the trees looking at the headstone and he has on a cheap black suit now. He twists the hat, tormented . . . and he starts to say something out loud but he can't because men don't talk to stones. So finally he gets up, slumped in defeat, and he puts a little bouquet of flowers on the grave and he turns away unhappily.[96]

Women in *Unforgiven* are largely assigned symbolic roles within a masculine mythos. The image of the female Munny can idolise, whereas a real woman proves to be a problematic issue. For instance, when Munny wakes from his fever to see Delilah nursing him he declares, 'I thought you was an angel.' He thereby identifies her as a religious idol, a Redeeming Feminine.

In another scene, Munny holds up a worn photograph of Claudia, regards her image (more idolatry) and then observes his old Starr .44 pistol. He puts down the photograph and picks up the gun, considering it intently. Like Tompkins suggests of the Western hero in general, Munny has now 'jettisoned' the feminine in preference for the role of the gunfighter. Even parental responsibility fails to persuade Munny to forgo a chance at reclaiming his old identity. He is not for farm labouring, and his attitude to the pastoral realm echoes Shane's unconvincing line to Joey: 'A man's gotta be what a man's gotta be. You can't break the mold, I tried it and it didn't work for me.' The point here is precisely that the few words that either Shane or Munny utter in this regard prove unconvincing; neither really tries to change and yet, in the course of favouring the gunfighter identity, both narratives betray the inadequacies of such a figure in general.

Tompkins further underscores the genre's apparent refusal of the feminine through the image of Eastwood's earlier role in *Josey Whales*. Here, the feminine is conceived within terms of Evangelical Christianity:

> [S]trength counts more than prayer ... when Clint Eastwood sees the homemade cross he has put on the grave of his son fall over, he picks up a gun from the charred ruins of his house ... and starts shooting maniacally at a tree, one two three four five six seven eight nine ten times, every shot ramming home his rejection of Christian forgiveness as a way of dealing with injury, and promising the audience more violence to come.[97]

Tompkins' description of Whales, or, rather, Eastwood, for she makes no distinction between character and actor, provides a strong contrast to the initial depictions of Munny (although I shall argue below that such a contrast is eventually collapsed).

The lure of the weapon – the way of the gun – becomes too great an existential pull for Munny, who is in the torturous process of questioning his very identity. In fact, it would appear that any possible hope of redress is wilfully closed off in preference to the stable subjectivity promised by the simplicity of the myth of the gunfighter. This is suggested from early on in the narrative when, having initially rejected the Kid's offer to go on the bounty hunt with him to Big Whiskey, the camera holds Munny's face as he gazes longingly after the receding image of the Kid. And as the Kid disappears over the horizon it can be said that, along with him, goes what Munny feels is his last, best hope for his future: his past. In this, Munny is looking longingly into his past because his future, surrounded by fever-ridden hogs and condemned to abject failure, is evidently too depressing an eventuality to even contemplate. Munny and, by extension, Eastwood, is now 'just a broke-down old pig farmer', and that is simply too much for him (or us) to bear. So, far from a more progressive narrative such as *The Gunfighter*, which sees the protagonist, Jimmy Ringo (Gregory Peck), tragically discover all too late that his identity resides in the importance of his family as his future, Munny seems tragically all too eager to abandon his family in favour of his past and his own selfish needs.

Initially, *Unforgiven* seems intent on a providing a revisionist account of the gunfighter through an ironic reversal of the more typical image of the Eastwood hero. The first such moment establishes Munny's woeful inadequacy with his pistol. Inverting Whales' brutal efficiency, Munny aims at a tin can and misses shot after shot after shot before finally relenting and blasting it into oblivion with a shotgun. Such pathetic displays of marksmanship, combined with his parodic inability to mount his horse and his advanced years, all work to emasculate the tradition of Eastwood's star persona as it has been established through a character like Whales or The Preacher. Munny's emasculation is such that even his children, all shame-faced, wonder aloud to each other whether 'paw really used to kill folks?' The fact that the narrative seems at pains to undermine this image is one of the main reasons that caused so many critics and scholars to hail its revisionist status. However, I argue that such undermining is depicted in *Unforgiven* solely for the purposes of engendering our desire for the return of the gunfighter. Munny's post-gunfighter existence is predicated on economic failure, a deceased wife, single parenthood and fever-ridden hogs. As such, it does not posit a workable (much less attractive) alternative to the myth of the gunfighter. In other words, and to borrow psychoanalytical terminology, it serves only to encourage the audience's longing for the 'return of the repressed', for the re-emergence of the uber-masculine on-screen persona of Clint Eastwood. We desire the return of No Name, The Preacher, Josey Whales, even the diabolical Drifter (*even* 'Dirty' Harry Callaghan), anyone but the sorry figure cut by William Munny.

By abandoning farm and family, Munny is essentially abandoning the woman's 'iron rule' that has kept him 'domesticated'. This surely confirms my above suggestions that women be read as some kind of symbol, icons to be either venerated or deplored, but never *real*, and all the while thoroughly emasculating to a mythic manhood. So Munny wanders back into the wilderness to, ironically, become the protector of another woman – Delilah, in her symbolic role as the proverbial damsel in distress, the captive of savage villains.

The account of Delilah's tragic episode with Mike is itself exaggerated beyond all recognition, first by the Kid in an effort to entice Munny, and then by Munny in an effort to entice Logan. The tales of her scars, although clearly severe enough, escalate out of all proportion to their reality. This Chinese-whisper effect is compounded by Munny, 'Cut her eyes out, cut her tits off, cut her fingers off . . . everythin' but her cunny, I guess.' This wilful collusion in exaggeration provides an important foretaste of *Unforgiven*'s particular narrative concern with the process of mythmaking: how fact is embellished and transformed into myth even as it is unfolding. Plantinga pointedly notes that 'when Munny and Ned actually meet Delilah and see that her wounds have been greatly exaggerated, the two continue their killing plans nonetheless. Apparently, their own momentum is enough to motivate them at this point.'[98] (I argue below that the lack of effect that this revelation has on Munny, Ned or the Kid relates to a concept of them being 'stuck' in the mythic roles already prepared for them by the myths of the past.) Perhaps more explicitly, such embellishment acts to justify in the minds of the bounty-hunters their plans to murder Davey and Mike. 'Well, I guess they had it coming', becomes the film's most repeated and least convincing statement. It resonates with a typical Westerner's attitude: his love for the gun and the image of the gunfighter far outweigh his love for a woman (who acts as a mere cursory reason for his desire for violent actions).

We might also remind ourselves that Logan's idyllic farmstead and wife (the diametric opposite of Munny's fever-ridden swine and dilapidated adobe hut) similarly fails as impetus to discourage him from leaving for Big Whiskey with his old partner. Logan is also clearly still in thrall to the image of the gunfighter of his youth. 'You still got the Spencer rifle?' Munny asks Logan. Logan grins back at him and boasts 'Yeah, an' I could still hit a bird in the eye flying.'

VII

John G. Cawelti once famously stated that, if established in the correct manner, the Western hero's act of violence becomes 'graceful, aesthetic and, even, fun'.[99] *Unforgiven*'s manner of depicting violence has, justifiably, received a lot of scholarly attention and not all of it is in consonance, either with each other or with Cawelti's assertion that Western violence is 'fun'. One scholar who has hailed the film's revisionist stance on violence is Scott D. Emmert. Emmert includes *Unforgiven* in a group of Westerns where 'violence affects all the characters negatively; rather than an unambiguous solution, their complicity in violent acts becomes a moral burden that the characters must bear'.[100] Quite apart from the dubious assumption that violence in Westerns is typically 'an unambiguous solution' to issues raised in the narrative, Emmert's assertion that *Unforgiven* stands as an ideologically revisionist 'repudiation of violence' is not as convincing as it may at first seem.[101]

It is true that we might feel little sympathy when the Kid executes the brutal and unrepentant Mike, ignominious as his fate is – unarmed and while sitting on a latrine (which, in a perverse sense, might just be considered 'fun'); however, Munny's murder of Davey is something else entirely. It emphasises the point that Davey *did not* 'have it coming' at all. Any moral justification for his killing is therefore removed. And it is with undeniable disappointment that Delilah reacts upon learning of Munny's and the Kid's act of cold-blooded murder. 'I didn't think they'd really do it . . . that kid . . . he's just a . . . boy. And that other one, Bill, being so true to his wife . . .' Alice finally corrects her misperception, 'He don't have no wife, not above ground, anyhow.'[102] *Unforgiven* is certainly deliberate in making this one thing clear: Davey's fate is both protracted and painful to watch. It is established thematically through his aforementioned offer of 'penance', and is articulated formally through the shot construction of his death scene. As the camera lingers on Munny's own uncomfortable reactions to what he has just done, Davey's forlorn cries for help echo throughout the Bar-T canyon. The Kid, beginning to doubt the very myths of heroism through which his understanding of the world is mediated and, in an effort to convince himself as much as anybody else, cries out, 'Yeah. Well. You . . . you shouldn't of cut up no whores, you son-of-a-bitch!'

In consonance with Emmert, Grist elaborates further on the issue of violence in *Unforgiven*:

> This emphasis on the disturbing nature of violence contests its more familiar generic representation. While most Westerns deal with the ideological motivations and consequences of violence, far fewer examine the destructive reality, the actual effects of violent acts. Since the sixties,

violence in the Western has been represented with differing degrees of explicitness, but the intention has rarely been to convey pain.[103]

Grist alludes here in particular to the blood-drenched films of Sam Peckinpah and to Eastwood's earlier collaborations with Leone, where, as I have already suggested, violence was often amplified and excessive so as to appear comic or even 'fun'. By contrast, Grist considers violence in *Unforgiven* as 'brutal, dreadful, squalid: anything but noble or ennobling'.[104] Such an account, of course, assumes a pure archetype of the hero's code that *Unforgiven* purposefully deconstructs. Moreover, it also assumes that such a thing ever existed within the genre in the first place. On this issue, Plantinga correctly notes that 'only the most simplistic Westerns ... draw an unproblematic distinction between the hero's good violence and the villain's bad'.[105] He then cites (among others) *The Searchers* as an example of narrative complexity, praising the film for its 'examination of the hero's motives and/or his use of violence'.[106]

Grist's account of the killings of Mike and Davey, and his assessment of *Unforgiven*'s overall attitude towards violence up till this point, is supported by McVeigh who, as I have already mentioned, reads *Unforgiven* as a post-modern deconstruction of the archetypal narrative of *Shane*. I have also mentioned how he insists that *Shane*, of all the descendants of what Slotkin terms 'renaissance' Westerns, marks the most radical shift in the depiction of the gunfighter. Accordingly, Shane is the first of the existential heroes who 'establishes himself in the role', and whose own chivalrous values became progressively undermined within the genre – 'along with the possibility of heroic leadership' – in the wake of Kennedy's assassination.[107] And such pronounced cultural pessimism was, according to McVeigh, 'compounded by American involvement in Vietnam'.[108] I suggested above that I feel this interpretation gives too much credence to the conjectural assumption of a prophetic political–ideological connection between Shane and Kennedy. If anything, I feel *Unforgiven* more likely has its thematic roots in that derivative of the renaissance Western that Slotkin termed 'psychological', more to do with the personal traumas of a film like Raoul Walsh's *Pursued* (1947), than it does with the wider historical issues of US settlement that concern a film like *Shane*. According to Slotkin, the psychological Western's main focus was on the motivation of the protagonist and was 'accompanied by the de-emphasis of the social/historical formulas of motivation'.[109] This interpretation is supported by Kitses, who suggests that 'Eastwood's ultimate iconic meaning generally has to do with an image of masculinity rather than national ethos, with a fusion of the dirty Westerner and Dirty Harry, figures in an existential landscape.'[110] He also reinforces masculinity as the narrative's catalyst, suggesting in a wilful play on Freud that *Unforgiven*'s chief axiom might just be 'masculinity and its discontents'.[111]

By its climax, *Unforgiven*'s plot has also segued into the 'revenger' plot. This plot type typified the narratives of the Westerns directed by Anthony Mann, and Kitses informs us that '[c]haracteristically, the Mann hero is a revenge hero'.[112] Thus, it is with Mann's existential heroes rather than Stevens' introspective Shane that we can forge the strongest thematic-narrative link, or a 'point of origin' as McVeigh has it.[113] In a further link with Munny, Kitses remarks on 'the schizophrenic style of the [revenge] hero, the violent explosions of passion alternating with precarious moments of quiet reflection'.[114] This is not to say that this descriptive *does not* apply to Shane, for indeed it does; it also fits numerous others, Ethan Edwards especially. My point of contention is the singular nature of McVeigh's assertion of *Shane* as a 'point of origin' for the Western and for the films that followed its release.

Furthermore, McVeigh's over-emphasis on an ideological analysis based on political allegory has the effect of underplaying *Unforgiven*'s own sense of generic intertextuality, which is (paradoxically) something that he claims for his reading. Indeed, it is where his analysis is at its strongest:

> The only positive aspect in the whole cycle of violence is the Schofield Kid's breaking out from it when confronted with its reality. This is another element of the deconstruction of Shane, or more precisely Joey. The Kid is fascinated by stories of the 'Old Days' in a way reminiscent of Joey's hero worship of Shane ... His break from the cycle is completed in the symbolic act of giving up the Schofield pistol, the icon ... by which legend would have 'remembered' his exploits. The stark realities from which the myth grew affect the Kid as it does the audience into re-examining the grounds for their fascination with screen violence and Western mythology.[115]

Intertextual referencing is, of course, nothing new in the Western and nor is a critiquing of the mythology through which it finds its terms of expression. After all, Ford sought just such a critique through an undermining of the genre's semiotic codes in *Fort Apache*. In the end, Colonel Thursday's reckless arrogance leads to the slaughter of his command at the hands of Cochise's Apaches. The film is itself often regarded in terms of allegory, as Ford's version of 'Custer's Last Stand'. Indeed, the images we see on-screen are replaced in the end by the 'official' history of what we might call 'Thursday's Last Stand'. Through the romance of a Remington-style painting, together with the collusion of Captain York, Thursday's memory – and that of the slaughtered regiment – are preserved and immortalised through this heroic re-imagining of the historical record. With York remarking that the painting is 'Exact in every detail', the myth of heroic leadership is re-endorsed with no small trace of irony after its exposure as fallacious. (We might remind ourselves that *Fort Apache* was released years before *Shane* even went into pre-production and so, too, it must be added, before Ford's own *Liberty Valance* supposedly initiated the era of the so-called revisionist Westerns.)

Ford was, in the words of Mitchell, one of 'the most incisive analysts of the genre's capacity to alter history', and in this capacity, he suggests, resides the belief that myths do not misrepresent, but 'actively comprise history'.[116] *Liberty Valance* provides another strong example of Ford's attitude to myth and history. It exposes the lie that the eastern 'dude' lawyer, Stoddard, managed to kill the notorious outlaw, Liberty Valance, in a fair shootout, in the process taming the town of Shinbone and ensuring both the coming of civilisation and his own future career as a Washington senator. The film's (perhaps also the Western's) most quoted phrase – 'When the legend becomes fact, print the legend' – actually belies the fact that the film does precisely the opposite. This is intentional on Ford's part, of course, and it exposes the unpalatable fact behind the official history that informed the myth of the frontier. But it goes much further than this, with Mitchell suggesting that fact and legend are 'mutually sustaining imperative gestures':

> The legend insidiously belies Ransom Stoddard's self-righteous touting of law over brute force, in an irony that draws attention to the incoherence of the Western's customary resolution (with masculine violence forced to establish the terms by which violence can be declared illegitimate). Yet Ford . . . delights in how such lies do not simply misrepresent but actively comprise history, and refuses in *Liberty Valance* to allow fact instead to stand in for the legend. The historical record, after all, embodies a legacy of powerful lies more than of countless irrelevant truths.[117]

The ending of *Liberty Valance* is, I believe, intentionally ambiguous. The film appears not to doubt the progressive elements of the creation of the promised Garden out of a Desert, as Hallie (Vera Miles) makes clear to her husband (even using the very terms laid out by Henry Nash Smith). Although the overall tone is, perhaps, ironic, with the train's smokestack polluting the Garden with its smog; the train is no longer the symbol of progress but one of Leo Marx's 'Machines' in the Garden.[118] Indeed, it would seem to suggest the coming of modernity as a historical necessity, as the *price* paid for progress.[119] However, with its monochrome photography, stage-set interiors rather than 'real' Western locations, ambivalence towards modernity and, by extension, civilisation, it is also a profoundly elegiac film. *Liberty Valance* seems concerned with mourning the loss of the generically endemic concept of wilderness itself.

Unforgiven's own self-conscious attempts at myth deconstruction and exploring the way history and myth inform each other are altogether more obvious. They are most particularly evident in the character of Beauchamp. As mentioned earlier, Beauchamp is the enthusiastic producer to the Kid's equally enthusiastic consumer of myths. He is initially engaged in writing the Duke's biography until Daggett beats Bob down both physically and, more significantly, psychologically. He thereby deconstructs the Duke's image as an heroic gunfighter in the most degrading of fashions: 'The *Duck* I says.' Grist writes in this regard:

> [Bill] corrects Beauchamp's floridly written description of English Bob's killing of Corky Corcoran. Where Beauchamp's account constructs English Bob as a gallant defender of women and heroically quick on the draw, Little Bill tells how a drunken English Bob had shot a powerless Corcoran in cold blood after Corcoran had shot himself in the toe and his pistol had exploded.[120]

Such vitriolic reassessment on the part of Daggett makes one wonder whether or not his account of what 'really happened' to Corky Two-Gun Corcoran (that is, that Bob shot Corcoran over a dispute regarding a woman) 'corrects' a falsity by finally revealing a true account, or is merely more self-serving mythology on his part. With his obvious delight in correcting Bob's tall tales, before subsequently going on to detail his own 'heroic' endeavours to an avid listener in Beauchamp, it is more likely that Daggett's stories are merely replacing one myth with another, more self-serving but, in the final analysis, just as fantastical. As an adjunct to this, Daggett's 'correction' of Bob's exploits also builds on the narrative's concern with masculinity and violence by linking alcoholism as a catalyst for aggressive action in men. It is a concern compounded when Munny responds to the Kid's constant nagging about what it was really like in the 'Old days'. 'I don't remember,' replies Munny. 'I was drunk most of the time.' Furthermore, such wilful collusion – the clichéd Western 'sit-in' between Bill and Beauchamp, subject and scribe, teacher and student – highlights a critical component in the Western's relation to myth and history: self-promotion of legend.

David Hamilton Murdoch points out that the various narratives that had developed from the myth of the heroic gunfighter were not the sole preserve of the eastern dime novelists or of 'yellow' journalists like Beauchamp. Such narratives were actually endorsed by many Westerners themselves who stood to benefit financially from either selling their own 'real-life' adventures or by writing their own 'genuine' accounts. In fact, 'virtually from the very beginning', he tells us, 'the real West took the myth and solemnly endorsed it'.[121] Murdoch continues:

> Journalistic excess was credited as truth, repetitions turned stories into folktales, wish-fulfilment made legends. Not centuries after their death, but within their lifetimes Daniel Boone was the torchbearer of civilisation in the wilderness, Kit Carson a superhuman scout and Jesse James the American Robin Hood.[122]

The critical analysis of Westerners' self-promotion is certainly an engaging aspect of *Unforgiven*'s narrative, but it is, as Mitchell puts it, 'hardly a new tack'.[123] With specific reference to *Liberty Valance* and *Unforgiven*, Mitchell insists that 'unlike Ford . . . who exposed how fully legend and fact create one another, Eastwood relies on a more conventional transition from initial debunking to mythic restoration'.[124] I would similarly seek to deny *Unforgiven*'s self-conscious deconstruction as evidence of an avowedly revisionist stance, also with reference to *Liberty Valance*, specifically through the figure of the gunfighter.

Plantinga (along with other scholars) seeks to make clear that Munny's and the Kid's murder of Davey and Mike, respectively, 'break every traditional rule for the hero's violence and are designed as a painful spectatorial experience'.[125] If this is so, then what is one to make of Tom Doniphon – the real man who shot Liberty Valance? Aiming at Valance unseen in the shadows of an alleyway, he assassinates the villain and thus initiates the fraudulent legend that grows up around Stoddard. 'Cold-blooded murder'. muses Doniphon beforehand, 'but I can live with it.' But, of course, his bitter life and lonely, marginalised death after Hallie leaves him for the 'heroic' Stoddard prove just the opposite. This might just be because, for the honourable Doniphon, his actions amount to what Plantinga insists on as *the* 'greatest of all Western cowardices, shooting someone in the back'.[126] I could answer this in turn by recourse to the scene from *The Searchers* where Ethan uses the unsuspecting Marty as bait in order to set an ambush for Futterman (Peter Mamakos). Ethan will go on to shoot the duplicitous Futterman and his two cohorts in the back. Of course, my point here is not to suggest that Munny's and the Kid's actions were honourable; rather, I am suggesting that *Unforgiven* should not be considered so formally or thematically revisionist in this particular respect. Westerns have always been replete with heroes interested only in profit or revenge no matter how ethically or otherwise it is obtained; men whose selfish purposes diminish any greater concern for civilisation that they might once have had. This analysis is supported by the events of the final shootout at Greeley's which, I suggest, undermines any such revisionist potential that the film may have initiated along the lines of a critical re-evaluation of the gunfighter's violence and its implications.

VIII

I shall now focus on the figure of the gunfighter in *Unforgiven*, specifically Munny's existential nature, by analysing the shootout at Greeley's and addressing Eastwood himself as a cultural icon and actor in the Western.

Upon hearing Little Sue's revelation of Logan's death, Munny lapses, regresses into his past of 'drink and wickedness'. The unforgiven and *unforgiving* reputation of his own legend re-emerges: 'a known thief and murderer, a man of notoriously vicious and intemperate disposition'. His regression to what he always was occurs the instant Sue repeats Logan's dying words to Daggett, that he was really 'William Munny out of Missouri . . . how he killed women and children . . . and was more cold-blooded than William Bonney, or Clay Allison, or the James brothers', and how he 'shot a US marshal in '73'. While Munny's association through reputation with such 'esteemed' company is being relayed by a frightened, tearful Sue, the camera holds a shot in close-up on the Kid's face, his gaze fixed firmly on Munny. We cut to a point-of-view shot from the Kid's perspective that reveals Munny gulping down whiskey, his last pretence of puritanical abstinence now finally abandoned. Despite having sworn to forgo violence following his slaying of Mike ('I'm not like you, Will'), the Kid's gaze remains one of sublime awe as he hands over his Schofield pistol to Munny at the latter's request. 'Don't worry, Kid,' says Munny, noting the Kid's apprehension. 'I'm not gonna kill you. You're the only friend I got.' While McVeigh quite fairly observes in this episode 'the only positive aspect in the whole cycle of violence', I would argue that this aspect of Munny's legend *still* holds appeal for the Kid. By extension, it appeals to us as well – Munny's legendary status threatens, or promises, to return. As enthusiasts of the Eastwood persona, we cannot wait to see it. Furthermore, I suggest that the film does little to dissuade us from this fascination with violence.

Unforgiven teases us, makes us wait in anticipation for the coming of this moment. We might lament Munny's personal failure, his atavistic regression, but the narrative has really been setting up this moment from the outset. We have followed Munny's tortured existence, been aligned with him throughout and, as the protagonist, we have come to care what happens to him. By riding into Big Whiskey on a dark, rain-swept night to indulge in 'vengeance duty', Munny will reward us with the realisation of our nightmare wish fulfilment. In addition, I contend that this wish fulfilment is *not* a Freudian assertion of our unconscious desires, for the deadly violence Munny unleashes at Greeley's receives social sanction on a fully-conscious narrative level.[127] Consider Sheriff Daggett. In order to justify Munny's actions, the film collapses his character from his position as complex arbiter of frontier justice into the stock-role of villain. With the narrative having spent so long trying to build up a balanced, somewhat sympathetic account of Daggett, any justification for his violent outbursts is finally undermined when, having caught Logan in his attempt to ride home, he indulges in wanton sadism. Under the thin guise of a police interrogation, Daggett tortures Logan to death by bull-whipping him, all the while cooing into his victim's ear: 'I'm gonna hurt you, not gentle like I've been doing, but bad . . .'[128]

Of course, this type of character is dramatically attractive in its own right, but warrants destruction at the hands of the hero. Consider, for example, Kitses' analysis of the villains that populate the Westerns of Anthony Mann:

> The insanity we sense in [the villainous] characters . . . derive from the rational and efficient way they break rules they are aware of and disdain. The attractiveness of these characters is that they are so purely out of joint . . . [N]aked power without a moral dimension, self-interest breeding totalitarianism – are persuasive arguments for the existence of evil. Faced with them, a society cannot but sanction force, killing if necessary,

the doer freed from blame by virtue of his instrumental role as vehicle for social justice.[129]

This astute piece of analysis recalls Tompkins' explanation of how the hero's violence against the villain receives moral justification. As discussed in Chapter 1, Tompkins writes that at a certain point 'retaliatory violence becomes not simply justifiable but imperative: now, we are made to feel, *not* to transgress the interdict against violence would be the transgression'.[130]

Daggett's violent outbursts – always threatening to spiral out of control and into hysteria – are seen here to have crystallised into a tyrannical but ultimately 'rational' use of brute force that lacks any moral or social sanction. Indeed, they can even be said to lack a *mythic* sanction, as even Beauchamp squirms and looks away from this violent spectacle. Once again, it is as if the reality of violence cannot be recuperated into the black-and-white morality of the chivalrous tales that Beauchamp actually writes. In turn, Daggett's abuse of Logan helps to sanction Munny's violent act of retribution. As if further justification were needed, Daggett has Logan's corpse propped up in an open coffin outside Greeley's in a spectacle akin to the aftermath of a racist lynch mob. A placard is shown hanging around the cadaver's neck: 'This is what we do to assassins around here.'

Grist, among others, has argued that the bull-whipping of Logan is, indeed, symptomatic of Anglo-America's racist legacy of slavery. He writes that 'the representation of [Logan's] oppression relates it to the history of American racism ... whipping [was] a traditional punishment for runaway slaves'.[131] This may well be true, but curiously enough the film does seem at pains to make little of the issue of Logan's race. I argue instead that our attitude towards his fate feeds into the main narrative concern with the figure of the gunfighter. Ergo, his untimely and brutal death echoes that of Davey's. Although not entirely blameless, neither Logan nor Davey are responsible for the acts to which they are fatally held to account. In the final instance, Logan is certainly innocent of the murder of which he is accused and, therefore, his fate rouses our deepest sympathies and desire for retribution. Furthermore, our desire is for Munny to administer it despite him being, at one and the same time, essentially responsible for Logan's death. It is at this point, I argue, that *Unforgiven* ultimately betrays its revisionist pretensions.

As we cut to the interior of Greeley's, Daggett is in the process of organising a posse to track down Munny and the Kid. Emboldened by hard liquor, Munny's masculinity has now been fully restored and, as he stands at the front door of the saloon, his shotgun symbolically erects in the foreground of the frame. In a carefully choreographed scene, and in what seems highly improbable considering the sad, incompetent figure Munny has presented thus far, he proceeds to dispatch Desbois, Daggett and three of the Sheriff's armed deputies with a consummate ease without receiving *any* wounds himself. In many ways, *Unforgiven*'s shootout is more fantastical, more improbable than is *Shane*'s. After all, Shane's competence as a gunfighter is never in doubt, and he is, at the very least, seriously injured in his fight with Wilson and the Rykers. Admittedly, while not being the display of superhuman speed we would expect to see from No Name or The Preacher, Munny's actions during the gunfight serve as an ironic vindication of Daggett's own earlier assurances to Beauchamp that coolness under fire beats those who panic (as Corcoran apparently did) and draw too fast. It also undermines Munny's own assertions to the Kid that 'It's a hell of a thing to kill a man.' For Munny, at least, it seems all too easy. The 'last man standing' routine (honed to perfection throughout Eastwood's career) when under fire from multiple directions ensures both his survival and cements his mythic status, his archetypal gunfighter identity.

As mentioned above, the shootout is also a personal loss for Munny, as justice segues into retribution. He first shoots Desbois who is unarmed; a deplorable action that prompts Daggett to call him a 'cowardly son-of-a-bitch'. Munny would have done the same to the Sheriff but for his shotgun misfiring. This could be interpreted as a further instance of irony, echoing as it does that part of Daggett's explanation to Beauchamp that Corcoran's Colt similarly misfired ('which was a failin' common to that model!'). More interestingly, it plays into the post-structuralist notion of a fault-line, or slippage, whereby the attempt by Munny to murder a defenceless Daggett (who, it must be said, shows great courage in staring death in the face) highlights the film's problem with depicting the reality of violence. Much like *Unforgiven*'s depiction of women, real violence proves to be unrepresentable. Therefore, after this slippage, the gunfight plays out in a manner rather typical of Eastwood's other Westerns. That is to say, he goes and gets the 'bad guys' who are all armed and in a fair fight; the weapon of choice, inevitably the six-gun (courtesy of the Kid's Schofield pistol).

In deferring the final showdown until the last possible moment, *Unforgiven* offers the audience what they have been waiting for – spectatorial catharsis by regeneration through violence. I have already discussed the problematical relation that the Western has had with this trope with regard to *Shane* and *The Searchers*, and it is worth quoting Slotkin's summarisation of it:

> The supreme value which the myth assigns to the climactic battle or gunfight is not simply a function of the ideological rationale that frames the fight. It derives its emotional force and irrational appeal from its role in the narrative structure of the myth. Specific versions of the myth may vary in their ideological rationale, hero type, and choice of happy or fatal ending; but they do not vary in their representation of a consummatory act of violence – *whatever* its motivation – as the *necessary* and *sufficient* resolution of all the issues the tale has raised.[132]

Munny's, more specifically, the cultural icon Clint Eastwood's, return as the instrument of retribution and his embracing of the 'consummatory act of violence' is in keeping with the Puritanical Angel of Vengeance that he embodied in No Name, The Drifter and The Preacher. It is precisely this kind of character intertextuality that causes the audience's delight in such recognisable Eastwood quips as, 'Who's the fella' that owns this shithole?' Such statements provide a base-alloy of farce to gloss over the more tragic elements at work within the narrative, working to make the final shootout an appealing spectacle, justifiable and, moreover, 'fun'.

IX

Overall, I have suggested that *Unforgiven* is a far cry from a film that forces the 'audience into re-examining the grounds for their fascination with screen violence and Western mythology', as McVeigh has it. Shorn of the (conscious) historical dimension of either *Shane* or *The Searchers*, it lacks even a counter-narrative of nation. I also conclude that it stands opposed to O'Brien's assertion that, despite the finale's 'collapse', the film's 'meditation on violence . . . is provocative and largely successful'.[133] In a similar vein to Greenberg's sentiments with which I opened this chapter (though divorced somewhat from his concerns with the wider scope of frontier history), Grist concludes his summary of the film thus:

> Even if perpetrated in revenge for Ned's suffering, the carnage is such as to overwhelm any moral validation and constitutes perhaps the film's most significant revision of Western violence, which is thus reduced completely to a matter of power and circumstance rather than justice or right.[134]

It is difficult to see how Grist can interpret *Unforgiven*'s finale in this manner. Despite the film's overwhelming pretensions towards a revisionist stance, it does little to critique or problematise either the so-called classical Western or the mythic theme of regeneration through violence. The episode at Greeley's is less bloody than the stacks of corpses in earlier Eastwood films. Additionally, it increases *Shane*'s death-tally by just two. So, far from forcing a 're-examining' of our 'fascination with screen violence' in the manner of the Kid's renunciation of it, and far from giving lie to the myth of the gunfighter through the figure of Beauchamp, *Unforgiven* would seem to exist as a celebration of these very things – a celebration of the gunfighter identity.

It is clear also that the myth of the West will continue to flourish in the tall tales that Beauchamp will continue to write. Indeed, the shootout at Greeley's proves to be irresistible to the dime novelist, and he at once goes about turning it into the stuff of legend. In the immediate aftermath of the shooting Beauchamp attempts to apply mythic structure to the terrifying chaos of the violence. As he panders around Munny like an excited dog (much akin to the way he pandered around Daggett previously, and English Bob previous to that) he asks, 'Who did you shoot first?' He immediately answers his own question, self-assuredly declaring that, 'when confronted by superior numbers, the experienced gunfighter will fire on the best shots first'. 'Is that so?' replies Munny, before stating that he was simply 'lucky in the order', philosophically musing that he has 'always been lucky when it comes to killin' folks'. Quickly irritated by the dime novelist's incessancy, Munny turns the rifle on Beauchamp. 'All I know is whose gonna be last,' he threatens. Beauchamp dutifully scurries off. A distinct lack of braggadocio is what really distinguishes Munny from the other would-be heroes of the film. Bob and Daggett talk a good fight, if little else. Munny, in true Western tradition, *acts*. As he leaves, Munny takes a last look at Logan's corpse – still on display outside Greeley's – and declares to all the townsfolk cowering along the sidewalks, 'You better bury Ned right . . . and you better not carve up nor otherwise harm no whores . . . or I will come back an' kill every last one of you sons of bitchs!'

Tall in the saddle of his pale horse amid a dramatic thunderstorm, a low-angle shot holds Munny with a US flag in plain view behind him, his grizzled face catching the rain. Jim Kitses states that '*Unforgiven* insists on the construction of its drunken killer as cowboy, Western hero, America.'[135] Taking the associations of Munny *as* America, he is precisely possessed of (or maybe by) what D. H. Lawrence once claimed as the 'essential American soul', which is 'hard, isolate, stoic, and a killer'.[136] As an instrument of death, we may also recall Megan Wheeler's (Sydney Penny) prayer in *Pale Rider*, the voicing of which brings forth the mysterious Preacher into the Carbon Canyon: 'And behold a pale horse, and the name that said on him was Death, and Hell followed with him.'

It seems clear to me that Eastwood has not revised or abandoned this character. As he rides off, Beauchamp gazes after Munny with an expression of awe, similar to that which earlier adorned the Kid. He furiously scribbles down notes in between quick glances at Munny's receding figure, notes that will no doubt continue the legend of William Munny. One of Murdoch's boastful Westerners he may not be, but the spectral figure Munny resembles here ends up supporting rather than undermining the florid prose of writers like Beauchamp.

During such moments in *Unforgiven* – the writing of history as myth – one is encouraged to recall Linda Hutcheon's assertion that our access to history 'is entirely conditioned by textuality'.[137] However, the post-modern implications of this claim are undermined when one considers that *Unforgiven*, as a whole, exists as a wilful instance of celebratory mythography. Or, and if I may use such redundant terms, its self-reflexivity is put to work in the service of a more classical agenda than a revisionist one. To put it another way, at the epic moment, Munny *fulfils* rather than undermines his own legend. Here, legend is not revised as fact only to be cynically covered up as is the case in *Liberty Valance*, where such cynicism purposefully undermines the cover-up that the chronicler of official history seeks to enact. In *Unforgiven*, legend is merely revised as more legend, and written as such. Whatever fiction Beauchamp may write about that fatal night at Greeley's, there will be little to distinguish it from the truth as it is presented to us.

Moreover, Grist's argument that *Unforgiven*'s reduction of Western violence to 'power and circumstance' over 'justice' constitutes a 'significant revision of Western violence' is to misinterpret the figure of the gunfighter within the history of the genre as a whole. Slotkin has said that gunfighters often operate 'in a "terminal" environment', and that, as a concept, the gunfighter describes a certain 'world-view . . . rather than a specific social role in a particular historical frame'.[138] He continues his description thus:

> The outward form of the gunfighter style emphasises artistic professionalism in the use of weapons, but what justifies and directs that professionalism is a particular state of mind, a 'gunfighter' understanding of 'how the world works.' That understanding is essentially 'hard-boiled': the world is a hostile place, human motives are rarely good, and outcomes depend *not on right but on the proper deployment of might*.[139]

Slotkin's comments refer, not as one might think to the so-called revisionist efforts of the 1960s or 1970s, but directly to his analysis of the 'gunfighter' Westerns of the early 1950s; films working within the broader popular–cultural world of 'hard-boiled' detective fiction and film noir. *Shane*, *High-Noon* and *The Gunfighter* are, for him, chief among such Westerns. To this list I would also add *The Searchers*, *Winchester '73* and *Pursued* for their focus on individual 'psychology' and narrative concern over the 'revenger' plot.

Such sentiments are also easily applied to *Unforgiven*. As Munny succinctly puts it to a mortally wounded Daggett, '"Deserves" got nothin' to do with it.' Daggett's last words are a clichéd spit of defiance moments before Munny wastes him with Logan's reclaimed Spencer rifle: 'I'll see you in Hell, William Munny.' Munny nods knowingly, 'Yeah.' Clearly, Munny proves to be extremely 'capable' in this regard and, in so being, can be related to the concept of the transcendent hero whose roots can be traced back at least as far Cooper's Leatherstocking tales. Douglas Pye writes that such a figure is 'invulnerable, endowed with almost superhuman skill, unencumbered by most human limitations – a fantastic impossible figure'.[140] The expression of Munny's transcendent power fulfils audience desires as well as providing a justification for a final mythologised, fantastical 'consummatory act of violence'. Furthermore, McGee notes that Munny's journey from reformed killer and back again fulfils the trajectory of a Calvinist morality tale. He expands upon Slotkin's 'terminal environment':

> Though no one is forgiven, sooner or later retribution will come in this Calvinist world; and its instruments are not those who are good or who

have been victimised or who have shown wisdom but are those capable of the violence retribution requires.[141]

According to this logic, the film thus 'justifies violence . . . through an appeal to transcendence'.[142] The Calvinist vision of *Unforgiven* offered by McGee would, through its particular concept of predestination, play into the idea that the film's characters appear to be 'stuck', as it were, in 'roles' already prepared for them in advance; roles endemic to frontier mythology and the figurative language of the Western genre (I will continue exploring this notion of 'roles' in Chapter 5). Munny's transformation from broken-down pig farmer into fantastical gunfighter would make little logical sense otherwise. And yet, far from scrutinising such roles, *Unforgiven* appears to exploit them.

To my mind, the film shows little awareness of its inability to revise these aspects of itself, which is surprising considering Eastwood's own protracted legacy within the genre. Alexandra Keller suggests that Eastwood may even have been held hostage by his own star persona. She suggests that, his 'status as icon of the individual's right to take matters into his own hands when the institutions whose job that is fail him had by 1992 ossified into something practically nonnegotiable to the public'.[143] She argues that this is one reason why '*Unforgiven* is in many ways a far less successful revisionist western than the older *Outlaw Josey Whales*.'[144] Given Eastwood's own conservative politics, however, I would be inclined to think that perhaps it would be more accurate to suggest that this inability is more an instance of unwillingness (*Josey Whales* excepting). In any case, *Unforgiven* is clearly less patently revisionist than his Italian Westerns with Leone, his own *Josey Whales* or Ford's *Liberty Valance* before it. (It is also less post-modernist than his 1960s collaborations with Leone.)

A major point with which to take issue with regard to McVeigh's assumed post-modern status for the film would be the idea of narrative closure. In general, post-modernists tend to be wary of the whole notion of closure, identified as it is with forms of dogmatism and exclusivity. There is a certain irony, therefore, in McVeigh suggesting that, '[u]ltimately, *Unforgiven* is a closed narrative . . . The audience knows where [Munny] came from, and now knows where he goes to.'[145] This last is in reference to the final crawl, which McVeigh uses to justify narrative closure and '*Unforgiven*'s deconstruction of *Shane*'.[146] The crawl suggests that Munny had 'long since disappeared with the children . . . some said to San Francisco where it was rumoured he prospered in dry goods'. I find in this little proof of 'knowing' anything beyond hearsay and rumour at least. The fact is that we cannot say with any degree of certainty what fate befell Munny; that we 'know' nothing would surely be a more postmodern aspect to impress.

Overall, as a frontier legend, Munny, like Shane and Ethan before him, is an enigmatic and, ultimately, contradictory figure. The ending of *Unforgiven* is ambiguous in many ways, providing little in the way of 'a closed narrative'.

Still, far from '*the*' post-modern status awarded the film by McVeigh, I contend that Munny's final resurrection through a regression into his past, through the isolation of 'the private dimension' which, as Slotkin has suggested, often 'determines the whole significance of the [gunfighter] story', fulfils, if anything, more of a modernist sensibility. It, therefore, provides a modernist perspective on history.[147] This must be distinguished from the inference that the film is also beholden to a modernist *aesthetic*; *Unforgiven*, like the bulk of commercial cinema, remains ensconced in an essentially realist narrative structure (although we should always bear in mind that the film does show a tendency towards reflexivity concerning its own nature, status and role as a Western). Pericles Lewis suggests that the defining trope of artistic modernism is the 'continual striving for a bright future ... forever undercut by the force or tradition of history ... which continually turns our forward-looking present into an unalterable past'.[148] As a literary example of this, Lewis turns to F. Scott Fitzgerald's, *The Great Gatsby* (1925):

> Gatsby believed in the green light, the orgastic future that year by year recedes before us. It eluded us then, but that's no matter – tomorrow we will run faster, stretch out our arms further ... And one fine morning – So we beat on, boats against the current, borne ceaselessly into the past.[149]

Fitzgerald's metaphorical 'boats' labour wilfully (but futilely) 'against the current' in search of an 'orgastic future ... borne ceaselessly into the past'. How fitting this is when applied to *Unforgiven*, with Munny's future 'borne back' into his own 'unalterable past'. The individual, hopelessly committed to the tropes of a mythic 'tradition', stuck in a 'role', suffers an ironic reversal in the tides of history. 'When we reach toward the future', argues Lewis, 'we find ourselves already living in the past.'[150] And it is this that ensures, at one and the same time, William Munny's mortal damnation *and* his mythical transcendence.

NOTES

1. Harvey R. Greenberg, 'Unforgiven', *Film Quarterly*, 46(3) (1993): 52–6. In support of Greenberg, see also the essay by Leighton Grist, '*Unforgiven*', in Ian Cameron and Douglas Pye (eds), *The Movie Book of the Western* (New York: Continuum, 1996), pp. 294–301.
2. Daniel O'Brien, *Clint Eastwood: Film-Maker* (London: Batsford, 1996), p. 178.
3. Michael Coyne, *The Crowded Prairie: American National Identity in the Hollywood Western* (London: I. B. Tauris, 1997), p. 188.
4. Patrick McGee, *From Shane to Kill Bill: Rethinking the Western* (Oxford: Blackwell, 2007), pp. 133–40.
5. It is worth mentioning that David Webb Peoples' script for *Unforgiven* was originally written in 1976 and many have therefore established the film's connection to a decade dominated politically and culturally by the fall-out from Vietnam.

6. Patricia Nelson Limerick, *The Legacy of Conquest: The Unbroken Past of the American West* (London: W. W. Norton, 1987), p. 19.
7. Alan Lovell, 'The Western' (1967), reprinted in Bill Nichols (ed.), *Movies and Methods, vol. 1: An Anthology* (London: University of California Press, 1976), pp. 164–75, quote on p. 175.
8. Ibid., p. 175.
9. James K. Folsom, 'Westerns as Social and Political Alternatives' (1967), reprinted in Jack Nachbar (ed.), *Focus on the Western* (Englewood Cliffs, NJ: Prentice-Hall, 1974), pp. 81–4, quote on p. 82
10. Ibid., p. 82.
11. Ibid.
12. Ibid., p. 83.
13. Will Wright, *Six-Guns and Society* (Berkeley: University of California Press, 1975), p. 23.
14. Janey Place, 'Structured Cowboys', *Jump Cut: A Review of Contemporary Media*, 18 (1978): 26–8.
15. Ibid., p. 26.
16. Ibid., p. 26.
17. McGee, *From Shane to Kill Bill*, p. xiv
18. Ibid., p. xvi.
19. Thomas Schatz, *Hollywood Genres: Formulas, Filmmaking, and the Studio System* (New York: Random House, 1981), pp. 50–1.
20. Stephen McVeigh, *The American Western* (Edinburgh: Edinburgh University Press, 2007), p. 203 (emphasis in original).
21. Tag Gallagher, 'Shoot-Out at the Genre Corral: Problems in the "Evolution" of the Western' (1986), reprinted in Barry Keith Grant (ed.), *Film Genre Reader III* (Austin, TX: University of Texas Press, 2003), pp. 262–76.
22. Fredric Jameson, *The Political Unconscious: Narrative as a Socially Symbolic Act* (London: Methuen, 1981).
23. Rick Altman, *The American Film Musical* (Bloomington, IN: Indiana University Press, 1989); Steve Neale, 'Questions of Genre' (1995), reprinted in Grant (ed.), *Film Genre Reader III*, pp. 160–84.
24. Neale, 'Questions of Genre', p. 179.
25. Jameson, *The Political Unconscious*, p. 17.
26. Ibid., pp. 76–7 (emphasis in original).
27. Ibid. (emphasis in original).
28. Ibid., p. 99.
29. Robert Warshow, 'Movie Chronicle: The Westerner' (1954), reprinted in Leo Braudy and Marshall Cohen (eds), *Film Theory and Criticism: Introductory Readings* (Oxford: Oxford University Press, 1999), pp. 654–68, quote on p. 654.
30. Richard Slotkin, *Gunfighter Nation: The Myth of the Frontier in Twentieth-Century America* (Norman, OK: University of Oklahoma Press, [1992] 1998), p. 379.
31. Ibid., p. 380.
32. Ibid.
33. Ibid., p. 379.
34. Ibid., p. 380 (emphasis in original).
35. Ibid.
36. Ibid. See also, p. 728 fn. 5.
37. Ibid., pp. 303–4.
38. Schatz, *Hollywood Genres*, p. 50.
39. Gallagher, 'Shoot-Out at the Genre Corral', p. 272 (emphasis added).
40. Schatz, *Hollywood Genres*, p. 50.

41. John H. Lenihan, *Showdown: Confronting Modern America in the Western Film* (Urbana, IL: University of Illinois Press, [1980] 1985), p. 23.
42. McVeigh, *The American Western*, p. 203.
43. Ibid., pp. 118–25; on *Shane* as archetypal Western, see pp. 161–8; on *Unforgiven* specifically, see pp. 202–13.
44. Ibid., p. 155.
45. Ibid.
46. Ibid., p. 122.
47. Ibid., p. 155.
48. Ibid., pp. 155–6.
49. Ibid., p. 155.
50. Ibid.
51. Ibid., p. 156.
52. Ibid.
53. Ibid., p. 159.
54. Slotkin, *Gunfighter Nation*, pp. 381–2.
55. Ibid.
56. John Tuska, *The American West in Film: Critical Approaches to the Western* (London: Greenwood Press, 1985), pp. 7–8.
57. Richard White, Review (untitled), *Journal of American History*, 80(3) (1993): 1039–41, quote on p. 1040.
58. McVeigh, *The American Western*, p. 206.
59. *Will Penny*, directed by Tom Gries, featuring Charlton Heston, Donald Pleasance, Joan Hackett, Lee Majors (Paramount Pictures, 1968).
60. McGee, *The American Western*, p. 195.
61. Carl Plantinga, 'Spectacles of Death: Clint Eastwood and Violence in *Unforgiven*', *Cinema Journal*, 37(2) (1998): 65–83, at p. 68.
62. The Biblical connotations of the name Delilah, the Philistine emasculator of Sampson, should not be overlooked.
63. Similar and related violent episodes are repeated twice more during the course of the narrative, with Bill beating a feverish Munny half to death, before going one step further with his fatal and sadistic bull-whipping of Ned Logan.
64. Grist, '*Unforgiven*', p. 296.
65. Ibid., p. 297.
66. The saloon's name is undoubtedly a reference to Horace Greeley, the nineteenth-century editor of the *New York Tribune* who supported liberal policies towards settlers, famously stating: 'Go West, young man. Go West and grow up with the country.' Prior to *Unforgiven*, Greeley's words were restated most famously and directly in a cinematic Western by the eastern 'dude' lawyer Ranse Stoddard in *Liberty Valance*.
67. Greenberg, '*Unforgiven*', p. 52.
68. Ibid., p. 52.
69. Jim Kitses, *Horizons West: Directing the Western from John Ford to Clint Eastwood* (London: British Film Institute, [2004] 2007), p. 308.
70. Plantinga, 'Spectacles of Death', p. 68.
71. Schatz, *Hollywood Genres*, p. 80.
72. Gallagher, 'Shoot-Out at the Genre Corral', pp. 272–3.
73. Ibid., p. 271.
74. Schatz, *Hollywood Genres*, p. 67.
75. Ibid., pp. 50–1.
76. Plantinga, 'Spectacles of Death', p. 70. Kitses, *Horizons West: Directing the Western*, p. 311.
77. Tuska, *The American West in Film*, p. 235.
78. O'Brien, *Clint Eastwood*, p. 177.

79. Kitses, *Horizons West: Directing the Western*, p. 308.
80. Ibid., p. 308.
81. Ibid., pp. 308–9.
82. Ibid., p. 308. Plantinga, 'Spectacles of Death', p. 76. See also McVeigh, *The American Western*, p. 205, for a similar misreading.
83. Andrechuck, *The Golden Corral*, p. 163.
84. Plantinga, 'Spectacles of Death', p. 68.
85. Ibid., p. 69.
86. Grist, '*Unforgiven*', p. 301.
87. Ibid., p. 301. Parallels with Sally's 'look' noted.
88. McGee, *The American Western*, pp. 196–7.
89. Jameson, *The Political Unconscious*, p. 85.
90. Ibid., p. 86.
91. Ibid., p. 85.
92. Ibid., pp. 85–6.
93. Ibid., p. 86.
94. Ibid., pp. 86–7.
95. McVeigh, *The American Western*, p. 211.
96. *The William Munny Killings*, an original screenplay by David Webb Peoples, 1976, available at: http://www.screenwrite.in/Screenplays/Unforgiven.pdf, pp. 17–18.
97. Tompkins, *West of Everything*, p. 35.
98. Plantinga, 'Spectacles of Death', p. 75.
99. John G. Cawelti, *The Six-Gun Mystique*, 2nd edn (Bowling Green, OH: Bowling Green State University Popular Press, [1971] 1984), p. 16.
100. Scott Emmert, *Loaded Fictions: Social Critique in the Twentieth Century Western* (Moscow: University of Idaho Press, 1996), p. 38.
101. Ibid., p. 3.
102. In mentioning 'that kid', Delilah is undoubtedly referring to the Schofield Kid, however, one could also link it to Davey, for he is 'just . . . a boy' too.
103. Grist, '*Unforgiven*', p. 297.
104. Ibid., p. 297.
105. Plantinga, 'Spectacles of Death', p. 72.
106. Ibid., p. 72.
107. McVeigh, *The American Western*, p. 203.
108. Ibid.
109. Slotkin, *Gunfighter Nation*, pp. 381–2.
110. Kitses, *Horizons West: Directing the Western*, p. 307.
111. Ibid., p. 308.
112. Ibid., p. 142.
113. McVeigh, *The American Western*, p. 155.
114. Kitses, *Horizons West: Directing the Western*, pp. 142–8.
115. McVeigh, *The American Western*, pp. 206–7.
116. Lee Clark Mitchell, *Westerns: Making the Man in Fiction and Film* (Chicago, IL: University of Chicago Press, 1996), pp. 21–3.
117. Ibid., p. 24.
118. Leo Marx, *The Machine in the Garden: Technology and the Pastoral Ideal in America* (New York: Oxford University Press, 1964).
119. Joseph McBride, *Searching for John Ford* (New York: Faber, 2003), pp. 623–34.
120. Grist, '*Unforgiven*', p. 297.
121. David Hamilton Murdoch, *The American West: The Invention of a Myth* (Cardiff: Welsh Academic Press, 2001), p. 83.
122. Ibid., p. 19.
123. Mitchell, *Westerns*, p. 261.

124. Ibid., p. 261.
125. Plantinga, 'Spectacles of Death', p. 76. Andrechuck relays that the 'killing of the cowboys by Munny and the Kid is a deplorable act of double-murder'. Andrechuck, *The Golden Corral*, p. 163. See also McVeigh, *The American Western*, pp. 205–7.
126. Plantinga, 'Spectacles of Death', p. 77.
127. Significantly, and in terms of anti-revisionist thinking, this gunfight, the 'money shot' (Munny shot?) of *Unforgiven* is precisely what so-called classical Westerns such as *Red River* withhold.
128. Such sadism is reminiscent of the murderous Frank (Henry Fonda) in Leone's *Once Upon a Time in the West* (1968). Frank is a murderous brute – an archetypal villain – who goes beyond what is necessary in the act of killing; a textbook sadist who relishes in physical and psychological torture.
129. Kitses, *Horizons West: Directing the Western*, p. 149.
130. Tompkins, *West of Everything*, p. 228.
131. Grist, '*Unforgiven*', p. 297.
132. Slotkin, *Gunfighter Nation*, p. 612 (emphasis in original).
133. O'Brien, *Clint Eastwood*, p. 179.
134. Grist, '*Unforgiven*', pp. 297, 300.
135. Kitses, *Horizons West: Directing the Western*, p. 310.
136. D. H. Lawrence, *Studies in Classical American Literature* (London: Penguin Classics, [1923] 1990). Lawrence, discussed in Slotkin, *Regenration through Violence*, p. 2.
137. Linda Hutcheon, *The Politics of Postmodernism* (London: Routledge, 1989), p. 16.
138. Slotkin, *Gunfighter Nation*, p. 401.
139. Ibid., pp. 401–2 (emphasis added).
140. Douglas Pye, 'Genre and History: Fort Apache and The Man Who Shot Liberty Valance', in Ian Cameron and Douglas Pye (eds), *The Movie Book of the Western*, (New York: Continuum), p. 121.
141. McGee, *From Shane to Kill Bill*, p. 199.
142. Ibid., pp. 198–200. See also Mitchell, *Westerns*, p. 261.
143. Alexandra Keller, 'Generic Subversion as Counter-history: Mario Van Peebles's *Posse*', in Janet Walker (ed.), *Westerns: Films through History* (London: Routledge, 2001), pp. 27–47, quote on p. 45 fn. 22.
144. Ibid., p. 45.
145. McVeigh, *The American Western*, pp. 211–12.
146. Ibid., p. 204.
147. Slotkin, *Gunfighter Nation*, p. 382.
148. Pericles Lewis, *The Cambridge Introduction to Modernism* (Cambridge: Cambridge University Press, 2007), pp. 32–3.
149. F. Scott Fitzgerald, *The Great Gatsby* (London: Penguin, [1925] 1994), p. 123. Fitzgerald, discussed in Lewis, pp. 32–3.
150. Lewis, *Cambridge Introduction to Modernism*, p. 33.

PART TWO

4. WHAT COUNTS AS HISTORY AND WHOSE HISTORY IS IT?

'I'm awful sorry about Mel. He was a good Mexican.'

I

Patricia Nelson Limerick has argued that, for much of the twentieth century, Anglo-America has been 'fixed on the definition of the frontier drawn from the imaginative reconstruction of the story of the United States and its westward expansion'.[1] A prominent scholar of the New Western History, Limerick has sought to deconstruct the 'interpretive straightjacket' of Turner's Frontier Thesis and redefine the concept of the frontier.[2] Interestingly, she points out that, despite the 'spectre' of the Frontier Thesis, 'North America has, in fact, had two strong traditions in the use of the term'.[3] On the one hand, is the 'idea of the frontier' that, as an 'extremely well established ... cultural common property', pertains to a Turnerian ideal, a space 'where white settlers entered a zone of "free" land and opportunity'.[4] On the other hand, is a less familiar, though 'more realistic usage of *la frontera*', which describes the cultural complexities and individual experiences along 'the borderlands between Mexico and the United States'.[5]

As a concept *la frontera* stands opposed to the frontier's 'imaginative reconstruction' by giving lie to its grand narrative of optimism and simplistic binarism, of its tale of righteous pioneers carving a civilisation out of the wilderness. Instead, it exposes a darker, more complex 'legacy of conquest' (using Limerick's own terminology), which includes ethnic cleansing, expropriation of land and resources, and environmental despoliation. It is a story driven less by dashing Anglo-American heroes on horseback, than it is by brutal monopolists, exploiters and warmongers. According to Limerick, this is what constitutes the real history of the American West. Consequently, when it comes to a historical reassessment of the borderlands through *la frontera*, Limerick insists upon there being 'no illusion of vacancy, of triumphal conclusions, or of simplicity'.[6]

Limerick has continually declared erroneous the argument that the historical issues concerning the American West are a thing of the past. She draws her inspiration from Earl Pomeroy's 1955 essay 'Toward a Reorientation of Western History'. This essay is commonly regarded as a blueprint for many of the concerns that were to be taken up by the New Western History in the decades that followed. Perhaps of most influence is Pomeroy's refutation of a temporal border separating 'Old' and 'New' Wests, urging his contemporaries to 'disregard arbitrary borders in time and space'.[7] Unlike Pomeroy, however, who largely neglects mention of Spanish and Mexican cultures,[8] Limerick presses the importance of the history of the Hispanic borderlands as part of the cultural geography of the United States. For her, 'the [Anglo] American conquest of the borderlands [is] an essential element in the story of expansion, to be compared and contrasted with the conquest of Indians'.[9] She further suggests that, for much of the twentieth century, 'Hispanic history remained on the edges of Western American history'.[10] Her approach is one that seeks to highlight the cultural–ideological machinations that lay behind this elision from the official discourse, and which seeks to re-engage the reader with an Hispanic culture now in its 'proper place at the centre of Western American history'.[11]

Regarding *la frontera*, it is her belief that 'the conquered and controlled borderland continued to exist only in the imagination . . . the Mexican border was a social fiction that neither nature nor people in search of opportunity observed'.[12] She draws our attention to the contemporary borderlands as a troubled region with ongoing 'conflicts over the restriction of immigration, with disputes over water flow and environmental pollution', ultimately describing 'a zone where an industrialised nation shares a long land border with a nation much-burdened by poverty'.[13]

By insisting upon the significance of economic, environmental and racial issues in the history of the frontier, New Western historians sought a less culturally anaemic and more socially relevant set of discourses on the American West than those allegedly offered by Turner and his sympathisers.[14] They contend that, despite their obvious significance, the cultural complexities of the borderlands are rarely accounted for in the official histories that chronicle US westward expansion. As far as Limerick is concerned, such discourses remain predominantly ethnocentric in character and are written by and for Anglo-Americans. 'If the idea of *la frontera* had anywhere near the standing of the idea of the frontier', she argues, 'we would be well launched toward self-understanding, directed toward a realistic view of this nation's position in the hemisphere and in the world.'[15]

As I have previously suggested, when it comes to popular culture's role in facilitating this 'realistic view', Limerick's attitude is far from optimistic (an attitude shared by many of her peers). Briefly reiterated, it was her contention that the Western genre has done little to critique frontier mythology; on the contrary, the genre actively and straightforwardly endorsed *and* engendered a triumphalist Anglo-American perspective. Its imagined re-creation of the frontier is one that consistently fails to deal with what she calls 'the risks inherent in the word, [which reduce the] multisided convergence of various peoples into a model of the two sides of a frontier line'.[16] Where she places Hollywood's West as something firmly enthralled to the 'fantasy' of the mythic frontier, the complex 'reality' of *la frontera* typically remains, for her, outside of the genre's dominant ideological purview.[17]

As I have thus far demonstrated, however, the Western should not be considered either historically vacant or ideologically monolithic. This underestimates the enormous depth of complexity with which the genre deals with the myth of the West, and disregards the ideological contradictions inherent in even the most ostensibly triumphalist of film texts. I have already offered my opinions on the shortcomings of Limerick's arguments; suffice it to say that the film with which I am mainly concerned with here, *The Three Burials of Melquiades Estrada*, responds to Limerick in ways that problematises her attitude towards popular treatments of the frontier. I seek no corrective to her historical challenge to Turnerian paradigms; indeed, for the most part I agree with them. What I do object to – what I have been objecting to throughout – is the tendency, as I see it, of a great many film scholars and cultural historians to offer generalised simplistic (mis)readings of certain films, force whole periods of genre production to fit into arbitrarily defined categories, or elide discussion of certain other films altogether in order to support specious historiographic and cultural–ideological trajectories within popular cultural production as a whole.

Of course, Limerick is not oblivious to the complex movements within some spheres of popular culture, and I in no way wish to accuse her of a 'blinkered' perspective. In fact, the conclusion to chapter 2 in *Something in the Soil* makes both an appeal to, and a prediction of, historical transfers into North America's collective conscience:

> If the velocity of the movement of ideas from frontier historians to popular culture remains constant, somewhere in the next century, we might expect the popular usage of the word [frontier] to begin to reckon with the complexity of the westward movement and its consequences. Somewhere in the mid-2000s, the term might undergo a crucial shift, toward the reality of *la frontera* and away from the fantasy of the frontier. That shift in meaning will be the measure of great change in this nation's understanding of its own origins.[18]

In light of films like *Three Burials*, such a 'crucial shift' might occur sooner than Limerick thinks. However, it must be pointed out that this correlation between history and popular culture exists equally as a happy coincidence of a long-standing desire (in some quarters of cultural production at least) to depict a more rounded perspective on the American frontier.

I shall take just one example of this desire here. In one of the most engaging essays that I have yet read on the silent era Western, Jennifer E. Smyth alerts us to the fact that early treatments of the frontier in Hollywood were less ignorant of the racial and imperialistic aspects of nineteenth-century expansion than is often assumed. Her analysis of Wesley Ruggles' *Cimarron* (1931), an Academy Award winning silent epic whose narrative concerns the experiences of a pioneering family, the Cravats, and encompasses the cross-over of two centuries (the late nineteenth and early twentieth) of westward expansion, teaches us that (at least some of the time) popular culture industries at least as far back as the early sound period 'began to fathom the mythic undercurrents propelling the rhetoric of western history'.[19] The film begins with the ambitious lawyer and newspaper editor, Yancy Cravat (Richard Dix), moving his wife, Sabra (Irene Dunne), and family from Kansas and into the newly opened up territories in Oklahoma. Despite becoming a leading citizen in the new township of Osage, Yancy abandons his family in search of yet 'greater' glories in the newly emerging settlements of the Cherokee Strip. In short, Smyth argues that Yancy is overcome by greed, and even a touch of megalomania, and *Cimarron* therefore reveals how the desire to advance Anglo-American civilisation quickly segues into the hubris of greed and warmongering. In the process, it implies that, as an approach to the history of the West, the New Western History is not so new after all.

My reading of *Three Burials* follows in a similar vein. I should point out that it is not my intention to offer a critique of the New Western historical approach in general, or of Limerick's in particular. On the contrary, it is my express belief that *Three Burials* exists as a film that offers an imaginative and a highly critical reassessment of the myth as 'the story of the United States' by intentionally foregrounding the formal and thematic limitations of its terms. Smyth's insights into the formal and thematic resonances of *Cimarron* suggest that, while this is not necessarily a new thing in and of itself, however, it remains a sober observation that serious considerations of the effects of the myth of the West on Mexican America are lamentably scarce in either socio-political discourse or America's popular culture industries. I suggest that *Three Burials* seeks to address this cultural silence and, in so doing, it indicates the capability of the Western in this regard. By applying the concept of *la frontera* we can interpret the film's ideological agenda as one that explores the traumatic 'legacy of conquest' (using Limerick's terminology again) by which the United States–Mexico border has been historically and geopolitically constructed asymmetrically along cultural and racial lines. In my opinion, the film offers an extremely engaging vision of the region's cultural geography that resonates with the concerns of the New Western History. Analysis along these lines allows me to explore how this border has been ideologically reified as a binary divide through frontier mythology and used as a prism for historical (mis)understanding.

In what follows I offer a close textual analysis of *Three Burials*, exploring some of the different narrative strategies employed by the film's director and star, Tommy Lee Jones, and of its writer, Guillermo Arriaga. I consider the film's formal characteristics and its thematic content, suggesting that both narrative aspects utilise the plot motifs and iconography of the Western in order to self-consciously address the relationship held by the myth to the borderlands. I argue that these two interrelated (though hardly indistinguishable) aspects of *Three Burials* constitute a deliberate deconstruction of this mythology; specifically, those aspects concerning the figure of the Anglo-American hero, the culturally constructed 'border' separating civilisation from wilderness (with Anglos on the former side and with Mexicans on the latter), and the idea of Mexico itself in the North American 'imaginary'.[20] The film's own ironic sense of history is similarly revealed through both its content and its form. Overall, such an approach not only allows me to explore *Three Burials'* take on the relationship between myth and history, and therefore extend the arguments of the previous chapter, it also illuminates the film's transnational revisioning of the region's cultural geography in terms that suit the outlook of historians like Limerick.

II

Perhaps the most immediately apparent of *Three Burials'* narrative strategies is the peculiar temporal and spatial disjuncture apparent in the first part of the film. This section of the story is pieced together by interspersing contemporary action with sequences from the past, so that we learn only gradually what happened to the eponymous Melquiades 'Mel' Estrada (Julio Cesar Cedillo), follow ranch foreman Pete Perkins' (Tommy Lee Jones) reactions of grief and anger over his friend's untimely death, and build up a picture of their initial meeting and developing friendship.

Disjointed plots, typically narrated through multiple perspectives, which challenge the conventions of so-called 'mainstream' filmmaking have become something of an authorial trademark for Arriaga. His other notable credits as screenwriter include a trilogy of collaborations with the Mexican director Alejandro González Iñárritu: the critically acclaimed *Amores Perros* (2000), *21 Grams* (2003) and, most recently, *Babel* (2006). Arriaga's particular style translates into the semiotic code of the films produced from his scripts, actively confusing their visual grammar and forcing audiences to reassess their conceptualisations of time and space. In the case of *Three Burials* it is not unusual for up to three different temporal and spatial frames to be simultaneously intermingled through multiple characters' perspectives.

It is well known how sound, continuity editing, causally coherent narrative and closure have all developed to become the established conventions of cinematic realism, the so-called classical narrative cinema. This style of filmmaking has come to dominate film production in Hollywood, and sought to feature 'a fictional world governed by spatial and temporal verisimilitude', aligning the audience with the 'centrality of the narrative agency of psychologically-rounded characters'.[21] Obviously, such narratives threaten (whether consciously or not) to undermine their own sense of 'wholeness', but if Barthes was correct in claiming that, in effect, ideology works as a contemporary mythology, then the overall ideological *aim* of a realist aesthetic is to efface its own constructed nature as language and to pass itself off as somehow 'natural'.

The narrative strategies apparent in the first half of *Three Burials* actively seek to undermine such pretensions and, initially, draw us away from the story towards the way the story is being told, towards its arbitrariness as a textual construct. This is undeniably a post-modern trait; however, the filmmakers' style here is not to be regarded as a mere pastiche of self-conscious irony. On the contrary, and as I go on to argue below, its portrayal of the myth of the West as a romantic delusion possessing destructive power for contemporary Americans is rendered in terms that are too intensely serious to be regarded as pastiche. Therefore, the question impressed upon us in the early stages of the narrative is not so much what is happening (or, rather, what has *happened*), but why is it being relayed to us in the fashion that it is?

Taking Barthes' now commonly held position that realism does not reflect but rather *constructs* reality, we might say that counter-narrative, or alternative cinematic styles, react against the conventions of realism, typically serving to make us more aware of these conventions and to question their ideological assumptions.[22] We should, of course, also consider the ideological implications of the counter-narrative itself. To this end, *Three Burials* displays a highly self-reflexive attitude towards the so-called classical Western's alleged collusion between cinematic realism and the myth of the West. As I have previously argued, such an attitude is not new of course, and is actually a systemic aspect of the genre. Consequently, there is a strong intertextual relay apparent in *Three Burial*'s confrontation with, and contestation of, these various modes of ideological expression. The film's aesthetic is, as a result, essentially anti-mythic. However, as I have already discussed in Chapter 3 in relation to *Unforgiven*, such a position is no guarantor of extrication from the discourses of myth or mythmaking; nor, indeed, is it an exemption from the assertion of an ideological position. Such assertion is, of course, usually denied by the producer of artistic realism as surely as it is denied by the historiographer; however, it seems axiomatic to me that the revelation of an ideological position is one that is actively sought by the producer of alternative cinemas, as something wilfully exposed through counter-narrative techniques rather than disavowed through 'causally coherent' narrative realism.

There is a frenetic pace engendered by *Three Burials*' formal structure which makes it difficult to establish a coherent sense of either time or space. When related to its thematic and ideological content, these formal aspects of the film represent (in ways that are peculiar to the cinema) time and space in terms that encompass not only the geographical, but the political, the cultural and the historical as well. *Three Burials* being set in both southwest Texas and northern

Mexico, and including a cast of characters from both these regions, actively confuses the concept of a homogeneous American national identity. It does this by highlighting the arbitrary nature of such identities inasmuch as they are defined historically by culture and race, and geopolitically through borders. It addresses these thematic concerns in terms of the myth through its recourse to certain tropes, formulas and stereotypes of the Western: the hero's code, the revenge motif, the shootout, the cowboy, horses, guns; physical location, the southwest desert, the Rio Grande and the journey into a Mexico of the North American Imaginary. Ultimately, the film depicts communities inhabiting a cultural and geographical space that is not officially recognised by US political institutions or typically explored through the discourses that narrate its history. As a consequence, it is difficult to think of the borderlands with much sobriety, and because of this I further suggest that *Three Burials* exemplifies the approach adopted by David Harvey towards a philosophy of cinema.

'Of all the art forms', writes Harvey, '[cinema] has perhaps the most robust capacity to handle intertwining themes of space and time in instructive ways.'[23] He elaborates by suggesting that 'the serial use of images, and the ability to cut back and forth across space and time, frees it from many of the normal [artistic] constraints'.[24] In support of his assertions, Harvey draws directly from the work of the French philosopher Gaston Bachelard, particularly his concept of 'poetic space' in relation to the narrative construction of individual identity. He quotes Bachelard to the effect that 'We think we know ourselves in time, when all we know is a sequence of fixations in the spaces of the being's stability.'[25] Bachelard states very clearly that even if we want to 'detach from our own history the always too contingent history of the persons who have encumbered it, we realise that the calendars of our lives can only be established in its imagery'.[26] Harvey extends these ideas to encompass the cinema by suggesting that time is represented 'as memories of experienced places and spaces' and, furthermore, that 'history must indeed give way to poetry, time to space, as the fundamental material of social expression. The spatial image (particularly the evidence of the photograph) then asserts an important power over history.'[27]

Harvey's approach enables him to highlight important insights with regard to the specific *potential* of cinema to signify history in terms of emotion and memory through its unique recourse to visual imagery and the editing process. If we apply this sentiment to *Three Burials*, one can discern the appearance of a modernist (or, more properly, post-modernist) collage of fractured memories that can be understood as attempts at capturing a 'sequence of fixations in the spaces of the being's stability'. These images are juxtaposed to shape a narrative complexity that weaves together a number of seemingly disparate temporal events by focusing on a single, violent act: the death of Melquiades at the hands of a border patrolman called Mike Norton (Barry Pepper). This fatal incident serves as a plot device, providing the necessary impetus behind the film's narrative trajectory, and of the various character motivations and actions contained within it.

It is significant to note that our access to Melquiades is largely mediated through the subjective memories of Pete who acts as a prism through which we interpret and attempt to decipher the unfolding events of the narrative. Other than that, we know him only posthumously as a corpse. It is also significant to note that these memories arise from a grief-stricken man whose own grasp on reality progressively deteriorates following his shock at the news of Melquiades' death. Therefore, the act of remembering in *Three Burials* is essentially unreliable and is accompanied by the process of mourning as an attempt to recover from a personal trauma. But for Pete, it is his very memories of Melquiades that actively constitute his trauma.

In an illuminating essay on traumatic capture in the cinematic Western, Janet Walker relays this trope's commonality within the genre as a whole. Analysing such diverse films as *The Searchers, Pursued, Once Upon a Time in the West* and *Lone Star*, she outlines in some detail the effect that the concept of trauma has on cinematic realism in its profound potential for reinterpreting the history of the American West through film:

> A prominent subgroup of westerns [are] made up of what I'll call 'traumatic westerns,' in which past events of a catastrophic nature are represented so as to challenge both the realist representational strategies of a genre that so often trades on historical authenticity and the ideological precepts of Manifest Destiny. Traumatic westerns, it might be said, are counter-realistic and counter-historical. They are those films in which the contradictions of American conquest – a kind of generalised trauma – become invested in particular narrative scenarios.[28]

There are strong *a priori* grounds for suggesting that *Three Burials* continues in this 'prominent subgroup', and I will argue below that Pete's memories (relayed in the form of a series of flashbacks) operate not only as another counter-narrative strategy against realism, but also (by utilising the approach taken by Harvey) as cinematic examples of Bachelard's concept of 'poetic space'. This is to say, as a 'sequence of fixations' through which Pete attempts to place his friend, as it were, and construct a sense of psychological 'stability', an identity for Melquiades and, ultimately, himself. It is an attempt to determine 'spaces of the being's stability' that are removed from temporality, contingency and chance; 'fixations' expunged from the chaotic flux of 'real' experience and recast or, rather, re-remembered in mythic terms.

The film's self-reflexivity proves to be fundamental in this respect for it highlights the process whereby identity is constructed through the narrative. An indicative moment includes a tender scene where Pete and Mel are herding cattle together. Cinematographer Chris Menges' camera encompasses the epic landscape of the Texas southwest in slow, broad sweeps; heat-hazed long shots 'fix' these attractive images 'as memories of experienced places and spaces', while composer Marco Beltrami's gentle music plays over the soundtrack, giving the whole scene a romanticised, timeless air. (Such scenes are visually reminiscent of some of the famous 'cattle-driving' Westerns of Ford and Hawks, and the painted canvases of Remington and Charles Russell.) We then cut to a contemporary shot of Pete sitting, brooding in his lodging, at once indicating that this has been his subjective memory of Mel and not objective reality. This is soon followed by another such flashback when, in an endearing act of friendship, Mel gives Pete his best horse. To Pete's protestations that the gift is 'too much . . . it's the best horse I ever saw,' Mel responds with, 'Mine, yours . . . what's the difference? He's got "Pete" branded on his brain!'

Recollections like this seek to provide a 'sequence of fixations in the spaces of the being's stability' and are, as indicated above, presented in mythic terms. This is to say, shot in a traditionally realist style, they are devoid of the disjointed editing of the film's contemporary action sequences within which they are framed and are, instead, permeated throughout with a mixture of nostalgia, eulogy and a 'black-and-white' simplistic morality. Even Pete's engineering of a tryst for himself and Mel with two married women, the local waitress Rachel (Melissa Leo) and Norton's own wife Lou Ann (January Jones), when depicted (or, more properly, remembered) in such terms, takes on an innocent air, despite the obvious moral issue of crossing the 'border' of marital fidelity. When Mel and Lou Ann are alone together in a motel room, they do not have sexual intercourse, but merely dance; the mood of the scene is one of tenderness rather than carnal lust.

Such narrative simplicity is, of course, undercut by framing Pete's flashbacks within and (on occasion) throughout with the chronologically disjointed scenes showing the actions and memories of other prominent characters, Norton chief among them. Norton's memories clearly differ from those of Pete's in both mood and composition. Here the mythic simplicity is replaced by a series of complex, often repetitive flashbacks of the circumstances leading up to his part in Mel's death. These are relayed in disorientating fashion with staccato bursts of varying lengths, which invade the contemporary action of the narrative at seemingly random points. For instance, in one scene we see Norton responding to the sound of rifle fire. He is aiming at something off-screen, but there is no accompanying reverse-shot to illuminate what (if anything) is contained within his point-of-view. Another such moment revealed earlier in the narrative sees a panicked Norton burying Mel's body in a scratch-dug hole. (Of course, this is chronologically illogical as it is revealed *before* the revelation of his shooting of Mel.) Another such moment is framed between shots of Norton gazing after Lou Ann as she heads into a shopping mall, the colour of her red miniskirt apparently enough to trigger his memory: a very brief hand-held shot reveals Norton looking at his shaking, blood-stained hands as he kneels over Mel's body. A cut forward in time to a close-up shot showing Norton's pained expression, his eyes watering, not only frames the flashback, it also reveals his trauma regarding the dreadful psychological consequences of taking another man's life.

Walker suggests that, in 'traumatic westerns . . . past events elude the realist register to suggest another way of knowing, one marked by ellipsis, uncertainty, and repetition'.[29] Such 'marks' are apparent in *Three Burials*, relayed through its numerous flashbacks and multi-layered diegesis. Indeed, in one particular moment, the film itself becomes involved in the process of constructing historical memory, for significantly included as a (disembodied) flashback is the single scene shot solely from Mel's perspective – this is the moment of his death. As the camera pans downward to provide an overhead shot of Mel dismounting from his horse, it is revealed that he was protecting his goats from a prowling coyote (hence, the gunshots heard by Norton) and is himself subsequently gunned down by Norton's 'return-fire'. The tragic nature of his death is thus enhanced with the realisation that not only did he not deserve such an end, but that as he lay dying Melquiades never knew who or what hit him.

When taken together (and accepting that the structure of the film would deliberately seek to deny this possibility), these sequences constitute what one would typically refer to in generic terms as the 'shootout'. But far from merely repeating this convention, *Three Burials* denies us both the immediacy and the catharsis of regeneration through violence; compared with Shane's shootout with Wilson, for instance, this epic moment is anything but. I have, throughout, argued against the implication that regeneration through violence occurs in all Westerns, however. Chapter 2, for instance, detailed how *The Searchers*, a purportedly classical Western, points out that following this path leads not to redemption of the spirit, but to the loss of spirit, as is Ethan's fate.

In both real and mythic terms, therefore, not only is Mel's death senseless, but it becomes apparent that Norton does not really see who he is firing at either: busy masturbating to *Hustler* when he is first alerted to the sound of rifle fire, he panics and responds with shots of his own. And, if we are to believe that he fired out of a genuine sense of self-defence, then his assigned mythical role as villain is hereby rendered problematic. Despite his generally objectionable personality, Norton, like everybody else in the borderlands, exists within the chaotic, intersecting flux of emotion and action that constitutes real life in the diegetic world of *Three Burials*. One can no more 'fix' him generically than Pete can 'fix' Melquiades' identity through subjective recollections.

The quality of memories, according to Bachelard, is that they 'are motionless', and 'the more securely they are fixed in space, the sounder they are'.[30] It is important to point out though that none of the flashbacks in *Three Burials* – Pete's or Norton's – serve a traditional purpose. This is to say, none of these perspectives give us any objective clarity on events as they serve to confuse rather than to elucidate. Norton's recollections are rendered as trauma through staccato editing and disorientating camera movement, while Pete's are, as the product of trauma, acts of attempted displacement, re-imaginations through a romantic aesthetic that is itself profoundly undermined by the confusing nature of the film's spatial–temporal narrative patterns. The issue then arises as to how much we really know about Melquiades. Nothing terribly objective at any rate; however, such subjective spatial 'fixations' within the narrative as offered through Pete's memories work to emphasise his bond with Mel as something almost innocent and pure, at least this is the indication – as something removed from the complexities and frustrations of real experience and laced with the harmonious simplicity of myth. They act as a counter-point to the recollections of Norton, but despite their ostensible realism they remain very much a product of the same trauma, what Walker refers to as 'the catastrophic past event'.[31]

Bachelard's and Harvey's views are perhaps best illustrated in *Three Burials* in what proves to be the last, most significant, of Pete's subjective flashbacks. In a scene established by a smooth panning shot of a flock of birds breaking into flight across a lake at sunset, we find Pete and Mel sitting together gazing out at the calm waters. It is here that we gain crucial knowledge of Mel's proud boast to Pete of a home and family back in his native Mexico, a small village he calls Jimenez. Harvey's idea of the significance of the 'spatial image', specifically the 'evidence of the photograph', finds a powerful consonance here as Mel shows Pete a photograph purporting to depict himself, his wife Evelia, and their three children. It is Mel's assertion of both an identity and of a history for himself through visual recourse to a family that he claims not to have seen in over five years. Mel goes on to note with unmistakable pride that his youngest son is 'gonna be a damn good cowboy', and yet this pride is tempered by a constant fear of the possibility of death – a fear that we know to have been already realised. As a 'wetback' Mel worries about being arrested or, worse still, shot by the border patrol. And it is at this point in the narrative that he asks Pete to promise that, should he die 'over here', he will return his body to Jimenez. But, of course, this scene is, like the others, a moment selected by Pete and re-enacted for us at a particular point in the narrative to suit a particular purpose. And its purpose is both to explain and to justify Pete's kidnapping of Norton, the disinterring of Mel's body, and his immanent embarking on a quixotic journey across the border into Mexico. It is not, then, strictly speaking, Mel's own assertion, rather, it is Pete's attempt to give his dead friend a voice – 'stability' – to speak for him as it were.

In addition to the above, this scene provides the narrative impetus for Pete to assume the mythic role of the hero, who will head into the wilderness in order to deal justice to his dead friend's killer before fulfilling his promise to return Mel's body to Jimenez. Before the flashback draws to a close, Mel draws Pete a map so he can locate his claimed birth place and, as the narrative segues into its second act – 'The Journey/*El Viaje*' – Pete will use this map and the photograph in his attempt to locate Jimenez, inform Mel's wife of her husband's passing, and honour his pledge to his dead friend.

III

Pete's occupation as a ranch foreman, together with his assumption of the role of heroic defender of his dead friend's honour, comprises two key elements of the Western: these are the image of the cowboy and the revenge motif. The film trades on these elements in order to present us with its particular deconstruction of the myth of the West.

The significance of the cowboy in relation to the frontier lies at the heart of Anglo-America's myth of itself. As I have already detailed in previous chapters, the cowboy is typically envisioned as a lone hero on horseback, one who lives by his own code of honour: tough, courageous and quick on the draw. He justly defends the pioneers of civilisation against the various representative forces of the wilderness. However, the hero is also a part of the world of the villain. His past, if not exactly the same, is in many ways related to this figurative savage. Consequently, the embryonic civilisation, whose very existence depends upon such a figure, ultimately rejects his violence once he has vanquished the savage forces that have threatened it. The wilderness provides the hero with the territory in which he can live out this mythic identity; its destruction is therefore his own. The cowboy is thus a profoundly existential figure in a profoundly existential landscape.

I have already discussed how the counter-narrative style engendered by the peculiar editing techniques and spatial–temporal disjuncture in the first part of *Three Burials* offer a brutal deconstruction of the demands cinematic realism places on verisimilitude and its need for 'psychologically-rounded characters'. Therefore, it is perhaps in keeping with the film's ironic tone that, in many ways, its most interesting aspect (as far as the Western is concerned) comes at the moment that this counter-narrative style is completely abandoned. At this intermediate point, the film segues into a more traditional aesthetic style of cinematic realism.

Having overheard a conversation between Sheriff Belmont (Dwight Yoakam) and Border Patrol Captain Gomez (Mel Rodriguez) that implicates Norton in the killing of Melquiades, Rachel comes to inform Pete 'who killed that Mexican'. Pete gazes out into the surrounding wilderness of his lonely farmstead and the romantic backdrop – much akin to Munny's adobe hut in *Unforgiven* – subsumes Pete; almost as if it is importing the knowledge of what he must do into his person, etching it into his very soul. The mythic West is to provide him (or so he thinks) with the method by which Norton will be brought to justice. This is confirmed in Pete's mind when Belmont refuses his angry demand that he arrest Norton. The killing of his best friend is to be ignored by the forces of law and, with this realisation, Pete, the man who has been brought to a standstill by his grief, is transformed into the vengeful hero. We are now in recognisable 'Western territory': when the lawful representatives of civilisation are unable or, in this case, unwilling to mete out justice, the gunfighter springs into action.

It is, of course, the borderlands that provide the geography in which Pete can live out his mythic role as the hero. Its constitution of deserts, mountains and canyons likens itself to the historical epic and immediately begs comparison with the aesthetic qualities of Westerns past, the Monument Valley terrain of Ford or the apocalyptic deserts of Leone and Sam Peckinpah; perhaps also with the southwestern novels of Cormac McCarthy. The film's intertextual relay makes clear the role that the Western narrative plays, not only in structuring mythic accounts of the historical past, but also its creation of a sense of individual identity. In this regard, *Three Burials* once more refers back to the Westerns of the past: fusing existentialism with the historical epic, incorporating at once the thematic legacies of Bud Boetticher, Anthony Mann and Hawks, and once again Ford.

A journey into such a territory evokes a journey back in time. Pick-up trucks are replaced by horses and roads give way to mountains and desert tracks. At times this effect of a temporal shift is depicted in *Three Burials* with no small sense of humour. Belmont, who hates Pete primarily because both men share a relationship with Rachel (Belmont's resentment perhaps grows in the knowledge of his own sexual impotency), accidentally drives his truck into a ditch. The pursuit of Pete is to be a horseback affair. The Sheriff's prowess as leader of the manhunt is quickly ridiculed. When discussing plans to detain Pete before he can make it into Mexico, Belmont enquires hopefully of Gomez, 'What about the heat-seeking radar ya'll got?' With perfect comic timing, Gomez replies, 'It don't work.'

Pete's journey is accompanied by striking long-takes of mountainous terrain which dwarf his small convoy of three horses and a pack-mule, enveloping them all in a primordial environment. It is at this moment that Pete's own associations with the wilderness become visually manifested. Belmont, crouching unseen from a vantage point, trains his rifle sight on Pete. He hesitates, and then releases his finger from the trigger before finally watching Pete disappear behind a rock face, as if he is merging with the landscape itself. Belmont's failure to shoot reaffirms his impotency. More significantly, he is quick to realise the ethical consequences should he kill Pete. He subsequently extricates himself from the manhunt. In a more abstract sense, he extricates himself from the myth, and his role in the narrative comes to an end.

Meanwhile, Pete's journey becomes increasingly perverse. Melquiades' corpse inevitably begins to rot in the desert heat, resembling less and less the person that it once was. Pete's vain attempts to preserve the body become increasingly farcical: burning off ants with kerosene, pouring anti-freeze down the cadaver's throat, and even attempting to comb its hair with a garden fork while drunk. Such dark humour is accompanied in equal measure by more traditional moments of danger and fear. While trekking round a gorge, one of Pete's horse's panics, slips and falls to its death in the valley below. In another, particularly upsetting scene, an unnamed old blind man (Levon Helm), whom Pete and Norton come across on their journey, asks Pete to shoot him because his son 'has got of cancer' and 'won't be comin' back' to look after him – a life lived alone and in darkness is more than he can bear. Norton in turn gets bitten by a rattlesnake and Pete has to rely on Mexican villagers to extract the poison. The healer woman, reluctant to help a 'gringo' of the Border Patrol, is swayed only by Pete's desperate plea for a higher purpose: 'I *need* him. I don't want him to die.' (It is quickly revealed that this is a woman whom Norton had, earlier on in the narrative, punched in the face as she attempted to cross the border. She returns the 'favour' in kind by pouring coffee on his crotch and then smashing the kettle across his face, breaking his nose in the bargain.)

As already mentioned, it is once Pete decides to adopt the role of the hero and cast Norton in the role of the villain that the complex temporality that has dominated the narrative of the film's first part is completely abandoned. *Three Burials*' assumption of the form and iconography of the Western in its second part seems to be undertaken with the self-conscious, deconstructive agenda. The narrative complexity remains, but in its second part it is in the contrast between form and meaning that the film acquires its depth and seriousness. That is to say, the self-conscious irony of the film's ideological agenda would be lost if the film merely replicated the narrative and iconography of a so-called traditional Western. Of course, as I have already outlined, and whether they intend to or not, Westerns not only propound the myth, they question it also. *Three Burials* both deconstructs the myth and shows, in an imitative form, the fate of the man who follows it. This fate, hinted at throughout Pete's journey, is finally laid bare when he arrives in Coahuilla. To his dismay, none of the locals seem to have heard of Jimenez. When Pete finally tracks down 'Evelia' (her name turns out to be Rosa), she claims never to have heard of Melquiades Estrada, let alone admit to being his wife. Upon presentation of the photograph, Rosa angrily demands how Pete managed to get hold of a picture of her and her children. She does not acknowledge the figure of Mel and demands that Pete leaves before he gets her into trouble with her husband, finally reasserting, 'We don't know any Melquiades!' Rosa's angry reaction suggests that she may indeed have encountered Mel in a sexual capacity, but not that of husband and wife.

After days of fruitless searching, Pete comes across a dilapidated old shack in the middle of the desert and proclaims it to be Jimenez. Pete's obsessive delusion has, by this point, convinced him of the reality of Mel's photograph. Harvey writes that 'photographs are now construed as evidence of a real history, no matter what the truth of that history may have been. The image is, in short, proof of the reality, and images can be constructed and manipulated.'[32] We now know that Pete's only reference to the 'real' – the photograph purporting to depict Mel with his wife and children – is revealed to be a lie. As if to confound his delusions further, he produces the photograph once more and holds it out to Norton. A reverse-shot from Norton's perspective reveals it to us in detail for the first time. (In the flashback, which constitutes Pete's memory, there is a split-second shot on the photograph as Mel hands it over.

I would suggest that, at this point in the narrative, we have no real reason to question its legitimacy.) Aside from the fact that Pete is holding it sideways, disorientating our perception from the outset, upon close inspection it depicts only Rosa and her three children – one has to look hard to see a shadowy figure in the far background (we presume this is Mel, but it could just as easily be anybody).

This harsh reality is as clear to Norton as it is to the audience, and we begin to feel a tremendous sense of sympathy for Pete's increasingly desperate situation. He is unable or, perhaps, unwilling to accept the truth of the situation as this would involve denying the validity of the heroic role in which he has cast himself. As Pete and Norton go about 'recreating' Jimenez, it is just as Harvey relates, 'a willingness to search for identity, home, and history'.[33] Mel may not have any of these things, but Pete is determined to create them for him. His final act is to reconstruct in the flimsiest of forms the home that Mel claimed, but which did not exist. It is his final attempt to create a space of 'stability' for the doomed man, a final resting place for his friend.

What of the enigma of Melquiades himself? I have already discussed how our access to him is mediated almost exclusively through the subjective memories of Pete, and it is, as a consequence of this, difficult to ascertain much of his personal history. Nevertheless, we can hypothesise, and it does indeed become evident that Mel created an imaginary home and family – a mythic 'space' for himself – something he desired, but which never actually existed. In relation to the North American Imaginary, Octavio Paz notes how the United States has defined Mexico as a place onto which its own imagined fantasies of cultural and racial otherness can be played out:

> In general, Americans have not looked for Mexico in Mexico; they have looked for their obsessions, enthusiasms, phobias, hopes, interests – and these are what they have found. In short, the history of our relationship is the history of a stubborn deceit, usually involuntary though not always so.[34]

If this can be said of 'Americans' cultural (mis)perceptions of Mexico, then the significance of *Three Burials* surely lies in the way it inverts this 'stubborn deceit', revealing it to work equally upon Mexico's cultural (mis)perceptions of the United States. If we reiterate Limerick to the effect that 'the Mexican border was a social fiction that neither nature nor people in search of opportunity observed', then we could say that when Mel first arrives at Pete's west Texas cattle ranch, he arrives out of two interdependent social fictions: the first of these is that which concerns the 'conquered and controlled borderland', which Mel has crossed over presumably in search of work; the second constitutes the mythic discourse that has influenced popular cultural perceptions of the American West. When Mel declares – 'I'm just a cowboy' – he is not only looking for employment, in mythic terms he is asserting an identity that has its roots firmly in the rhetoric of popular frontier mythology and its attendant cultural, political and historical functions. In seeking economic and social 'opportunity', he is playing into the American Dream, itself, of course, a 'social fiction' that, like the cowboy, is firmly rooted in the popular cultural mindset of America. In existential terms, Paz also relates that, in any civilisation, '[t]here is no meaning, there is a search for meaning'.[35] Such sentiments relate to *Three Burials*' complex use of narrative, juxtaposing the human desire for meaning with the absence of meaning.

For his part, Norton is purged by confrontation with his own shortcomings. His brutal and torturous journey ends with him being forced at gunpoint by Pete to beg forgiveness for the killing of Melquiades. Indeed, his heartfelt and pained outpourings of grief and regret leave us with little doubt that, despite Lou Ann's declaration, he is *not* 'beyond redemption'. Instead of meeting his end at Pete's hands Norton is let go. Pete cannot bring himself to kill Norton probably because this would mean a violation of the code by which Pete has constructed his heroic persona. By the same token, Norton is the enemy whose existence has defined Pete and given meaning to his mythic quest. He is also, in the final instance, the closest thing to family that Pete has. (In this, his relationship with Norton bears a thematic resemblance to the conflicting emotions felt by Ethan Edwards towards Marty Pawley in *The Searchers*.)

In a final touching scene moments before he leaves, Pete says to Norton, 'You can keep the horse . . . son.' As if to confirm his redemption, Norton calls after Pete, asking if he is 'gonna be alright?' A close-up of Norton's battered face showing genuine compassion for his erstwhile captor is thus the last image we see. (We are also left to ponder how he will make his way back across the border to his empty home – parted from Lou Ann, the wife who has left him to go back to the city life she had abandoned in Cincinnati.)

So Pete rides off, betrayed by a mythic identity that did not exist as surely as Mel's professed identity did not exist either. He wanders into a borderland that is neither myth nor reality, nor even a conflicted mixture of the two, lying in between; a nowhere man, a fugitive cut-off from both the United States and Mexico. He has also lost his relationship with Rachel, who refuses to leave her husband Bob (Richard Jones) for either Belmont or Pete. Actually, Rachel comes across as the most philosophical of the characters in the film. Unlike Pete, she accepts the complex and contradictory identities that reflect the complexities of the borderlands; to her they seem complimentary rather than contradictory, a state of mind that completely eludes Pete (and most of the other characters for that matter); as she says to Pete, 'You just don't understand.' Such an attitude enables her to accept Belmont's impotence and Bob's mixture of jealousy and complacency, all the while assuring Pete that 'You're the one for me. The only one I love!' She will not exchange this tangible reality, nor buy into Pete's fantasy of marriage, an offer he makes from across the border when drunk. Thus, Rachel shatters Pete's last-ditch effort to realise a mythic identity, it completes his personal failure. He has become a lost soul, like

Ethan at the conclusion of *The Searchers*, unmoored in a figurative borderland, unable to adapt to civilisation and, ultimately, lost in the wilderness.

IV

As the preceding chapters have sought to make clear, the separation of history from myth is a difficult task to undertake. In the final instance, it may even be an impossible one. From Turner onward, the terms by which the history of the nineteenth-century American West have been rendered share more in common with the language of fictional narratives than most historians would care to admit. I have indicated above that opening a discussion of *Three Burials'* relation to frontier mythology necessarily opens up a discussion of its relation to frontier history, as well as confronting us with the constructed nature of historical discourse itself. It is to such a discussion that I now turn.

This chapter began by describing how the New Western historians have charged Turner with engendering a false historical consciousness, a fanciful theory driven by myth at the expense of historical reality. However, it is precisely the elusive nature of reality that comes under scrutiny here. In an astute critique of the New Western History, Forrest G. Robinson points out that 'it is telling . . . that Limerick came to the study of history convinced that it gave her unmediated access to real things, real events, real people, and *not to their constructions in thought and word*'.[36] Or, as Stephen McVeigh asks, are not history and literature 'both stories that emerge from certain contexts to answer specific problems or circumstances and face the same problems of language and meaning?'[37] If this is so, then one must always consider the nature and function of culture, language and narrative in all forms of historiography; at the same time, one must consider the historiographic element of popular culture.

Relating *Three Burials'* narrative and visual style to the question of historical reality must, therefore, take into account the indelible mark of myth on historiography. If we recall, Henry Nash Smith once described the frontier in terms of myth and symbol, as 'intellectual construction[s] that fuse concept and emotion into an image'.[38] And this 'image' was actually of great importance in 'exert[ing] a decided influence on practical affairs' in the historical West.[39] Despite assuming a discernable difference between myth and reality, in other words, how the *reality* of the frontier has been written into history as *myth*, Smith identifies the constructed image of the West as a mediator of historical experience. He points out the fundamental necessity of a 'continuous dialectic interplay between the mind and its environment', one that privileges 'perception' as a barometer of the real:

> History cannot happen – that is, men cannot engage in purposive group behaviour – without images which simultaneously express collective desires and impose coherence on the infinitely numerous and infinitely varied data of experience. These images are never, of course, exact

reproductions of the physical or social environment. They cannot motivate and direct action unless they are drastic simplifications, yet if the impulse toward clarity of form is not controlled by some process of verification, symbols and myths can become dangerous by inciting behaviour grossly inappropriate to the given historical situation.[40]

In *Three Burials* 'the impulse toward clarity of form' is undermined throughout the narrative and 'verification' is denied its protagonist. In Jones' and Arriaga's tragic vision, the myth and the man whose 'perception' is shaped by that myth, has become not the hero of legend, but a deluded individual 'dangerous' in his actions. Laudable as Pete's intentions may be, they have become 'grossly inappropriate' in the film's 'given historical situation'.

In alluding to the potential sociological dangers inherent in the terms symbol and myth, Smith also causes us to recall Slotkin's sentiments with which he began *Regeneration through Violence*. Regarding 'the sense of coherence and direction in history that myths give to those who believe in them' Slotkin writes:

> The mythology of a nation is the intelligible mask of that enigma called the 'national character.' Through myths the psychology and world view of our cultural ancestors are transmitted to modern descendants, in such a way and with such power that our perception of contemporary reality and our ability to function in the world are directly, often tragically affected.[41]

Sacvan Bercovitch further elaborates upon the cultural–ideological implications of this interrelationship between myth and history. 'Myth may clothe history as fiction', he writes, 'but it persuades in proportion to its capacity to help men act in history. Ultimately, its effectiveness derives from its functional relationship to facts.'[42] Throughout this study we have borne witness to the multifarious ways in which the Western has responded to the issues raised by the frontier and of its oft-times keen awareness of its own role and culpability in shaping historical perceptions and (mis)understandings. The Western, undoubtedly, has its own 'functional relationship to facts'.

One of the most convincing arguments for the intermixing of historiography and genre theory in the study of the Western comes from Walker. She maintains that, while it is true that Westerns frequently take dramatic license, 'it is also true that [they] take *historical license* [and] the rejection of the western's historicity on the basis of its dramatic license is specious; and falsity is not grounds for dismissal'.[43] Following a rigorous critique of genre studies, which she describes 'as a text-dependent form of analysis', giving little 'play' to ethnic voices and histories within the 'symbolic drama' of a white male 'fantasy', Walker accuses genre criticism of evincing 'a tendency to recapitulate the [racial] bias it pretends only to reveal'.[44] It allows, instead, for 'historical interpretation presented in narrative form to parade as mere myth'.[45] Hers is an approach that highlights the benefit of studying film texts and historical accounts in 'concert', claiming that 'history and myth are related and textual'.[46] Walker goes further, suggesting that 'the western is a profoundly historical genre [one that] repays a historical approach to its analysis'.[47]

That I have been dealing primarily with audio-visual representations of the West requires me to engage with the *form* that the Western as an 'historical genre' may take. Hayden White's 1988 essay, 'Historiography and Historiophoty', proves relevant in this regard. Walker makes fleeting reference to this essay in her study; however, I feel that a more in-depth analysis is necessary.[48]

White sought to contextualise contemporary approaches to historiography with a well-considered and sympathetic appeal to what was fast becoming a new subdiscipline within the field. He defines historiophoty as 'the representation of history and our thought about it in visual images and filmic discourse'.[49] According to White, historiophoty raises a troublesome challenge to historical purists, whose reservations regarded the degree to which 'it is possible to "translate" a given written account of history into a visual-auditory equivalent without significant loss of content'.[50] This reservation brought forth two major charges (simultaneous yet paradoxical) against the capacity of visual narratives to be historically valid. When it came to issues of verisimilitude, historical films were considered to be both 'too detailed' and 'not detailed enough'. Although White does not use these specific terms (he concedes to 'not know[ing] enough about film theory to specify more precisely the elements, equivalent to the lexical, grammatical, and syntactical dimensions of spoken or written language'[51]) when a filmic discourse is perceived to be 'too detailed' (that is, 'in what it shows when it is forced to use actors and sets that may not resemble perfectly the historical individuals and scenes of which it is a representation'), we can relate this to the formal aspects of its *mise-en-scène*. The contrariwise charge that historical film is often 'not detailed enough' (that is, 'when it is forced to condense a process that might have taken years to occur ... into a two or three-hour presentation'[52]) we can relate directly to the process of editing (the spatial and temporal elisions typical of the filmmaking process which Harvey branded 'unique' to the cinema). As *Three Burials* makes clear, the editing process can add a level of complexity that makes redundant such charges as the 'poverty of the "information load"' with regard to the shaping and presentation of past events through visual images.[53]

One way of approaching the complexities of the relationship between visual and written history is to consider White's own answer to the above academic charges. In *Metahistory* (1973), he relates the practice of historiography to the artistic-creative processes of literary narrative forms. Like Fredric Jameson, White's overall opinion has always been that history is consciously *emplotted* as a narrative. This is to say, that it is always a work of interpretive historiography and, therefore, necessarily engages with, and is a product of, a philosophy of history. Following in the tradition of Northrop Frye, White outlines the process of historical emplotment by utilising the traditional literary modes available to western discourse. Romance, tragedy, comedy and satire are thus employed in order to reveal how historians express them using one or more of the major linguistic tropes. Metaphor, metonymy, synecdoche and irony thus provide ways of *explaining* events as historical facts and, simultaneously, imbuing them with cultural meaning.[54]

In language that is evocative of the Barthes of *Mythologies*, White elucidates the ideological machinations that lay behind historical 'facts':

> Events happen or occur; facts are constituted by the subsumption of events under a description, which is to say, by acts of predication . . . not 'facts' in general, but 'facts' of a specific kind (political facts, social facts, cultural facts, psychological facts).[55]

'The historian *shapes* his materials', claims White, 'in response to the imperatives of narrative discourse in general.'[56] If this is so, then the historian also necessarily engages with ideology in his or her act of historical emplotment, suggesting 'the constructivist nature of the historian's enterprise'.[57] White further suggests that '[j]ust as every ideology is attended by a specific idea of history and its processes, so too . . . is every idea of history attended by specifically determinable ideological implications'.[58]

For his part, White draws little distinction between literary or visual modes of historical representation as both (invariably) constitute a form of narrative that draws its intelligibility from the same cultural–ideological traditions. In his own discussion of White's approach, Kerwin Lee Klein concludes that there can be no exact science to history. As I have indicated above, each history *depends* on a speculative philosophy of history, on poetic over cognitive bases, hence, Klein writes that 'the best reasons for choosing one history rather than another are moral or aesthetic rather than epistemic'.[59] He puts forward the notion of a 'plot' of history, which constitutes a cognitive and linguistic act, drawing a variety of disparate items into some larger, intelligible whole. Like Smith's approach to image, this plot explains itself by 'individuating an event out of the historical flux'.[60] He then turns this method to Turner's Frontier Thesis, posing and then answering two important questions: 'what is the frontier?' and 'how does the frontier explain?' In response to the first question: the frontier is a 'concatenation of different places and processes, from ethnic interaction to migration to community building, which historians abstract from the chaos of sense data and synthesise into an individual concept'.[61] In response to the second question: it explains by providing 'the middle in a narrative whose beginning point is non-democratic European society and whose endpoint is twentieth-century American democracy'.[62] This brings us once more to the vital question of history in relation to myth. Drawing directly from the structural anthropology of Claude Lévi-Strauss, White assesses the fundamental role of myth in the shaping of historical narrative and, therefore, the structuring of what Klein dubbed our 'historical imaginations':

> [History] is constituted, Lévi-Strauss thinks, by virtue of a conceptual strategy that is *mythic* in nature, and which identifies the 'historical' with the experiences, modes of thought, and praxis peculiar to modern Western civilisation ... stories of the founding of cities or states ... whether presented under the aspect either of social science or of history, partake of the mythical inasmuch as they 'cosmologize' or 'naturalise' what are in reality *nothing but* human constructions which might well be other than what they happen to be.[63]

From this perspective history is unavoidably conjoined with myth. Consequently, for White, 'thus envisioned, to *historicize* any structure, to write its history, is to mythologize it'.[64] Furthermore, he insists that history 'is never only history *of*, it is always also history *for*'.[65] That is to say, any history is always written for the interests of a specific social group, race or class, and with a certain perspective in mind (that is, it necessarily asserts an ideological position as an actual *fact*). 'For Lévi-Strauss', White argues, 'the impulse to mythologize [is] in the very nature of language itself.'[66] Taken to its logical conclusion, this approach suggests that historical form is determined not only by any given culture's narrative traditions, but also by the inherent *nature* of language.

Such opinions regarding the nature of language do not enjoy universal agreement, and it is worth noting here some disputations. For one, Slotkin suggests that such archetypal approaches (particularly the structural anthropology of Lévi-Strauss) tend 'to obscure the importance of historical experience and change in the shaping of specific myth/ideological systems and in the social life of the communities the systems serve'.[67] For Slotkin, 'myths are formulated as ways of explaining problems that arise in the course of historical experience'.[68] Hence, he considers 'both myth and genre as phenomena shaped by historical contingency, rather than as archetypes generated either by "the nature of things" or "the nature of language"'.[69] In *Narration and Knowledge* (1985), Arthur C. Danto presses these implications further by mapping the presence of narrative onto our own, individual lives. Again, like Jameson, Danto's philosophical approach suggests that '[n]arration exemplifies one of the basic ways in which we represent the world ... to so great a degree that our image of our own lives must be deeply narrational'.[70] As we have seen, however, *Three Burials* uses narrative in order to evoke the underlying tension afflicting all narratives: the human desire for meaning and the very absence of meaning. The film's narrative apes Smith's notion of 'continuous dialectic interplay between the mind and its environment', but there is no synthesis in evidence for the 'interplay' between Pete's 'mind' and the 'environment' in which he operates *undermines* human 'perception'. For if Pete's *viaje* had succeeded and drawn to a heroic conclusion, then the film would surely have failed to live up to the promise of its counter-narrative beginnings. But, of course, this is not the case.

In terms of its own brand of historical representation, I suggest that *Three Burials* forms part of a small (but growing) number of transnational Westerns that are concerned with both 'sides' of the United States–Mexico border, and that seek to bring forth the latent history of the borderlands; an historiophotic example of *la frontera*. The borderlands – as a problematic in between space of racial antagonisms, liminal identities and violence – prove fertile ground for scrutinising Anglo-America's national mythology and, therefore, its own sense history. Of course, the notion of transnationalism is not new to the Western genre. On a broader scale, and in response to those who see the Western primarily as an American genre, it has, in fact, always been influenced by an extended historical legacy of European conquest from which it has drawn and adopted its recognisable tropes and plot motifs. Specifically, from the various narratives related to that legacy: popular literary fictions including pulp, dime novels, literature, poetry, song; religious sermons; political speeches; historiographies; and, of course, the cinema.

In historical and racial terms, Slotkin writes of the transnational origins of the United States, reminding us that, from its very inception, '[American] history in the West and in the East, was shaped from the beginning by the meeting, conversation, and mutual adaptation of different cultures.'[71] Susan Kollins presses an issue already implicit in Slotkin's own treatment of the genre. 'In perceiving how the Western borrows its faraway setting and redeeming male hero from the plots of colonial novels', she writes, 'critics can no longer argue that the genre operates as a quintessential American form but instead must recognise that its sensibilities have been shaped by a larger history of imperialism.'[72] Furthermore, she argues that Western narratives that draw attention to this 'colonial unconscious' act to restore 'the history of empire to the genre'.[73] I suggest that a film like *Three Burials* forces us to consider one of the major problems posed by numerous Westerns, whether one wishes to demarcate them in classical or revisionist categories, and that is the enigmatic concept of a homogeneous and stable Anglo-American national identity.

To date, *the* prominent and oft-cited example of transnationalism in the cinematic Western remains John Sayles' masterful *Lone Star*. This film highlights the intersections among racial, ethnic and social groups by locating itself geographically along the Rio Grande in a fictional Texas border town aptly named, Frontera. In a representative scene, the town's history teachers answer angry parents' protestations regarding the possible import into the school's curriculum of Mexican and Hispanic cultures extending beyond anything other than cookery classes. 'We're not changing anything,' one replies, 'We're just trying to present a more complete picture.' In the end, this is what *Lone Star* tries to articulate – 'a more complete picture' – a breaking down of borders, both geographical and cultural, as they have been established by the binarism of the myth of the West. It is, therefore, representative of the fact that the United States is a polyglot society as well as being culturally diverse generally; its identity 'shaped' by the interaction of different cultures.[74]

I contend that *Three Burials* can be read along similar lines. To a certain degree, the film does depict the borderlands as an in between space, one that is not simply defined as a line drawn between two distinct and wholly different countries, societies and cultures. Instead, it is depicted as a space with its own character and meaning, one that is inseparable from history and myth. And, like *Lone Star*, it renders its own transnational characteristics in terms that encompass not only the political and the geographic, but the cultural and the ethnic as well. A number of the actors, creative contributors and technicians, including the screenwriter Guillermo Arriaga, are Hispanics. Aside from such collaboration on the film's production there is a stylistic acknowledgement of transnationality in the fact that the film's dialogue is in both English and Spanish. It must be conceded that only English subtitles are provided. The Mexican pastel-coloured chapter headings that announce the different sections of the film are provided in both English and Spanish. Occasionally, there is Spanish dialogue unaccompanied by English translation.

As I have suggested above, the film can also be considered transnational in its presentation of cultural identity for, in part, *Three Burials* deals with the various ethnic groups – Hispanic, Chicano, Mestizo and Mexican – that the official history of the borderlands so often neglects, and that (so the charge goes) the myth and the Western genre often reduce to orientalist, unflattering or outright insulting stereotypes: the bordello 'senorita' (as witnessed briefly in *The Searchers*); the savage 'bandit' or the lazy 'greaser'. Not only does *Three Burials* explode such stereotypes, it explodes the notion of a border through its presentation of the various characters and their relationships, all of whom cross 'borders' of one kind or another: racial, marital, lawful, political, social, economic and cultural.

Most directly, however, *Three Burials*' overall theme seeks to draw the history of the borderlands onto the contemporary moment with the extremely controversial issue of 'border jumping'. Mexicans desperate to escape their poverty-stricken situation by 'crossing-over' into the United States in search of economic opportunity is, of course, another repressed aspect of Anglo-America's triumphalist version of the history of frontier settlement. The New Western History is surely correct in suggesting that, for the most part, so-called official history sought to conceal the brutal acts of conquest required in advancing US claims of national, cultural and racial hegemony throughout the southwest. This historical elision is of fundamental importance if we are to consider both the national and individual identities of the borderlands. One of the most important writers in this regard is Gloria Anzaldúa.

Anzaldúa writes a poetic and highly personalised account of her upbringing along the borderlands. In *Borderlands – la Frontera: the New Mestiza* (1987), she shifts the traditional parameters of historiographic concern, displaying a sense of frustration and fear held by the local communities – the 'little people' – among whom she lived and grew up, and with whom she identifies her personal history. Her reminiscences of her childhood and self-identification with cultural otherness as a *mestiza* share pages with long passages of non-translated Spanish dialogue, thus ramifying the reality of the borderlands as linguistically polyglot, a 'melting pot' of myriad cultures, identities and voices; voices that have, themselves, invariably become subsumed under the official Anglo-American discourse. The result of her work is part poetry, part literary criticism and part history. This in itself can be considered a part of *la frontera* and in keeping with the spirit of historiophoty: a breaking down of the borders between various modes of artistic and historical expression.[75] Of course, the fact that Anzaldúa does write in Spanish as well as English (and other indigenous languages such as Nahua) provides us with an analogue to *Three Burials'* own dialogism. But this is not the only point of comparison.

Anzaldúa writes from the perspective of an intellectual who is at once a woman, a *Tejana* and a lesbian. Therefore, for her borders are primarily cultural; just as the border between the United States and Mexico defines in geopolitical terms the two nations, so it symbolises the imagined borders separating cultural identities. Her perspective is that of a member of several ethnicities who have suffered from discrimination and who continue to struggle for recognition. She also identifies herself as a Chicana – one of the 'dispossessed' – whose ancestors 'lost their land and, overnight, became foreigners' after the 'white imperialist takeover', and who are now regarded as interlopers in their own land.[76] In order to consolidate their hegemony, the Anglo-American population has either forgotten that the Chicanos once 'owned' the country, or else bluntly claim that the southwest is theirs by right of conquest and is to be protected by force from the 'incursion' of the Mexican 'other'.

What she seeks to remind us is that 150 years ago the border separating Mexico and the United States simply did not exist, and the people of the area moved across the Rio Grande at will; in some indigenous cultures they still do. Her account of the contemporary borderlands, however, is one of trauma for those '*mojados*' who, 'without the benefit of bridges . . . float on inflatable rafts across *el rio Grande*, or wade or swim across naked, clutching their clothes over their heads'.[77] For her, the United States–Mexico border,

> *es una herida abierta* where the Third World grates against the first and bleeds. And before a scab forms it hemorrhages again, the lifeblood of two worlds merging to form a third country – a border culture. Borders are set up to define the places that are safe and unsafe, to distinguish *us* from *them*. A border is a dividing line, a narrow strip along a steep edge. A borderland is a vague and undetermined place created by the emotional residue of an unnatural boundary. It is in a constant state of revision. The prohibited and forbidden are its inhabitants. *Los atravesados* live here: the squint-eyed, the half-breed, the half-dead; in short, those who cross

over, pass over, or go through the confines of the 'normal.' Gringos in the US Southwest consider the inhabitants of the borderlands transgressors, aliens – whether they posses documents or not . . . The only legitimate inhabitants are those in power, the whites and those who align themselves with whites. Tension grips the inhabitants of the borderlands like a virus. Ambivalence and unrest reside there and death is no stranger.[78]

Anzaldúa's language elicits a powerful imagery of the border as an open wound – *'una herida abierta'* – her emotive language exploding the repressed history of the United States–Mexico border. This finds a consonance with Limerick's idea of the border as a 'social fiction'. However, for the tens of thousands of people – *'los atravesados'* – who attempt to cross it illegally year-in year-out, this fiction seems all too real:

> Barefoot and uneducated, Mexicans with hands like boot soles gather at night by the river where two worlds merge creating what Reagan calls a frontline, a war zone. The convergence has caused a shock culture, a border culture, a third country, a closed country.[79]

Anzaldúa conflates the personal with the political, victims in Reagan's so-called 'frontline', thereby casting doubt over the possibility of a stable subjectivity. Identity proves as porous and uncertain as the concept of a border that cleanly and unambiguously separates nations, the 'Third World' from the 'first'. Her conception of a 'border culture', borne painfully of an uneasy synthesis between 'two worlds merging', is one that highlights the fallacy of geopolitical attempts to establish a border along national or racial lines, a binary to 'distinguish *us* from *them*'. In *la frontera*, nothing could be further from Turner's 'closed' frontier.

An attempt to distinguish *'us* from *them'* is personified (and undermined) in *Three Burials* through the character of Norton. Norton clearly sees himself as a defender of Anglo-American territory by resisting with violence the Mexican 'transgressors'. For him the border must be defended with a paranoid (even pathological) zeal. In one particularly telling scene, we find Norton involved in a round-up of Mexicans attempting to cross the border illegally. During the group's detainment, Norton pursues a woman who attempts to flee; after a lengthy chase he launches himself at her, roughly tackling her to the ground and punching her in the face, breaking her nose. Norton's extreme actions are the product of fear, the fear of the racial other that lies at the heart of racism. They are also the product of his sexual frustrations, which serve only to fuel his aggressive behaviour, at once linking sex (or rather the lack of it) with violence. (Norton is masturbating to *Hustler* moments before his call to duty, an action which is, as mentioned above, replicated moments before his fatal shooting of Melquiades.)

Similarly related to the effort to maintain the sanctity of the border is Captain

Gomez, Norton's commanding officer. In racial terms, Gomez problematises the binary that the border would otherwise seek to establish, the *'us* from *them'*. He is either a Mestizo or a Chicano (though this is, perhaps fittingly, never made clear), but he is also a US citizen born and a part of the establishment; one of those 'who align themselves with whites'. He is caught between the opposed forces of the two worlds to which he belongs and which conflict in the 'border culture' in which he operates. As a servant of the white power structure he enforces US immigration law, yet he also reprimands Norton for 'beating up on' the Mexicans he apprehends. (One suspects, however, that this ostensible concern has less to do with protecting their human rights than it does with him avoiding trouble with his own superiors.) His offhand remark regarding the few of the group who escaped implicitly reveals the southwest's economic dependency on illegal labour from Mexico: 'Well, I guess somebody's gotta pick strawberries.' More significantly, Gomez also knows that Norton killed Melquiades, but conspires with Belmont to cover it up.

Overall, the film's depiction of the brutalisation of illegal immigrants at the hands of the Border Patrol, combined with the establishment's callous attitude towards Mel's death, comprise a shocking indictment of the United States' relationship with Mexico. Indeed, the official response to Mel's death exposes a cynical racist dictum: 'Your life only matters if you are white.' The metonym is reinforced during the scene at the graveyard. When asked by the grave digger what Mel's surname is, Deputy Antonio (Brent Smiga) merely shrugs his shoulders and replies, 'Mexico?' It is as if, as a nation, Mexico is to be regarded as one homogeneous mass; as an individual, one Mexican is the same as another and, perhaps, at a stretch: 'The only good Mexican is a dead Mexican'? This callousness is summarised neatly in a subsequent scene that depicts Pete sitting miserably beside Mel's grave. The smallest of markers simply reads: 'Melquiades, Mexico'.

Three Burials conflates the personal with the political. Mel's ill-treatment thus becomes a mirror for the reflection of broader social truths about relations between the United States and Mexico. In other words, the film's ideological concern with the mythic themes of justice, morality, violence and redemption become focused on the individual. Looked at in this way, Mel's pauper's life and ignominious death comes to symbolise social attitudes as a whole. In his own way, Pete tries to rectify this by inverting the terms under which oppressor and oppressed operate. He takes Norton to Mel's adobe hut, forces him sit in his chair, wear his work clothes, and even makes him drink from his cup. It is as if by forcing Norton to exist in Mel's 'space', he can force him to see from Mel's perspective. But it is Mel's decaying body which best exemplifies this conflation, representing as it does the ultimate sign of putrefaction: the corpse of an unwanted and unknown *vaquero*, a horrible, rotting *memento mori* for Anglo-America to reflect upon.

However, we should not be too quick to reassert our own binary, depicting (albeit in inverted terms) one nation simply as victims of another's brutal oppression. Such a reading would overlook the intelligent way in which *Three Burials* operates as an historiophotic text. Aside from Gomez, the film exposes Mexican complicity in the oppression of Mexicans. As Limerick rightly points out, one should not slip into the habit of 'taking point[s] of view for granted' and she reminds us that 'Hispanics – like Indians, Anglos, and every other group – could be victims as well as victimisers, and [that] the meanings of the past could seem, at times, to be riding a seesaw.'[80] Again, it is *Three Burials'* narrative concern with borders and the crossing of those borders that illustrates this intelligence. The film is also ironic in that it inverts a historical phenomenon by having its Anglo-American protagonist attempt to enter Mexico illegally. Pete enlists the help of a Mexican (the same man who, earlier, we see 'helping' the group who are detained by the Border Patrol) who smuggles illegal Mexican immigrants over the Rio Grande – for a fee. Upon quoting Pete $1,000 for his assistance, Pete scoffs, 'I don't have a thousand dollars.' 'No, not one thousand,' replies the smuggler. 'Three thousand: one for you, one for the Gringo, and one for the dead guy!' Pete eventually bargains his horse for passage, but, in a broader sense, what this scene reveals is the extortionate amount 'wetbacks' are charged by gangsters in this regard. As an organised crime, people trafficking is a booming economy, intimately connected to cross-border drug trafficking, and largely set up by unscrupulous Mexicans in order to financially exploit the desperation of their fellow countrymen and women.

V

Interpreting *Three Burials'* stylistic and thematic peculiarities in tandem with the writings of Anzaldúa has the additional and more significant consequence of forcing us to re-engage our conceptual barometer of what counts as history or, more properly, what counts as historiography.

As outlined above, such an appeal was made by White in 1988 with the consideration of historiophoty. However, in his much-celebrated earlier essay, 'The Burden of History' (1966), White responded to the reasons behind the growing anti-historicist sentiment apparent from the early twentieth century onwards. In many ways this essay acted as a precursor to his essay on historiophoty.[81] He argued that the reasons behind this anti-historicism lay in the fact that historians of the period were wedded to 'antiquated' nineteenth-century approaches to both science and the arts; approaches that were more in line with the realism of William Makepeace Thackeray than they were with the modernism of either Henrik Ibsen or James Joyce.[82] 'When [historians] say they are artists', he wrote, 'they certainly don't mean to identify themselves with action painters, kinetic sculptors, existentialist novelists, imagist poets, or *nouvelle vague* cinematographers.'[83] In essence, White's accusation was that many 'historians continue to treat their "facts" as though they were "given" and refuse to recognise . . . that they are not so much "found" as "constructed" by the kinds of questions which the investigator asks of the phenomena before him'.[84] He deemed such an approach to be inadequate to the task of representing contemporary society. As Klein succinctly puts it, '[i]nvented in an earlier age, "realist history" no longer served its original purpose: it could not adequately represent the authentic chaos of modernity'.[85] Even more succinctly than this: '"Historical realism" was no longer "realistic".'[86] In his appeal for the development of a conceptual language capable of representing history for the modern world, White lamented that, so far, 'there have been no significant attempts at surrealistic, expressionistic, or existentialist historiography in this century (except by novelists and poets themselves) for all the vaunted "artistry" of the historians of modern times'.[87]

To White's exceptions I would include certain contemporary film texts such as *Lone Star* and *Three Burials*. Indeed, it seems to me that, writing more than a generation ago, White must have had the sort of aesthetic formal qualities displayed in *Three Burials* in mind when he concerned himself with the concept of historiophoty. Consequently, my approach to the film has viewed it as an historiophotic document adequate to the task of representing Klein's 'authentic chaos of modernity', satisfying Anzaldúa's demand for personal history, and realising Limerick's regional appeal through the concept of *la frontera* in the history of the American West.

NOTES

1. Patricia Nelson Limerick, *Something in the Soil: Legacies and Reckonings in the New West* (London: W. W. Norton, 2000), p. 87.
2. I borrow the phrase 'interpretive straightjacket' from Richard W. Etulain. See Richard W. Etulain (ed.), *Does the Frontier Experience Make America Exceptional?* (Boston, MA: St Martin's Press, 1999), p. 108.
3. Limerick, *Something in the Soil*, p. 87.
4. Ibid., p. 87.
5. Ibid., pp. 87–8.
6. Ibid., p. 88.
7. Earl Pomeroy, 'Toward a Reorientation of Western History: Continuity and Environment', *Mississippi Valley Historical Review*, 41(4) (1955): 579–600, quote on p. 599. Pomeroy's essay is also discussed in Richard W. Etulain, *Re-imagining the Modern American West: A Century of Fiction, History, and Art* (Tucson, AZ: University of Arizona Press, 1996), pp. 163–8.
8. Pomeroy, 'Toward a Reorientation of Western History', p. 590: 'The role of Spanish culture in the Southwest has been exaggerated . . . Actually the native Spanish and Mexican elements in many parts of the West – particularly California, where they are most revered today – were small and uninfluential, often fairly recent arrivals themselves; the typical American settler was ignorant of their language and despised their institutions.'
9. Patricia Nelson Limerick, *The Legacy of Conquest: The Unbroken Past of the American West* (London: W. W. Norton, 1987), p. 254.
10. Ibid., p. 254.
11. Ibid., p. 255.
12. Ibid., p. 251.
13. Limerick, *Something in the Soil*, p. 88.
14. See especially Ray Allen Billington, *Westward Expansion: A History of the*

American Frontier, 2nd edn (New York: Macmillan, [1949] 1960); Ray Allen Billington, *Fredrick Jackson Turner: Historian, Scholar, Teacher* (New York: Oxford University Press, 1973); Ray Allen Billington (ed.), *The Frontier Thesis: Valid Interpretation of American History?* (Malabar, FL: Krieger, [1966] 1977), esp. the essays by Everett S. Lee, David M. Potter and Harry C. Allen.

15. Limerick, *Something in the Soil*, p. 88.
16. Ibid., p. 94.
17. Ibid., pp. 88–92.
18. Ibid., p. 92.
19. J. E. Smyth, 'The New Western History in 1931: RKO and the Challenge of *Cimarron*', in Peter C. Rollins and John E. O'Connor (eds), *Hollywood's West: The American Frontier in Film, Television, and History* (Lexington, KY: University of Kentucky Press, 2005), pp. 37–65, quote on p. 52.
20. I borrow this last term from Margarita de Orellana's 'The Incursion of North American Fictional Cinema 1911–1917 into the Mexican Revolution'. This excellent essay analyses US cinematic efforts to cover the armed phase of the Mexican revolution, together with its deployment of a range of racial and gendered stereotypes by which Anglo-Americans could 'read' the Mexican 'other'. See in John King, Ana M. Lopez and Manuel Alvarado (eds), *Mediating Two Worlds: Cinematic Encounters in the Americas* (London: British Film Institute, 1993), pp. 2–14.
21. Pam Cook and Mieke Bernink (eds), *The Cinema Book* (London: British Film Institute, [1985] 1999), p. 226.
22. See Robert Lapsley and Michel Westlake (eds), *Film Theory: An Introduction* (Manchester: Manchester University Press, 1988), see especially the chapters 'Narrative', 'Realism' and 'The Avant-Garde'.
23. David Harvey, *The Condition of Postmodernity: An Enquiry into the Origins of Cultural Change* (Oxford: Blackwell, 1990), p. 308.
24. Ibid., p. 308.
25. Gaston Bachelard, *The Poetics of Space* (1964), discussed in Harvey, *The Condition of Postmodernity*, p. 217. See also Neil Leach (ed.), *Rethinking Architecture: A Reader in Cultural Theory* (London: Routledge, 1997), pp. 81–94.
26. Leach, *Rethinking Architecture*, p. 85.
27. Harvey, *The Condition of Postmodernity*, p. 218.
28. Janet Walker (ed.), 'Captive Images in the Traumatic Western: *The Searchers, Pursued, Once Upon a Time in the West*, and *Lone Star*', in *Westerns: Films Through History* (London: British Film Institute, 2001), pp. 220–1.
29. Walker, 'Captive Images in the Traumatic Western', p. 220.
30. Harvey, *The Condition of Postmodernity*, p. 217.
31. Walker, 'Captive Images in the Traumatic Western', p. 220.
32. Harvey, *The Condition of Postmodernity*, p. 312.
33. Ibid.
34. Octavio Paz, 'Mexico and the United States' *The New Yorker*, 17 September 1979, in Octavio Paz, *The Labyrinth of Solitude* (London: Penguin, [1950] 1990), p. 358.
35. Ibid., p. 353.
36. Forrest G. Robinson (ed.), 'Clio Bereft of Calliope', in *The New Western History: The Territory Ahead* (Tucson, AZ: University of Arizona Press, 1998), p. 68 (emphasis added). Robinson, discussed in Stephen McVeigh, *The American Western* (Edinburgh: Edinburgh University Press, 2007), p. 147.
37. McVeigh, *The American Western*, p. 147.
38. Henry Nash Smith, *Virgin Land: The American West as Symbol and Myth* (London: Harvard University Press, [1950] 1978), p. xi
39. Ibid., p. xi
40. Ibid., pp. ix–x

41. Richard Slotkin, *Regeneration through Violence: The Mythology of the American Frontier, 1600–1860*, new edn (Norman, OK: University of Oklahoma Press, 2000), p. 3.
42. Sacvan Bercovitch, *The American Jeremiad* (London: University of Wisconsin Press, 1978), p. 11.
43. Walker, *Westerns: Films through History*, p. 7.
44. Ibid., pp. 9–10.
45. Ibid., p. 10.
46. Ibid., pp. 10, 13.
47. Ibid., p. 10.
48. Ibid., pp. 8–9.
49. Hayden White, 'Historiography and Historiophoty', *American Historical Review*, 93(5) (1988): 1193–9, quote on p. 1193.
50. Ibid., pp. 1193–4.
51. Ibid., p. 1196.
52. Ibid., p. 1194.
53. Ibid., p 1195. Here White references the historian Ian Jarvie. In relation to the 'essence' of historiography (as opposed to film's tendency to rely on 'narration'), Jarvie suggests that it consists less of 'descriptive analysis' than of 'debates between historians about just what exactly did happen, why it happened, and what would be an adequate account of its significance'. See Ian Jarvie, 'Seeing through Movies', *Philosophy of the Social Sciences*, 8 (1978): 374–97.
54. Hayden White, *Metahistory: The Historical Imagination in Nineteenth-Century Europe* (Baltimore, MD: Johns Hopkins University Press, 1973), pp. 1–42; White, 'Historiography and Historiophoty', p. 1196.
55. White, 'Historiography and Historiophoty', p. 1196.
56. Hayden White, 'Historicism, History, and the Figurative Imagination', *History and Theory*, 14(4) (1975): 48–67, at p. 49.
57. White, 'Historiography and Historiophoty', p. 1196.
58. White, *Metahistory*, p. 24.
59. Kerwin Lee Klein, *Frontiers of Historical Imagination: Narrating the European Conquest of Native America, 1890–1990* (London: University of California Press, 1997), p. 53.
60. Ibid., p. 52.
61. Ibid.
62. Ibid.
63. White, 'Historicism, History, and the Figurative Imagination', p. 51 (emphasis in original). See also Claude Lévi-Strauss, *The Savage Mind* (London: Weidenfeld & Nicolson, [1962] 1966), pp. 245–69.
64. White, 'Historicism, History, and the Figurative Imagination', p. 51 (emphasis in original).
65. Ibid.
66. Ibid., p. 52.
67. Richard Slotkin, *Gunfighter Nation: The Myth of the Frontier in Twentieth-Century America* (Norman, OK: University of Oklahoma Press, [1992] 1998), p. 6.
68. Ibid., p. 7.
69. Ibid., p. 8.
70. Arthur C. Danto, *Narration and Knowledge* (New York: Columbia University Press, [1985] 2007), p. xiii.
71. Slotkin, *Gunfighter Nation*, p. 655.
72. Susan Kollins, 'Genre and the Geographies of Violence: Cormac McCarthy and the Contemporary Western', *Contemporary Literature*, 42(3) (2001): 557–88, quote on p. 568.

73. Ibid., p. 568
74. For in-depth analyses of these issues in *Lone Star*, see the essays by Kim Magowan, '"Blood Only Means What You Let It": Incest and Miscegenation in John Sayles' *Lone Star*', *Film Quarterly*, 57(1) (2003): 20–31, and Kimberley Schultz, 'Challenging Legends, Complicating Borderlines: The Concept of "Frontera" in John Sayles's *Lone Star*', in Rollins and O'Connor (eds), *Hollywood's West*, pp. 261–81.
75. It is worth noting that Anzaldúa was initially rejected by the academic community because she did not hold the title of PhD. Her current acceptance is the breaking down of another 'border'. See Klein, *Frontiers of Historical Imagination*, pp. 266–73.
76. Gloria Anzaldúa, *Borderlands – la Frontera: the New Mestiza*, 2nd edn (San Francisco, CA: Aunt Lute Books, 1999), p. 28.
77. Ibid., p. 33 (emphasis in original).
78. Ibid., pp. 25–6 (emphasis in original).
79. Ibid., p. 33.
80. Limerick, *The Legacy of Conquest*, p. 257.
81. Hayden White, 'The Burden of History', *History and Theory*, 5(2) (1966): 111–34.
82. Ibid., pp. 126–7.
83. Ibid., p. 126.
84. Ibid., p. 127.
85. Klein, *Frontiers of Historical Imagination*, p. 270.
86. Ibid., p. 270.
87. White, 'The Burden of History', p. 127.

5. ACTORS TRANSCENDING
THE DARKNESS

'Well it's a mess ain't it, Sheriff.'
'If it ain't it'll do till the mess gets here.'

I

This chapter continues my concerns with recent cinematic treatments of the borderlands by focusing on Joel and Ethan Coen's *No Country for Old Men* (2007). The film is adapted from Pulitzer Prize winning author Cormac McCarthy's 2005 novel of the same title.[1] The book engages with McCarthy's long-standing metaphysical concerns, presenting a meditation on mortality as a terrifying contest between an ageing West Texas sheriff and an implacable killer. The Coen's *No Country* successfully adapts such concerns to the cinema and has achieved a good deal of both critical and commercial acclaim, garnering, among numerous other prizes, four 2008 Academy Awards, including one for Best Motion Picture and another for Best Achievement in Directing. In this regard, a Hollywood Western has not been so successful since *Unforgiven*, which similarly won multiple Oscars back in 1993. Like *Three Burials* and *Lone Star* before it, *No Country* reminds us that the cinema has depicted the United States–Mexico border as a real place and a set of myths associated with that place – a mythic terrain, adjunct to the myth of the West. The borderlands are therefore a term of both geographical *and* ideological reference for many Americans, including historians, political figures and producers of popular culture. As such, I develop the previous chapter's concern with the concept of national identity in specific relation to the Western genre.

As I have already outlined, the concept of an American national identity draws from frontier historiography, especially the 'mystical entity' Turner and Roosevelt both called the 'national character'.[2] Throughout the twentieth century the Hollywood Western has disseminated this construct to cinema audiences both in the United States and around the world. It has provided the United States with some of its greatest cultural heroes, both real and fictitious – and all thoroughly re-imagined through its mythology. At the same time, the genre has also critically interrogated and deconstructed such mythic themes as the domestication of the wilderness, the Rooseveltian and Turnerian versions of frontier history, and such hero figures as the cowpuncher and the gunfighter through the forms and themes available to it: open landscapes, deserts, mountains, prairie; the wilderness–civilisation binary, the epic moment, redemptive violence, the captivity narrative, and the revenge motif. The Western has long provided the form through which these various tropes could be articulated, and yet, more often than not, it becomes apparent that Westerns are contradictory in their narrative meanings, existing as platforms for debating the impact and scope of the myth of the West on US culture, rather than acting as a mouthpiece which univocally celebrates a particular version of American history – that is to say, 'the white man's story'.

The kind of post-structuralist analyses already discussed alert us to the possibility that all texts (filmic or otherwise) promise latent meanings that potentially contradict the surface messages of the narrative. However, as my analyses have revealed, a reading 'against the grain' is not always necessary as the intertextual relay and self-reflexivity apparent in many Westerns is striking, and *No Country* is no exception. Through the figure of Sheriff Ed Tom Bell (Tommy Lee Jones), *No Country* re-engages us with the figure of the lawman. Aligning the audience with him through narrative screen-time, it keeps him as a sympathetic protagonist while self-consciously seeking to undermine his heroic trajectory. The lawman has been depicted in the Western in both positive and negative terms (and every which way in between). From the many incarnations of one-time sheriff, Wyatt Earp, through to the notorious, 'Judge' Roy Bean, the Western has taught us that heroic or corrupt arbiters of frontier justice need not be mutually exclusive character traits. People act in history in complex and contradictory ways, and this is often reflected in their mythic cinematic avatars. As my discussion in Chapter 3 of *Unforgiven*'s Sheriff Little Bill Daggett suggested, the good and the bad often exist simultaneously in the same character, even if it is eventually collapsed into one or the other for the sake of narrative closure. A certain level of ambiguity therefore seems apparent in many Western characters, if one cares to look closely enough. Such a reading would align itself with the New Western historians who have forwarded 'complexity' as one of their key words in discussing the American West. Limerick writes:

A major project of the New Western History [has] to be the assertion that benefits often came packaged with injuries, good intentions could lead to regrettable outcomes, and the negative aspects of life wove themselves into a permanent knot with the positive aspects. The deeply frustrating lesson of history in the American West and elsewhere is this: human beings can be a mess – contentious, conflict loving, petty, vindictive, and cruel – *and* human beings can manifest grace, dignity, compassion, and understanding in ways that leave us breathless.[3]

Limerick's sentiments with regard to human complexity would be well applied to popular culture, but it is also, perhaps, no surprise that such character complexities apparent in Westerns such as *The Searchers* are overlooked in those whose first and foremost concerns are with 'real' history. As we know, when it comes to the popular imagination, Limerick argues that the 'desire for a telling of Western history in which good guys are easily distinguished from bad guys is deep and persistent'.[4] While this is undoubtedly true in many instances, the films analysed thus far in this study have surely illustrated that the popular imagination is itself a complex and, often, unpredictable thing. I shall discuss these various narrative complexities as they appear in *No Country* throughout the course of this chapter. This is done in conjunction with the wider scope of frontier mythology and its import in constructing the historical memory informing the US cultural mindset – America's national identity.

I am acutely aware of the fact that like *Three Burials*, *No Country* is set in a more contemporary period and, also like *Three Burials*, it has been regarded by the few critics and journalists who have discussed the film as an example of a 'neo', or a post-Western. I shall scrutinise this appellation and discuss *No Country*'s commentary on social, cultural and historical issues that affect the present-day United States. I conclude with another look at the New Western credentials of *No Country*; specifically, Limerick's preference to 'place Western American history back into history with an explicit and honest use of the word "conquest"', is considered by offering a brief assessment of the continued significance of the frontier mythology that the Western genre propounds in relation to those aspects of US political discourse which it still informs – for good or ill. Specifically, I discuss *No Country*'s ideological significance in (de)constructing the cultural rhetoric behind twenty-first-century US foreign policies, specifically those in Afghanistan and Iraq.

While certainly not comprising the whole of *No Country*'s significance, the historical issue does provide me with an inroad to my primary focal point; once again, the figure of the Western hero – for so many a portal through which the United States entered into a fantasy about itself and its place in the world – shall provide the lens by which I observe how *No Country* assesses the role of myth in history and its sociopolitical role in the contemporary world. Moving beyond the concerns of the previous chapter, we could argue that if *Three Burials* seeks to critically assess the notion of a homogeneous 'American self' in relation to the Mexican as its foreign 'other', then *No Country* utilises the same mythological tropes and generic conventions in order to affect a critique of the influence that the myth of the West holds over the sociopolitical trajectory of the present-day United States in its role as the world's figurative lawman. In this last regard, I take as my starting point the historian Harold Rosenberg's

1959 essay 'The Resurrected Romans'.[5] My application of Rosenberg's essay to my reading of *No Country* is combined with a comparative analysis of Ford's *The Searchers*, which was, of course, the subject of Chapter 2. Both Rosenberg and Ford provide me with suitably comparative texts with which to elucidate *No Country*'s attitude towards the Western genre, American history and the myth of the West. First, however, I shall outline Rosenberg's essay and expand the theoretical context of this chapter before working to align its focus with *No Country*.

II

Rosenberg offers a detailed analysis of Karl Marx's 1852 treatise, *The Eighteenth Brumaire of Louis Bonaparte*.[6] Central to Rosenberg's analysis is Marx's peculiar concept of how history repeats itself, the first time as tragedy, the second time as farce. Specific to my purposes is Marx's insistence on how the repeating history always comes back to haunt and influence the decisions of those acting in the present. As with White and Arthur C. Danto (discussed in Chapter 4), Rosenberg views history as deeply narrational and he identifies two continuities in what he describes as 'the plot of history'. The first concerns the various 'circumstances in which historical acts take place', and thus 'constitute an external continuity'; the second forms an 'inner continuity between the men who are to act historically in the present and other actors who once trod the stage ... men who in a situation sufficiently resembling the present one played their part with greatness'.[7] We can say that these two continuities set up a distinction between macro- and micro-political scenarios; between the general flow of historical movement itself and those individual 'actors' who themselves move within it and draw from the past their inspiration for acting in the present and imagining their future. And it is these individual actors, asserts Rosenberg, who suffer from history's ironic 'Reversal': as noble intentions grind into their very opposite, the teleological flow of history continues unabated. This is especially apt for my reading of *No Country*, dealing as it does with the film as an individual (micro) unit, which is defined (if not entirely determined) within the larger (macro) movements and language of the myth of the West and its contingent relation to social, cultural and historical movements.

'The question of myth in history', claims Rosenberg 'is the question of the hero. And the question of the hero is the question of resurrection.'[8] So it is that this dead hero is resurrected, disinterred, as it were, from the grave, his role assumed by the individuals acting in the present as they 'anxiously conjure up the spirits of the past to their service and borrow from them names, battle slogans and costumes'.[9] However, just as myth seeks to eradicate the historicity of things, as Barthes has suggested, so too does the historical element become lost on the hero whose awareness is only of 'eternal forms'. It is this that leads Rosenberg to concur with Marx that this 'invasion by the "dead

generations" is what makes a "nightmare" out of history'.[10] It would be pertinent at this point to reiterate (once again) a similar sentiment made by Slotkin
in the opening paragraphs of *Regeneration through Violence*. As I have mentioned, Slotkin writes that 'the mythology of a nation is the intelligible mask
of that enigma called the "national character"', and it is the transference of
this 'mask' to the modern descendants of our cultural ancestors that ensures
that 'our perception of contemporary reality and our ability to function in the
world [is] directly, often tragically affected'.[11] Slotkin provided subsequent
chroniclers of the relationship between myth and history in American studies
with a national context for exploring what Sacvan Bercovitch described as
frontier mythology's 'functional relationship to facts' in its 'capacity to make
men act in history'.[12] In another thematic link to Rosenberg, it is Slotkin's
contention that the poets of the early years of the American republic looked
backwards into antiquity, into the founding epics of ancient Greece and Rome,
in their attempt to 'fabricate an "American epic"' that would mark the beginning of a national mythology, 'providing a context for all works to come after':

> Their concept of myth was essentially artificial and typically American:
> they believed, in effect, that a mythology could be put together on the
> ground, like the governments of frontier communities or the national
> Constitution, either by specialists or by the spontaneous awakening of
> the popular genius. Like the Constitution, such myth-epics would reflect
> the most progressive ideas of American man, emphasising the rule of
> reason in nature and in human affairs, casting aside all inherited tradi-
> tions, superstitions, and spurious values of the past. The freedom and
> power of man were to be asserted against the ideas of necessity, of his-
> torical determinism, of the inheritance of guilt and original sin.[13]

Slotkin highlights an inherent contradiction in the thinking behind the
American epic. The context by which the New World was to 'be liberated
from the dead hand of the past' and, in the process, become 'the scene of a new
departure in human affairs', remained intractably tied to the very influence
of this 'dead hand'. This was so both in its adaptation of the movements of
European history and its mythological traditions, specifically its structural and
thematic reliance on the likes of Homer and Virgil.[14]

This can all in turn be related to Fredric Jameson's conception of dialectical
movements in history. Jameson insists that the various modes of production
in the process of history comprise a diachronic framework that provides the
'cultural machinery' informing the dialectical struggle between human 'desire'
(for a utopian future of 'freedom' within collective unity along Marxist lines)
and of the painful and contradictory socioeconomic effects that we experience
as a historical 'necessity'. As with Slotkin, 'freedom' stands opposed to 'necessity' as the overall dialectic of history. And, as with Rosenberg, this struggle
is bestowed upon contemporary society as a 'product ... of the actions of

past human agents'.[15] Central to the cultural expression of this dialectic is the all-important concept of narrative, to which (as I have already mentioned) Jameson ascribes the supreme potential for concrete action in history itself. 'History', he assures us, 'is *not* a text, not a narrative (master or otherwise) but that, as an absent cause, it is inaccessible to us except in textual form.'[16] Linked to this claim is the concept of the text coming before us as the 'always-already-read'.[17] In other words, we do not receive texts anew, or freshly, instead we receive them through interpretive traditions and sedimented reading habits. It is also strongly inferred that the various narratives through which we speak and understand our world are, themselves, comprised and cannibalised from these same traditions and habits.

Fundamental to the survival of the utopian desire in narratological expressions of history is the importance Jameson places on situating the various cultural artefacts (as modes of its expression) 'within the unity of a single great collective *story*'. Further adding that 'only if, in however disguised and symbolic a form, they are seen as sharing a single fundamental theme [and are] grasped as vital episodes in a single vast unfinished *plot*'.[18] This 'plot' was, of course, history itself, and Jameson's philosophy of history stood-off against emergent post-modern trends of the time, typified as they were by a declaration of a 'crisis of narratives'. The self-proclaimed object of Jean-François Lyotard's study, for instance, is a definition of the post-modern condition as one that is 'incredulous' towards master narratives. This would obviously include (and oppose) Jameson's neo-Marxist philosophy of history, defined as the dialectical struggle between 'freedom' and 'necessity'.[19]

White describes the predicted cultural consequences of a failure of Jameson's 'single fundamental theme':

> In those works of literature in which narrativity is either refused or breaks down, we are met with the traces of despair that is to be assigned, not to the moral weakness or lack of knowledge of their authors, but rather to the apperception of a shape of social life grown old. The breakdown of narrativity in a culture, group, or social class is a symptom of its having *entered into a state of crisis*. For with any weakening of narrativising capacity, the group loses its power to locate itself in history, to come to grips with the Necessity that its past represents for it, and to imagine a creative, if only provisional, transcendence of its 'fate'.[20]

If, as Jameson and others suggest, culture, identity and, above all, history are determined and structured by narrative, then it is fair to say that the national character, or identity, has been structured by the myriad narratives that fed into and shaped frontier mythology, including, particularly, the creation of the myth of the West towards the close of the nineteenth century. By harnessing the power of myth, those who consciously helped to create the myth of the West were able to create compelling narratives that guided and energised cultural attitudes, social action and political decisions; in other words, they affected history and those who 'act' in history. These narratives frequently justified historical movements which would otherwise be morally compromised. The nineteenth-century conquest of the North American interior by the US military, pioneers and other settlers can be seen as such a movement. As discussed previously, this settlement, justified by the myth of bringing civilisation – the domestication of the wilderness – was, in effect, a savage war for land, eventuating in the slaughter, expropriation and ethnic cleansing of the Native Americans from their ancestral homelands: racially other and, therefore, savage, atavistic; evil agonist in a mythic struggle of Good against Evil.

The traditions and ideologies that have been central to American thinking for hundreds of years undoubtedly found their pre-eminent voice in the twentieth century through the cinema, and it is not too difficult to see why White's sentiments as they are outlined above can be related to the kind of Westerns that were being produced during the late 1960s and 1970s. There has always been a strong tendency in genre scholarship – and, in particular, scholarship of the Western – to try to 'read' films for underlying meaning. It is this concentration on interpretation that has given rise to the critical models typically associated with the genre: broadly speaking, the assertion that Westerns are *about* the epic moment and the domestication of the wilderness. As we have seen, theories extolling the revisionist model typically see Westerns of the 1960s and 1970s operating as a critique of the classical model of the 1940s and 1950s, as reflections of societal change and social unrest, as well as a growing national disillusionment with the conflict in Vietnam. More specifically, they are seen as an open attack on the triumphalist brand of frontier mythology that fuelled that conflict's political rhetoric and cultural symbolism. A 'breakdown of narrativity' through the 'apperception of a shape of social life grown old' seems to have informed the thinking behind most critical responses to the film texts of this period. For instance, the so-called 'spaghetti' Westerns from directors like Leone, Sergio Corbucci, etc. are often read in terms of generic disillusionment, as post-modern blank parodies of Western tropes. While turn-of-the-decade films such as Sam Peckinpah's *The Wild Bunch* (1969), Arthur Penn's *Little Big Man*, and Ralph Nelson's *Soldier Blue* (both 1970) are usually read as thinly veiled allegories of atrocities committed by US Marines in Vietnam. Either that or they are read as an exposé of the US policy of foreign interventionism as imperial conquest thinly veiled as liberation. Perhaps such a 'breakdown' finds its ultimate expression in the almost schizophrenic (non) narrative of Alejandro Jodorowsky's *El Topo* (1970).

In this profoundly ideological reading of the Western, social and cultural factors external to the films proper predominate, acting as the critical barometer. In this regard, Kitses is surely right to warn us that 'the thrust of ideological and psychoanalytic analyses can be to suggest a sick culture, a cinema of symptoms, toxic elements and pathologies', while reminding us that, far from being exclusive, 'ideology and aesthetics are inextricably bound up'.[21] Neale is supportive of this belief, writing that 'the ideological significance of any text – or any genre – is always to be sought in a context-specific analysis'.[22] He further suggests that, typically, the ideological approach 'pay[s] little attention to aesthetics ... form is always, and only, a wrapping for the cultural or ideological content in which [advocates of such an approach] are almost exclusively interested'.[23]

The belief that, by this point in history, the mythic narrative that had informed the classical Western had 'entered into a state of crisis' is indeed a powerful one, and one with which the contemporary, or so-called post-Western, must contend. This chapter must do likewise. Situated in this way, I shall use Rosenberg's approach to argue that *No Country*'s attitude towards the effects of the myth upon the history of the United States is profoundly negative. However, like *Three Burials*, I shall also argue that, at one and the same time, it relies upon the established traditions and conventions of the Western in order to enact its critique. As such, it suggests once more the profundity of the genre's scope through its problematic relationship with the myth of the West. The popular tropes elicited by the Western's brand of the myth prove vital in the film's shaping of its own ideological position. *No Country*, like numerous Westerns before and since, is not so much anti-Western as it is anti-myth, and, as I have been discussing throughout, this so-called anti-myth seems to be as much a part of the myth itself, rather than an oppositional discourse. I also argue that *No Country* understands political–ideological situations and attitudes affecting the contemporary United States in terms of a direct consequence of the 'product' of the actions of past 'agents' who have drawn their inspiration from this same mythology. And it is through a study of the film's narrative characteristics that we can begin to deal with the consequential effects that such a historical necessity has on the assertion of the 'freedom and power of man', together with America's sense of history and its sense of 'place' on the international 'stage'.

III

Despite being regarded by many reviewers as a fairly straightforward literary adaptation of McCarthy's novel, the cinematic version of *No Country* does differ in its thematic emphasis in several key aspects. I argue that the reasons for this (aside from the more commonplace transformative necessities that typically occur in the adaptation process) are to be found in the legacy of the cinematic Western itself.

Like the novel, the film opens with the protagonist Ed Tom Bell's narration, given in the form of a voice-over by Jones. It is delivered over a montage of shots depicting the landscapes of the Texas southwest: semi-arid plains, rolling hills, a short barb-wire fence, and a dawn-shot of a tall metal windmill revolving familiarly and somewhat forlornly. However, there is here a significant difference in purpose to be discerned between the novel's initial monologue and the film's opening voice-over. Condensed from Bell's first three observations in the novel, it constitutes the one and only such voice-over in the entire film. The reasons for this are partly practical. Since the novel is approximately 50 per cent comprised of Bell's narration, its virtual deletion in the film can be put down to the requirements of the medium of commercial narrative cinema (such an amount of voice-over would be considered excessive). Most interestingly, as far as the Western goes, however, it is the effect of generic intertextuality that the voice-over narration creates. Bell expresses the thoughts and emotions of a man approaching retirement:

> Voice-over: I was Sheriff of this county when I was 25 years old. Hard to believe. Grandfather was a law man. Father too. Me and him was sheriffs at the same time, him up in Plano and me out here. I think he was pretty proud of that. I know I was.

In *Cormac McCarthy and the Myth of American Exceptionalism* (2008), John Cant has traced McCarthy's struggle with the so-called fathers of the American literary tradition: Melville, Faulkner, Eliot, to name but a few. In Cant's opinion, such a struggle is articulated by McCarthy in terms of eclecticism, as an acknowledgement of the 'ugly fact' that books are made out of other books (the 'always-already-read'?).[24] Similar sentiments can be related to Bell's voice-over in the film where the literary fathers can be exchanged for what one might call the cinematic or, perhaps better still, the fathers of the generic tradition; a group in which we would undoubtedly place the likes of Ford, Boetticher, Peckinpah (again), to name but a few.

Accordingly, Bell's recourse to times and peoples past extend beyond the level of plot function, beyond the introspective concerns of the familial (that is, in his touching comments regarding his dead father's and his own sense of pride), and delves into the legacy of an extensive generic tradition:

> Voice-over: Some of the old time sheriffs never even wore a gun. A lot of folks find that hard to believe. Jim Scarborough never carried one. That's the younger Jim. Gaston Boykins wouldn't wear one. Up in Comanche County. I always liked to hear about the old timers. Never missed a chance to do so. You can't help but compare yourself to the old timers. Can't help but wonder how they woulda operated these times.

As far as the traditions of the Western are concerned, the significance of this part of the monologue is worth discussing. With the revelation that some of the 'old time sheriffs never even wore a gun', the narrative acts to deconstruct the genre's long-held 'six-gun mystique' (to borrow the title of Cawelti's study), despite 'a lot of folks (read audience) find[ing] that hard to believe'.[25] The apparent attempt to dispel this aspect of the myth so long articulated by the cinematic past is married to an antonymic desire to 'hear about the old timers', Bell stating that he '[n]ever missed a chance to do so.'

What appears to be going on here is a dialectic that, when colligated with the simultaneous montage of Western landscapes on display, feeds off of the Western genre. It is an acknowledgement of the need to reference the diverse wealth of Westerns and associated filmmakers of the past. It also suggests that any attempt to move beyond the dictates of the past cannot but acknowledge its influence, reaffirming Jameson's insistence that the text comes before us as the 'always-already-read'. It is also in this regard that one can echo, perhaps with no small amount of dilution, the Karl Marx of *The Eighteenth Brumaire*: the tradition of the dead generations weighs 'like a nightmare upon the brain of the living'. This conceptual belief in history as an encumbering force has been advanced by many in the field of historiography, most notably White. In 'The Burden of History', we may recall that White lamented the (then) growing sentiment that the discipline of history had outlived its usefulness. He critically assessed the growing understanding of history as a 'substantive burden imposed upon the present by the past in the form of outmoded institutions . . . *the way of looking at the world* which gives to these outmoded forms their specious authority'.[26] Such an argument continued along the lines that 'it is only by disenthralling human intelligence from the sense of history that men will be able to confront creatively the problems of the present'.[27]

The concept of history as a burden, and even the notion of a 'sense of history' are, of course, issues that the contemporary Western has to confront if it is to conceive of set of symbols beyond a tragic or farcical repetition of the past, its chosen metaphors and tropes doing more than what Rosenberg describes as merely 'mimicking the engraving of a hero on one of history's old playbills'.[28] The symbolic struggle with regard to *No Country* concerns the past generations of Westerns and their mythic heroes, the allegorical 'old timers', to whom Bell compares himself. I argue that such a struggle encompasses both the implicitly micro-political and the explicitly macro-political in the figure of the hero as an individual and of the Western genre as a whole. Such an interpretation provides testament to the continuing importance of the cinematic Western as a medium whereby such complex issues, which include concepts of nation, history, race and identity can be played out, deconstructed and commented upon.

Of course, the overriding allegorical sensibility of this film (which draws directly from McCarthy's oeuvre) would appear to be the sense of the betrayal of the myth's promise: the domestication of the wilderness. This idea has been ingrained in frontier mythology since the earliest Puritan colonists' 'errand into the wilderness', and was carved into the American Imaginary in the late nineteenth century by the likes of Cody, Turner and Roosevelt in their formulation of the myth of the West. This mythic promise has, of course, been articulated, legitimated *and* critiqued throughout numerous Westerns over the past century. *No Country* may, indeed, exist as a sombre reminder of what the Garden 'made' by such frauds as *Liberty Valance*'s Ranse Stoddard and *Fort Apache*'s Colonel Owen Thursday has become. After all, the country as depicted in *No Country* is far from 'A fine good place to be'.

In the case of *No Country*, none of the Western tropes is more important than the issue of individual identity and the mythic mode of its expression – the archetypal hunter-hero, Llewellyn Moss (Josh Brolin); the lawman, Sheriff Bell; and the savage force representing the myth's figurative wilderness, Anton Chigurh (Javier Bardem). This sets up what Rosenberg describes as an 'inner continuity between the men who are to act historically in the present and other actors who once trod the stage . . . heroes living in the memory'.[29] In revisionist terms, the undermining of the assertive status of the hunter-hero, as embodied by the character of Moss, and the passivity and lack of agency displayed by Bell, spring instantly to mind. Neither of them is master of their own fate nor, significantly, can either man domesticate the wilderness, much less can they defeat the terrifying Chigurh.

This sense of 'inner continuity' extends to the very geography of the borderlands and is reflected in the film's *mise-en-scène*. From the outset we are provided with a poetic collage of images and desolate impressions, evocative of the sublime landscapes and narrative themes of Ford's Monument Valley and the Spanish-come-southwestern deserts of Leone. If it is the mythic landscapes of Ford that evoke this sense of 'inner continuity', then it is surely the agonists in Leone's films in particular that lend themselves to such a reading. As indicated above, the typical assertions that the characters are devoid of depth and emotion give rise to accusations that they are merely post-modern simulacra of generic Western stereotypes. If we accept this interpretation, then characters like Harmonica (Charles Bronson), No-Name (Clint Eastwood) and Frank (Henry Fonda) 'were thrown into roles prepared for them in advance', selected from the Western's gallery of stock-types and regurgitated into a world of blank-parody (a similar observation that I made in Chapter 3 in relation to *Unforgiven*).[30] However, as with *Three Burials*, I contend that the characters of *No Country* cannot be so easily described in such a fashion.

It is the recapitulation of such Western themes that becomes of particular importance when considering the cinematic adaptation of *No Country* as a Western. This is especially so if we remind ourselves that Hollywood's West is often considered to be largely confined to the short period between 1865 and 1890, with only a handful of notable 'deviations' from this (totally) arbitrary norm (see Introduction). As many of the most distinguished of the films that constitute the artistic hub of the post-Cold War Western are set in a more contemporary (though no less mythic) period, the erstwhile fetishisation of this fleeting moment in US history becomes one more among many Western tropes to be viewed through a critical lens.

Again, this posits the spirit of my argument in relation to many of the tenets of those affiliated with the New Western History. 'After all', asks Limerick, 'are Geiger counters and airplanes less "frontier-like" than picks and shovels?'[31]

(This statement is made in reference to the numerous uranium 'rushes' during the 1940s and 1950s.) In a similar vein to this, and relating more specifically to *No Country*, one could ask whether or not a pick-up truck is any *less Western*-like in its signification than a horse? How exactly do we value such traditional visual signifiers against more deep-rooted generic themes? After all, both truck and horse symbolise the desire for enfettered freedom, be it on the road or on the range. Therefore, one could argue that both truck and horse adhere in this respect to the prevalent mythological tropes of the Western. In this regard the purposes of applying this aspect of the New Western History to the so-called post-Western is to erase the notion of a Rubicon to be crossed when considering popular cultural treatments of the 'Old' and the 'New' West(s).

If we were to remain purist in our generic categories, then we would have to dismiss such significant films as Martin Ritt's *Hud* (1963), Terence Malik's *Badlands*, James William Guercio's *Electra Glide in Blue* (both 1973) and, of course, the magnificent *Lone Star*. *Hud* is especially relevant as its narrative concerns the legacy of the frontier in modern America; therefore, it holds a thematic concern with the myth of the West. The film follows the character of Hud Bannon (Paul Newman), the hedonistic son of an aging rancher, Homer (Melvyn Douglas). Faced with financial ruin as a result of unwittingly purchasing diseased cattle from Mexico, Homer is encouraged to allow oil exploration on his ranch. The conversation that follows Hud's sarcastic remark that 'My daddy thinks oil is something you stick in your salad dressing' is telling with regard to the socioeconomic impact of the myth on the twentieth-century United States:

Homer: If there's oil down there, you can get it sucked up after I'm under there with it. There'll be no holes punched in this land while I'm here. They ain't gonna come in and grade no roads so the wind can blow me away. What's oil to me? What can I do with a bunch of oil wells? I can't ride out every day and prowl amongst them like I can my cattle. I can't breed them or tend them or rope them or chase them or nothing. I can't feel a smidgen of pride in them cause they ain't none of my doing.

Hud: There's money in it.

Homer: I don't want that kind of money. I want mine to come from something that keeps a man doing for himself.

All the films mentioned above draw upon frontier mythology and Westerns past for their narrative significance, and all in my opinion are to be classified *as* Westerns. Equally, they all share a sociological concern for the way both frontier mythology and the Western genre affected the cultural outlook of the twentieth-century United States.

As already discussed, the main theoretical thrust advanced by advocates of revisionism is to put forward Vietnam as the last phase in the development of the mythology of the American frontier in its relation to this cultural outlook. It was also for many the death-knell of the Western genre itself. The political and social fall-out from Vietnam and the failure of frontier rhetoric to 'speak' that conflict adequately, as it were, led to what Slotkin termed the 'crisis of public myth'.[32] No longer, he believed, could the Western articulate *meaning* in the contemporary United States:

> We are in a 'liminal' moment of our cultural history. We are in the process of giving up a myth/ideology that no longer helps us to see our way through the modern world, but lack a comparably authoritative system of beliefs to replace what we have lost.[33]

If we take seriously the 'crisis of public myth' that Slotkin outlines, then the tripartite relationship between myth, ideology and genre that he highlights as informing and mediating 'historical memory' rightly becomes our main focus of attention.[34] This is especially so as we are considering the role of the hero, the attendant cult of heroic leadership, and their respective relations to historical movements in US politics and culture. As I have already detailed, many scholars have discerned a loss of faith in the image of the mythic hero in the cultural mindset. Slotkin claims that this was evidenced by the declining popularity of the Western during and after the Vietnam War, where the idealisation through myth of a violent, regenerative past did not marry well to the brutal *degenerate* realities of US imperialism in southeast Asia. According to Slotkin, this sense of disillusionment was replicated in 'the intellectual establishment' at the time. 'A good deal of [its] creative energy', he writes, went 'into criticism and demystification of old myths. This critical mood both reflects and adds to a public scepticism that is the product of hard experience.'[35] Consequently, he maintains that the tenuous thread that linked this long-running myth–ideology system to history began to come apart. This, he reasoned, caused a breakdown in the narrative of the Western genre itself. Likewise, the end logic of the revisionist argument maintains that, by the 1970s, the hero's role in mediating historical memory had become obsolete.

Despite the popularity of such presentist attitudes in both film theory and frontier historiography, the Western remains a genre that has resolutely refused to die. The Western, therefore, is defying such rigorous, almost Turnerian, assertions that it has passed away into Hollywood history. The genre has revealed an ongoing ability to reshape its version of history and, at the same time, reflect or critique contemporary values as well as the values of the past. To take just one example, after watching Andrew Dominik's *The Assassination of Jesse James by the Coward Robert Ford* (2007), one was struck by the deft handling whereby both Jesse's (Brad Pitt) and Robert's (Casey Affleck) status as hero and coward, respectively, are undermined. The film is centred on the figure of Jesse James, whose legend is wholly at odds with most sober accounts of his actual life. There is thus a certain irony in a large-scale international production, relying for commercial success on the appeal of its star, Brad Pitt, being devoted to a critique of the cult of celebrity. In a further irony, it is Casey Affleck whose performance as the hero-worshiping Ford steals the film. In his 1986 study of the James phenomenon in cinema, Christopher Anderson argues that, as a 'cultural figure . . . James is an inevitable intertextual signifier'.[36] He bases this belief on the fact that twenty-nine films had (as of 1986) been based on or around Jesse James. He continues that, as 'intertextual signifier', James 'exists at the junction of social, institutional, and ideological contexts, appealing to a viewer with knowledge of the figure's intertextual resonances'.[37] In providing one of the most compelling depictions of such drab historical figures as Jesse and Bob, Dominik has ensured that the signifier, Jesse James, still has something to say, the trope maintaining cultural currency at the end of the first decade of the twenty-first century.

Of course, none of this has prevented numerous commentators and critics from pronouncing that the Western has been in terminal decline since the 1960s. I argue that, far from being 'dead', the Western's protean ability to adapt and improvise is, as Slotkin himself concedes, essential to both the survival of any mythological discourse and its connection to contemporary socio-historical trends. More importantly than this and, despite his assertions of the severity of the 'crisis of public myth' that was evidenced in the Westerns of the 1960s and 1970s, he states the following:

> The beliefs and practices that hold society together are the product of a long historical interaction between ideas, experience, and remembering. To propose significant social change without recourse to that language renders the proposal unintelligible; to impose change as if from outside of culture, appealing to authority to values that the culture has not generated and accepted for itself, is to assert dictatorship.[38]

On this understanding, any change in sociopolitical ideology *must* take place from within the mythological traditions of a nation and, therefore, within the narratives that have helped to shape that tradition. The relevant question now becomes: how far is this achievable within the Western? As far as the proposition of 'significant social change' goes, it is important to note that *No Country* does more than merely deconstruct that aspect of the myth that deals with the construction and promotion of the cult of heroic leadership. This alone would be nothing new. Neither, it should also be noted, was all of this mythic deconstruction peculiar to the counter-cultural efforts of the younger generation of Hollywood directors of the 1960s and 1970s. In fact, as is usually the case in the Western if one cares to dig deep enough, Ford was there first.

I have argued in Chapter 2 how *The Searchers* goes some way to deconstructing the image of the individualist hero and, by extension, the cult of heroic leadership such a figure has historically embodied. The iconic screen persona of John Wayne in the role of ex-Confederate and unregenerate racist Ethan Edwards brings forth the dark complexities latent in Shane and is mercilessly inverted by Ford, who refused to separate the light from the dark in this, one of his most infamous and complex characters. It is worth reminding ourselves here of one of the film's more memorable scenes. Shortly after the Edwards family massacre, Ethan disinters the body of a Comanche and, in an act of base sadism, shoots the dead man through both eyes. To the disgusted protestations of the Revd Captain Clayton, 'What good did that do you?!' Ethan retorts, 'By what you preach, none. What that Comanch' believes – he ain't got no eyes; he can't enter the spirit world. He's doomed to wander forever between the winds! You get it Reverend.' As also discussed previously in Chapter 2, in the final instance it is young Marty and *not* Ethan who kills his implacable enemy, the Comanche chief, Scar. Likewise, it is the 'old fool', Mose Harper who pinpoints the Comanche encampment, thereby locating Debbie in the process. Not only is Ethan a failure in his professed role as a searcher (read hunter), as is evidenced in his ineffectiveness in pinning down Scar despite several years spent hunting him, but he is also, until the penultimate moment, an active threat to the community that he is supposed to serve. More particularly, he is an outright threat to Debbie, with the spectator unsure of Ethan's intentions – whether Debbie is the captive white woman to be rescued from savages, or a proxy-Comanche tainted by the blood of the other and, in Ethan's eyes, a legitimate target for extermination.

So a question now becomes, if *No Country* in any way answers Ford (surely the most significant of the cinematic fathers) then how so? As far as the undermining of heroic leadership is concerned, something approaching an adequate answer would be the abject failure of individual action on the part of Moss. It is, after all, the spirit of individual action, so long cherished in American ideology, which inspires his theft of the $2 million in cash found abandoned at the drug deal massacre site. But this does not really satisfy as an answer and forces an additional question of its own: why, after all, does Moss take something that he knows full well will be ruthlessly searched for? True, he could not have reckoned on the furious brand of pursuit employed by Chigurh, and yet the futility of his actions, their anti-progressive nature in mythic terms, is tellingly revealed as he remarks to his wife, Carla-Jean (Kelly Macdonald), 'Honey, at what point would you quit looking for your $2 million?' If one were to follow Moss' illogic to the final extreme, then his act of theft could be understood as an act of protracted suicide, as some kind of nihilistic endeavour symptomatic of the failure of the myth's promise of a Garden from a Desert. There does not, after all, appear to be any place for the likes of Moss – the hunter-hero – in the world of *No Country*. By the same token, the world it depicts, with its backdrop of cross-border drug trafficking and relentless, brutalising murder is, again, anything but 'A fine good place to be'.

Surely, then, the most likely figure that answers Ford in this respect has to be Bell. As a protagonist, let alone a hero or lawman, he is something of a curiosity. Never initiating the action or propelling the narrative forwards, he instead pursues the ever-destructive and despairing exchanges of violence between Moss, Chigurh and the various Mexican drug dealers searching for the stolen money. In fact, not once does Bell give the impression that he is in control of events, is capable of bringing Moss into protective custody or, indeed, that he is realistically any match for Chigurh. As he says at one point in the narrative, 'I guess . . . I feel overmatched.'

So, how does *No Country* differ from *The Searchers*' repudiation of Ethan's brand of destructive pathology? How does it initiate a narrative that advances upon a deconstruction of traditional heroism? The simple answer to both of these questions would be that, unlike Ethan, Bell manages to extricate himself from a potentially similar oscillating spiral of violence and counter-violence, revenge and counter-revenge to that in which Ethan and Scar are permanently and, therefore, fatally entangled. Sheriff Bell manages to transcend this fate by recognising his own limitations as a lawman, and the realisation too that he is not a hero (at least, not a hero in the tradition of the myth). Bell can, therefore, be understood to have had a moment of clarity impossible to a character like Ethan. And in so doing, he goes some way towards unburdening himself of the weight of the 'dead generations' by provisionally transcending the 'nightmare' of history.

One of the overall aims of this study has been to uphold the contention that in the Western there has always been a fine line discernable between the hero and the villain. This is a much finer line than is suggestive in those stock types who wore the white hats and the black hats 'so as you'd know who was on which side', as Ronald Reagan was so fond of stating.[39] As we know, the hero has to have more than a little touch of the savage about him, for he typically uses the methods of the wilderness against itself, in turn paving the way for the coming civilisation 'before whose face he must disappear'. Robert C. Cumbow remarks, 'Show me a hero and I'll show you a villain with good excuses.'[40] This is, of course, another way of saying that the road to Hell is paved with good intentions, and Bell, for his part, seems to recognise the fine line that he is treading in his literal and mythic function as lawman and, by extension, his mythological role as hero.

Bell's recognition is combined with the apparent self-acknowledgement of the fate that awaits him if he commits himself fully to the course of the violent events that he trails. There are several examples of such recognition strewn, as it were, throughout the narrative; however, one will suffice to illustrate the point succinctly. When Bell and his deputy, Wendell (Garret Dillahunt), break into Moss' abandoned trailer the Sheriff spies a carton of milk that Chigurh had been holding moments before during his own search for Moss. Bell picks up the milk, pours himself a glass, and sits down on Moss' cheap sofa in exactly the same spot that Chigurh had occupied moments before. His silhouetted reflection stares back at him from the blank television screen, again, exactly the same shot which held Chigurh's opaque expression in the previous scene. These two separate moments thus combined have the effect of a graphic-match, the delayed nature of which would appear not only to symbolise Bell's inability to initiate the narrative action, that is to say, he is always in Chigurh's brutal wake, but also to operate metaphorically as a visual association between himself and Chigurh. It is almost as if Bell knows where this will lead, knows that, in his own words, such an endeavour would force him to 'put his soul at hazard'. This is, of course, precisely what Ethan ends up doing through his pathology and his obsession; failing or refusing to recognise on a personal level his own associations with Scar. He who puts souls at hazard ('ain't got no eyes, can't enter the spirit world') is forced to 'wander forever between the winds' like the soul of the dead Comanche that Ethan condemns. Putting one's 'soul at hazard' is, of course, something Bell assuredly informs us he would never do. 'You think this fella, Moss, has any idea of the sorts of sons-of-bitchs that are huntin' him, Sheriff?' asks Wendell. 'Well, he ought to,' replies Bell while gazing at his 'mirrored' reflection in the television screen with a forceful intent. 'He's seen the same things that I have, and it's certainly made an impression on me.'

Upon a closer inspection of the film it would appear that this recognition is made from the very outset as we are shown Chigurh for the first time. He is being taken into police custody by a patrol officer who he will soon strangle to death in a vicious paroxysm of fury. (As an aside, given what we soon learn of Chigurh's brutal capacities, we might indeed wonder how Chigurh was ever apprehended in the first place, unless, for some reason, he wanted to be.) Bell puts the statement of putting one's 'soul at hazard' into context as he concludes his opening monologue thus:

> Voice-over: The crime you see now, it's hard to even take its measure. It's not that I'm afraid of it. I always knew you had to be willin' to die in order to even do this job. But, I don't wanna push my chips forward, stand up, and go out and meet something I don't understand. A man would have to put his soul at hazard. He'd have to say: 'Ok. I'll be a part of this world.'

With the benefits of hindsight, this seems a more obvious connection to make. Bell refuses to 'be a part of this world', the world that he does not 'understand', the world of cross-border drug trafficking, gangsters, hit-men, brutal massacres and random death forced at the toss of a coin; in other words, the world of Chigurh. This is suggested after Moss' death at the hands of the Mexican drug-dealers (the spectacle of which, not incidentally, is denied us as Bell, typically, arrives to see not the event itself but its aftermath). While in conversation over coffee with another County sheriff, Roscoe Giddens (Rodger Boyce), Bell laments what he sees as a world degenerating into violence. Giddens moans about young people with 'green hair' and 'bones through their noses':

Bell:	Signs and wonders. But I think once you stop hearin' sir and ma'am the rest is soon to follow.
Giddens:	It's the tide. It's the dismal tide. It is not the one thing.
Bell:	Not the one thing. I used to think I could at least some way put things right. I don't feel that way no more . . . I don't know what I do feel like.
Giddens:	Try 'old' on for size.
Bell:	Yessir. It may be that. In a nutshell.

At first it would appear that Bell is out of touch, focusing on trivial matters such as teenage rebellion and bad manners as the foretaste of apocalypse. However, maybe it is precisely because he *does*, in fact, understand the nefarious machinations of Chigurh's world that he seeks to preserve his 'soul' in a manner that so many heroes of Westerns past have failed to do: doomed to wander forever between the winds like Ethan, swept away by the tides of history like *Liberty Valance*'s Tom Doniphan (perhaps the most tragic of all Ford's heroes), or forced into exile like Shane, Harmonica and *Clementine*'s Wyatt Earp.

In the final instance, Bell returns to the motel where Moss was killed. At the moment he is about to enter a series of shot/reverse-shots indicate that Chigurh is there, waiting for him in the shadows. We as the audience are anticipating the long-standing Western tradition of the gunfight, though, having several times borne witness to Chigurh's murderous prowess, we are in this case justifiably fearful for Bell's chances. Death is about to be visited on the sheriff. But as he enters, he is alone in the dark room. Chigurh is not there. In either spatial or temporal terms this makes no logical sense, of course, but what is a failure at the level of realism is a success at the level of allegory. In an allegorical sense it works perfectly: Bell has refused the mythic route of violent resolution, perhaps because he realises all too well that such confrontations do not resolve anything, and that to engage in such an endeavour he would have to 'put his soul at hazard' and risk becoming as Chigurh is – a killer with no apparent soul of his own.

Arguably, and certainly ironically, it is his uncle Ellis (Barry Corbin) – one of the so-called 'old timers' – who weaves the disparate strands of Bell's recognitions into a verifiable whole. Ellis, a former lawman himself, was paralysed in a past gunfight. When questioned what he would do if the man who shot him was ever to have been released from prison, Ellis responds by explaining to Bell the pitfalls of vengeance, 'I don't know. Probably nothin' . . . All the time you spend tryin' to get back what's been took from you there's more going out the door. After a while you just try and get a tourniquet on it.' It is a piece of impromptu sermonising that Ethan Edwards would have done well to listen to. Bell looks at his uncle and Ellis recognises his look, adding knowingly, 'Your granddad never asked me to sign on as deputy.' Ellis does not blame the 'old timers' for how his life turned out, he does not live with a vengeful mind burdened by the events of the past and, by extension, he impresses the same sentiments onto Bell.

IV

As this study has argued, for successive generations of US Americans the myth of the West has provided a grid, or cultural matrix, whereby complex sociopolitical historical (and even economic) events have been shaped to fit a grand narrative that, in its most successful moments, naturalised the myth of American exceptionalism; under the religious auspices of Manifest Destiny it justified the conquest of the West and the destruction of the Native American, recasting it as the domestication of the wilderness; essentially, it helped to legitimate the idea of the United States as the 'redeemer nation', the original vision of the 'City on the Hill' of Puritan lore. For the first European settlers, North America was a New World, a New Eden, a pastoral realm for the new all-American Adam. The power of this mythology has hardly diminished in the twenty-first century. As Cant suggests:

> Any thoughts that postmodernism's assertion of the end of the 'grand narratives' of western culture might have undermined the power of America's identifying myth will have been dispelled by reactions to the attack on the significantly named World Trade Centre [sic]. The incomprehension that greeted this grievous event was clearly informed by the view that America is still the 'City on the Hill' standing as an example that can redeem the world.[41]

Stephen McVeigh relates such sentiments to the cinematic Western. Declaring that 'a new century, launched by a shocking event, has brought the Western back into focus in a way that it had not been since the Cold War'.[42] It is worth elaborating on these comments and bringing them up to date with a more contemporary political period defined by the terminology or war.

With the Bush administration's announcement of the so-called 'War on Terror' immediately following the events of 11 September 2001 – most vividly demonstrated by the notoriously controversial 2003 invasion of Iraq – the conservative traditions of extreme masculinity and heroic individualism that have informed much of the Rooseveltian brand of the myth have increasingly gained sociopolitical currency. With George W. Bush's comments regarding Osama Bin Laden as 'Wanted: Dead or Alive' – the common 'old poster out West, as I recall . . . remembering when I was a kid . . .' – the 43rd President of the United States of America was invoking a well-known and clichéd visual signifier of the Western film. As McVeigh argues, 'Bush's response to the events of 11 September and America's reaction to his leadership, demonstrate the ongoing and central importance of Western mythology in America.'[43] This mythological charge went even further in an address to the Joint Session of Congress. A mere nine days later, on 20 September, Bush famously stated: 'You are either with us or you are with the terrorists. This is civilisation's fight.' By reducing what must be one of the most complex political issues in modern history to such a simplistic binary opposition, Bush (whether consciously or not) was utilising one of the most archetypal foundational constructs of the myth's grand narrative: the agonistic struggle between the forces of civilisation and savagery.

Of course, what Bush was articulating through his own 'remembering' is not lived history, but rather a personal history shaped by mythological resonances of the frontier. One is obliged to bear in mind when regarding the concept of history (both in relation to the frontier and, by logical extension, the purposes of this study) a short and insightful remark by David M. Wrobel. 'We are dealing here with perceptions', he writes, 'often with myths.'[44] The myth of the West – that firmly entrenched system of beliefs otherwise masquerading as the US myth of origins – has informed successive generations of its citizens in their comprehension not only of their own history, but of their immediate environment and sociopolitical culture as well. From this, it is enough to suggest that it was a mythic, probably even cinematic 'remembering', rather than any tangible historical experience that Bush was drawing upon. The very concept of 'Wanted: Dead or Alive' itself acts to conjure in the mind an image of the lone gunfighter – the vindicator – as representative of such a Redeemer Nation, one that would take on the 'evil-doers' and 'smoke 'em out', leading the way in 'civilisation's fight'.

Despite the persuasive power of such rhetoric, I have, of course, argued that the Western's best efforts have often questioned these same legitimating ideologies, the genre's responses to the informing myth of the West never uniform, often confused, contradictory and complex. This being said, as a Western, *No Country* is not such a libratory text in or of itself. It does not deal with issues of gender and race in such a way as to satisfy the full spectrum of demands outlined by the New Western History. It is less progressive than both *Lone Star* and *Three Burials* with regard to both gender and race. Women are largely marginalised in the film, although one must acknowledge the fact that it is a woman, the trailer park manager (Kathy Lamkin), who remains the *only* person in the film who answers back to Chigurh and survives. In terms of race, Chigurh is, in the final analysis, played by the Spanish actor, Javier Bardem, which adds to his 'Mexicanness'. This figure most directly associated with the wilderness is, therefore, still racially 'other'. (A point worth noting is that there is no indication of Chigurh's nationality or ethnicity in McCarthy's novel.) The film's protagonists are still Anglo-American males, still touched with a conservative ideology and a Christian ethic, if only if they lament these as culturally absent. As Bell says to Ellis, 'I always thought when I got older God would sort of come into my life in some way. He didn't. I don't blame him. If I was him I'd have the same opinion about me that he does.' To such self-depreciating sentiments Ellis replies, 'You don't know what he thinks.' It is, I believe, a rebuke to such a conservative ideology as Bell professes.

I suppose one ultimately agrees with Mitchell's insistence that a text's power resides in its 'margins'. In the case of *No Country*, this marginal figure appears to be Ellis. In his own way, Bell's uncle gives the lie to both aspects of the myth that promote American exceptionalism and Manifest Destiny. He says to Bell that 'what you got ain't nothin' new. This country is hard on people. This statement echoes *The Searchers*' Lars Jorgenson's insistence that 'it was this country' rather than Comanches what killed his son, Brad. Ellis' own damning prognosis on the United States follows his retelling of how Bell's uncle Mac was gunned down on his porch by 'Injuns' in 'nineteen zero and nine'. This thematic link between *The Searchers* and *No Country* suggests that America's history of violence is something that the Western genre has always taken into account; at its best it may even be said to hold it to account.

It also suggests this violence as an ongoing 'nothin' new' that would dispel any notion that Bell may have had that the country's tendency towards brutality is somehow getting worse ('The crime you see now it's hard to even take its measure'). These are wise words indeed in light of the antithetical neo-conservative project that, during the Bush Administration, manipulated and elevated the same symbols and ideological traditions of the myth of the West into the type of decisions that propelled the United States into justifying, despite initiating, the invasive violence in both Afghanistan and Iraq.

In *The Terror Dream* (2007), Susan Faludi offers a sociopolitical study of the cultural effects of the aftermath of the terrorist attacks on 11 September. In the process she provides us with important insights into the US cultural mindset at the time. She both reveals and comments upon a set of sociopolitical attitudes still shaped and defined, not only within terms of frontier mythology, but by the Western specifically and, by inference, these attitudes reinforce Marx's assertion that history is an invasion by the dead generations. 'One potential insight', she remarks, 'involves learning to live with insecurity, finding accommodation with – even drawing strength from – an awareness of vulnerability.'[45] Ultimately, in the immediate aftermath of 11 September, the 'nation refused to venture down that path. Presented with a chance to free itself from the thrall of a dangerous myth, the country balked and summoned John Wayne and his avenging brethren instead.'[46] This marries well with Rosenberg's cautionary statement that 'man has not acquired the capacity for the historical; in crisis his response is still – the mask'.[47]

The issues that *No Country* raises would appear to relate to how the myth affects the United States – socially, politically and historically. Such issues comprise the very 'content' expressed through the various cultural 'forms' available. Rosenberg again: 'In vain are the dead of every period disinterred in nations old and new. The effect is not a heroic transcendence of "the limitations of the historical content" but of mixing the "nightmare" of the past into the "sober reality" of the present.'[48] Perhaps now, however, years after the attacks of 11 September, these attitudes are being openly questioned again and workable political alternatives provided – the forging of a 'mindful future' rather than 'succumb[ing] to the hauntings of a fabricated past'.[49] I have argued that *No Country* is a popular cultural product of the former rather than the latter.

Bell accepts his place by realising that, in such a place, one cannot simply close the door on the wilderness, as is the ostensible signification of that famous final shot of *The Searchers*. But as with Ford's film, *No Country* understands that this very figurative wilderness is a part of us, of our society, of our more sinister potential. Ellis warns Bell that he 'can't stop what's coming', but consoles him with the caveat that, at the same time, 'it ain't all waiting on you', because, tellingly, 'that's vanity'. Bell finally accepts his own limitations and refuses to be defined by the cultural 'mask' that has shaped the dominant attitudes of the past. Ellis can be said to reassure Bell in his concern of feeling 'overmatched'. The latter's decision to retire from his job as sheriff, and therefore give up on the symbolic roles of heroic lawman, is not comprehended thus as defeat. Rather, it is what Slotkin describes as incorporation into the myth of Anglo-America's 'experience of defeat and disappointment, [an] acquired sense of limitation', which he feels essential for the very survival of a viable and functioning mythology. This is opposed to the alternative, which is a continuation of 'the rigid defence of existing systems, the refusal of change, which binds us to dead or destructive patterns of action and belief that are out of phase with social and environmental reality'.[50] This, of course, relates directly to Jameson's conception of history as 'the collective struggle to wrest a realm of Freedom from a realm of Necessity' and of the fundamental role of narrative in this task.[51] As White reiterates, this specifically distinguishes 'between ideologies that conduce to the effort to liberate man from history and those that condemn him to an "eternal return" of its "alienating necessities"'.[52]

Perhaps it is too much for me to suggest that, through the figure of Bell, the narrative of *No Country* achieves what Jameson describes as a 'struggle to wrest a realm of Freedom from a realm of Necessity'. But it does suggest that the Western hero *can* make a choice within what Marx describes as 'circumstances directly found, given and transmitted from the past'. In accepting his own limitations and conceding to defeat, Bell manages to escape the 'destructive patterns of action' that would lead him to an 'eternal return' of history's 'alienating necessities'. I would suggest that it is through recognition of his own historical insignificance that Bell avoids being 'crushed by the Reversal' of history's 'plot'.[53] For 'history', Rosenberg informs us, 'is not susceptible to the fatalities of individual existence', and it is through a willingness to acknowledge and learn from the 'plot' of history that Bell saves himself through accepting the fact that 'it ain't all waiting on [Him]'.[54] He accepts that to feel 'overmatched' is not shameful, rather it is something that he needs to incorporate and come to terms with – his terms, not those of the myth that would see him doomed. In essence, what I suggest is that Bell becomes more than a mere 'effect' of history; in refusing the 'mask' of the dead generations he manages to 'come to grips with the necessity that [history's] past represents . . . and to imagine a creative, if only provisional, transcendence of [his] fate'.[55]

In the summary of his discussion of McCarthy's novel *No Country*, Cant discusses what he sees as Bell's epiphany regarding 'his acknowledgement of his own insignificance by insisting on facing the truth of his own life, accepting responsibility for that truth and resting on the life-giving support of his wife'.[56] Analogous to my own assessment of the film, he suggests that, 'if his inability to apprehend Chigurh is a "failure" at the level of plot, allegorically it is a "success," for the sheriff "chooses life" by avoiding Death personified'.[57] In terms of the Western genre, it is Bell's final monologue (the final scene in the film), his recalling of a dream involving his own long-dead father that he recounts to his wife, Loretta (Tess Harper), which for him encapsulates this unburdening of history's 'nightmare':

> It was like we was both back in older times and I was on horseback goin' through the mountains of a night; goin' through this pass in the mountains. It was cold and there was snow on the ground. He rode past me and kept on goin'. Never said nothin goin' by. Just rode on past. He had his blanket wrapped around him and his head down and when he rode past I seen he was carryin' fire in a horn the way people used to do and I could see the horn from the light inside of it. About the colour of the moon. And in the dream I knew that he was goin' on ahead and that he was fixin' to make a fire somewhere out there in all that dark and all that cold. And I knew that whenever I got there he would be there. And then I woke up.

If we relate this final moment from the film to the concerns that have structured this chapter, then we could argue that Bell has paid heed to a message from his unconscious, relayed to him (and then to us) in the form of a lucid dream. If his father could be said to represent the past, the 'old timers' to whom Bell cannot help but 'compare' himself, then we see final confirmation of the film's narrative trajectory. Bell's past and, by extension, America's past is no longer to be comprehended as a burden invading the present at inopportune moments like a nightmare. Instead, the past can now be considered (to a certain degree) with a sense of peace, an affirmation of continuance, of life; the metaphorical 'fire' that Bell's father carries ensures that the past will be in the future; Faludi's 'mindful future', that is, with Bell 'finding accommodation with – even drawing strength from – an awareness of vulnerability'. Bell transcends the darkness around him. He survives.

NOTES

1. Cormac McCarthy, *No Country for Old Men* (London: Picador, 2005).
2. Richard Slotkin, 'Nostalgia and Progress: Theodore Roosevelt's Myth of the

Frontier', *American Quarterly, Special Issue: American Culture and the American Frontier*, 33(5) (1981): 608–37.

3. Patricia Nelson Limerick, *Something in the Soil: Legacies and Reckonings in the New West* (London: W. W. Norton, 2000), p. 21.
4. Ibid., p. 21.
5. Harold Rosenberg, 'The Resurrected Romans' (1959), reprinted in Harold Rosenberg, *The Tradition of the New* (London: Paladin, 1962), pp. 140–58.
6. Karl Marx, *The Eighteenth Brumaire of Louis Bonaparte* (London: International Publishers, [1852] 1994).
7. Rosenberg, *The Tradition of the New*, p. 141.
8. Ibid., p. 141.
9. Ibid.
10. Ibid., p. 142.
11. Richard Slotkin, *Regeneration through Violence: The Mythology of the American Frontier 1600–1860*, new edn (Norman, OK: University of Oklahoma Press, 2000), p. 1.
12. Sacvan Bercovitch, *The American Jeremiad* (London: University of Wisconsin Press, 1978), p. 11.
13. Slotkin, *Regeneration through Violence*, pp. 3–4.
14. Ibid., p. 3.
15. Fredric Jameson, *The Political Unconscious: Narrative as a Socially Symbolic Act* (London: Methuen, 1981), pp. 1–102. See also Hayden White, 'Getting Out of History: Jameson's Redemption of Narrative', in *The Content of the Form* (Baltimore, MD: Johns Hopkins University Press, 1987), pp. 147–8.
16. Jameson, *The Political Unconscious*, p. 35.
17. Ibid., p. 9.
18. Ibid., pp. 19–20(emphasis in original).
19. Jean-François Lyotard, *The Postmodern Condition: A Report on Knowledge*, trans. Geoff Bennington and Brian Massumi (Manchester: Manchester University Press, [1979] 1984), p. xxiii
20. White, *The Content of the Form*, p. 149 (emphasis added).
21. Jim Kitses, *Horizons West: Directing the Western from John Ford to Clint Eastwood* (London: The British Film Institute, [2004] 2007), p. 21.
22. Steve Neale, 'Questions of Genre' (1995), reprinted in Barry Keith Grant (ed.), *Film Genre Reader III* (Austin, TX: University of Texas Press, 2003), pp. 160–84, quote on p. 179.
23. Ibid., p. 179.
24. John Cant, *Cormac McCarthy and the Myth of American Exceptionalism* (London: Routledge, 2008), pp. 3–17.
25. John G. Cawelti, *The Six-Gun Mystique* (Bowling Green, OH: Bowling Green State University Popular Press, [1971] 1984).
26. Hayden White, 'The Burden of History', *History and Theory*, 5(2) (1966): 111–34, quote on p. 123 (emphasis in original).
27. Ibid., p. 123.
28. Rosenberg, *The Tradition of the New*, p. 141.
29. Ibid., p. 141.
30. Ibid., pp. 141–2.
31. Patricia Nelson Limerick, *The Legacy of Conquest: The Unbroken Past of the American West* (London: W. W. Norton, 1987), p. 24.
32. Slotkin, *Gunfighter Nation*, p. 624.
33. Ibid., p. 654.
34. Ibid., pp. 5–8, 624–63.
35. Ibid., p. 654.
36. Christopher Anderson, 'Jesse James, the Bourgeois Bandit: The Transformation

of a Popular Hero', *Cinema Journal*, 26(1) (1986): 43–64, quote on p. 45.

37. Ibid., p. 45.
38. Slotkin, *Gunfighter Nation*, pp. 655–6.
39. See Karen R. Jones and John Wills, *The American West: Competing Visions* (Edinburgh: Edinburgh University Press, 2009), pp. 100–9.
40. Lee Clark Mitchell, *Westerns: Making the Man in Fiction and Film* (Chicago, IL: University of Chicago Press, 1996), p. 222.
41. Cant, *Cormac McCarthy*, pp. 252–3.
42. Stephen McVeigh, *The American Western* (Edinburgh: Edinburgh University Press, 2007), p. 212.
43. Ibid., p. 215.
44. David M. Wrobel, *The End of American Exceptionalism: Frontier Anxiety from the Old West to the New Deal* (Lawrence, KS: University Press of Kansas, 1993), p. viii.
45. Susan Faludi, *The Terror Dream: What 9/11 Revealed about America* (London: Atlantic Books, 2007), p. 286.
46. Ibid., p. 286.
47. Rosenberg, *The Tradition of the New*, p. 152.
48. Ibid., p. 158.
49. Faludi, *The Terror Dream*, p. 286.
50. Slotkin, *Gunfighter Nation*, p. 655.
51. Jameson, *The Political Unconscious*, pp. 19–20.
52. White, *The Content of the Form*, p. 148.
53. Rosenberg, *The Tradition of the New*, p. 144.
54. Ibid., p. 144.
55. White, *The Content of the Form*, p. 149.
56. Cant, *Cormac McCarthy*, p. 250.
57. Ibid., p. 250.

CONCLUSION

I

Throughout this study I have attempted to describe through recourse to a small but significant number of Westerns some of the contexts within which the genre has engaged with the myth of the West. Clearly this study is not definitive, but it was never intended to be. Its intention has always been to scrutinise existing film scholarship on the Western and to highlight the complexities of some of the genre's most celebrated examples – even the most ostensibly triumphalist – and observe the complex of ways in which such films have interacted with contemporary culture, politics and historical perspectives. I have taken up the critical thread of those like Janet Walker, who have argued for a strong historiographic element in the Western. I have also sought to assess the interdependent relationship held between history and myth. Above all, I have sought to repudiate the widely held belief in a pattern of consistent development within the genre as it has been defined within terms of popular evolution theories that tend to categorise groups of film texts rather bluntly into classical, revisionist and post-Western phases.

Some of the 'classical' Westerns that I have discussed (and the many more that I have not) often come across as more complex than most of those that have followed, including the allegedly 'revisionist' exemplars, *Unforgiven* and *Dances with Wolves*; both of which are less complex than *The Searchers*. This is not to deny that there is such a thing as a revisionist Western, rather, it is to suggest that, from the outset, the Western has been a very self-conscious, self-reflexive and diverse genre capable of a variety of opinion. Furthermore, the period in which a particular film was released does not necessarily determine the nature of its relationship to the myth or, indeed, to prevailing political and cultural ideologies. Individual film texts could be supportive, oppositional or, more often than not, a combination of both stances. Consider (as I have done) for example, John Ford. Anyone who has followed the line from *Stagecoach* and *My Darling Clementine* through to *The Searchers* and *The Man Who Shot Liberty Valance* should be aware of the ambivalence, ambiguity and complexity of these films. As I have argued, a sense of narrative confusion permeates such Westerns and the genre as a whole has never been consistent. Recall Ford's 'counter-evolutionary' depiction of Native Americans in his Cavalry Trilogy: *Fort Apache*, *She Wore a Yellow Ribbon* and *Rio Grande*; the complex depiction of the Comanche in *The Searchers*. Even within the 'confines' of a single filmmaker's oeuvre, *inconsistency* in critical vision would appear to prevail over all else.

Perhaps it is inevitable that the sort of approaches to the Western that I have discussed and critiqued – those that try to discern and assert general generic principles before attempting to 'explain' individual films by reference to these principles – often result in over-simplified interpretations. Within such broad schemas, effacement or distortion appears to be the fate of those all too numerous films that deviate from self-serving and self-inscribed norms. Seeking unity through a 'grand narrative', where the overall system of interpretation is privileged over the individual films (which are essentially employed as singular instances with which to 'prove' the system's validity), cannot help but omit the details, contradictions, ambiguities and idiosyncrasies that go into the individual films themselves. As we have seen, Will Wright's attempt to apply a structural study to the Western based upon cultural–ideological shifts and, indeed, Thomas Schatz's attempt to discern a formal evolution within the genre, depends upon a near total abandonment of considerations of individual character psychology and motivation; aspects which, I have argued, are of fundamental importance to any considerable appreciation of the films themselves.

In spite of the ever-growing wealth of rich and insightful material on the genre, it seems that the evolution argument together with the classical, revisionist and post-Western readings will persist. For instance, Carlton Smith (who I discussed in the Introduction) uses *Shane* as an example against which to foreground the post-modern credentials of Leone's 1960s Italian Westerns. Smith places these films within a Cold War context and sees them as wilful examples of post-modern blank-parody: 'There is no meaning to the landscape . . . and there is no one way to read the film[s]. There are only codes, tropes, and images that have become detached from any stable signifier.'[1] The problem with such an analysis lies not in Smith's assessment of the Dollars Trilogy themselves (which I happen to agree with), but rather his use of *Shane* as a classical contrast to these later, revisionist films. The legendary image of *Shane* as a distillation of mythic archetypes appears so powerful in scholarship on the Western *and* within popular culture that it seems to have led Smith (and others) towards inaccurate plot description. He writes that Leone's films 'compound the very structure of *Shane*. It is no longer possible, suggests Leone, for Alan Ladd, as Shane, to ride off happily into the sunset.'[2] It is difficult to see how the conclusion of *Shane* could be described in such a fashion. Shane is seriously wounded and leaves behind a domestic setting that he covets and a woman whom he desires but can never have. He leaves trying his best to ignore the pleas of a boy who idolises him. He may even be dead (or at least dying) in the saddle – hardly riding off 'happily into the sunset' then! Surely Smith's assessment is based on a culture of genre evolution theory which cannot but see these older Westerns through a myopic lens, one where, to reiterate Tag Gallagher, 'rich lodes of ambivalence are overlooked in order to bolster a specious argument that "classic" westerns are simple and naive'.[3]

Similarly, I have attempted to show that related political–allegorical approaches by the likes of John G. Cawelti, John H. Lenihan, Richard Slotkin, Michael Coyne and Stephen McVeigh, which posit Vietnam as a nexus shaping cultural attitudes and the products of that culture, and which regarded and repudiated an ever-declining Western idealism, also exhibit significant shortcomings. First and foremost, is the questionable assertion that the 'destruction' of the myth through critique of US policies in Vietnam is the same thing as the 'destruction' of the genre itself. It is not. No more than the prevailing Western theme of the 'end of the frontier' signals the 'end of the Western'. Smith adheres closely to the political–allegorical reading himself, claiming that Leone's films imply that the 'very idyllic act' of happy endings in films like *Shane* were 'complicitous in the disaster of the cold war'.[4] Although Smith is not wrong in claiming that the 'idyllic act' of frontier triumphalism is, politically and culturally, deeply 'complicitous in the disaster of the cold war', he *is* wrong in his assertion that *Shane* embodies this mythic idyll in unproblematic terms through a 'happy ending'. Indeed, the homesteader's suspicions of Shane highlight another sort of problem. Shane may be seen as the idealised version of the Cold War warrior by many, but the complexities and contradictions of his own psychology can be extended in equal measure to his political–allegorical connotations. As Patrick McGee writes, 'Shane may be the embodiment of the theory of nuclear deterrence; but if he is, he also signifies US society's fear of its own defence and of the men who transformed themselves into the agents of state violence.'[5] This interpretation is borne out by the harsh fact that, despite Wright's claim to the contrary, Shane cannot stay to be a part of the community he has helped create through his violence.

I sought to demonstrate in Chapter 2 that the formal and thematic impact of significant Westerns does not so much come from the theme of the myth of the West, but rather from the complexities by which the films themselves *deal* with this theme and its attendant mythic discourses. In *The Searchers*, it is the narrative's focus on the captivity narrative and miscegenation, the problematic nature of the hero as outrider of Manifest Destiny, and of its depiction of the race war as a necessary phase in the domestication of the wilderness. Furthermore, the film suggests that the values espoused by the myth could never be anything but myths; historically devastating and destructive because they operate in the context of a violent and death-obsessed 'will to power' that provides a corrupting vehicle for their misappliance.

Following a critical account of the origins of the revisionist phase of the genre, Chapter 3 used Clint Eastwood's previous Westerns to argue that the causes surrounding *Unforgiven*'s struggle to assert its revisionism in the face of the classical elements of its story, setting and characters can be related more generally to the cultural prominence and power of the actor's star persona. It can be said to partly explain *Unforgiven*'s inability to offer a more complex picture of the Western hero. It is unclear if the film is a self-consciously unsuccessful attempt to escape from the conventions of the genre (and the persona of the film's star), whether it is just confused, or whether it is, in fact, dishonest. In any case, it highlights a curious dynamic when considered alongside the dubious sort of hero played by the equally celebrated and associated Western persona of John Wayne in the earlier, more supposedly classical, *The Searchers*. In other words, through a scrutiny of the Western hero, along with *Unforgiven*'s asserted 'feminist' perspective and its dilapidated frontier community, Chapter 3 sought to further problematise the assumed chronological development that the genre underwent as it supposedly evolved from celebratory classicism to a critical revisionist stance; and of the gunfighter himself as he moved from celebrated hero to dangerous anachronism.

II

Part Two of this study focused on the contemporary-set 'border' Western and sought to do two related things. First, it aimed to initiate critical discussion of the so-called post-Western by offering case studies of two films that have (so far) received little scholarly attention. Secondly, it aimed to draw thematic links to the Western's complex engagement with notions of race and national identity, as well as the various iconography and tropes of the genre as a whole that were discussed throughout Part One.

By focusing on *The Three Burials of Melquiades Estrada*, Chapter 4 initiated enquiry into this topic by analysing the Western's potential for highlighting the violence and complexities of the borderlands. Patricia Nelson Limerick has argued that, for much of the twentieth century, 'Hispanic history remained on the edges of Western American history.'[6] Her account is one that highlights the cultural–ideological machinations that lay behind this elision from the official historical discourse, and she seeks to re-engage the reader with a Hispanic culture now in its 'proper place at the centre of Western American history'.[7] However, if the fates of *all* the characters in *Three Burials* teach us anything, it is that we should be wary of claiming a 'centre' of history, especially along the borderlands. As Octavio Paz suggests, by the mid-twentieth century, social alienation 'is now a condition shared by all men':

> We Mexicans have always lived on the periphery of history. Now the centre or nucleus of world society has disintegrated and everyone – including the European and the North American – is a peripheral being. We are all living on the margin because there is no longer any centre.[8]

The idea of a 'disintegrated' social centre and of the individual as a 'peripheral being', of course, relates to Gloria Anzaldúa's *la frontera*. I proposed that such identities are apparent in many of the characters that populate the world of *Three Burials* – particularly illustrated in the fates of Pete Perkins and Melquiades Estrada himself – as they play out international issues as personal traumas while searching in vain for stable identities through the romantic promises of the myth.

Overall, I have tried to argue that *Three Burials* offers us a compelling examination of the myth of the West in both historiography–historiophoty and popular culture – ultimately blurring the border between these modes of discourse. To paraphrase the full title of Turner's Frontier Thesis, we can say that *Three Burials* re-engages us with the following question: how do individual experiences relate to the broader scope of the significance of the frontier in American history? John Higham insists that American historiography must move beyond the 'tenacity of nationalism', and suggests that the 'need to rethink the vehicles of tradition and the agencies of authority in a chaotic world is upon us'.[9] How fitting this is if applied to *Three Burials*, where the transnational nature of the film – both in terms of its narrative and production – engages us with the question of what it means to be an American, ultimately enriching our notions of such an ideological construct. Equally, it utilises the recognisable tropes and motifs of the Western in order to suggest an inclusive *and* broad telling of one of the most controversial and disputed areas of the present-day United States.

Chapter 5's primary focus on *No Country for Old Men* sought to connect the film to some of the contemporary sociopolitical issues affecting the United States. At its core it drew from Gallagher's insistence that the Western genre has always reflected or commented upon such concerns. In my reading, *No Country* reflected both a sense of generic introspection though its reference to the Westerns of the past *and* made broader cultural reference to the so-called 'War on Terror'; furthermore, it suggested that, as a political ideology, the War on Terror is intimately related to the myth of the West. Again, this reading is in no way definitive. That is to say, it does not suggest itself as *the* constitutional theme above all others, for if Westerns (like other genres) reflect the cultural climate within which they are produced, then it is more likely than not that a diverse and complex set of attitudes will arise to match what is, and always has been, a diverse and complex culture.

One could argue that *No Country* is in fact dominated by Chigurh and that it demands that he is the figure who should be read. I have suggested Chigurh as an allegory of the wilderness, although he does seem far more at home in an urban setting and seems more like a hit-man from a crime story than a Western outlaw. While I would not wish to argue against this, I think that Bell is a more interesting character and the notion of the savage wilderness within, threatening to put one's 'soul at hazard', struck me as the film's most powerful aspect. I suggested that *No Country's* attitude towards the ongoing effects of the myth upon the United States is one of profound negativity. And yet, like *Three Burials*, at one and the same time, it relies upon the multitude of established traditions and conventions of the genre in order to enact its critique. As such, it supports the argument that has run throughout this book: the Western has often had a problematic relationship with the myth of the West, just as often as it lauded it, the genre displays its opposition.

To return to the introductory sentiments with which I opened this study, films like *Three Burials* and *No Country* are a part of the current and growing crop of Westerns being produced. We may also recall that, despite this, I suggested that the Western is generally regarded as a somehow diminished generic form – post-Western. Overall, I have argued against the implications of this term. Indeed, throughout this study, I have suggested that, as a genre, the cinematic Western metamorphoses according to the exigencies of a given time and the visions of individual artists, but as a whole it has refused any defined pattern of continuous development. The release of films like David Von Ancken's *Seraphim Falls* (2006), James Mangold's *3:10 to Yuma* (2007) and Ed Harris' *Appaloosa* (2008) – which we might regard as 'unregenerate' Westerns – are evidence of this refusal, coming across as patently less revisionist than they do classical. They add a further corrective to those who consider that the genre has long since been deconstructed and revised in gunfighter Westerns like *Unforgiven*. Equally, films like Wim Wenders' *Don't Come Knocking* and David Jacobson's *Down in the Valley* (both 2005), continue the theme of Westerns with a contemporary setting; both providing rich sources for analysing the myth and the Western's articulation of the concept of a national identity in the modern era.

The genre's output seems set to continue, occasionally taking some very intriguing paths. *Django Unchained* (2012), written and directed by Quentin Tarantino, fuses blaxploitation cinema with the generic legacy of the fictional character, Django – a tradition first established by Sergio Corbucci in 1966 and made famous by actor Franco Nero – to tell the story of a freed slave, the eponymous, Django (Jamie Foxx). A brutal tale of abuse and revenge, the narrative revolves around the attempts of Django and his German bounty-hunter companion, Dr King Schultz (Christoph Waltz in an Academy Award winning role), to rescue his wife, Broomhilda Von Schaft (Kerry Washington), from a notoriously brutal Mississippi slave plantation nicknamed 'Candyland'.

Furthermore, the release of such films as the aforementioned *The Assassination of Jesse James by the Coward Robert Ford* and, subsequently, the Coen brothers' *True Grit* (2010) indicate that the Western is far from 'post' anything, and, indeed, that further scholarship on the rich diversity of the genre (rather than a post mortem on it) should and will continue.

III

Following in the tradition of the New Western History, scholars like Neil Campbell have suggested that the West is 'always relational, dialogic, engaged in or capable of reinvention – and, therefore, contradictory, irreducible, and hybrid'.[10] To me this complex descriptive could well be applied to the cinematic Western. For even in the most apparently ideologically uniformed of times, the United States has hosted a vast range of opinion and visions of the world, and this has always been reflected in Hollywood. The idea that the Western has ever had such an ideological uniformity has never been true. It is the failure to take this into account, the desire to produce unifying theories, which leads so many scholars astray. While it remains necessary to analyse a set of films that do fit a particular theoretical framework, this remains so only as long as this, itself, is not taken to be the whole picture. Such scholars discount the exceptions, whereas they should include them, marked as exceptions, as evidence of the permanent ongoing ideological contest that exists everywhere. Such disunity has always characterised the narratives Hollywood has produced. For, *if* the Western ever was an attempt to provide a mythic set of values and a version of history around which the United States could unite, the creative imagination never admits of, much less *allows* for, such uniformity and certainly the public's desire for innovation often ironically undermines the desired result. Indeed, as I have shown in this study, one often finds that any given Western draws introspectively upon elements and conventions of the genre from both past and present along with numerous other cultural themes in a process of reinvention.

Let us consider for a moment the case of Howard Hawks' *Red River*. For some this is an exemplar of the classical Western; it was certainly one of the most successful. *Red River* is set in the context of the development of the (short-lived) cattle-ranching industry of the nineteenth century, a development associated with the growth of the eastern cities and the railroads that served them. Within the context of the first use by drovers of the 'Chisholm Trail', the film encapsulates the role played by sheer violence in the appropriation of the land. In that sense we can draw thematic links with the earlier films *Cimarron*, *Stagecoach* and *My Darling Clementine*, and a few years later with *Shane* and *The Searchers*; further into the future still, we can retroactively relate it to films such as Kevin Costner's *Open Range* (2004). It is clear that Hawks deliberately addresses the historical aspect of the film, particularly in the initial sequences in which we learn that this story is from 'Early Tales of Texas' and Tom Dunson (John Wayne), who 'claims' his territory by means of his prowess with a gun. This is possible due to the fact that its Mexican owner lives so far away that he cannot exercise effective power over his domain. What we see is, in effect, a change of feudal overlordship brought about by force of arms. (The film does not represent the historical details accurately, particularly with respect to dates, but the process is essentially what occurred.) For many *Red River* expresses the myth of the West in political–allegorical terms that mirror the confidence of a country recently victorious in the Second World War. While there is no revisionist West here, it is equally the case that there is no civilised community established either, even in embryo. In addition to the open acknowledgement of 'land-grabbing', the film also reveals Dunson, the embodiment of late-nineteenth-century US capitalist expansion, as a fascist, ready to lynch those who dare oppose his tyranny. It is fair to say that the 'classical' *Red River* displays both narrative confusion and 'revisionist' traits in its assertion of the myth of the West.

To return to another pair of scholars who I discussed in the Introduction, Karen R. Jones and John Wills re-emphasised a key point regarding the double-edged nature of the myth of the West within the popular imagination. This re-emphasis goes hand-in-hand with what we might refer to as the double-edged nature of contemporary accounts of the American West which, in part, use the cinematic Western as a source of reference. With regard to the myth of the West, Jones and Wills suggest that, at the same time that its triumphalist rhetoric was being expounded upon by artists, journalists, religious leaders and politicians alike, there existed significant anti-mythic discourses. Notwithstanding 'that damned cowboy' epithet by Roosevelt's political enemies, Jones and Wills highlight that 'for critics and satirists, the cowboy moniker serviced accusations that harked back to the myth of the lawless West'.[11] Furthermore, that none other than Mark Twain offered a cautionary voice in the face of the overwhelming drive towards late-nineteenth-century US expansionism. Twain 'quipped that Roosevelt was "clearly insane . . . and insanest upon war and its supreme glories"'.[12] (Farther back yet, in 1851, Herman Melville had completed his magnum opus, *Moby Dick*. Through Captain Ahab's monomaniacal pursuit of the white whale, Melville can be said to have given an early literary voice against what I described earlier as the hubristic condition of US self-righteousness.)

It is unfortunate to note, therefore, that in having correctly highlighted anti-mythic sentiment from the outset of the cultural and political ascendancy of the myth of the West, Jones and Wills doubt the capacity of the cinematic Western to the task of mythological critique. Here, for instance, is their use of *High Noon* in order to illustrate the historical reality of the West:

> Frontier imaginings of the dime novel and Hollywood showed the West as a land of conflict – the sheriff with pistols cocked, facing off against his outlaw nemesis across a dusty main street. This brand of High Noon-style violence – heroic, redemptive and honourable – offered an unproblematic narrative of the winning of the West: all glory and gun-play without gory details or moral qualms. In reality, violence in the nineteenth-century West proved to be far more inglorious, atavistic and disturbing. Ethnic, racial and religious issues fostered hatred, social conflict, community

feuds and contests for resources; all promoted a brand of violence that was far less endearing to celluloid.[13]

By way of conclusion, I would hope that throughout this study I have indicated convincingly enough that the Western cannot simply be described as 'heroic, redemptive and honourable', and that, as often as it celebrated the myth of the West, it betrayed the more 'inglorious, atavistic and disturbing' elements of American national identity and the domestication of the wilderness. I suggest that the genre's attitude towards the myth has, therefore, always itself been double-edged; with myth and anti-myth often merging into the forms and themes of the same film text to create what Mitchell described as an 'exhilarating narrative mix', and that I have described as a mosaic of varied narratives that reflect not only different times, but also different attitudes existing within any given time.

NOTES

1. Carlton Smith, *Coyote Kills John Wayne: Postmodernism and Contemporary Fictions of the Transcultural Frontier* (Hanover, NH: University Press of New England, 2000), p. 97.
2. Ibid., p. 97.
3. Tag Gallagher, 'Shoot-Out at the Genre Corral: Problems in the "Evolution" of the Western' (1986), reprinted in Barry Keith Grant (ed.), *Film Genre Reader III* (Austin, TX: University of Texas Press, 2003), pp. 262–76, quote on p. 272.
4. Smith, *Coyote Kills John Wayne*, p. 98.
5. Patrick McGee, *From Shane to Kill Bill: Rethinking the Western* (Oxford: Blackwell, 2007), p. 19.
6. Patricia Nelson Limerick, *The Legacy of Conquest: The Unbroken Past of the American West* (London: W. W. Norton, 1987), pp. 253–4.
7. Ibid., p. 255.
8. Octavio Paz, *The Labyrinth of Solitude* (London: Penguin, [1950] 1990), p. 159.
9. John Higham, 'The Future of American History', *Journal of American History*, 80(4) (1994): 1289–309, quote on p. 1295.
10. Neil Campbell, *The Cultures of the American New West* (Edinburgh: Edinburgh University Press, 2000), p. 164.
11. Karen R. Jones and John Wills, *The American West: Competing Visions* (Edinburgh: Edinburgh University Press, 2009), p. 98.
12. Bernard DeVoto (ed.), *Mark Twain in Eruption* (New York: Harpers, 1940), p. 8. Twain and DeVoto, discussed in Jones and Wills, *The American West*, p. 98.
13. Jones and Wills, *The American West*, p. 171.

BIBLIOGRAPHY

Texts

Abel, Richard, *The Red Rooster Scare: Making Cinema American, 1900–1910* (London: University of California Press, 1999).

Altman, Rick, *Film/Genre* (London: British Film Institute, 1999).

Altman, Rick, *The American Film Musical* (Bloomington, IN: Indiana University Press, 1989).

Anderson, Christopher, 'Jesse James, the Bourgeois Bandit: The Transformation of a Popular Hero', *Cinema Journal*, 26(1) (1986): 43–64.

Anderson, Perry, *The Origins of Postmodernity* (London: Verso, 1998).

Andrechuck, Ed, *The Golden Corral: A Roundup of Magnificent Westerns* (London: McFarland, 1997).

Anzaldúa, Gloria, *Borderlands – la Frontera: the New Mestiza*, 2nd edn (San Francisco, CA: Aunt Lute Books, 1999).

Baker, Bob, '*Shane* through Five Decades', in Cameron and Pye (eds), *The Movie Book of the Western*, pp. 214–20.

Barthes, Roland, *Mythologies*, trans. Annette Lavers (London: Vintage, [1972] 1993).

Bazin, André, 'Évolution du western', *Cahiers du Cinéma*, 55 (1955), reprinted in Bill Nichols (ed.), *Movies and Methods*, vol. 1, pp. 150–7.

Beebee, Thomas O., *The Ideology of Genre: A Comparative Study of Generic Instability* (University Park, PA: Pennsylvania State University Press, 1994).

Bercovitch, Sacvan, *The American Jeremiad* (London: University of Wisconsin Press, 1978).

Billington, Ray A. (ed.), *The Frontier Thesis: Valid Interpretation of American History?* (Malabar, FL: Krieger, [1966] 1977).

Billington, Ray A., *Fredrick Jackson Turner: Historian, Scholar, Teacher* (New York: Oxford University Press, 1973).

Billington, Ray A., *Westward Expansion: A History of the American Frontier*, 2nd edn (New York: Macmillan, [1949] 1960).

Bird, Robert M., *Nick of the Woods; or, Adventures of Prairie Life* (Hamburg: Tredition Classics, [1837] 2007).

Braudy, Leo and Marshall Cohen (eds), *Film Theory and Criticism: Introductory Readings* (Oxford: Oxford University Press, 1999).

Brooks, James F., '"That Don't Make You Kin!": Borderlands History and Culture in *The Searchers*', in Eckstein and Lehman (eds), *The Searchers: Essays and Reflections on John Ford's Classic Western*, pp. 265–89.

Browne, Nick (ed.), *Refiguring American Film Genres: Theory and History* (Berkeley, CA: University of California Press, 1998).

Brown, Dee, *Bury My Heart at Wounded Knee: An Indian History of the American West* (New York: Henry Holt, 1970).

Buscombe, Edward (ed.), *The BFI Companion to the Western* (London: British Film Institute, 1988).

Buscombe, Edward and Roberta E. Pearson (eds), *Back in the Saddle Again: New Essays on the Western* (London: British Film Institute, 1998).

Cameron, Ian and Douglas Pye (eds), *The Movie Book of the Western* (New York: Continuum, 1996).

Campbell, Joseph, *The Hero with a Thousand Faces* (New York: Meridian Books, 1949).

Campbell, Neil, *The Cultures of the American New West* (Edinburgh: Edinburgh University Press, 2000).

Cant, John, *Cormac McCarthy and the Myth of American Exceptionalism* (London: Routledge, 2008).

Cawelti, John. G., *The Six-Gun Mystique Sequel* (Bowling Green, OH: Bowling Green State University Popular Press, 1999).

Cawelti, John. G., *The Six-Gun Mystique*, 2nd edn (Bowling Green, OH: Bowling Green State University Popular Press, [1971] 1984).

Cawelti, John. G., 'Myths of Violence in American Popular Culture', *Critical Inquiry*, 1(3) (1975): 521–41.

Cawelti, John G., 'Savagery, Civilisation and the Western Hero' (1971), reprinted in Nachbar (ed.), *Focus on the Western*, pp. 57–64.

Churchill, Ward, *Fantasies of the Master Race: Literature, Cinema and the Colonisation of American Indians* (Monroe, ME: Common Courage Press, 1992).

Cixous, Hélène, 'Sorties' (1975), reprinted in Lodge and Wood (eds), *Modern Criticism and Theory*, pp. 263–71.

Coyne, Michael, *The Crowded Prairie: American National Identity in the Hollywood Western* (London: I. B. Tauris, 1997).

Cook, David A,. *A History of Narrative Film* (London: W. W. Norton, [1981] 2004).

Cook, Pam and Mieke Bernink (eds), *The Cinema Book* (London: British Film Institute, [1985] 1999).

Cooper, James F., *The Pioneers* (New York: Signet Classics, [1823] 1964).

Colonese, Tom G., 'Native American Reactions to *The Searchers*', in Eckstein and Lehman (eds), *The Searchers: Essays and Reflections on John Ford's Classic Western*, pp. 335–43.

Creekmur, Corey K., 'Buffalo Bill (Himself): History and Memory in the Western Biopic', in Walker (ed.), *Westerns: Films through History*, pp. 131–51.

Crèvecoeur, J. Hector St John de, *Letters from an American Farmer* (New York: Oxford University Press, [1782] 1998).

Danto, Arthur C., *Narration and Knowledge* (New York: Columbia University Press, [1985] 2007).

Devlin, William J., '*No Country for Old Men*: The Decline of Ethics and the West(ern)', in McMahon and Csaki (eds), *The Philosophy of the Western*, pp. 221–41.

DeVoto, Bernard (ed.), *Mark Twain in Eruption* (New York: Harpers, 1940).

Drinnon, Richard, *Facing West: The Metaphysics of Indian-Hating and Empire-Building* (New York: Meridian, 1980).

Eagleton, Terry, *Literary Theory: An Introduction* (Oxford: Blackwell, [1983] 1995).

Eagleton, Terry, *Ideology: An Introduction* (London: Verso, 1991).

Eckstein, Arthur M., 'Introduction: Main Critical Issues in *The Searchers*', in Eckstein and Lehman (eds), *The Searchers: Essays and Reflections on John Ford's Classic Western*, pp. 1–47.

Eckstein, Arthur M., 'Darkening Ethan: John Ford's *The Searchers* (1956) from Novel to Screenplay to Screen', *Cinema Journal*, 38(1) (1998): 3–24.

Eckstein, Arthur M. and Peter Lehman (eds), *The Searchers: Essays and Reflections on John Ford's Classic Western* (Detroit, MI: Wayne State University Press, 2004).

Emmert, Scott, *Loaded Fictions: Social Critique in the Twentieth Century Western* (Moscow, ID: University of Idaho Press, 1996).

Esselman, Kathryn C., 'From Camelot to Monument Valley: Dramatic Origins of the Western Film' (1974), reprinted in Nachbar (ed.), *Focus on the Western*, pp. 9–19.

Etulain, Richard W. (ed.), *Does the Frontier Experience Make America Exceptional?* (Boston, MA: St Martin's Press, 1999).

Etulain, Richard W., *Re-imagining the Modern American West: A Century of Fiction, History, and Art* (Tucson, AZ: University of Arizona Press, 1996).

Faludi, Susan, *The Terror Dream: What 9/11 Revealed about America* (London: Atlantic Books, 2007).

Fenin, George N. and William K. Everson, *The Western: From Silents to the Seventies* (New York: Penguin, [1973] 1977).

Fiedler, Leslie A., *Love and Death in the American Novel* (London: Penguin, [1960] 1984).

Fiedler, Leslie A., *The Return of the Vanishing American* (London: Jonathan Cape, 1968).

Fitzgerald, F. Scott, *The Great Gatsby* (London: Penguin, [1925] 1994).

Fojas, Camilla, 'Hollywood Border Cinema: Westerns with a Vengeance', *Journal of Popular Film and Television, Special Issue: The Western*, 39(2) (2011): 93–101.

Folsom, James K., 'Westerns as Social and Political Alternatives' (1967), reprinted in Nachbar (ed.), *Focus on the Western*, pp. 81–4.

Foucault, Michel, *The Archaeology of Knowledge* (London: Routledge, [1969] 2002).

Foucault, Michel, *The Order of Things: An Archaeology of the Human Sciences* (London: Tavistock, [1966] 1970).

French, Philip, *Westerns: Aspects of a Movie Genre* (New York: Viking, 1974).

Frye, Northrop, *Anatomy of Criticism* (Princeton, NJ: Princeton University Press, 1957).

Fussell, Edwin, *Frontier: American Literature and the American West* (Princeton, NJ: Princeton University Press, 1965).

Gallagher, Tag, 'Shoot-Out at the Genre Corral: Problems in the "Evolution" of the Western' (1986), reprinted in Grant (ed.), *Film Genre Reader III*, pp. 262–76.

Grant, Barry K. (ed.), *Film Genre Reader III* (Austin, TX: University of Texas Press, 2003).

Greb, Jacqueline K., 'Will the Real Indians Please Stand Up?', in Yoggy (ed.), *'Back in the Saddle': Essays on Western Film and Television Actors*, pp. 129–44.

Greenberg, Harvey R., *'Unforgiven'*, *Film Quarterly*, 46(3) (Spring, 1993): 52–6.

Griffin, Ruth, 'Writing the West: Critical Approaches to *Shane*', *Literature Compass*, 4(1) (2007): 24–47.

Grimsted, David, 'Re-Searching', in Eckstein and Lehman (eds), *The Searchers: Essays and Reflections on John Ford's Classic Western*, pp. 289–343.

Grist, Leighton, *'Unforgiven'*, in Cameron and Pye (eds), *The Movie Book of the Western*, pp. 294–301.

Grossman, James R. (ed.), *The Frontier in American Culture* (Berkeley, CA: University of California Press, 1994).

Gultang, Johan, 'The Meanings of History: Enacting the Sociocultural Code', in Rüsen (ed.), *Meaning and Representation in History*, p. 98

Gwynne, S. C., *Empire of the Summer Moon: Quanah Parker and the Rise and Fall of the Comanche Tribe* (London: Constable & Robinson, 2010).

Harvey, David, *The Condition of Postmodernity: An Enquiry into the Origins of Cultural Change* (Oxford: Blackwell, 1990).

Hearne, Joanna, 'The "Ache for Home": Assimilation and Separatism in Anthony Mann's *Devil's Doorway*', in Rollins and O'Conner (eds), *Hollywood's West: The American Frontier in Film, Television, and History*, pp. 126–60.

Heidler, David S. and Jeanne T. Heidler, *Manifest Destiny* (London: Greenwood Press, 2003).

Henderson, Brian. '*The Searchers*: An American Dilemma', *Film Quarterly*, 34(2) (1980/1): 9–23.

Higham, John, 'The Future of American History', *Journal of American History*, 80(4) (1994): 1289–309.

Hine, Robert V. and John Mack Faragher, *The American West: A New Interpretive History* (New Haven, CT: Yale University Press, 2000).

Holtz, Martin, *American Cinema in Transition: The Western in New Hollywood and Hollywood Now* (Oxford: Peter Lang, 2011).

Hutcheon, Linda, *The Politics of Postmodernism* (London: Routledge, 1989).

Hutson, Richard, 'Sermons in Stone: Monument Valley in *The Searchers*', in Eckstein and Lehman (eds), *The Searchers: Essays and Reflections on John Ford's Classic Western*, pp. 93–109.

Jaimes, M. Annette (ed.), *The State of Native America: Genocide, Colonisation, and Resistance* (Boston, MA: South End Press, 1992).

Jameson, Fredric, *The Geopolitical Aesthetic: Cinema and Space in the World System* (Indiana: Indiana University Press, 1992).

Jameson, Fredric, *Postmodernism or, the Cultural Logic of Late-Capitalism* (London: Methuen, 1991).

Jameson, Fredric, *The Political Unconscious: Narrative as a Socially Symbolic Act* (London: Methuen, 1981).

Jarvie, Ian, 'Seeing through Movies', *Philosophy of the Social Sciences*, 8 (1978): 374–97.

Jauss, Hans, R., *Towards an Aesthetic of Reception* (Brighton: Harvester Press, 1982).

Jones, Karen R. and John Wills, *The American West: Competing Visions* (Edinburgh: Edinburgh University Press, 2009).

Kaplan, Amy, *The Anarchy of Empire in the making of US Culture* (Cambridge, MA: Harvard University Press, 2002).

Kasson, Joy S., 'Life-Like, Vivid and Thrilling Pictures: Buffalo Bill's Wild West and Early Cinema', in Walker (ed.), *Westerns: Films through History*, pp. 109–31.

Keller, Alexandra, 'Generic Subversion as Counter-history: Mario Van Peebles's *Posse*', in Walker (ed.), *Westerns: Films through History*, pp. 27–47.

King, Geoff, *New Hollywood Cinema: An Introduction* (New York: Columbia University Press, 2002).

King, Geoff, *Spectacular Narratives: Hollywood in the Age of the Blockbuster* (London: I. B. Tauris, 2000).

King, John, Ana M. Lopez and Manuel Alvarado (eds), *Mediating Two Worlds: Cinematic Encounters in the Americas* (London: British Film Institute, 1993).

Kitses, Jim, *Horizons West: Directing the Western from John Ford to Clint Eastwood* (London: British Film Institute, [2004] 2007).

Kitses, Jim, *Horizons West: Anthony Mann, Bud Boetticher, Sam Peckinpah*

– *Studies of Authorship within the Western* (London: Secker & Warburg/ British Film Institute, 1969).

Klein, Kerwin L., *Frontiers of Historical Imagination: Narrating the European Conquest of Native America, 1890–1990* (London: University of California Press, 1997).

Kollins, Susan, 'Genre and the Geographies of Violence: Cormac McCarthy and the Contemporary Western', *Contemporary Literature*, 42(3) (2001): 557–88.

Kroker, Arthur and David Cook, *The Postmodern Scene: Excremental Culture and Hyper-Aesthetics* (London: Macmillan, [1986] 1988).

Lapsley, Robert and Michael Westlake (eds), *Film Theory: An Introduction* (Manchester: Manchester University Press, 1988).

Lawrence, D. H., *Studies in Classical American Literature* (London: Penguin Classics, [1923] 1990).

Leach, Neil (ed.), *Rethinking Architecture: A Reader in Cultural Theory* (London: Routledge, 1997).

Lehman, Peter, '"You Couldn't Hit It on the Nose": The Limits of Knowledge in and of *The Searchers*', in Eckstein and Lehman (eds), *The Searchers: Essays and Reflections on John Ford's Classic Western*, pp. 239–65.

Lehman, Peter, 'Looking at Look's Missing Reverse Shot: Psychoanalysis and Style in John Ford's *The Searchers*', *Wide Angle*, 4(4) (1981): 65–71.

Lenihan, John H., *Showdown: Confronting Modern America in the Western Film* (Urbana, IL: University of Illinois Press, [1980] 1985).

Lévi-Strauss, Claude, *The Raw and the Cooked*, trans. John and Doreen Weightman (London: Jonathon Cape, 1969).

Lévi-Strauss, Claude, *The Savage Mind* (London: Weidenfeld & Nicolson, [1962] 1966).

Lewis, Pericles, *The Cambridge Introduction to Modernism* (Cambridge: Cambridge University Press, 2007).

Limerick, Patricia N., *Something in the Soil: Legacies and Reckonings in the New West* (London: W. W. Norton, 2000).

Limerick, Patricia N., *The Legacy of Conquest: The Unbroken Past of the American West* (London: W. W. Norton, 1987).

Lodge, David and Nigel Wood (eds), *Modern Criticism and Theory: A Reader* (London: Longman, [1988] 2000).

Lovell, Alan, 'The Western' (1967), reprinted in Bill Nichols (ed.), *Movies and Methods*, vol. 1, pp. 164–75.

Lyotard, Jean-François, *The Postmodern Condition: A Report on Knowledge*, trans. Geoff Bennington and Brian Massumi (Manchester: Manchester University Press, [1979] 1984).

Magowan, Kim, '"Blood Only Means What You Let It": Incest and Miscegenation in John Sayles' *Lone Star*', *Film Quarterly*, 57(1) (2003): 20–31.

Maltby, Richard, 'A Better Sense of History: John Ford and the Indians', in Cameron and Pye (eds), *The Movie Book of the Western*, pp. 34–49.

Marsden, Michael, 'The Modern Western', *Journal of the West*, 19 (1980): 54–61.

Martin, Waldo E., Jr, *Brown v. Board of Education of Topeka: A Brief History with Documents* (Boston, MA: Palgrave Macmillan, 1998).

Marx, Karl, *The Eighteenth Brumaire of Louis Bonaparte* (London: International Publishers, [1852] 1994).

Marx, Leo, *The Machine in the Garden: Technology and the Pastoral Ideal in America* (New York: Oxford University Press, 1964).

Melville, Herman, *Moby Dick; Or, The Whale* (London: Penguin, [1851] 2003).

McBride, Joseph, *Searching for John Ford* (New York: Faber, 2003).

McBride, Joseph and Michael Wilmington, 'The Prisoner of the Desert', *Sight and Sound*, 40(4) (1971): 210–14.

McBride, Joseph and Michael Wilmington, *John Ford* (London: Secker & Warburg, 1974).

McCarthy, Cormac, *No Country for Old Men* (London: Picador, 2005).

McGee, Patrick, *From Shane to Kill Bill: Rethinking the Western* (Oxford: Blackwell, 2007).

McMahon, Jennifer L. and B. Steve Csaki (eds), *The Philosophy of the Western* (Lexington, KY: University of Kentucky Press, 2010).

McVeigh, Steven, *The American Western* (Edinburgh: Edinburgh University Press, 2007).

Mitchell, Lee C., *Westerns: Making the Man in Fiction and Film* (Chicago, IL: University of Chicago Press, 1996).

Miller, Lee (ed.), *From the Heart: Voices of the American Indian* (London: Random House, 1995).

Modleski, Tania, *Old Wives' Tales: Feminist Re-Visions of Film and Other Fictions* (London: I. B. Tauris, 1998).

Morris, Edmund, *Theodore Rex* (New York: Random House, 2001).

Moses, Michael Valdez, 'Savage Nations: Native Americans and the Western', in McMahon and Csaki (eds), *The Philosophy of the Western*, pp. 261–91.

Murdoch, David H., *The American West: The Invention of a Myth* (Cardiff: Welsh Academic Press, 2001).

Mulvey, Laura, 'Visual Pleasure and Narrative Cinema', *Screen*, 16(3) (1975): 6–19.

Nachbar, Jack (ed.), *Focus on the Western* (Englewood Cliffs, NJ: Prentice-Hall, 1974).

Nachbar, Jack (ed.), 'Introduction', in *Focus on the Western*, p. 8.

Nachbar, Jack (ed.), 'Riding Shotgun: The Scattered Formula in Contemporary Western Movies' (1973), reprinted in *Focus on the Western*, pp. 101–13.

Neale, Steve (ed.), *Genre and Contemporary Hollywood* (London: British Film Institute, 2002).

Neale, Steve, *Genre and Hollywood* (London: Routledge, 2000).

Neale, Steve, 'Questions of Genre' (1995), reprinted in Grant (ed.), *Film Genre Reader III*, pp. 160–84.

Neale, Steve, 'Vanishing Americans: Racial and Ethnic Issues in the Interpretation and Context of Post-War "Pro-Indian" Westerns', in Buscombe and Pearson (eds), *Back in the Saddle Again: New Essays on the Western*, pp. 8–29.

Nichols, Bill (ed.), *Movies and Methods, vol. 1: An Anthology* (London: University of California Press, 1976).

O'Brien, Daniel, *Clint Eastwood: Film-Maker* (London: Batsford, 1996).

Orellana, Margarita de, 'The Incursion of North American Fictional Cinema 1911-1917 into the Mexican Revolution', in King, Lopez and Alvarado (eds), *Mediating Two Worlds: Cinematic Encounters in the Americas*, pp. 2–14.

Patterson, John, 'Whatever Happened to the Heroes?', Culture section, *The Guardian*, 16 November 2007.

Paz, Octavio, *The Labyrinth of Solitude* (London: Penguin, [1950] 1990).

Perez, Gilberto, 'House of Miscegenation', *London Review of Books*, 32(22), 18 November 2010, pp. 23–5.

Pippin, Robert B., *Hollywood Westerns and American Myth: The Importance of Howard Hawks and John Ford for Political Philosophy* (New Haven, CT: Yale University Press, 2010).

Place, Janey, 'Structured Cowboys', *Jump Cut: A Review of Contemporary Media*, 18 (1978): 26–8.

Plantinga, Carl, 'Spectacles of Death: Clint Eastwood and Violence in *Unforgiven*', *Cinema Journal*, 37(2) (1998): 65–83.

Pomeroy, Earl, 'Toward a Reorientation of Western History: Continuity and Environment', *Mississippi Valley Historical Review*, 41(4) (1955): 579–600.

Prats, Armando J., *Invisible Natives: Myth and Identity in the American Western* (London: Cornell University Press, 2002).

Propp, Vladimir, *The Morphology of the Folktale*, trans. Laurence Scott (Austin, TX: University of Texas Press, [1928] 1968).

Pye, Douglas, 'The Western (Genre and Movies)' (1977), reprinted in Grant (ed.) *Film Genre Reader III*, pp. 203–18.

Pye, Douglas, 'Double Vision: Miscegenation and Point of View in *The Searchers*', in Cameron and Pye (eds), *The Movie Book of the Western*, pp. 229–35.

Pye, Douglas, 'Genre and History: Fort Apache and The Man Who Shot Liberty Valance', in Cameron and Pye (eds), *The Movie Book of the Western*, pp. 111–22.

Robinson, Forrest G. (ed.), 'Clio Bereft of Calliope', in *The New Western History: The Territory Ahead* (Tucson, AZ: The University of Arizona Press, 1998).

Robinson, Forrest G., *Having it Both Ways: Self-Subversion in Western*

Popular Classics (Albuquerque, NM: University of New Mexico Press, 1993).

Rollins, Peter C. and John E. O'Conner (eds), *Hollywood's West: The American Frontier in Film, Television, and History* (Lexington, KY: University of Kentucky Press, 2005).

Roosevelt, Theodore, *The Winning of the West, vol. 1: From the Alleghanies to the Mississippi, 1771–1783* (Lincoln, NE: University of Nebraska Press, 1995).

Roosevelt, Theodore, *The Rough Riders* (New York: Da Capo Press, [1902] 1990).

Roosevelt, Theodore, *The Strenuous Life*, from *The Works of Theodore Roosevelt in Fourteen Volumes* (New York: P. F. Collier, 1901).

Roosevelt, Theodore, *The Winning of the West*, 6 vols (New York: G. P. Putnam, 1900).

Roosevelt, Theodore, *Ranch Life and the Hunting Trail* (New York: Century, [1888] 1899).

Roosevelt, Theodore, *American Ideals, and Other Essays, Social and Political* (New York: G. P. Putnam, 1897).

Rosenberg, Harold, 'The Resurrected Romans' (1959), reprinted in Harold Rosenberg, *The Tradition of the New* (London: Paladin, 1962), pp. 140–58.

Rüsen, Jörn (ed.), *Meaning and Representation in History* (Oxford: Berghahn Books, 2006).

Rydell, Robert W. and Rob Kroes, *Buffalo Bill in Bologna: The Americanization of the World, 1869–1922* (Chicago, IL: University of Chicago Press, 2005).

Schaeffer, Jack, *Shane* (London: Bantam Pathfinder, [1949] 1963).

Schatz, Thomas, *Hollywood Genres: Formulas, Filmmaking, and the Studio System* (New York: Random House, 1981).

Schultz, Kimberley, 'Challenging Legends, Complicating Borderlines: The Concept of "Frontera" in John Sayles's *Lone Star*', in Rollins and O'Connor (eds), *Hollywood's West: The American Frontier in Film, Television, and History*, pp. 261–81.

Slotkin, Richard, *Regeneration through Violence: The Mythology of the American Frontier 1600–1860*, new edn (Norman, OK: University of Oklahoma Press, 2000).

Slotkin, Richard, *Gunfighter Nation: The Myth of the Frontier in Twentieth-Century America* (Norman, OK: University of Oklahoma Press, [1992] 1998).

Slotkin, Richard, *The Fatal Environment: The Myth of the Frontier in the Age of Industrialisation, 1800–1890* (Norman, OK: University of Oklahoma Press, [1985] 1998).

Slotkin, Richard, 'Nostalgia and Progress: Theodore Roosevelt's Myth of the Frontier', *American Quarterly, Special Issue: American Culture and the American Frontier*, 33(5) (1981): 608–37.

Smith, Carlton, *Coyote Kills John Wayne: Postmodernism and Contemporary*

Fictions of the Transcultural Frontier (Hanover, NH: University Press of New England, 2000).

Smith, Henry N., *Virgin Land: The American West as Symbol and Myth* (London: Harvard University Press, [1950] 1978).

Smyth, J. E., 'The New Western History in 1931: RKO and the Challenge of *Cimarron*', in Rollins and O'Connor (eds), *Hollywood's West: The American Frontier in Film, Television, and History*, pp. 37–65.

Simon, William G. and Louise Spence, 'Cowboy Wonderland, History and Myth: "It ain't all that Different in Real Life"', in Walker (ed.), *Westerns: Films through History*, pp. 89–108.

Staiger, Janet, 'Hybrid or Inbred: The Purity Hypothesis and Hollywood Genre History' (1997), reprinted in Grant (ed.), *Film Genre Reader III*, pp. 185–99.

Studlar, Gaylyn, 'What Would Martha Want?: Captivity, Purity, and Feminine Values in *The Searchers*', in Eckstein and Lehman (eds), *The Searchers: Essays and Reflections on John Ford's Classic Western*, pp. 171–97.

Szaloky, Melinda, 'A Tale N/nobody Can Tell: The Return of the Repressed Western History in Jim Jarmusch's *Dead Man*', in Walker (ed.), *Westerns: Films through History*, pp. 47–71.

Tompkins, Jane, *West of Everything: The Inner Life of Westerns* (New York: Oxford University Press, 1992).

Thompson, David, 'The Cowboy's Last Stand', *The Independent on Sunday*, 30 April 2006.

Tudor, Andrew. 'Genre and Critical Methodology' (1974), reprinted in Nichols (ed.), *Movies and Methods*, vol. 1, pp. 118–26.

Turner, Frederick J., 'The Significance of the Frontier in American History' [1893], in *The Frontier in American History* (Tucson, AZ: University of Arizona Press, [1920] 1986), pp. 1–38.

Tuska, John, *The American West in Film: Critical Approaches to the Western* (London: Greenwood Press, 1985).

Walker, Janet (ed.), *Westerns: Films through History* (London: Routledge, 2001).

Walker, Janet (ed.), 'Introduction: Westerns through History', in *Westerns: Films through History*, pp. 1–27.

Walker, Janet (ed.), 'Captive Images in the Traumatic Western: *The Searchers, Pursued, Once upon a Time in the West*, and *Lone Star*', in *Westerns: Films through History*, pp. 219–53.

Watts, Sarah, *Rough Rider in the Whitehouse: Theodore Roosevelt and the Politics of Desire* (Chicago, IL: University of Chicago Press, 2003).

Warshow, Robert, 'Movie Chronicle: The Westerner' (1954), reprinted in Braudy and Cohen (eds), *Film Theory and Criticism: Introductory Readings*, pp. 655–67.

White, Hayden, 'Historiography and Historiophoty', *American Historical Review*, 93(5) (1988): 1193–9.

White, Hayden, *The Content of the Form* (Baltimore, MD: Johns Hopkins University Press, 1987).

White, Hayden, 'Getting Out of History: Jameson's Redemption of Narrative', in *The Content of the Form*, pp. 147–8.

White, Hayden, 'Historicism, History, and the Figurative Imagination', *History and Theory*, 14(4) (1975): 48–67.

White, Hayden, *Metahistory: The Historical Imagination in Nineteenth-Century Europe* (Baltimore, MD: Johns Hopkins University Press, 1973).

White, Hayden, 'The Burden of History', *History and Theory*, 5(2) (1966): 111–34.

White, Richard, 'Frederick Jackson Turner and Buffalo Bill', in James R. Grossman (ed.), *The Frontier in American Culture* (Berkeley, CA: University of California Press, 1994), pp. 7–67.

White, Richard, Review (untitled), *Journal of American History*, 80(3) (1993): 1039–41.

Williams, Alan, 'Is a Radical Genre Criticism Possible?' *Quarterly Review of Film Studies*, 9(2) (1984): 121–5.

Winkler, Martin M., 'Homer's Iliad and John Ford's *The Searchers*', in Eckstein and Lehman (eds), *The Searchers: Essays and Reflections on John Ford's Classic Western*, pp. 145–71.

Winkler, Martin M. (ed.), 'Tragic Features in John Ford's *The Searchers*', in *Classical Myth and Culture in the Cinema* (Oxford: Oxford University Press, 2001), pp. 118–47.

Wister, Owen, *The Virginian: A Horseman of the Plains* (Oxford: Oxford University Press, [1902] 1998).

Worland, Rick and Edward Countryman, 'The New Western, American Historiography and the Emergence of the New American Westerns', in Buscombe and Pearson (eds), *Back in the Saddle Again*, pp. 182–97.

Wright, Will, *The Wild West: The Mythical Cowboy and Social Theory* (London: Sage, 2001).

Wright, Will, *Six Guns and Society: A Structural Study of Myth* (Berkeley, CA: University of California Press, 1975).

Wrobel, David. M., *The End of American Exceptionalism: Frontier Anxiety from the Old West to the New Deal* (Lawrence, KS: University Press of Kansas, 1993).

Xie, Shabo, 'History and Utopian Desire: Fredric Jameson's Dialectical Tribute to Northrop Frye', *Cultural Critique*, 34 (1996): 115–42.

Yoggy, Gary A. (ed.), *'Back in the Saddle': Essays on Western Film and Television Actors* (London: McFarland, 1998).

Žižek, Slavoj, *The Plague of Fantasies* (London: Verso, 1997).

Žižek, Slavoj, *The Sublime Object of Ideology* (London: Verso, 1989).

Films

Appaloosa, director Ed Harris, featuring Ed Harris, Viggo Mortensen, Renée Zellweger, Jeremy Irons (New Line Cinema, 2008).

Amores Perros, director Alejandro González Iñárritu, featuring Emilio Echevarría, Gael García Bernal, Goya Toledo, Álvaro Guerrero (Nu Vision/ Lions Gate Films, 2000).

Assassination of Jesse James by the Coward Robert Ford, The, director Andrew Dominick, featuring Brad Pitt, Casey Affleck, Mary-Louise Parker, Sam Sheperd (Warner Bros, 2007).

Babel, director Alejandro González Iñárritu, featuring Brad Pitt, Cate Blanchett, Mohamed Akhzam, Peter Wight (Paramount Vantage, 2006).

Black Robe, director Bruce Beresford, featuring Lothaire Bluteau, Aden Young, Sandrine Holt, August Schellenberg (Alliance Communications Co., 1991).

Broken Arrow, director Delmer Daves, featuring Jimmy Stewart, Jeff Chandler, Debra Paget, Basil Ruysdael (20th Century Fox, 1950).

Buffalo Bill and the Indians; or, Sitting Bull's History Lesson, director Robert Altman, featuring Paul Newman, Burt Lancaster, Joel Grey, Harvey Keitel (Lion's Gate Films, 1976).

Chisum, director Andrew V. McLaglen, featuring John Wayne, Forrest Tucker, Ben Johnson, Christopher George (Warner Bros, 1970).

Cimarron, director Wesley Ruggles, featuring Richard Dix, Irene Dunne, Estelle Taylor, Nance O'Neil (RKO, 1931).

Dances with Wolves, director Kevin Costner, featuring Kevin Costner, Rodney A. Grant, Graham Greene, Wes Studi (Orion Picture Corp., 1990).

Devil's Doorway, director Anthony Mann, featuring Robert Taylor, Louise Calhern, Paula Raymond, Marshall Thompson (Metro-Goldwyn-Mayor, 1950).

Django Unchained, director Quentin Tarantino, featuring Jamie Foxx, Christoph Waltz, Leonardo DiCaprio, Kerry Washington (Columbia Pictures, 2012).

Don't Come Knocking, director Wim Wenders, featuring Sam Shepard, Jessica Lange, Sarah Polley, Tim Roth (Sony Pictures Classics, 2005).

Down in the Valley, director David Jacobson, featuring Edward Norton, Evan Rachel Wood, David Morse, Rory Culkin (ThinkFilm, 2005).

El Topo, director Alejandro Jodorowsky, featuring Alejandro Jodorowsky, Brontis Jodorowsky, José Legarreta, Alfonso Arau (Producciones Panicas, 1970).

Fistful of Dollars, A, director Sergio Leone, featuring Clint Eastwood, Marianne Koch, John Wels, Joe Edger (20th Century Fox, 1964).

For a Few Dollars More, director Sergio Leone, featuring Clint Eastwood, Lee Van Cleef, Gian Maria Volonte, Klaus Kinski (20th Century Fox, 1965).

Good, the Bad, and the Ugly, The, director Sergio Leone, featuring Clint Eastwood, Lee Van Cleef, Aldo Giuffre (20th Century Fox, 1967).

Great Train Robbery, The, director Edwin S. Porter, featuring A. C. Abadie, Gilbert M. 'Bronco Billy' Anderson, George Barnes, Justus D. Barnes (Edison Manufacturing Co., 1903).

Gunfighter, The, director Henry King, featuring Gregory Peck, Helen Westcott, Millard Mitchell, Karl Malden (20th Century Fox, 1950).

Hell Bent, director John Ford, featuring Harry Carey, Duke R. Lee, Neva Gerber, Vester Pegg (Universal Film Manufacturer's Co., 1918).

High Noon, director Fred Zinnemann, featuring Gary Cooper, Katy Jurado, Grace Kelly, Thomas Mitchell (United Artists, 1952).

High Plains Drifter, director Clint Eastwood, featuring Clint Eastwood, Verna Bloom, Marianna Hill, Mitch Ryan (Malpaso/Universal Pictures, 1973).

Hondo, director John Farrow, featuring John Wayne, Geraldine Page, Ward Bond, Michael Pate (Warner Bros, 1953).

Hour of the Gun, director John Sturges, featuring James Garner, Jason Robards, Robert Ryan, Albert Salmi (United Artists, 1967).

Last of the Mohicans, The, director Michael Mann, featuring Daniel Day-Lewis, Wes Studi, Madeleine Stowe, Jodhi May (20th Century Fox, 1992).

Life of Buffalo Bill, The, director Paul Panzer, featuring William F. Cody, William J. Craft, Irving Cummings, Pearl White (Pawnee Bill Film Co., 1912).

Little Big Man, director Arthur Penn, featuring Dustin Hoffman, Chief Dan George, Faye Dunaway, Richard Mulligan (Cinema Center Films, 1970).

Lone Star, director John Sayles, featuring Chris Cooper, Elizabeth Pena, Kris Kristofferson, Matthew McConaughey (Columbia TriStar, 1996).

Man Who Shot Liberty Valance, The, director John Ford, featuring John Wayne, Jimmy Stewart, Vera Miles, Lee Marvin (Paramount Pictures, 1962).

No Country for Old Men, director Joel Coen, featuring Tommy Lee Jones, Javier Bardem, Josh Brolin, Kelly MacDonald (Miramax-Paramount Vantage, 2007).

Once Upon a Time in the West, director Sergio Leone, featuring Charles Bronson, Henry Fonda, Claudia Cardinale, Jason Robards (Paramount, 1968).

One-Eyed Jacks, director Marlon Brando, featuring Marlon Brando, Karl Malden, Katy Jurado, Ben Johnson (Paramount Pictures, 1961).

Ox-Bow Incident, The, director William A. Wellman, featuring Henry Fonda, Dana Andrews, Mary Beth Hughes, Anthony Quinn (20th Century Fox, 1943).

Pale Rider, director Clint Eastwood, featuring Clint Eastwood, Michael Moriarty, Carrie Snodgrass, Sydney Penny (Warner Bros, 1985).

Pursued, director Raoul Walsh, featuring Teresa Wright, Robert Mitchum, Judith Anderson, Dean Jagger (Warner Bros, 1947).

Red River, director Howard Hawks, featuring John Wayne, Montgomery Clift, Joanne Dru, Coleen Gray (United Artists, 1948).

Searchers, The, director John Ford, featuring John Wayne, Henry Brandon, Ward Bond, Nathalie Wood (Warner Bros, 1956).

Seraphim Falls, director David Von Ancken, featuring Liam Neeson, Pierce Brosnan, Michael Wincott, Xander Berkeley (Icon Productions, 2006).

Shane, director George Stevens, featuring Alan Ladd, Brandon De Wilde, Van Heflin, Jean Arthur (Paramount Pictures, 1953).

Soldier Blue, director Ralph Nelson, featuring Candice Bergen, Peter Strauss, Donald Pleasance, Jorge Rivero (AVCO Embassy Pictures, 1970).

Three Burials of Melquiades Estrada, The, director Tommy Lee Jones, featuring Tommy Lee Jones, Barry Pepper, Julio Cedillo, January Jones (EuropaCorp., 2005).

Track of the Cat, director William A. Wellman, featuring Robert Mitchum, Teresa Wright, William Hopper, Diane Lynn (Warner Bros, 1954).

True Grit, director Joel Coen, featuring Jeff Bridges, Hailee Steinfeld, Josh Brolin, Matt Damon (Paramount Pictures, 2010).

Unforgiven, director Clint Eastwood, featuring Clint Eastwood, Gene Hackman, Morgan Freeman, Richard Harris (Malpaso/Warner Bros, 1992).

Virginian, The, director Victor Fleming, featuring Gary Cooper, Walter Huston, Richard Arlen, Mary Brian (Paramount Pictures, 1929).

Wild Bunch, The, director Sam Peckinpah, featuring William Holden, Ernest Borgnine, Robert Ryan, Warren Oates (Warner Bros, 1969).

Wild and Woolly, director John Emerson, featuring Douglas Fairbanks, Eileen Percy, Walter Bytell, Joseph Singleton (Douglas Fairbanks Pictures, 1917).

Winchester '73, director Anthony Mann, featuring Jimmy Stewart, Shelley Winters, Dan Duryea, Stephan McNally (Universal Pictures, 1950).

3:10 to Yuma, director James Mangold, featuring Russell Crowe, Christian Bale, Logan Lerman, Ben Foster (LionsGate Films, 2007).

21 Grams, director Alejandro González Iñárritu, featuring Sean Penn, Naomi Watts, Danny Huston, Benicio Del Toro (Focus Features, 2003).

INDEX